THE GLOBAL GUN EPIDEMIC

THE GLOBAL GUN EPIDEMIC

From Saturday Night Specials to AK-47s

Wendy Cukier
and
Victor W. Sidel

PRAEGER SECURITY INTERNATIONAL
Westport, Connecticut · London

Library of Congress Cataloging-in-Publication Data

Cukier, Wendy, 1956–
    The global gun epidemic : from Saturday night specials to AK-47s / Wendy
Cukier and Victor W. Sidel.
        p. cm.
    Includes bibliographical references and index.
    ISBN 0–275–98256–4 (alk. paper)
1. Gun control.   2. Firearms and crime.   3. Violence.   4. Violent deaths.   I.
Sidel, Victor W.   II. Title.
    HV7435.C85   2006
    363.33—dc22   2005019185

British Library Cataloguing in Publication Data is available.

Library of Congress Catalog Card Number: 2005019185
ISBN: 0–275–98256–4

First published in 2006

Praeger Security International, 88 Post Road West, Westport, CT 06881
An imprint of Greenwood Publishing Group, Inc.
www.praeger.com

Printed in the United States of America

∞™

The paper used in this book complies with the
Permanent Paper Standard issued by the National
Information Standards Organization (Z39.48–1984).

10 9 8 7 6 5 4 3 2 1

Contents

List of Tables

List of Figures

Foreword

As I write this, I am in my favorite place in the whole world, the living room of my house. Out one side of the room is the Atlantic Ocean, and out the other side tranquil Silver Lake. I am on the Delmarva Peninsula, a broad spit of land surrounded by water—the Atlantic Ocean on one side, the Chesapeake Bay on the other.

I cherish this place to a great extent because of the serenity it gives me and my husband, Jim. That's funny. Thirty years ago, we went to great lengths, he and I, to *avoid* serenity. Our lives were great adventures. We were in campaign politics, which is a world of frenzied activity and high stress.

Jim rose to the top tier of his professional world. If you're a press secretary, the top job in the trade is to speak for the president of the United States. I was, and still am, extremely proud of him, and I know how proud Jim was to serve.

They call press secretaries "flaks" behind the scenes, because you're expected to "take the flak" for the boss. In war, "taking flak" means being shot at. And in 1981, Jim literally did take flak for the boss. He was shot, along with President Ronald Reagan, by a lunatic who shouldn't have been allowed to buy a gun.

Jim lived, but his recovery was long and hard and incomplete. He'll be in a wheelchair forever, and he's in pain frequently. How we got from there to here—writing an introduction to a book about guns—is a long story. You are welcome to buy my book to hear it, but this is about another book, so pardon me if I just say we became activists against gun violence, were deeply honored to become somewhat successful as activists, and amused to become somewhat famous in the bargain. I honestly believe we remain pretty humble, however, and rightfully so: There is so much more work to be done in our chosen cause, and instead of making progress on reducing gun violence, the country that Jim and I both love with all of our hearts and souls is sliding backwards.

Recently, the American television news program *60 Minutes* broadcast a story on an Eastern European man who helped his kin wage civil war by smuggling fifty-caliber sniper rifles into the former Yugoslavia from the United States. I say that he smuggled them into his homeland, rather than saying that he smuggled them out of the United States, because if you're a U.S. citizen and not a felon, you can take all the guns you want just about anywhere you want to take them. You can buy all the fifty-caliber sniper rifles, military-style assault weapons and powerful handguns you want. You can have a hundred weapons, or a thousand, and a hundred rounds of ammunition, or a hundred thousand rounds. It is legal, and it is obscene.

Why is this? Why does the rest of the world gasp when they hear about how easy it is to buy all the firearms you want in America? Why does the United States serve as the global flea market for every other nation's illegal gun market? Well, it's cultural, and it's not quickly explainable. But it has something to do with the pioneer history of the United States and the tortured and bloody battle to tame a continent and wage a war for freedom and independence, and it also has something to do with the makeup of the American political system that resulted. The way our politics and government work leads to a fascinating dynamic where a minority can have a disproportionate amount of political power. Built to safeguard against tyrannical majorities, our system now means that an organization called the National Rifle Association can wield tremendous force to block progress, or even to roll back the clock.

Jim and I were able to help accomplish some steps forward in the United States partly because of what some call the "Nixon in China" phenomenon: We were Republicans working on a cause that had been somewhat dominated by Democrats, and as a result, the news media thought we brought something new to the debate. But the truth is that gun violence prevention has not been primarily a partisan political issue in the United States, but rather a geographical one. Most supporters of tougher gun laws live in cities and city suburbs, while the most passionate supporters of unrestricted access to firearms either live in rural areas or were raised in rural areas. In the country, a gun is a tool for everyday life: Shooting or scaring away pests and predators, or hunting for game. In the cities, a gun is a tool for dangerous days: Committing a crime or protecting oneself from a world that can sometimes seem terrifying and lawless.

Wendy Cukier and Victor Sidel have spent a great deal of time compiling a global snapshot of gun laws and policies. It's a terrific piece of work and a compelling one to read, and they deserve praise for how much work obviously went into it. What you'll read here will make certain things very clear. The most important of all will be that for the most part, where it's easier to obtain a gun, it's also easier to be shot. Guns are not going away. But the world has too many guns, and the United States deserves its fair share of the blame.

Is there hope for progress? Of course there is. Perhaps it's just that I'm an optimist, but I believe progress on this crisis is inevitable. The cost of firearm violence in the United States is profound, and the measures my husband and I have advocated (promoted by the Brady Campaign to Prevent Gun Violence and the Million Mom March organization) would really just move the United States toward firearm regulations already well established in other industrialized countries. But the gun problem in the United States is like a leaky faucet—eventually, someone with the right tools is going to pay attention. We can—and do—work hard to put the right tools in the right hands, but the human costs of the crisis are permanent and profound, and mounting by the hour. It's a crisis of global significance, on a global scale, leaving no nation and no one untouched.

I need to say a special word about Wendy Cukier, whom I have long regarded as a heroine, a truly remarkable woman. She proves that one person can make a huge difference. In her home country of Canada, where guns are culturally revered much as they are in the United States, her measured, persistent, fact-based advocacy has led to stronger gun laws—laws that have proven to reasonable people that you can regulate firearms in a way that stops them from being readily available to criminals. Unfortunately, too many cheap, illegal guns are still crossing the relatively open border with the United States to the south, leading to gun crimes that might otherwise be prevented.

Her co-author, Dr. Victor Sidel, contributes to academic scholarship and works as a tireless advocate. As past president of both the International Physicians for the Prevention of Nuclear War and the American Public Health Association, he has shown that fact-based advocacy can advance the public health agenda both in the United States and abroad.

The American people have a duty to be good neighbors to the rest of the world, and one of the ways we have to work to be better neighbors is to stop being the world's convenience store for firearms. We, as a nation, criticize some countries for not being aggressive enough to stop the flow of weapons of mass destruction. We criticize other nations for not halting the flow of drugs. We have to stop supplying the world's criminals with cheap handguns. I truly believe that in the years to come, we will.

Sarah Brady
August 2005

Preface

In recent years, the problem of firearm death and injury has attracted international attention, but approaches to the issue have tended to be fragmented. Scholars interested in disarmament and conflict prevention have tended to focus on the flow of weapons to war zones, while those interested in crime have tended to concentrate on high-income countries, often the United States. The public health perspective has been brought to bear on the issue of firearms as part of national studies and is often referred to in larger studies of violence but is less often as a single focus point. In addition, many writers have focused on a particular aspect of the issue, for example, the supply or the demand for firearms or regulation. In this book we provide a comprehensive overview of all these aspects.

The public health perspective begins with an analysis of a problem in order to identify the causal links that lead to an illness or injury. Based on an analysis of those causal links, interventions are developed, aimed at breaking the chain at its weakest point. The interventions are implemented and continuously evaluated in order to refine and improve them. The public health perspective helps separate fact from fiction and focuses on the evidence: What is the nature of the problem of gun violence? What factors contribute to gun violence? What interventions can break the cycle, and do they work? Regardless of the context—crime, conflict, domestic assault, suicide—firearms increase the number of victims and the potential for children to become killers. Firearms also undermine long-term efforts to build civil society by fueling internal arms races, whether in war zones or in inner cities. While social science is not hard science and analyses of causes and effects are not simple or unambiguous, our interpretation is based on integrating a wide range of sources and perspectives. The data provided in the book are a snapshot. Current data will be available at www.ryerson.ca/SAFER-Net.

Understanding violence and systematically developing strategies to deal with it are the focus of a number of disciplines, including public health, peace studies and criminology. We have tried to integrate work from these perspectives. Because violence is a complex, multifaceted problem, simple solutions are seldom widely effective. Public health models have been used to try to understand the problem of firearm injury and death and to develop strategies to reduce death and injury. In public health models developed to address other problems, a range of interventions are possible. Despite the debate in the literature, there is no single "public health approach" to the problem of firearms.

We felt that it was important to write a book that applied the public health lens to the problem of firearms on a global scale, in order to draw attention to the obvious but silent reality: The American approach to guns is anomalous in the industrialized world, and the world, not just Americans, pays a high price for this. In every chapter, we highlight the U.S. situation and how it compares to that of the rest of the world. For example, the Americas have 14 percent of the world's population, but more than a third of the world's guns are owned by civilians in the United States. More firearm deaths occur in countries "at peace" than in those at "war" and more than half of those are in the Americas. The United States plays a central role in the global gun epidemic: It is a major producer of legal guns. It has the highest rate of gun ownership in the world (almost one gun per citizen). Unlike other nations, industrialized and developing, it has fragmented and limited regulations of firearms. The United States has the highest rate of gun death and injury of any industrialized country. But U.S. guns do not kill only American citizens—the United States is also a major source of illegal guns, which jeopardize the safety of citizens in other countries. In spite of growing momentum to establish international standards to regulate firearms, the United States has used its political might to block such efforts. At a time when the "security" agenda has shaped many aspects of our lives, it is important to reflect on the effects that American guns and American gun culture have on human security worldwide.

Programs for peace building, public health and crime prevention all have models for intervention that address the root causes of violence through social development and value building. Once crime, injuries or conflicts occur, there is recognition of the need to intervene with policing, enforcement and "treatment." Controls on firearms are an intermediate step. By reducing the opportunity for violence or conflict using deadly weapons, and by controlling the supply of firearms, it is possible to lessen the severity of violent encounters. While it is possible to kill with other means, firearms are particularly efficient and are more likely than other easily accessible weapons to cause death or severe injuries and involve multiple victims. In addition, firearms enable children, who might otherwise lack the strength to kill, to kill more readily. Fundamental to this book is the belief that unregulated access to firearms is a major factor in the global gun epidemic.

Models for preventing injury, crime and conflict often have common elements and consist of several well-defined steps. These begin with understanding the problem, analyzing the contributing causal factors, developing interventions, monitoring and evaluation. We used these models as a framework for structuring our analysis and for examining some of the approaches to reducing firearm death and injury that have been proposed and adopted. Research into these interventions has tended to suggest that modifying the voluntary behavior of individuals, by focusing, for example, on raising awareness and education, is less effective than other approaches. Options in public health increasingly focus on modifying products to reduce the harm they cause, in effect shifting the responsibility to the manufacturers of dangerous products and away from the users. After years of focusing on driver training, for instance, efforts of traffic safety advocates have shifted, due to the efforts of consumer advocates such as Ralph Nader, to the automobile industry, forcing improvements to products through regulation of mandatory seat belts, shatterproof glass and, more recently, air bags. Similarly, in the fight to reduce smoking, the focus has shifted to an ecological model of smoking in an effort to understand what factors lead large numbers of people to smoke, and away from a focus on the choices of individual smokers. For example, attention has progressively focused on measures to control the manufacture, advertising and promotion of tobacco, rather than on educating smokers regarding the risks.

Efforts to address the problem of firearms at the regional, national and international level are relatively new, but in recent years, governments, nongovernmental organizations and academics have begun to turn their attention to the global gun epidemic. The public health approach focuses on a systematic process to develop contextually appropriate interventions rather than cookie-cutter prescriptions. Solutions to the firearms problem need to address specific contexts; however, at the same time, we believe, international norms are emerging, and the book traces their development. We find that countries with the most firearms tend to have the highest rates of gun death but also the strongest opposition to stronger regulation. Ironically, countries such as Japan, the United Kingdom and Australia, which account for a fraction of the world's gun problems, are able to move decisively. In the last five years more than fifty countries have strengthened their laws; once again the United States stands alone in relaxing its laws.

There is no doubt that this book will stir controversy and the "more guns, less crime" advocates will make their case. But we think the evidence, though imperfect, is compelling: It has shown us that with more guns, we see more deaths. At the end of the day, we believe that there is enough information to move forward in our efforts to combat the global gun epidemic. As Sir Austin Bradford-Hill commented on the need to control tobacco products forty years ago, "All scientific work is liable to be upset or modified by advancing knowledge. That does not confer upon us a freedom to ignore the knowledge we already have, or to postpone the action that it appears to demand at a given time."[1]

Acknowledgments

Writing *The Global Gun Epidemic* involved the combined skills and resources of many people over a number of years. To them, we are profoundly grateful. Special thanks to our editor, Hilary Claggett, whose infinite patience was matched only by her belief in the project. We also want to thank Nicole Azze for her efforts to keep production on track. In addition, our production editor Carla Talmadge took enormous time to rework the manuscript and made many helpful suggestions.

We also would like to thank Antoine Chapdelaine, Quebec Public Health; David Hemenway, Harvard University; David Meddings, World Health Organization; James Sheptycki, York University; Tom Diaz, Violence Policy Centre; Josh Horowitz, Coalition Against Gun Violence; Ed Laurence, Monterey Institute; Adele Kirsten, Gun Free South Africa; Rebecca Peters, International Action Network on Small Arms (IANSA); and Peter Hamm, Brady Campaign, for their help at various stages.

In addition, our research and editorial assistants did much of the leg work and nitpicking: Karen Poetker, Alison Kooistra, Steve Joyce, Sara Rodrigues, Eva Nesselroth, Ward Eagen, Justyna Susla, Anne Warner, Eli Malinsky and David Lochhead all assisted with the work.

Finally, we wish to express our gratitude and appreciation to our families for their continuing encouragement, support and love.

1

Guns: A Global Perspective

Tragedies with firearms dominate newspaper headlines around the world on a daily basis. The context and circumstances may vary, but the lethal consequences of the misuse of guns appear time and time again. Certainly the United States has more than its share of violence, suicides and "accidents" involving guns. But there are few places in the world immune to the global gun epidemic. Examples appear in headlines around the globe:

In the United States

- October 22, 2004: In North Point, Maryland, a man fatally shot his estranged wife and wounded her friend before turning the gun on himself.[1]
- October 24, 2004: Two Arby's employees were shot to death in an apparent robbery in West Milwaukee, Wisconsin.[2]
- November 24, 2004: A hunting dispute in Wisconsin left six dead when a hunter armed with a Chinese-style SKS semiautomatic rifle shot at other hunters.[3]

In Canada

- August 26, 2004: The estranged husband of a woman fired a sawed-off rifle at her in a crowded downtown food court in Toronto but missed. He beat her with the gun and fled the scene. When pursued by police, he took a woman passerby hostage. After several hours of negotiations the man was shot and killed by a police sniper and the hostage escaped unharmed.[4]
- November 4, 2004: A man was charged with killing three and wounding two on the Penticton First Nation Reserve in British Columbia.[5]

- March 3, 2005: Four Royal Canadian Mounted Police officers were shot with an H&K 303, prohibited in 1995 in Canada but imported from the United States in 1993.[6]

In Brazil

- October 4, 2004: A twenty-eight-year-old Brazilian forward who played for FC Zurich of Switzerland was shot and killed in Rio de Janeiro by thieves apparently trying to steal his car.[7]

In Haiti

- October 1, 2004: In Port-au-Prince, shooting broke out between police and demonstrators. Demonstrators shot and killed three officers and were believed to have kidnapped a fourth.[8]

In Argentina

- September 28, 2004: A fifteen-year-old boy in Carmen de Patagones opened fire in his classroom, killing three fellow students and wounding five others. The handgun he used belonged to his father.[9]

In England

- October 11, 2004: In Hackney, a suburb of East London, an eighteen-month-old girl was shot and two men seriously wounded when a gunman fired into a car. The attack came only two days after fourteen-year-old Danielle Beccan was killed in a drive-by shooting in Nottingham. She was shot as she walked with friends.[10]

In Russia

- July 9, 2004: In Moscow, Paul Klebnikov, the editor of the Russian edition of *Forbes* magazine was shot and killed.[11]
- September 3, 2004: The siege at the secondary school in Beslan, Russia, ended in a series of explosions and gunfire that left at least 330 people dead and more than 500 injured. Many of the victims were children.[12]

In Bangladesh

- August 21, 2004: An attack with grenades and guns on a public rally in Dhaka left twenty-one people killed and hundreds injured. The opposition political party Awami League said the attack was an assassination attempt on party leader Sheikh Hasina.[13]

In the Philippines

- October 19, 2004: Radio host Eldy Gaginales was shot dead, becoming the eighth journalist murdered that year in the Philippines.[14]

While conflicts and wars are fueled by the arms trade, the shocking reality is that more people are killed with guns each year in countries not at war. The circumstances of these deaths vary—some are in the context of street crime or robberies, some relate to domestic violence or disputes among friends and some are political violence. Most of them occur in countries not at war and many of them occur in the United States. The victims are primarily male and mostly young, as are the shooters. But the one factor that links each and every one of these shootings is the weapon. While the sources of the weapons are not defined in each of the cases described above, we know that in many of them, the guns originated in the United States, home of one-third of the guns in the world and a leading manufacturer of firearms for both military and commercial markets. Whether a handgun, a rifle or an AK-47, in each of these cases, a firearm played a role in the tragedy.

THE FIREARM EPIDEMIC

Firearms have been recognized as a public health problem in the United States for many years, yet attention to the issue on a global basis is relatively recent. It was not until 1996 that the World Health Organization labeled violence a pandemic.[15] This was the same year that the International Committee of the Red Cross went on record, stating simply, "Weapons are bad for people's health," and, "health professionals have been slow to recognize that the effects of weapons are, by design, a health issue, and moreover constitute a global epidemic mostly affecting civilians."[16]

This book considers, from the public health perspective, the "global gun epidemic." It begins with an examination of the dimensions of this epidemic and the factors that fuel firearm death, injury and crime. The effects of the misuse of firearms extend far beyond the statistics of gun death, injury and crime. Rather, they have far-reaching impacts on democratic institutions, economic development, culture and ultimately the health of individuals, nations and the global community. While there are no simple solutions to complex problems, this book aims to demonstrate what we know about the supply of and demand for firearms, as well as detail the possible interventions that may reduce the death and injury toll. Finally, it considers the emergence of a global movement for stronger controls on firearms and the impediments to effective responses to the "global gun epidemic."

A firearm, according to the United Nations Firearms Protocol, is any portable, barreled weapon that expels a shot, bullet or projectile, by the action of an explosive. This includes revolvers and pistols (handguns), rifles and shotguns, as well as machine guns. Historically, the term "small arm" has been applied to firearms and other weapons capable of being carried by an individual (such as rocket launchers), particularly those designed for military specifications. For example, the UN expert panel on small arms referred to "revolvers and self-loading pistols; rifles and carbines; submachine guns; assault rifles; and light machine guns." While some have attempted to differentiate "civilian firearms" from "military specification firearms," this is virtually impossible, as over time weapons primarily produced for military markets are often adapted to civilian markets. For the purposes of the book, we will use the terms firearms and small arms interchangeably to refer to the full range of revolvers, pistols, rifles, shotguns and machine guns. Issues related to definitions will be discussed in more detail later in the book.

It is not surprising that the terms *epidemic* and *pandemic* are now being used in association with firearms. A look at the impact of firearms on human lives in terms of homicide, suicide, accidental death and injury illustrates the magnitude of the public health challenges posed by guns. Globally, approximately 200,000 people are estimated to have been killed annually in homicides, suicides and accidents with firearms, with thousands more killed in military conflicts. Although the exact number of small arms casualties in military conflicts is a matter of debate, there is no doubt that small arms are the weapons of choice in armed conflicts today and that the secondary impacts of these conflicts are immense. A large percentage of casualties are civilians, conservatively estimated by the International Committee of the Red Cross at more than 35 percent.[17] In Iraq, for example, civilian casualties actually outnumber combatant deaths. While there has been intense focus on the deaths from small arms in the context of conflict, there are more deaths annually from firearms in the hands of civilians in countries not engaged in conflict. To put it bluntly: From a public health perspective, a dead child is a dead child, whether it is a child soldier in Uganda, a crime victim in Soweto or a student in Columbine High School in the United States. There is evidence that the threat to children from firearms is as great in some countries considered to be at peace as it is in conflict zones.[18]

Fatality rates for suicides attempted with firearms tend to be much higher than those for attempted homicide; consequently, the rate of injury associated with suicide attempts is much lower. Of course, the impact of firearms is not restricted to fatalities. For every death caused by a firearm there are additional injuries requiring hospitalization. Studies in Brazil and South Africa, for example, report almost ten times more firearm injuries than fatalities, while in countries such as Finland and Canada, the reported mortality and injury rates are roughly equivalent.[19] This difference may be related to the context in which the death and injury occur. Research shows that in Brazil and South Africa, the person firing the weapon is most likely attempting a homicide, while in Canada and Finland, the person is probably attempting suicide.

Some segments of the population are particularly hard hit, in both industrialized and developing countries. Women are seldom users of firearms but are often victims, both in the context of war and in domestic violence. A recent comparative study showed that guns figure prominently in the cycle of violence against women and children in Canada, Australia and South Africa.[20] The patterns of weapons use in domestic violence are also remarkably consistent across cultures. In many industrialized countries, firearms are a leading cause of mortality among children and youth, with these groups representing a large percentage of the victims of conflict, both as combatants and as casualties.[21] Furthermore, a number of studies have revealed that the poor are more likely to be victims of violence.[22]

The secondary impacts of firearm violence are also staggering. For countries in conflict, violence is a major threat to democratic governance and sustainable peace.[23] The continued availability of weapons often produces other lasting consequences, such as the breakdown of civil order and dramatic increases in lawlessness, banditry and illicit drug trafficking. Firearms can change the balance of power within a state and raise the level of violence overall. Even if in the short term firearm use is for self-defense, its effect over the long term may be to limit, if not negate, peaceful avenues for conflict resolution.[24] Criminal violence involving firearms in South Africa, for example, has been defined as "the greatest threat to human rights" facing the young democracy.[25] In Central America, the United Nations has been very successful in peacekeeping, yet the proliferation of light weapons presents challenges to long-term stability and reconciliation.[26] Indeed, throughout Latin America, criminal violence dwarfs political violence and has a huge impact on individual security, economic development and governance.

The economic costs of violence, including costs of policing and the value of life lost, are staggering on a global level. In Latin America, for example, the effects of violence have been estimated to consume 14 percent of the gross domestic product (GDP).[27] Even in industrialized countries, where gun violence is generally less prevalent, the economic costs are high. In Canada, for example, the annual costs associated with firearm death and injury (including murder, suicide and unintentional deaths and injuries) have been estimated (in U.S. dollars) at $195 per person, or almost $5 billion per year, compared to $495 per person in the United States, or $125 billion annually.[28] In addition to the costs armed violence incurs, measured in terms of the economic value of lost life, injury and disability, it diverts health, policing and social resources from other problems.

Violence and the prevalence of weapons also create psychological stress that fuels other health problems and creates insecurity. Arms-infested environments yield observable symptoms of post-traumatic stress disorder, such as overwhelming anxiety and a lack of motivation.[29] Other secondary effects include problems related to a country's blood supply. Not only are blood availability and facilities for transfusion key issues in developing countries, but emergency responses to large-scale violence often do not accommodate careful testing for HIV and result in additional public health problems.[30]

Violence has been identified as a major impediment to the provision of basic health care. Violence also diverts resources from other health and social services. In South Africa, scarce hospital resources are diverted from patients suffering from disease to deal with victims of gun violence. Even more troubling, health care personnel are themselves increasingly the target of violence because they attempt to save the lives of people who are the targets of violence. Furthermore, many injured victims die during transport rather than at treatment facilities, as the medical transportation infrastructure cannot carry the burden created by increased arms proliferation.

MORE GUNS EQUAL MORE DEATHS

The public health approach to injury prevention is multilayered and comprehensive and addresses the root causes of firearm death and injury at the individual and community levels. It also focuses our attention on the instrument of violence—the firearm—and the relationship between the availability of firearms and their misuse, particularly in industrialized nations. The link between accessibility of guns and levels of violence has been demonstrated in a number of contexts. Research does show, however, that high rates of gun ownership are generally related to high levels of arms-related violence in "conflict zones"[31] as well as in countries that are "at peace."

Studies comparing homes where firearms are present to those where they are not have concluded that the risk of death is substantially higher if firearms are in the home.[32] This is not to say that the presence of firearms in a home is the only contributing factor to violence. Certainly more research could illuminate the interactions of the range of factors shaping the demand for firearms, at the societal level and at the individual level, including criminal activity, drug use and parental factors.[33]

Nevertheless, a growing body of literature reveals a relationship between access to firearms, and firearm death rates and rates of firearm crime in industrialized countries.[34] The International Victimization Survey collected cross-national data on firearm victimization and ownership,[35] and a few scholars, notably Martin Killias, published comparative analyses of gun death rates among industrialized countries. International comparisons show that among industrialized nations, the United States has by far the highest rates of firearm ownership as well as firearm death and injury. In contrast, rates of other violence in the United States, including murders committed without firearms, are comparable to rates found in other countries. This underpins the notion that reducing access to firearms through regulation could lead to a reduction in the lethality of conflicts, assaults, suicide attempts and accidents.

THE GLOBAL GUN TRADE

While there is a general consensus that firearms are dangerous and need to be regulated, there is no international consensus regarding what would constitute an appropriate domestic or global approach to regulation. To understand the challenges of regulating firearms, it is first necessary to understand the global gun trade, including the production of firearms for state and commercial uses. The international market for firearms is large and complex in terms of both the markets served and the players in the distribution chain, from production through use. Almost 100 countries are engaged in some aspect of firearm manufacture, although much of the production is concentrated in a few countries, including the five permanent members of the UN Security Council—the United States, Russia, China, the United Kingdom and France—plus a number of other European, Asian and Latin American countries. In many cases, the production of firearms is state controlled. Firearms manufacturers fall into two general categories: Those whose production is state controlled and tied very closely to defense industries, and those who focus on "consumer markets." The latter group is extremely diverse in terms of scale of operations and range of product offerings.

GLOBALIZATION AND GUN-RUNNING

The global trade in firearms is not always transparent. It is well documented that legal firearms are diverted to illegal markets that fuel crime as well as political conflicts worldwide. Virtually every "illegal" small arm began as a legal one. An analysis of more than 200 reported incidents of illicit trafficking suggests that misuse and diversion occur through a variety of mechanisms that generally fall into three broad categories: (1) legally held firearms that are misused by their lawful owner (whether states, organizations or individuals); (2) legal firearms that are "diverted" into the "gray" market (sold by legal owners to unauthorized individuals, illegally sold, stolen or diverted through other means) and (3) illegally manufactured and distributed firearms (although these account for only a small fraction of the illicit gun trade).

There are more firearms in the possession of civilians worldwide than are held by governments and police,[36] and diversion of these firearms, particularly in the United States, fuels illicit firearm markets and deaths worldwide. In many parts of the world, firearms diverted from legal markets in one country into illegal markets in another are a significant problem. Many nations in southern Africa, for example, have strict domestic controls on firearms and correspondingly lower crime rates compared to those in South Africa, where gun controls are far less strict. As a result, countries near South Africa, such as Lesotho and Botswana, must contend with a high rate of gun smuggling across their borders.[37] In North America, U.S. guns are exported to the gray markets of neighboring countries Canada and Mexico. In Mexico, U.S. guns account for 80 percent of illegal firearms.[38] In Canada about 50 percent of illegal handguns used in crime come from the United States. Proximity to a country with less stringent gun controls is not a prerequisite for "importing" guns. Consider, for example, that many of the firearms possessed by the Irish Republican Army (IRA) originated in the United States, and that guns in Japan come primarily from the United States, China and South Africa.

GUN CULTURE AND THE DEMAND FOR FIREARMS

In the United States there are almost as many guns as people—roughly 220 million, almost one-third of all the guns in the world. In the United States people own guns for a variety of reasons—hunting, target shooting, collecting and self-protection. The rates of firearm ownership in the United States are not seen elsewhere in the world. Most industrialized countries have much lower rates of gun ownership, and few allow civilians to carry guns for the purposes of protection. Firearm ownership rates range from less than 1 percent of households in countries such as England, Wales, Germany and Japan to about 20 percent in countries such as Canada, Austria and France and closer to 40 percent in countries such as Finland and Switzerland. But only a small percentage of firearms in these countries are handguns. The purposes for owning firearms vary considerably—some countries, such as Canada, Austria, and the United States, have extensive recreational hunting. Others, such as Kenya, use firearms to protect herds from predators. Many permit sporting uses of firearms for target shooting and collecting. In many contexts firearms are possessed, legally or illegally, as a means of promoting a sense of security in the face of crime or political instability.

Globally, gun makers and sellers work closely with firearms user groups to promote firearm ownership and to build markets. The American National Rifle Association is one of the most powerful lobbies in the world and operates on a national as well as international level to fight efforts to more strictly regulate firearms.

Regardless of the differences among cultures, one factor is constant—firearm possession is a predominantly male activity. Men dominate armies and police forces, and the vast proportion of hunters and target shooters worldwide is male. The link between masculinity and firearms permeates many cultures, both industrialized and developing. A range of cultural carriers, from traditional practices such as songs through electronic media such as video games and movies, reinforce these links and promote demand. Again, firearms sellers exploit many of these beliefs and values in their efforts to sell more guns.

There is also an interesting and complex dynamic between the supply of and the demand for firearms. Increased weapon availability has been shown to fuel a "culture of violence." More weapons tend to promote armed violence, which in turn promotes fear, which drives demand. The militarization of culture in South Africa[39] illustrates this point. A number of studies have shown links between that country's culture of violence and civilian attitudes to firearms. Laws that control firearms both reflect and shape values, particularly the "culture of violence," in the same way legislation has been observed to have long-term effects on other behaviors.[40] The concept that what a society tolerates, and what it legislates, shapes its behaviors and attitudes was eloquently voiced by Martin Luther King, Jr., more than forty years ago: "By our readiness to allow arms to be purchased at will and fired at whim; by allowing our movies and television screens to teach our children that the hero is one who masters the art of shooting and the technique of killing . . . we have created an atmosphere in which violence and hatred have become popular past-times."[41] Consequently, it is not surprising that countries and regions with the highest levels of firearm violence and ownership are less able to address them than countries with low rates of firearm violence and ownership. Stricter controls on firearms both reflect and shape values, which is perhaps why countries with relatively low rates of gun ownership and crime are more able to move quickly to strengthen laws when tragedy strikes. The terrible irony is that countries with the highest rates of gun death and ownership are also the least able to effect change.

REGULATING FIREARMS

Faced with evidence that easy access to weapons fuels violence, governments around the world have adopted legislation to regulate firearms possessed by civilians. Most firearm controls are based on the assumption that controlling access will result in fewer deaths, injuries and crimes. Measures aimed at controlling access include the outright prohibition of certain firearms where the risks are considered to outweigh the utility, as well as measures to reduce the risk that legal firearms will fall into the wrong hands. These include regulating the sale of firearms and ammunition, licensing owners, registering firearms, defining the conditions under which firearms may be used or stored, and restricting the types and numbers of firearms that may be possessed.

The analysis of current approaches to regulating firearms provides insight into some of the emerging global norms around licensing and registration of firearms and civilian possession of military weapons. In recent years, the trend in both developed and developing countries has been in the direction of increasing regulation. Most countries require licensing of all firearm purchases and registration of some or all firearms. Import and export controls are virtually universal. There are safe-storage regulations in most countries. The vast majority of countries ban civilian possession of full automatic military weapons, and most also prohibit civilian possession of semiautomatic military weapons, although definitions of these weapons differ from country to country.

Canada prohibited fully automatic weapons in 1979, semiautomatic weapons that could be converted to fully automatic weapons in 1991, and semiautomatic versions of military weapons in 1995. In most cases, current owners were "grandfathered," or allowed to keep their weapons under certain conditions. Great Britain banned 90 percent of handguns in early 1997 and the remaining 10 percent with the change in government in June 1997. British gun owners were entitled to compensation, but possession of the prohibited weapons was illegal. Similarly, Australia banned semiautomatic firearms and shotguns except those owned by individuals who could demonstrate "good reason" for owning them, buying back more than 500,000 guns. The United States, in 1994, banned the sale of many semiautomatic assault weapons but lifted the ban in 2004.

While some countries have totally prohibited civilian ownership of all guns, most nations accept that some firearms serve some legitimate purposes. Generally, regulators agree on a compromise, allowing products that are inherently dangerous to be used under special circumstances. The end result is a set of regulations that reduce casual ownership by raising barriers to obtaining firearms and by improving screening processes such as criminal record checks, personal references, waiting periods and mandatory training programs.[42]

Examples of steps being taken to prevent impulsive use and unauthorized access include regulations to encourage safe-storage practices, such as the use of locked containers, trigger locks, disabling of firearms and separation of ammunition from guns. These safety precautions are standard in most industrialized countries but are the exception rather than the rule in the United States.[43]

Measures have also been undertaken to reduce demand for firearms by raising public awareness of the risks they pose, particularly in the home,[44] and developing programs such as amnesties and buybacks to encourage individuals to rid themselves of unwanted or unneeded firearms.[45] Education programs have also focused on raising public awareness of safe practices and on encouraging compliance with these practices.[46] Regulatory restrictions and litigation have also been used to encourage suppliers of firearms to control sales and assume a higher level of responsibility for their products.[47]

GLOBAL ACTION: THE RISE OF A GLOBAL MOVEMENT

On a global level, governments and civil society organizations or non-governmental organizations (NGOs) have begun working together to control the proliferation and stop the misuse of firearms worldwide. Many states and most NGOs,[48] including the International Action Network on Small Arms (IANSA),[49] maintain that much more needs to be done to prevent the diversion and misuse of firearms. A number of resolutions passed by various UN councils and commissions stress the importance of regulation of civilian firearm possession as a strategy to reduce conflict, crime and human rights violations. A 1997 resolution presented to the UN Crime Prevention and Criminal Justice Commission remains an important standard, as do other resolutions by the UN Security Council. The Firearms Protocol of the United Nations Convention on Transnational Organized Crime has established minimum standards for the import, export and transit of commercial shipments of firearms, but stopped short of establishing standards for national regulation. Since the 2001 UN Conference on the Illicit Trafficking in Small Arms and Light Weapons in All Its Aspects, the problem of regulating civilian possession is getting more attention. While explicit references to the regulation of civilian possession and use of firearms were deleted from the 2001 Conference Programme of Action (PoA) as a result of pressure from the United States,[50] a number of the recommendations that were agreed to clearly have implications for the regulation of civilian possession. An example is that the agreement to criminalize illegal possession of small arms implies standards for legal possession. Most recently, the UN Special Rapporteur on Human Rights stressed that countries have obligations to adequately regulate civilian possession of firearms under international human rights law. Many regional agreements have emerged that include harmonization of legislation regarding civilian possession.

These efforts reflect the change in attitude toward firearm regulation over the past ten years. Global awareness has increased to the point that there is less debate over the need to regulate firearms. The debate now focuses on how to regulate. We hope this book, with its public health approach to the issues, will add a fresh perspective to this important new direction.

2

The Firearm Epidemic

Gun violence is a problem in many nations around the globe. It is prominent in the headlines and dominates the news in many countries, even those considered to be generally peaceful. Although gun violence is a daily occurrence in many places, there are often high-profile events that attract and focus national and international attention on the issue of guns. Prominent in Western media, for example, have been:

- The assassination of John F. Kennedy on November 22, 1963,[1] the assassination of his brother Robert, on June 5, 1968,[2] and the assassination of Martin Luther King, Jr., on April 4, 1968.[3]
- The Montreal massacre in Canada, on December 6, 1989, when a man walked into an engineering school, separated the male from the female students, and shot twenty-seven people, killing fourteen young women.[4]
- The Dunblane killing in Scotland, on March 13, 1996, in which a licensed gun owner killed sixteen children and their teacher.[5]
- The Port Arthur massacre in Australia, on April 28, 1996, in which thirty-five people were killed.[6]
- The Columbine shootings in the United States, on April 20, 1999, in which two teenagers, Eric Harris and Dylan Klebold, walked into their school, Columbine High School in Colorado, and began a one-hour-long killing spree that ended in the death of twelve of their fellow students and one teacher, and left another twenty-eight students and teachers wounded. The shooters then took their own lives.[7]
- The Zug massacre in Switzerland, in which a lone gunman wielding an assault rifle wounded fourteen people and killed fifteen (including himself) in a regional parliament in September 2001.[8]

- The killing of an award-winning television journalist, Tim Lopes, in Brazil in June 2002.[9]
- The sniper shootings in Washington, D.C., which began on October 2, 2002. The shooting spree ended on October 22, 2002, with the arrest of two men for the killing of ten victims.[10]

These events may not, however, be "typical" of the problem. While high-profile shootings often become a focal point for public outrage, and in some cases swift political responses, people's perceptions of the risks and realities associated with firearms are often quite different. For example, in industrialized nations attention often focuses on high-profile serial killings or random violence in public places, while most homicides in these countries involve assailants and victims known to one another. Women, for instance, are often fearful of being attacked by strangers in the streets when the real threat to women is more often their intimate partners. Similarly, in industrialized countries children are more likely to be killed by their parents (often caught in the cross fire of domestic violence) than they are by random violence. Moreover, in all industrialized countries except the United States, the risk of suicide by firearm is far greater than the risk of homicide with a firearm.

Violence has been identified as a "pandemic" by the World Health Organization. Firearms figure prominently in such violence, whether in war or in crime. While the specific impacts of small arms in the context of conflict and violence are still being investigated, there is no doubt that their global impact is significant.

Firearm use has a variety of direct and indirect effects. The most serious is death, but for every death there are hundreds injured and the extraordinary psychological impact of victimization. Other effects that are also critically important but often receive less attention include the dislocation of people, the disruption of health and education, the diversion of resources and extensive economic impacts. In extreme cases, gun-fueled violence disrupts the ability of states to effectively govern or provide basic levels of security to their citizens. The unchecked proliferation of firearms can also promote a culture of violence, which in turn promotes fear, further arming and more violence.

The negative effects of firearms can be categorized in a variety of ways, including direct effects such as homicide and assault, suicide, unintentional injury, collective violence and crime. While some claim that there are also positive effects associated with firearms—for example, the claims that security is improved through arming civilians for self-protection as will be discussed in Chapter 3—most of the evidence suggests that arming for self-protection may produce a sense of security but generally does not make people safer.

DIRECT EFFECTS

Debates rage about the global toll of firearms and the direct versus indirect costs of armed violence.[11] Approximately 200,000 people die each year from firearms in homicide, suicide and unintentional injuries in nonconflict situations.[12] The World Health Organization has estimated that annually there are approximately 2.3 million deaths due to violence, of which 42 percent are suicides, 38 percent are homicides and 26 percent are war-related deaths.[13] Firearms account for almost 20 percent of these deaths. In some countries, the number of deaths from firearms matches or exceeds the number of deaths in automobile crashes, despite the fact that automobiles are used more frequently and by more people than are firearms. In terms of preventable deaths, firearms rank high on the list of global health priorities.

Global data concerning death and injury associated with firearms are limited. In industrialized countries different data sources yield different results: For example, emergency room (ER) codes taken from health records often produce different data than the Uniform Crime Reporting (UCR) codes taken from police records because of the interpretation of the circumstances of death. In addition, while homicide is one of the more reliably reported crimes, other crimes (or injuries) involving firearms may not be reported or accurately recorded even in highly industrialized countries.[14] Definitions also play a role in this—some countries count cases of involuntary manslaughter with homicides. Hospital records may be unreliable if coding is not a priority. In some countries reporting of injuries or deaths may be affected by fear of authorities. Cultural factors may come into play; for example, suicides are underreported when there is a religious taboo against them, while "accidents" may be overreported. Moreover, domestic violence in many contexts is still not considered a crime, and injuries that result from domestic violence may be unreported or reported as self-inflicted wounds or accidents.[15]

While data collection on firearms death and injury is incomplete, data on civilian and military deaths and injuries in armed conflicts are even more fragmented.[16] Nevertheless, it is maintained that small arms and light weapons are the weapons of choice in the vast majority of the world's conflicts.[17] International Committee of the Red Cross (ICRC) personnel working in conflict zones claim that these weapons are responsible for more than 60 percent of all weapons-related deaths and injuries in internal conflicts—far more than landmines, mortars, grenades, artillery and major weapons systems combined.[18]

As we have noted, while precise data are not available, murders, suicides and "accidents" with firearms in areas not at war exceed 200,000 per year.[19] Although this number has been challenged by gun advocates,[20] it is based on reliable data from several sources and has been validated by the most recent report of the *Small Arms Survey* and excludes many of the deaths directly or indirectly associated with conflict.[21] A WHO survey of fifty-two high- and medium-income countries documented a total of 104,492 deaths in 1998. Of these, 30,419 occurred in the United States, including homicides, suicides and unintentional injury (4.4 per 100,000 population).[22] More than sixty countries did not report data to the WHO, although we know some have high rates of firearm deaths. The WHO survey excluded lower-income countries with the highest mortality rates. For example, in 2002, Brazil reported 38,088 firearm deaths, South Africa 11,709 and Colombia 22,827, accounting for more than 72,000 deaths not included in the WHO estimate. Among 112 countries surveyed, the United States has the thirteenth highest rate of firearm deaths. (See Table 2.1, Countries with the Highest Rates of Reported Firearm Deaths in the World.)[23]

Certain subgroups are more likely to be victimized than others. In the United States, gun use is the leading cause of death among young African American men.[24] In Canada, firearm use is the third leading cause of death among fifteen- to twenty-four-year-olds (most of them in firearm suicides), exceeding deaths from falls, drowning and cancer combined.[25]

When considering crime and injury data, it is important to recognize that deaths are only the tip of the iceberg and tend to be better reported than nonfatal injuries or assaults. For every injury or crime that is reported, there are many more that are not reported (see Figure 2.2). For every firearm death, there are additional injuries requiring hospitalization, but data on these are even less available and reliable. Studies in Brazil and South Africa, for example, report almost ten times as many small arm injuries as fatalities, while in countries such as Finland and Canada, the reported mortality and injury rates are roughly equivalent.[26] This discrepancy appears to be related to the context in which the death or injury occurs: in Brazil and South Africa, homicide is the principal problem, while in Canada and Finland, suicide is. Fatality rates for suicides attempted with firearms tend to be higher than those for attempted homicide. Consequently, for each suicide there are relatively few injuries. In contrast, for each homicidal death there are often many nonfatal assaults.

In public health terms, the "costs" of firearm death and injury are particularly significant because the victims are often the youngest and healthiest members of the population. For example, health effects are often calculated in terms of disability-adjusted life years (DALYs), which measure the impact on survivors as well as the impact of the number of deaths in terms of the years of life lost.[27] Many of the deaths caused by firearms are considered to be preventable, making this "pandemic" a major concern for public health professionals.

For every death and injury, there are broader psychological effects that are hardly ever measured. The impacts of violence range from death to physical and psychological injury. Furthermore, violence and the prevalence of weapons often create psychological stress that fuels other health problems and creates insecurity. "Terrorist" attacks, random violence and serial killers, while statistically insignificant as causes of death and injury, in many contexts create elevated levels of psychological stress and anxiety among large segments of the population.

Table 2.1 Countries with the Highest Rates of Reported Firearm Deaths (per 100,000) in the World*

Ranking	Country	Year	Total Firearm Deaths (Minimum)	Total Firearm Death Rate (Minimum)	Gun Homicide Rate	Gun Suicide Rate	Accidental Firearm Death Rate	Undetermined Death Rate	Percent of Homicides with Firearms	Percent of Firearm Deaths That Are Homicides
1	Colombia	2002	22,827	55.7	51.8				86	93
2	Venezuela	2000	5,689	34.3	22.15	1.16	0.42	10.57	67	95
3	South Africa	2002	11,709	26.8	26.1				54	97
4	El Salvador	2001	1,641	25.8	25.3				71	98
5	Brazil	2002	38,088	21.72	19.54	0.78	0.18	1.22	64	97
6	Puerto Rico	2001	734	19.12	17.36	1.17	0.49	0.1	91	91
7	Jamaica	1997	450	18.6	18.2	0.37			58	98
8	Guatemala	2000	2,109	18.5						
9	Honduras	1999	1,677	16.2	16.2					
10	Uruguay	2000	104	13.91	3.11	7.18	3.53	0.09	63	22
11	Ecuador	2000	1,321	13.39	10.73	0.77	0.25	1.63	68	80
12	Argentina	2001	371	11.49	4.34	2.88	0.64	3.63	70	38
13	USA	2001	29,753	10.27	3.98	5.92	0.28	0.08	64	38

*Firearm death rate among 112 countries.

Source: Global Firearms Deaths (Toronto: Small Arms/Firearms Education and Research Network, 2005), http://www.ryerson.ca/SAFER-Net/issues/globalfirearmdeaths.html.

Figure 2.1 Firearm Death Rates for Twenty-Five High-Income Countries

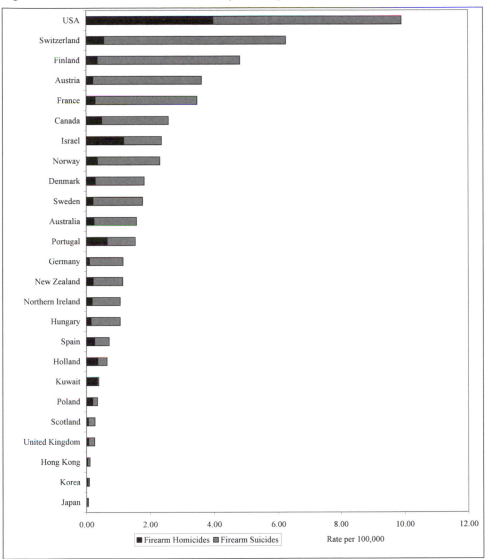

Source: *Global Firearm Deaths* (Toronto: Small Arms/Firearms Education and Research Network, 2005), www.ryerson.ca/SAFER-Net/issues/globalfirearmdeaths.html.

Homicide

Homicide rates are driven by a variety of factors, including demographics. The percentage of young males in a population is positively related to homicide rates. Young men tend to account for a substantial percentage of perpetrators as well as victims. Often the boundaries of criminal and polit-

Figure 2.2 Crime/Injury Pyramid

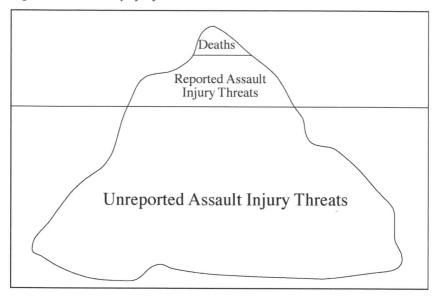

Deaths

Reported Assault
Injury Threats

Unreported Assault Injury Threats

ical violence are blurred so that the casualties of homicide versus "conflict" are difficult to discern. In contrast, domestic violence (discussed in the next section) is endemic in both industrialized and developing countries and is shaped by different factors. Because of the complexity of homicide determinants, it is often difficult to establish the specific role of firearms; nevertheless, most observers agree that the availability of firearms increases the lethality of violence and is tied to higher rates of firearm homicide. Studies of homicide across industrialized nations have shown consistently that, while rates of homicide involving other means are comparable, rates of homicide involving firearms are higher in the United States than in any other industrialized countries.[28] For example, in 2003 there were 11,700 gun homicides in the United States, a country with 300 million people (4.0 per 100,000). In Canada, a country with 30 million people, there were 161 gun murders (0.5 per 100,000) and in England and Wales 80 gun murders (0.15 per 100,000). (See Table 2.9.) We discuss these differences further in Chapter 3, but one factor certainly appears to be the availability of firearms.

Between 1985 and 1994, youth homicide rates increased in many parts of the world. Male homicide rates rose more than female homicide rates, and youth homicide increases were more pronounced in developing countries. During this period, there was a steep increase in homicides using guns in many countries. Colombia, a country in which criminal and political violence are intimately connected, has one of the highest reported gun homicide rates in the world—55.7 per 100,000 in 2002. South Africa, Brazil, Venezuela and El Salvador have rates higher than 20 per 100,000.

While in Canada youth homicides fell in this period from 2.1 per 100,000 to 1.9 per 100,000, rates rose in the United States from 8.8 per 100,000 to 15.6 per 100,000. One of the differences appears to have been related to firearms—in Canada only one-third of youth homicides involve guns, compared to 70 percent in the United States. Countries formed after the collapse of the Soviet Union also experienced significant increases in homicides with firearms—the proportion of deaths from firearms in this age-group more than doubled in Azerbaijan, Latvia and the Russian Federation during the 1990s. The other risk factors for youth violence include individual characteristics, relationship factors and family influences. Peer influence is considered to play a critical role, particularly in gang-related violence, as is substance abuse. Gangs, guns and drugs are a particularly lethal combination. Carrying weapons is a high-risk and predominantly male behavior in this age-group. Access to firearms is considered a particularly significant factor because much of the homicide in this age-group (as with suicide) is impulsive. In many societies, young people represent a high proportion of perpetrators and victims of violence. For example, in Rio de Janiero, where the majority of homicides are committed with firearms, the majority of victims and perpetrators are under twenty-five years old and drug dealing is often associated with victimization.[29]

Gender-Based Violence

The majority of victims of most crimes, including murder, are men, and in many countries firearms are the weapons of choice. According to WHO, of 115,593 deaths reported, women accounted for 11,110, including roughly 10 percent of homicides. However, in many countries death and injury data are not reported by gender.[30] In some forms of violence involving firearms, for example, domestic violence, women are more likely to be victims. The presence of firearms is a particular risk factor for domestic homicide. A number of studies have suggested that the risk of being murdered by an intimate partner increases with the availability of firearms. A study of women physically abused by current or former intimate partners in the United States showed a fivefold increased risk of the partner murdering the woman when the partner owned a firearm.[31] In Canada, access to firearms is one of the top five risk factors associated with domestic female homicide.[32] Family and intimate assaults involving firearms are twelve times more likely to result in death than intimate assaults that do not involve firearms.[33]

Worldwide, women are more at risk from violence at the hands of intimate partners, while men are more at risk from male acquaintances.[34] For example, in four out of five intimate partner homicides in Australia, the perpetrator is male and the victim female.[35] Women account for the majority of victims in domestic violence worldwide. Consistent with other international studies, research in South Africa suggests that more women are shot at home in domestic violence situations than are shot by strangers on the streets or by intruders.[36] In a ten-year period in the United States, over 70 percent of spousal homicides carried out by husbands or ex-husbands

Figure 2.3 Female Homicide Rates for Twenty-Five Populous, High-Income Countries, 1994–1999

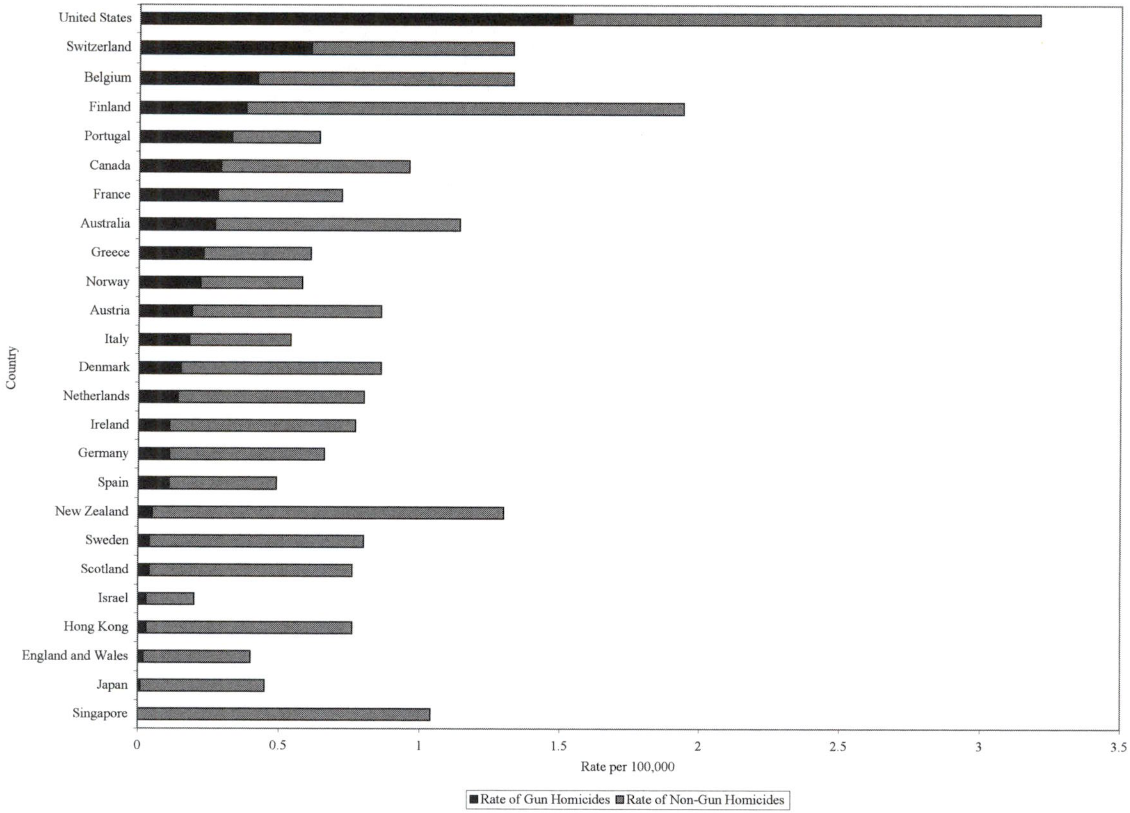

Rate per 100,000

■ Rate of Gun Homicides ■ Rate of Non-Gun Homicides

Source: D. Hemenway, T. Shinoda-Tagawa, and M. Miller, "Firearm Availability and Female Homicide Victimization Rates across 25 Populous High-income Countries," *Journal of the American Medical Women's Association* 57 (2002): 100–104.

involved firearms, and in 57 percent of all murders committed by boyfriends, guns were used.[37] Women are far more at risk from intimate partners than from strangers: Among female homicide victims, murders by spouses, ex-spouses and intimate acquaintances were more prevalent than murders by strangers. In fact, for every female killed by a stranger, four women were murdered by intimate partners using guns.[38] In Brazil, almost half (46 percent) of women killed by their husbands are shot; in Canada, 25 percent of female victims of domestic homicide are shot.[39] A recent study of female homicide in twenty-six countries with firearms showed a strong relationship between the rates of women killed and the availability of firearms.[40] (See Figure 2.3.)

Traditional constructions of "crime" and "the criminal element" in the media focus on random acts of violence and have tended to downplay domestic violence. Women's organizations have argued that these distinctions have little meaning when violence against women is concerned:

> Most homicides are not random acts of violence and most guns used to commit murder are not smuggled or illegally owned. In fact, in most cases they are owned by legitimate gun owners. [Is it not true] that domestic abuse and domestic homicide are criminal acts? The men who commit these crimes are usually perceived by their friends and neighbours as law-abiding, responsible people, and many of them own guns legally. But when a man abuses his spouse, he commits a crime, whether he is prosecuted or not.[41]

Domestic violence is widespread and not considered a serious crime in many countries. Under-reporting makes it difficult to track levels of gender-based violence or to protect women from firearm violence in their homes. Emerging research from Turkey recognizes the dangers that gun ownership poses for married women, as firearms are increasingly being used to harm or murder spouses.[42]

For every woman who is killed or injured with a firearm, many more are threatened. Even when a gun is not fired, people threatened with shooting may suffer serious psychological damage."[43] The patterns of threatening are astonishingly similar across cultures and include such behaviors as shooting the family dog as a warning or getting the gun out and cleaning it during an argument. Studies of abused women in many corners of the world—Australia,[44] South Africa[45] and Canada[46]—report remarkable similarities.

Sexual assault is a crime in which women represent a disproportionate number of victims. Many countries have very limited data-collection capacities and do not track victims by age or gender. Nevertheless, a variety of data sources suggest that the problem is widespread. While there are frequently methodological questions surrounding these sources, a number of victimization surveys indicate that the rate of reported sexual assaults by women is high in developing as well as industrialized countries. For example, a meta analysis of studies of women being assaulted by intimate partners showed one-quarter of women or more reporting physical violence in countries as diverse as Nigeria, South Africa, Mexico, Canada, the United States, Papua New Guinea, Switzerland, the United Kingdom and Egypt.[47] Many of the assaults are conducted by individuals known to the victim. Where guns are available, they are used extensively in armed sexual assaults on women, as evidenced by the significant increases in armed rape and sexual assault in South Africa.[48] Sexual violence is endemic during conflict, with much of it perpetrated by armed combatants. Women are strategic targets in conflict; rape and sexual abuse have been used as intimidation strategies in conflicts in Yugoslavia, Afghanistan, Sudan and elsewhere.[49] A recent study in Sierra Leone that surveyed 991 households revealed high levels of sexual violence. While 91 percent indicated that they were quite a bit or extremely worried about future sexual violence to themselves or their family members by combatants, a substantial proportion (39 percent) indicated that they were worried about future sexual violence to themselves or family members by "non-combatants," again reinforcing the fact that risks to women are not confined to war.[50]

Despite the fact that men are statistically more likely to be victims of violence, women often expressed more fear of being injured by firearms. For example, a Canadian study revealed that 36 percent of males and 59 percent of females feared that "you or someone in your household would be threatened or injured with a firearm."[51] The psychological trauma of firearms disrupts social cohesion and family safety, and it often impacts women in different ways than it does men, given their traditional roles in many societies and the family.

Violence Against Children

Children also account for a substantial percentage of firearm victims in conflict situations as well as in "peaceful" contexts. Firearms also enable children, who otherwise would lack the physical strength, to become combatants or killers. There are an estimated 300,000 child soldiers worldwide. There is ample evidence that children raised in conflict (or violence), particularly male children, demonstrate a willingness to use firearms to resolve disputes and so fuel the culture of violence.[52]

The evidence also clearly shows that the risk to children from firearms is not restricted to countries in conflict. Certainly in industrialized countries there are many examples of children using firearms against siblings, schoolmates or themselves. Children are also frequently targets of domestic violence and, where firearms are used, there are more likely to be multiple victims. A study from the Centers for Disease Control comparing firearm death rates in industrialized countries showed that the number of children under the age of fifteen killed annually in the United States equaled the total number of children killed in twenty-five other countries combined. The United States had a rate of firearms death among children that was higher than in conflict zones in Israel and Northern Ireland. American children were nine times more likely to die unintentionally from a firearm, eleven times more likely to die in a firearm suicide and sixteen times more likely to die in a firearm homicide than children in other industrialized countries.[53] Even countries such as Canada have regions in which the number of children under fifteen killed with firearms is higher than the number in Israel and Northern Ireland combined.[54]

Self-Directed Violence: Suicide

In industrialized countries, the mortality rates for suicide with firearms are greater than the mortality rates for homicide with guns. Firearms are the weapons of choice in many countries when men commit suicide, and the increased lethality of firearms often accounts in part for the gender differences in suicide rates. In most industrialized countries, suicide rates with firearms are much higher than rates of interpersonal violence. For example, in Canada, while there were 137 firearm homicides in 2002, there were 633 suicides. Switzerland, with one of the highest rates of firearm death and injury in Europe (see Figure 2.1), had only 36 firearm homicides in 1999 (0.5 per 100,000) but 412 firearm suicides (5.78 per 100,000). In developing countries, the trend is reversed; for example, Brazil reported only 1,383 firearm suicides compared to 37,606 firearm homicides in 2003. Bangladesh reported 14 firearm suicides in 2000 compared to 1,518 firearm homicides. Colombia reported 708 firearm suicides in 1999 compared to 19,553 firearm homicides. While this may in part reflect reporting problems, the pattern is fairly consistent.

The United States is unusual in that the rate of firearm homicide approaches the rate of firearm suicide. Every year in the United States, more than 30,000 people commit suicide, more than half of them with a firearm. In 2002, 17,108 Americans committed suicide with firearms. Young people (fifteen to twenty-four years of age) and the elderly (over sixty-five years of age) are particularly prone to using firearms for this purpose.[55] It should be noted that in the last thirty years firearms have replaced poisoning as the most frequently used method of committing suicide for women in the United States.[56]

While suicides can be committed by other means, firearm use is particularly lethal—93 percent of suicides attempted with firearms succeed.[57] Men are more likely than women to use firearms in suicide attempts, and this in part accounts for the higher rate of completed suicides. Results of epidemiological studies in the United States indicate that there is 4.7 times higher risk of suicide in a household where there is a firearm than in a household where there is no firearm.[58]

There is also a link between the availability of firearms and firearm suicide rates.[59] Indeed, one study suggested a 93 percent correlation between the rate of households with firearms and the firearm death rate (consisting mainly of suicides) in Canada.[60] This is also seen on a regional basis. For example, a 1990–1992 study revealed that nearly half of all suicides in rural regions in Quebec, Canada, involved firearms, while in urban areas such as Montreal, they accounted for only 14 percent. Other research has shown that the rate of suicide with firearms in Quebec has tended to vary with the rate of hunting licences issued. In areas of the province where the number of firearm hunting licences issued is high, the firearm suicide rate is also high.[61] Similar studies in the United States show a strong association between rates of firearm ownership and rates of suicide across regions.[62] Other factors may be at work here, but reducing the availability of firearms seems to be an important part of a suicide reduction strategy.

Data from industrialized countries shows that the correlation between gun ownership (i.e., percentage of households with one or several guns) and gun suicide rates is very strong, although the impact on overall suicide rates is less clear.[63] A number of studies have examined the impact of reducing access to firearms on suicide rates. Studies have tended to show that reducing access results in a reduction over time of both firearm and total suicides, with no evidence of substitution.[64] "The weight of the scientific evidence points to reduction in suicide when adequate gun control legislation is in effect, particularly in subgroups of the population where guns are 'culturally prescribed' methods of suicide as among males. This has led suicide experts to conclude that lives may be saved when effective gun control legislation is in place and conscientiously applied."[65] (This issue is discussed further in Chapter 3.)

Unintentional Injury: "Accidents"

Unintentional injuries or "accidents" account for the smallest percentage of firearm deaths worldwide. However, many of these deaths and injuries affect children and youth and are preventable. Unintentional injuries and deaths are often the result of unauthorized access to firearms, particularly by children. In the United States, 3 percent of firearm deaths, approximately 900 each year, are classified as unintentional. Approximately 400 of the victims are nineteen years of age or younger. Boys are particularly at risk; 80 percent of the shootings involve males, and many incidents occur when a child finds a firearm in the home. Given that 40 percent of American homes are thought to own firearms, it is not surprising that accidental shootings occur more often in the United States than in other industrialized countries. Finland, Canada and Switzerland, which among industrialized countries have high rates of gun ownership, have relatively high rates of unintentional injury and death associated with firearms.

Studies of unintentional injuries in a variety of contexts have suggested that reducing access to firearms is critical in promoting the safety of children. Despite an emphasis on efforts to educate or "train" children not to touch a firearm if they find it, repeated studies have shown that children who find a firearm will play with it in spite of prior firearm safety education, and that parents tend to overestimate the extent to which children will obey instructions not to touch a firearm.[66]

Crime

Firearms figure prominently in a wide range of crimes. In the United States, with a population of 300 million, there are more than 400,000 robberies each year, 40 percent of them with firearms, for a rate of 62 per 100,000 people.[67] In Canada, in contrast, with a population of 30 million, there were 21,751 robberies in 2001, 14.6 percent[68] of them with firearms, for a rate of 14 per 100,000. Yet the rates of robberies *without* firearms are roughly comparable in the two countries—74 per 100,000 in Canada and 87 per 100,000 in the United States. (See Table 2.9.) In a review of victimization data from industrialized countries, a similar pattern emerged. In eight of the nine countries studied, there was a very low reported rate of confrontation with a firearm during a robbery (fewer than 0.5 percent of the respondents). In contrast, among U.S. respondents, more than 1 percent had been a victim of at least one firearm-related robbery in the previous five years. About as many U.S. respondents (1.10 percent) said that they were confronted with a gun as Canadian respondents said that they were confronted with any weapon (1.09 percent).

In some developing countries, the situation is considerably worse. In South Africa, with a population of approximately 45 million, there were a staggering 88,178 robberies with firearms in the year 2000, for a rate of 196 per 100,000.[69] However, the problems of armed urban violence associated with gangs and organized crime transcend national borders. Countries as diverse as the United States, Great Britain, Cambodia,[70] Kenya and Brazil are among the many that have identified urban violence as a significant problem.

Even when robberies do not result in personal injury, the psychological impact can be severe. Robberies have a wide range of consequences for the health of victims.[71] People who live in arms-infested environments have been found to have symptoms of post-traumatic stress disorder, such as overwhelming anxiety and a lack of motivation.[72] Studies have shown that in high-crime areas, residents are more reluctant to venture out and become victims of a wide range of health problems.[73]

The consequences of criminal violence extend beyond their direct effects on victims and the fearfulness created in communities. As discussed below, crime has a variety of indirect effects, including discouraging the provision of basic services and economic development. Fear of crime is also a major factor in the expansion of armed private security, which in turn is linked to the proliferation of weapons and violations of human rights.[74]

Firearms do not in and of themselves "cause" crime, but the availability of firearms can increase the rates and escalate the violence of crime. The use of firearms in robberies in the United States, for example, has been linked to high homicide rates. This is not the case in countries such as Canada that have much lower rates of firearm ownership (particularly handguns). While claims have been made that arming citizens will provide protection from crime, there is little evidence to support these claims.

Collective Violence

The World Health Organization describes various forms of collective violence, including:

- Wars, terrorism and other violent political conflicts that occur within or between states;
- State-perpetrated violence such as genocide, repression, disappearances, torture and other abuses of human rights; and
- Organized violent crimes such as banditry and gang warfare.

Often the boundaries between political and criminal violence are unclear. For example, Colombia reports a high rate of firearm homicide. Of these reported homicides, many occur in the context of political violence. Calculating the deaths from small arms in "conflict zones" is difficult because of the lack of data as well as the imperfect definition. The WHO estimates that about 310,000 people died from war-related injuries in 2000.[75] Typically, deaths in armed conflicts are not differentiated according to the instrument of death, as they are in other contexts. Recent studies have claimed that in most conflicts, light weapons (handguns, rifles, shotguns, mortars and other small arms) are the principal cause of both civilian and combatant deaths.[76] More recent work has refined the estimate, distinguishing between those who are direct casualties killed by gunshots and those who die as a result of the secondary impacts of small arms violence. The Small Arms Survey estimates the number of direct conflict deaths for 2003 as between 80,000 and 108,000 with small arms and light weapons responsible for the majority (60 to 90 percent). Indirect deaths associated with these conflicts are much higher.[77]

Often the data regarding these deaths are not detailed in terms of the profiles of the victims; however, a large percentage of victims are believed to be civilians, conservatively estimated by the International Committee of the Red Cross at more than 35 percent. An analysis of the first 17,086 people admitted for weapon injuries and recorded in the ICRC surgical database reported that 35 percent were female, males under the age of sixteen, or males age fifty and over.[78] This figure has been cited as a conservative indicator of the proportion of people injured by weapons who were probably noncombatants. There is evidence that the proportion has been increasing over the course of the twentieth century.[79] A study in Croatia used death certificates and employment records to examine the civilian proportion of conflict-related fatalities and found that civilians could have accounted for 64 percent of the 4,339 fatalities studied.[80] Not only are data regarding deaths and injuries from gunshots unavailable, but there are also many more secondary deaths caused by small arms conflicts and the dislocation and diseases that follow.

It is important to note that the changing nature of conflict has put women and children more at risk, both during and after conflict, as the patterns of warfare and the weapons used have changed. In many of the conflicts of the 1990s, civilians have been the deliberate targets of violence and terror.[81] Fighting along tribal, religious and ethnic lines is often explicitly aimed at ethnic cleansing, forced displacement and killings, or a combination of the three.[82]

A study of 101 conflicts fought between 1989 and 1996 revealed that small arms and light weapons were generally the weapons of preference or even the only weapons used.[83] Another study estimated that 3.2 million deaths occurred in internal armed conflicts during the period 1990–1995 alone.[84] Quite apart from death and injury associated with firearms, there are many secondary impacts of conflict, including the creation of large migrations of people. The conditions in many of the resulting refugee camps are appalling and are coupled with constant threats from warring parties or criminal activity. The stability that is needed to raise a family is often completely disrupted. The stress and the psychological impact of being a refugee or displaced person can leave scars that last long after the hostilities have ended.[85]

Worldwide, the percentage of firearm deaths in what are deemed "terrorist acts" is quite small. Nevertheless, firearms are stockpiled by terrorist organizations worldwide to support a wide range of activities—robberies, kidnappings, armed conflicts and massacres. Many "terrorist" acts occur within the context of sustained political conflict, but "terrorist" acts of violence are generally distinguished by their deliberate targeting of civilians. When military weapons are used in a confined space against civilians (typical circumstances in terrorist attacks and other mass murders), the ratio of injuries to death decreases to less than 1 to 1.[86]

Firearms have been used in many mass attacks against civilians over the past thirty years. One of the first highly publicized attacks occurred on September 5, 1972, at the Munich Olympics, when eight members of Black September, a Palestine Liberation Organization splinter group, killed two Israeli athletes and took nine hostages, whom they eventually killed. Many other high-profile attacks on civilians have involved small arms.

Although comprehensive data are not available, an analysis of 400 recorded "terrorist" incidents during 1997–2001 revealed that firearms were clearly used in 119 of them and probably used in another 40 kidnappings and abductions.[87] Often, legal firearms are diverted to illegal markets to arm terrorists—for example, a review of illicit trafficking incidents reveals many cases in which firearms from U.S. gun shows were diverted to the Irish Republican Army (IRA). Decommissioning the IRA and collecting members' weapons has proved a major stumbling block to sustainable peace in the region. In Colombia, where fighting among factions labeled "terrorist" has resulted in the highest reported homicide rate in the world, 80 percent of deaths are caused by firearms. Although recent attacks by Al Qaeda have involved explosives and incendiaries, it has been reported that Al Qaeda training manuals instruct adherents to obtain military assault weapons and provide details about how to acquire them in the United States.[88]

INDIRECT EFFECTS

Economic Effects

The economic well-being of populations is significantly affected by firearm use and possession in many areas of the world. The direct effects include the cessation of direct medical care and rehabilitative services, the disruption of basic human services, the negative impacts on property values and tourism and the undermining of responsible governance. The indirect effects include economic downturns, lost growth and reduced productivity. In Latin America, criminal violence dwarfs political violence and has a huge impact on individual security, economic development and governance. The Inter-American Development Bank estimated the economic costs of all violence, including costs of policing as well as the value of life lost, at $140–170 billion (U.S. dollars) per year, or 14.6 percent of the GDP. In Brazil, 10 percent of the GDP is consumed by violence, and in Colombia the cost is 25 percent of GDP.[89] Firearms are used in more than 70 percent of homicides in Colombia and 88 percent of homicides in Brazil.

Estimates have long been made of the broad economic impacts of various public health problems, such as tobacco use,[90] AIDS, motor vehicle accidents and gunshots. Some studies have focused on tallying the direct costs (hospitals, police, etc.). For example, a 1997 study estimated the cost of treating firearm injuries in one South African hospital to be between 12 and 47 million rand (U.S. $1.9–7.3 million).[91]

The impact of gun violence in "peaceful" countries is also significant. The direct cost of deaths and injuries due to firearms in the United States has been calculated at $22,500 for each fatal gunshot and $30,500 for each injured person.[92] The total impact goes beyond emergency medical care and rehabilitation.

Other studies have added "indirect costs" to these direct costs, such as the value of lost life in terms of earning power. In some cases, "quality of life" has also been included. The "value" assigned to the loss of life varies considerably based on the earning power of the victim, which is affected by age, gender and other factors. Even in industrialized countries, the economic costs of violence are staggering. One study estimates that factoring in indirect costs and quality of life costs, the cost rises to $2.8 million per fatally wounded person and $249,000 per nonfatally injured person.[93] Ted Miller, a health economist, has estimated costs of firearm-related damage as being $195 per person per year in Canada and $495 per person per year in the United States.[94]

In Canada, the costs of firearm death and injury (including murder, suicide and unintentional injuries) have been estimated at $6.6 billion per year.[95] In addition to the costs measured in terms of the economic value of lost life, violence in the United States diverts health, policing and social resources from other problems. In the United States, the number of deaths and attendant costs are much higher.[96] The assumptions underlying these figures have, however, been challenged, since they assign monetary values to factors such as pain, burden of suffering, loss of livelihood and quality of life. Others maintain that attempting to assign a monetary value to human life is perverse.[97]

Violence may have a direct negative effect on property taxes and values.[98] Some studies have explored the effects of crime and violence on local businesses by assessing the impact of crime and disorder on the economic vitality of local areas. In addition to the direct costs of burglary, vandalism and theft, there are effects on retailing and hospitality industries, insurance costs and the ability to attract and retain employees.[99] Cook and Ludwig also maintain that living with the risk of gun violence leads private citizens, businesses and government agencies to spend money to reduce risk. They estimate that $5–8 billion per year is spent in the United States in avoidance and prevention costs, such as additional costs to the justice system, policing and private security.[100]

Impeding Sustainable Development

Studies of crime and conflict examine the "cycle of violence" as both a cause and an effect of violence. For example, some claim that violence is a key reason for the broadening chasm between industrialized and developing countries. Young people in many countries are socialized in cultures defined by war.[101] These systems give rise to greater poverty and inequality, conditions that in turn can lead to increased levels of crime and violence. Similar arguments are made about criminal subcultures in the United States and Canada. Victimization contributes to crime and violence, and instability impedes development. In many parts of the world, crime and violence have emerged as major obstacles to development objectives.[102]

There are additional costs of victimization. Victims of violence, out of a desire for retribution, become perpetrators themselves, fuelling the cycle of violence.[103] This cycle can also be understood in indirect terms: violent societies create insecurity, which leads to a greater level of arms ownership among the populace, which leads to more violence.[104] The long-term or ripple effects are also dependent in part on the availability of services for victims as well as the individual's financial capacity. In many countries, the poor are most often the victims of crime, and they are less likely to be able to absorb the costs (such as medical care or the inability to work).[105]

The Corporate Resources Group of New York rates cities around the world based on forty-two variables including political and social stability.[106] Crime levels are also one of the factors taken into account by similar bodies that rate cities as desirable tourist destinations or business locations.[107] Typically, high-crime-rate areas have higher insurance premiums for both businesses and residences.[108] At the same time, decision making is a function of perception as well as reality, and we need to explore the effects of perceived risk on decision making with regard to investment and consumer behavior.[109] The media's (mis)representation of violence plays an important role in shaping these perceptions (see Chapter 6).[110]

Disruption of Health Care

Violence has been identified as a major impediment to the provision of basic health care by diverting much-needed resources from health and social services.[111] In South Africa, scarce hospital resources are absorbed in dealing with violence, and health care personnel are increasingly finding themselves the target of violence. Treating firearm injuries absorbed considerable emergency room resources.[112]

In conflict zones, field personnel have observed that more injured victims die during transport than at treatment facilities. The medical transportation infrastructure and local personnel trained in first aid cannot carry the burden created by increased arms proliferation. Other secondary effects include problems related to the blood supply. Not only are blood availability and transfusion key issues in developing countries, but emergency responses to large-scale violence often do not accommodate careful testing for HIV and result in additional problems.[113]

In early 1998, a survey of staff of the International Committee of the Red Cross was undertaken to assess the impact on armed violence on their humanitarian missions. Most (60 percent) of respondents reported that ICRC operations were interrupted fairly frequently by armed security threats. Typically the incident involved firing weapons at or near ICRC staff, followed in prevalence by use of weapons to threaten ICRC personnel and use of weapons to commit a robbery. Approximately one-third of respondents believed that "roughly half" or more of the population lived in areas not accessible to the ICRC because of armed security threats.[114]

Fueling the Culture of Violence

The "culture of violence" is both a cause and an effect of small arms and light weapons availability. A culture of arms possession created and normalized during the militarization of societies can contribute to individuals resorting to guns as their first instruments for resolving problems. A Cambodian study reported that in areas with high levels of weapons possession, people are threatened with guns over simple conflicts such as traffic violations.[115] Increased weapon availability also fuels the "culture of violence." Relief workers have noted increases in the number of common thieves who are armed and the number of armed military and police personnel who are under the influence of alcohol or drugs and carrying firearms.[116] Similar effects have been observed in terms of the militarization of culture in South Africa.[117] In addition, arming in response to perceived threats to security was evident in the United States: firearm sales increased after the attacks of September 11, 2001.

The demand for firearms, particularly military weapons and handguns, may also be fueled by violent movies and television programs that tend to link masculinity and heroism with guns and violence.[118] The association of masculinity and guns is by no means a phenomenon limited to the United States, but has been reported in contexts as diverse as Papua New Guinea, Brazil and South Africa as well.

Scholars have also maintained that institutions and laws are important cultural carriers. For example, scholars have suggested that laws do not just reflect values, they can also shape them. In the same way, legislation has been observed to have long-term effects on other behaviors.[119] Capital punishment, for example, legitimizes violence, while laws controlling firearms reinforce values of non-violence.

Human Rights and Governance

Violence fueled by firearms also represents a significant threat to the reinstatement of democratic governance essential to sustainable peace.[120] The continued availability of weapons often produces other lasting consequences such as the breakdown of civil order and dramatic increases in lawlessness, banditry and illicit drug trafficking. Firearms can change the balance of power and may raise the level of violence. Even if in the short term their use is for self-defense, the long-term effect may be to limit, if not negate, other ways of addressing conflict resolution by peaceful means.[121] In Central America, for example, the United Nations has been very successful in peacekeeping, but the proliferation of light weapons presents challenges to long-term stability and reconciliation.[122]

Recently, the United Nation's Special Rapporteur on Human Rights reiterated the importance of recognizing the threat that the proliferation and misuse of firearms presents to human rights worldwide.

REGIONAL VARIATIONS

The problem of firearms must be framed through regional needs and contexts. Regional differences in the shape of the problem must be understood in order to develop appropriate strategies to address it. In some contexts, as in the Horn of Africa, conflict is a priority, while in others such as Brazil, crime is the most compelling problem. In countries such as Canada and Finland, on the other hand, prevention of suicide and injury is critical; in newly democratizing and economically transitioning countries such as South Africa and the former Soviet republics, conflict and crime are inseparable. The problem of firearms varies from region to region. Studies that have been undertaken in South Asia,[123] South Africa[124] and Central America[125] have reinforced the importance of reducing the availability of weapons.

North America and the Caribbean

The thirty-five countries that comprise the Americas include 800 million people—about 14 percent of the world's population. But these countries account for more than half the world's reported firearm deaths occurring in countries that are not at war. In total there are more than 40,000 deaths from firearms per year in North America and the Caribbean (see Table 2.2) and more than 50,000 per year in Central and South America. In the year 2000, the United States had almost 30,000 deaths from firearms—accidents, suicides and homicides (10.27 per 100,000)[126]—by far the highest rate in the industrialized world.[127] Of these, 10,820 were homicides, 17,108 were suicides and the rest were unintentional deaths.[128] The pattern in the United States, where 38 percent of firearm deaths are due to homicide, is similar to patterns found in third world countries such as Colombia, Brazil and Jamaica, where the firearm homicide rate is comparable to or surpasses the firearm suicide rate. Of homicides in the United States, two-thirds (66.7 percent) involve firearms.[129] Regional variations in firearms death and injury are pronounced. The effects on different populations are also significant. While African Americans account for 13 percent of the population of the United States, they account for 24 percent of total firearm deaths and over half of firearm homicide victims.[130] Because of the fragmentation of reporting, the United States still does not have a reliable national record of firearm injuries, but generally it is estimated that a comparable number of people require hospitalization for injuries with firearms each year.

Canada is similar to the United States in many ways, except when it comes to firearms. While rates of violent crime are comparable or higher, rates of homicide and particularly of firearm homicide are much lower. Suicides account for 80 percent of firearm deaths in Canada. In 2001, for example, a total of 816 firearm deaths (2.6 per 100,000) were reported. Of these, 31 were classified as unintentional (accidents), 633 as suicides, 137 as homicides, 5 as "justifiable homicides" and 10 as undetermined. A comparable number of people injured with firearms required hospitalization.[131] Although handguns now account for more than 60 percent of firearm homicides, rifles and shotguns are the weapons more likely to be used in suicides, unintentional injuries and domestic violence. A substantial proportion—about 50 percent—of handgun murders in Canada occur with firearms smuggled in from the United States. Despite media portrayals of gun violence as an urban phenomenon, the murder rate in communities in Canada with populations greater than 500,000 is half that in rural locations where guns are more prevalent.[132]

In Mexico, rates of firearm homicide are slightly higher than those in the United States, with about 6,000 people killed in 2001 (5.21 per 100,000). But reported suicides are lower (0.7 per 100,000). Consequently, Mexico has a lower rate of firearm deaths than the United States (6.69 per 100,000 in Mexico versus 10.27 per 100,000 in the United States). In Mexico, it is estimated that more than 80 percent of guns recovered in crimes are smuggled in from the United States.

Islands in the Caribbean are also a transit point in the illegal trafficking of firearms, often in exchange for drugs. Hardest hit in the region was Jamaica, where 450 people were murdered with firearms in 1997, for a rate of 18.6 per 100,000. "Justifiable" homicide in Jamaica—killings by police—are relatively high: 5.0 per 100,000.[133] Political violence in Haiti has taken a toll in recent years, although data on death by firearms are not available. In comparison, the Bahamas had less than 40 firearm murders in 2000, for a rate of 12.29 per 100,000, and the Dominican Republic has 314 firearm murders in a typical year, for a rate of 4 per 100,000.[134] There is no research data available for Haiti, but anecdotal reports suggest high levels of gun violence there.

South and Central America

Brazil has one of the world's highest rates of firearm homicide, four times higher than that of the United States.[135] (See Table 2.3.) In 2002, a total of 49,570 homicides were documented in Brazil (28.4 per 100,000); firearms were the weapons used in 68.8 percent or 34,085 homicides (21.7 per 100,000).[136] The homicide rate in Brazil more than doubled from 1980 to 2002, from 11.4 per 100,000 to 28.4 per 100,000.[137] In 2002, the Brazilian homicide rate was 53.1 per 100,000 among males and 4.3 per 100,000 among females, and adolescent (fifteen to nineteen years of age) and young adult (20 to 29 years of age) males accounted for 52.2 percent of homicide victims.[138] The homicide rate was highest among young adult males (121.0 per 100,000),[139] and for persons age fifteen to forty-four, homicide was the leading cause of death.[140] Brazil reports ten times as many injuries as fatalities from firearms.[141] In São Paulo, the homicide rate more than tripled, from 17.5 per 100,000 in 1980 to 53.9 per 100,000 in 2002.[142] A total of 5,719 homicides were reported in São Paulo in 2002,[143] and firearms were used in 62.0 percent of all incidents. The homicide rate for males was nearly 15 times that for females (105.1 compared to 7.2 per 100,000).[144] The largest portion of homicide victims (approximately 59.8 percent) were adolescent and young adult males.[145] The highest rate among males, approximately 227.4 per 100,000, was found among males age twenty to twenty-nine years of age.[146]

Increasing urbanization, expansion of illegal drug and firearms trafficking, a lengthy economic crisis, increased unemployment, and widening income inequality have been identified as contributing to increased

Table 2.2 Firearm Death Rates (per 100,000) in North America and the Caribbean

Country	Year	Total Gun Death Rate (Minimum)	Gun Homicide Rate	Gun Suicide Rate	Gun Accident Rate	Undeter-mined	Total Homicide Rate	Percent of Homicides with Guns	Total Suicide Rate	Percent of Suicides with Guns
Puerto Rico	2001	19.12	17.36	1.17	0.49	0.1	19.4	89.5	7.5	15.6
Jamaica	1995	18.6	18.2	0.37			32.2	58	1.49	25
Bahamas	2000	12.95	12.29	0.33	0	0.33	20.3	60.5	3.7	8.9
USA	2001	10.27	3.98	5.92	0.28	0.08	6.5	61.2	10.7	55.3
Saint Lucia	2001	6.44	6.44	0	0	0	14.8	43.5	4.5	0
Barbados	2000	6.02	6.02	0	0	0	10.2	59.0	3.8	0
Canada	2002	2.6	0.4	2.0	0.03	0.01	1.3	36.9	11.8	17.8
Cuba	2002	0.98	0.45	0.35	0.13	0.06	5.8	7.8	14.3	2.5

Source: Global Firearms Deaths (Toronto: Small Arms/Firearms Education and Research Network, 2005), http://www.ryerson.ca/SAFER-Net/issues/globalfirearmdeaths.html.

violence.[147] Homicide research in other urban areas worldwide is consistent with the strong negative correlation between monthly average income and homicide rates found in São Paulo.[148] The availability of firearms is also considered to be an important contributing factor.

In Colombia, political and criminal violence involving firearms has escalated dramatically over the last twenty years. The boundaries between the two are blurred as there is what is considered a civil war being waged between the Colombian government and the Revolutionary Armed Forces of Colombia (FARC). The drug trade, the illicit trade in firearms and political violence are also intertwined. In 2002 there were 22,827 firearm murders, more than 51.8 per 100,000 the highest rate in the world.[149] A large proportion of these occurred in the nation's capital, Bogotá, as well as in the cities of Cali and Medellín, historic centers of the cocaine trade.

Other Latin American countries also have a legacy of violence, as firearms have remained in circulation following civil wars. It has been estimated that in 1998–1999, the number of violent deaths from firearms in Nicaragua, El Salvador and Guatemala exceeded those that had occurred in the civil wars in Colombia. El Salvador had 1,609 in 2001 (25.3 per 100,000 in 2001), and 71 percent of El Salvador's murders are committed with firearms.[150] Seven percent of thirteen- to nineteen-year-olds admitted to carrying a gun to school. The vast majority of weapons in the country are pistols and revolvers.[151] In Guatemala, murder rates are also high, though current data is not available.[152] In Nicaragua, the reported firearm homicide rate was 8.02 per 100,000 in 1998, but by 2002 had declined to 3.04 per 100,000.[153] In Honduras, 1,677 firearm homicides were reported in 1999, a rate of 16.2 per 100,000.[154]

Western Europe

There is a significant variation in rate of firearm death in European countries, although in all of them in which data are available, suicides account for the majority of firearm deaths. The relaxation of border controls has meant that the flow of firearms among countries has increased. Great Britain's rates of firearm death are much lower than those of other countries. In 2002, England and Wales had 115 firearm suicides (a rate of 0.2 per 100,000), accounting for a small percentage of overall suicides. Firearms also account for a small proportion of homicides. In total, they had 80 firearm homicides in 2002–2003 for a rate of 0.15 per 100,000.

Germany also has low rates of firearm suicide and homicide. In 2001, there were 906 reported firearm suicides (1.1 per 100,000). There were 155 firearm homicides (0.2 per 100,000) among 720 total homicides (0.9 per 100,000).[155]

In Western Europe, the highest rates of firearm death are reported in Switzerland (6.4 per 100,000 in 1998) and Finland (4.89 per 100,000 in

Table 2.3 Firearm Death Rates (per 100,000) in Central and South America

Country	Year	Total Gun Death Rate (Minimum)	Gun Homicide Rate	Gun Suicide Rate	Gun Accident Rate	Undeter-mined	Total Homicide Rate	Percent of Homicides with Guns	Total Suicide Rate	Percent of Suicides with Guns
Colombia	2002	55.7	51.8				60.23	86.0	0	
Venezuela	2000	34.3	22.15	1.16	0.42	10.57	25.8	85.9	5.2	22.3
El Salvador	2001	25.8	25.3				31.54	80.2		
Brazil	2002	21.72	19.54	0.78	0.18	1.22	28.4	68.8	4.4	17.7
Guatemala	2000	18.5					44.9	0.6	0	
Honduras	1999	16.16	16.16	0	0	0	16.16	63.5	16.6	43.3
Uruguay	2000	13.91	3.11	7.18	3.53	0.09	4.9	68.3	4.2	18.3
Ecuador	2000	13.39	10.73	0.77	0.25	1.63	15.7	70.0	8.1	35.6
Argentina	2001	11.49	4.34	2.88	0.64	3.63	6.2	37.7	7.4	5.5
Belize	2000	9.09	8.26	0.41	0.41	0	21.9	64.6	2.7	23.0
Paraguay	2000	8.26	7.11	0.62	0.27	0.26	11	61.4	5.2	13.3
Panama	2002	8	7.25	0.69	0.07	0	11.8	61.3	3.7	18.9
Mexico	2001	6.69	5.21	0.7	0.48	0.29	8.5	56.8	6.9	18.8
Costa Rica	2002	4.87	3.18	1.3	0.07	0.32	5.6	46.8	6.9	7.0
Nicaragua	2002	4.51	3.04	0.48	0.97	0.02	6.5	37.3	10.1	10.9
Chile	2002	2.99	1.49	1.1	0.41	0	4	47.7	0.8	13.8
Peru	2000	1.8	0.62	0.11	0.94	0.13	1.3			

Source: Global Firearm Deaths (Toronto: Small Arms/Firearms Education and Research Network, 2005), http://www.ryerson.ca/SAFER-Net/issues/globalfirearmdeaths.html.

2003).[156] These countries also have the highest rate of women murdered with firearms and high rates of suicide with guns. These relatively high rates have been linked to the greater availability of firearms in homes although they are still less than half the rates of the United States.[157]

Eastern Europe and the Former Soviet Union

The breakup of the Soviet Union destabilized the region in a number of ways. Economic and social instability have increased crime and insecurity, and the explosion of private security organizations has fueled an increase in weapons carrying. Sectarian violence and terrorism with firearms plague some regions. (See Table 2.5.) In the turbulent period leading up to and following the collapse of the Soviet Union, homicide rates among ten- to twenty-four-year-olds in the Russian Federation increased by more than 150 percent, from 7.0 per 100,000 in 1985 to 18.0 per 100,000 in 1994. During the same period, the proportion of homicides with guns more than doubled.[158] Nevertheless, rates of firearm homicide vary significantly in the region.

The Russian Federation does not provide comprehensive data on firearm crime, so the specifics are vague, but there is no question that there is a significant problem. In 1998, as many as 18,500 crimes were committed using arms or explosives.[159] According to the Russian Interior Ministry, more than 30,000 crimes were committed using weapons in 1999. Of these, 6,000 were homicides and 7,500 were assaults committed during robberies.[160] In 2000, there were 20,890 homicides in Russia (20 per 100,000), but the proportion with firearms is not known, although some scholars estimate it is fewer than 20 percent. In the first half of 2002, there were 7,200 crimes involving firearms, and approximately half of these involved legally possessed weapons.[161] The problems of criminal violence in the Russian Federation have given rise to an explosion in private security forces and have undermined the confidence of foreign investors in the region. Political conflicts in Chechnya have also fueled terrorist attacks.

Some countries in the region have shown marked improvement, however. Estonia, for example, has shown a dramatic decline in reported homicides with firearms. In 1994, there were a total of 423 reported homicides (28.3 per 100,000), of which 121 involved firearms[162] (8.1 per 100,000), one of the highest firearm homicide rates among industrialized countries.[163] However, over the last few years, the firearm homicide rate appears to have declined dramatically. In the year 2002, there were only 160 homicides (11.7 per 100,000), and only 21 involved firearms, for a rate of 1.55 per 100,000.[164] Countries such as Lithuania and Latvia have similar statistics. In 2003, there were 346 murders in Lithuania, 21 of which were committed with a firearm (a rate of .06 per 100,000).[165] Latvia, like Lithuania, is relatively stable, with 21 firearm homicides in 2003 (0.9 per 100,000).[166] In 2002, 155 other crimes involving use of firearms were reported in

Table 2.4 Firearm Death Rates (per 100,000) in Western Europe

Country	Year	Total Gun Death Rate (Minimum)	Gun Homicide Rate	Gun Suicide Rate	Gun Accident Rate	Undetermined	Total Homicide Rate	Percent of Homicides with Guns	Total Suicide Rate	Percent of Suicides with Guns
Switzerland	1998	6.4	0.5	5.8	0.1					
Finland	2003	4.89	0.35	4.45	0.06	0.04	1.8	19.44	20.6	21.6
France	2001	3.95	0.28	3.19	0.06	0.43	0.7	40	16	19.33
Austria	2003	3.02	0.21	3.4	0.02	2.8	0.6	35	20	17
Norway	2002	2.34	0.35	1.96	0	0.02	0.9	38.89	10.62	18.46
Portugal	2002	2.13	0.65	0.89	0.2	0.4	1.4	46.43	11	8.09
Italy	1997	1.98	0.81	1.1	0.07					
Denmark	2000	1.91	0.28	1.54	0.02	0.07	1.2	23.33	13.6	11.32
Sweden	2001	1.84	0.21	1.56	0.02	0.04	0.9	23.33	13.4	11.64
Germany	2001	1.34	0.2	1.1	0.02	0.16	0.9	20	13.3	7.89
Northern Ireland	2002	1.06	0.18	0.88	0	0	1.2	15	9.5	9.26
Spain	2002	0.78	0.25	0.46	0.06	0.01	0.9	27.78	7.8	5.9
Netherlands	2003	0.64	0.35	0.29	0.01	0.01	1.2	29.17	9.2	3.15
Scotland	2002	0.32	0.06	0.2	0.02	0.04	2.3	2.61	12.4	1.61
England and Wales	2002	0.38	0.15	0.2	0	0.03	1.9	7.9	6.7	2.69

Source: Global Firearms Deaths (Toronto: Small Arms/Firearms Education and Research Network, 2005), http://www.ryerson.ca/SAFER-Net/issues/globalfirearmdeaths.html.

Latvia.[167] In contrast, the Ukraine has a lower rate of reported firearm homicides—only 173 in 2000, for a rate of 0.35 per 100,000.[168] This is lower than the rates for many European countries, although Poland is comparable, with under 200 firearm deaths in 2002, a rate of 0.48 per 100,000.[169] Further, only a small percentage of robberies in the Ukraine are committed with a firearm. In 1996, for example, of 5,361 reported robberies and thefts, only 326 were committed with a firearm.[170] Reporting of crime is of course variable but levels of violence in Eastern Europe (with the exception of the Russian Federation, Georgia and Maldova) are approaching the levels in other industrialized regions.

Africa

Casualties from small arms in African conflicts are difficult to estimate, and the impact of the conflicts is wide-ranging. The WHO estimates that 167,000 deaths from war-related injury occurred in Africa in 2000—more than half the deaths in conflicts worldwide (310,000) that same year. Worldwide, the highest rates of war-related deaths are found in the African region (32 per 100,000). Violence-related injuries (homicide, war wounds and suicide) account for 3 percent of all deaths in that region. There are no reliable estimates of the proportion of these caused by gunshots. Even when firearms are not the cause of death, they often play a role. For example, in Rwanda, where other weapons such as machetes may account for the majority of deaths, firearms were often used to round up potential victims.[171] The problem of small arms in the hands of child soldiers in the region has also received particular international attention. Between 2001 and 2004, armed hostilities involving children under the age of eighteen occurred in Angola, Burundi, Congo, the Ivory Coast, Liberia, Rwanda, Somalia, Sudan and Uganda. In Uganda, for example, it has been estimated that 80 percent of the Lord's Resistance Army were abducted as children. However, records of associated death and injury are limited and causes of death are not generally recorded. A 1998–2000 study from hospitals in Brazzaville (a city of 600,000 people), in the Republic of Congo, reported 1,354 firearm injuries for that time period.[172] Mortality rates in the Dafur Region of the Sudan are very high but there is no specific data available regarding the use of firearms.

South Africa's transition to a multiracial democracy occurred with relatively little violence, but the toll of overtly "political" conflict is dwarfed by the prevalence of other forms of violence: over 21,000 South Africans were murdered in 2002 alone (more than half of them with guns), while only 15,000 people were killed from 1990 to 1998 in acts deemed "political." Handguns are the weapons most often used. In 2000 alone, 375 children under twelve and 324 children between the ages of twelve and seventeen were killed by guns.[173] More people in South Africa die from gunshots than from car accidents, and for those older than fourteen, death by firearms ranks first among causes of death.[174]

Table 2.5 Firearm Death Rates (per 100,000) in Eastern Europe and the Former Soviet Union

Country	Year	Total Gun Death Rate (Minimum)	Gun Homicide Rate	Gun Suicide Rate	Gun Accident Rate	Undeter-mined	Total Homicide Rate	Percent of Homicides with Guns	Total Suicide Rate	Percent of Suicides with Guns
Albania	2002	4.29	4.29				5.68	75.5		
Slovenia	2003	4.01	0.4	3.46	0.05	0.1	1.4	28.57	28.1	12.31
Georgia	2001	3.83	2.97	0.04	0.15	0.66	3.9	76.15	2.2	1.82
Estonia	2002	3.53	1.55	1.55	0	0.44	11.7	13.25	27.3	5.68
Croatia	2003	3.15	0.61	2.43	0.07	0.05	1.4	43.57	18.2	13.35
Latvia	2003	2.49	0.9	1.29	0.04	0.26	10.6	8.49	26	4.96
Czech Republic	2003	2.44	0.36	2	0.03	0.05	1.1	32.73	16.5	12.12
Slovakia	2002	2.38	0.43	1.32	0.33	0.3	2.2	19.55	13.3	9.92
Lithuania	2003	1.91	0.58	0.9	0.17	0.26	9.5	6.11	42.1	2.14
Moldova	2003	1.47	0.86	0.39	0.11	0.11	9.3	9.25	17.2	2.27
Hungary	2003	1.11	0.15	0.91	0.03	0.02	1.9	7.89	27.6	3.3
Kyrgyzstan	2003	0.86	0.32	0.32	0.1	0.12	4.2	7.62	9.5	3.37
Poland	2002	0.48	0.19	0.15	0.02	0.11	1.7	11.18	15.4	0.97
Belarus	2002	0.38	0.38				9.96	3.82		
Ukraine	2000	0.35	0.35	0	0	0	8.99	3.91	29.4	0
Romania	2002	0.31	0.11	0.12	0.08	0	2.6	4.23	14	0.86

Source: Global Firearm Deaths (Toronto: Small Arms/Firearms Education and Research Network, 2005), http://www.ryerson.ca/SAFER-Net/issues/globalfirearmdeaths.html.

While other southern African countries report problems due in part to guns smuggled in from South Africa, their homicide rates are significantly lower. For example, in Zimbabwe 598 people were reported murdered in 2000 with firearms, a rate of 4.75 per 100,000.[175]

Asia

While Asia is the most populous continent in the world—accounting for 60 percent of the world's population—most countries on the continent have relatively low rates of reported firearm death and injury. In Japan, there is a relatively low incidence of firearm-related crimes compared to other countries. Most firearm-related crimes in Japan are committed with illegally imported, foreign-made handguns. Most of these incidents involve factional disputes within the Boryokudan (Japanese organized crime syndicate). Between 1992 and 1996, 73 percent of crimes involving handguns were related to Boryokudan activities. However, firearm offenses by non-Boryokudan individuals saw an increase over this period, while the overall incidence of firearm-related crimes decreased.[176] In 2002, according to WHO, there were approximately 24 firearm homicides, with 47 firearm suicides and 7 unintentional firearm deaths for a rate of 0.06 per 100,000, one of the lowest in the world.[177] Singapore also has extremely low rates of firearm-related death and injury. China does not report data and has strict controls over access to collected data. Thailand and Vietnam report relatively low rates. Cambodia does not report data to the United Nations, but anecdotal reports suggest that its rates are higher in part as a result of the postconflict weapons that remain in circulation. Thailand had a reported rate of 4.82 deaths per 100,000, which is higher than many countries in the region, but lower than many European countries.

In South Asia firearms figure in both criminal and sectarian violence, but data in the region are very incomplete. Overall India reported 9,284 firearm homicides for 1 billion people in 1999 (0.93 per 100,000) and less than one quarter of all homicides involve firearms. In India, tensions between Hindu and Muslim groups are one of the country's major sources of sectarian violence, particularly in the Kashmir region. Although a "ceasefire" was in effect through the first three months of 2001, 87 militants and 151 civilians were killed during that period.[178]

Bangladesh is the one country in the region with fairly comprehensive statistics. In Bangladesh, there are approximately 1,500 firearm homicides each year (1.11 per 100,000) among a total 1,900 homicides (1.44 per 100,000). Of 6,328 robberies, about 17 percent involve firearms. There are approximately 1,995 reported hospitalizations for firearm injuries. As in other parts of the region, Bangladesh is plagued by a combination of political and criminal violence. For example, in an average year in Bangladesh, there are 111 shooting deaths by police, security forces and the Indian Border Security Force (BSF).[179]

Table 2.6 Firearm Death Rates (per 100,000) in Africa and the Middle East

Country	Year	Total Gun Death Rate (Minimum)	Gun Homicide Rate	Gun Suicide Rate	Gun Accident Rate	Undeter-mined	Total Homicide Rate	Percent of Homicides with Guns	Total Suicide Rate	Percent of Suicides with Guns
South Africa	2002	26.8	26.1				47.5	55		
Lesotho	1997	23.8	23.8				42.7	56		
Zimbabwe	2000	4.85	4.75	0.11	0	0	8	66	0	0
Zambia	1995	2.59	4.6	0.05	0.02		9.2	50	0.6	8
Israel	2000	2.7	1.2	1.18	0.21	0.17	2	59	5.2	23
Jordan	1997	1	1				5	19		
Tanzania	1997	0.6	0.6	0	0.02	0	7.9	7	0.9	
Kuwait	2002	0.4	0.3	0.04	0	0.04	1.1	31	2	2
Bahrain	2000	0.3	0.3	0	0	0	1.3	23	4.3	
Egypt	2000	0.23	0.02	0.03	0.12	0.06	0.1	20	0.1	30

Source: Global Firearm Deaths (Toronto: Small Arms/Firearms Education and Research Network, 2005), http://www.ryerson.ca/SAFER-Net/issues/globalfirearmdeaths.html.

It has been claimed that on average 25,000 people have been killed with guns in Pakistan each year for the last twenty years[180] (17 per 100,000), but there are no official data to support this claim. In the southern city of Karachi, with 13 million people, the annual death toll has been estimated at about 1,000 per year (7.6 per 100,000).[181] A more recent study has estimated firearm injuries of 15.9 per 100,000 population and a firearm mortality rate of 9.8 per 100,000 population in the city.[182]

Australia and the South Pacific

In 2002, Australia reported 333 firearm deaths (3.6 per 100,000). As in countries like Canada, the majority of firearm deaths in Australia are suicides 261 (78 percent), with homicides numbering 47 (14 percent) and accidents 18 (5 percent). The rest (7, or 2 percent) are accounted for by undetermined cases and deaths caused by legal interventions.[183] The type of firearm was reported in 179 of the cases of firearm deaths. Where the type of firearm was known, the majority were rifles (54) and shotguns (76), while handguns were used in 49 cases.

In New Zealand, in 2000 there were 53 firearm deaths (1.35 per 100,000) including 8 homicides, 36 suicides and 4 accidents. The most commonly used firearms in homicides were rifles and shotguns.[184]

In many of the smaller Pacific countries the levels of firearm-related crime are very low. For example, in the Federated States of Micronesia, with an approximate population of 124,000, there were 7 homicides committed between 1997 and 2001, none involving a gun. Six other Pacific island nations, including the Cook Islands, Kiribati, Micronesia, Palau, Tonga, Tuvalu and Vanuatu, report no firearm homicides between 1997 and 2001.[185]

CONCLUSION

In virtually every nation, with very few exceptions, the proliferation and misuse of firearms presents a challenge. The impact of gun violence goes far beyond the number and "cost" of the lives lost and can strike at the very heart of citizens' sense of security, their economic and social well-being, and the basis of democracy itself. Simply put, "gun violence reduces the quality of life for everyone."[186] A small number of countries, most of them in the Americas, account for a disproportionate number of the world's gun deaths. The United States ranks thirteenth among 112 countries reporting firearm death rates and has rates of homicide that are not seen in other industrialized countries. Even in countries with statistically low rates of firearm death and injury—for example, countries such as Japan, Great Britain and Germany—high-profile incidents have raised concerns about

Table 2.7 Firearm Death Rates (per 100,000) in Asia

Country	Year	Total Gun Death Rate (Minimum)	Gun Homicide Rate	Gun Suicide Rate	Gun Accident Rate	Undetermined	Total Homicide Rate	Percent of Homicides with Guns	Total Suicide Rate	Percent of Suicides with Guns
Thailand	2002	4.82	3.22	0.41	0.13	1.05	4.40	73	7.2	6
Sri Lanka	1997	3.01	3.01	0.00			9.90	30		
India	1999	1.20	0.93	0.06	0.24		3.72	25	8.9	1
Bangladesh	2001	1.11	1.11	0.00	0.00		1.44	77		
Taiwan	1994	0.38	0.15	0.12	0.11					
Vietnam	1999	0.17	0.11	0.02	0.04		0.74	15		
Singapore	1998	0.17	0.90	0.60	0.23		45.00	2	10.6	6
Hong Kong	2002	0.12	0.04	0.07	0.00	0	0.90	4	15.3	
Korea	2002	0.10	0.05	0.04	0.01	0.01	1.70	3	17.9	
Japan	2002	0.06	0.02	0.04	0.00	0	0.50	4	23.7	

Source: Global Firearm Deaths (Toronto: Small Arms/Firearms Education and Research Network, 2005), http://www.ryerson.ca/SAFER-Net/issues/globalfirearmdeaths.html.

Table 2.8 Firearm Death Rates (per 100,000) in Australia and the South Pacific

Country	Year	Total Gun Death Rate (Minimum)	Gun Homicide Rate	Gun Suicide Rate	Gun Accident Rate	Undeter-mined	Total Homicide Rate	Percent of Homicides with Guns	Total Suicide Rate	Percent of Suicides with Guns
Philippines	1996	3.35	3.35				15.67	21		
Australia	2001	1.68	0.24	1.34	0.09	0.01	1.5	16	12.60	11
New Zealand	2000	1.35	0.21	0.93	0.1	0.1	1.3	16	11.90	8

Source: Global Firearm Deaths (Toronto: Small Arms/Firearms Education and Research Network, 2005), http://www.ryerson.ca/SAFER-Net/issues/glob-alfirearmdeaths.html.

Table 2.9 Canada and the United States: Comparing Firearm-Related Deaths and Crimes

	Year	Canada	United States	United States/ Canada
Population	2003	32.2m	290m	9×
Number of all firearms	1998	7.4m	222m	30×
Number of handguns	1998	.5m	76m	
Firearms per capita	1997	.25	.82	3.3×
Crime statistics (rate per 100,000)				
Total homicides	2003			
Number		548	16,500	
Rate per 100,000		1.73	5.7	3×
Homicides with firearms	2003			
Number		161	11,700	
Rate per 100,000		0.51	4.0	6.5×
Homicides without firearms	2003			
Number		387	4800	
Rate per 100,000		1.22	1.7	1.4×
Robberies with firearms				
Number		3877	172,800	
Rate per 100,000	2003	12	59	4.4×
Robberies without firearms				
Number		24,455	240,600	
Rate per 100,000	2003	78	83	1.1×

Source: Kwing Hung, Firearm Statistics: Updated Tables. Department of Justice Canada, Ottawa, January 2005.

gun violence. Indeed, some countries such as Australia and Great Britain have responded decisively to isolated tragedies, while the United States appears to be paralyzed even in the face of mass shootings, which seem to occur with alarming frequency. From a global perspective, the Americas—North, Central and South—have a disproportionate number of guns, and they pay a price—almost half the world's reported firearm deaths occur in the continents that are home to only 14 percent of the world's population.

3

More Guns Equal More Deaths

UNDERSTANDING VIOLENCE

Violence committed with firearms is one strain of the violence pandemic. Ecological models have increasingly been used in an effort to understand the complex interplay of individual, relationship, social, cultural and environmental factors that give rise to violence. An "ecological" model identifies several levels of risk factors, which include societal, community, relationship and individual factors (see Figure 3.1).

Individual behavior, for example, is shaped by both biological and personal history. Among the strongest predictors of violence are age and gender. Most violence worldwide is perpetrated by young men (fifteen to twenty-four years old), but clearly there are other pertinent factors, including impulsivity, substance abuse, a prior history of aggression or victimization, and low educational levels. Understanding victim-aggressor relationships is consequently critically important to addressing violence. In many forms of violence, the same groups at risk for perpetrating violence are at risk for being victimized.

Relationships with peers, intimate partners and family members also play an important role, particularly when it comes to youth and gang violence, intimate partner violence, child abuse and suicide. In many forms of violence, victim and aggressor are bound in a relationship. In peaceful, industrialized countries such as Canada, for example, 85 percent of homicide victims know their killer, and 85 percent of women murdered are killed by their intimate partners.[1] Similarly, in these contexts children are more likely to be abused or killed by family members than by strangers.

Social relationships in communities are also important. In many cities, for example, particular neighborhoods or segments of the population are disproportionately affected by violence. Socioeconomic disparity, political

Figure 3.1 Ecological Model for Understanding Violence

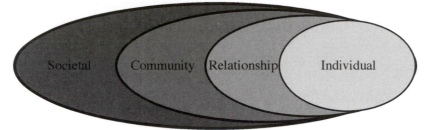

Source: Étienne G. Krug, Linda L. Dahlberg, James A. Mercy, Anthony B. Zwi, and
Rafael Lozano, eds., *World Report on Violence and Health* (Geneva: WHO, 2002),
310, 312, 316, 318, 322, 323. Available at: http://www.who.int/violence_injury_
prevention/violence/world_report/wrvheng.

instability, inequality, lack of democratic processes, health, social and educational policies and cultural norms and the availability of drugs, alcohol
and weapons are all contributing societal factors. Social cohesion at the
community level and involvement in local schools or religious institutions
can help mitigate the effects of these factors and thereby play an important role in preventing violence.

The public health model can be adapted to each specific form of violence.[2] The recent WHO *World Report on Violence*, for example, applies
the model to youth violence, child abuse and neglect, violence by intimate
partners, elder abuse, sexual violence, self-directed violence (suicide) and
collective violence. However, it is important to note that while there are
common elements, there are also important differences. For example,
domestic violence against women seems less affected by age and socioeconomic status than are other forms of violence. Similarly, while interpersonal violence tends to increase with socioeconomic disparity, suicide
rates are positively correlated with socioeconomic status. As discussed in
Chapter 2, in richer nations suicides tend to account for a higher percentage of firearm deaths than in poorer nations. Moreover, there are also
interactions between different forms of violence. Periods of conflict, for
example, are often followed by elevated rates of interpersonal violence.
Male victims of child abuse are more likely to be violent themselves, and
suicide risk factors are strongly associated with other forms of violence.[3]
In Canada, for example, 50 percent of men who kill their partners with
firearms kill themselves.

In considering violence, then, it is essential to remember the complex nature of the causal factors. "[T]he root causes of ethnic, religious and sectarian conflicts around the world are quite complex and varied, typically
involving historical grievances, economic deprivation, inequitable distribu-

tion of resources, human rights abuses, demagogic leadership and an absence of democratic process."[4]

ANALYSING THE RISK FACTORS

As discussed in the previous chapter, the forms of violence with firearms are varied, ranging from homicide, suicide, youth violence, intimate partner violence and unintentional injuries to collective violence, all of which have different dynamics. Nevertheless, when one considers violence with firearms, there are some common factors that seem evident. For example, societal factors include economic disparity, ethno-cultural heterogeneity, social marginality, weak institutions and the availability of firearms. At the community level, issues include low social cohesion, negative peer influences and isolation. At the family level, dysfunctional relationships, poor family cohesion and supervision of children, male control of the household and firearms in the home have been identified as factors. At the individual level, those most at risk to misuse firearms or to be killed with firearms are young (fifteen to twenty-four years old), male, involved with alcohol or drugs, previous victims of violence and in possession of firearms.[5]

Prevention models in public health are based on an analysis of the elements that create an illness, or in the case of gun violence, an injury. For example, when considering malaria, preventive action may focus on the agent (the parasite), the vehicle or vector (the mosquito) and the host (the patient). These agents, vehicles and hosts interact in a particular physical or sociocultural environment.[6] The nature of this environment can also affect the probability of disease. When considering gun injuries, the agent is the ammunition, the vector is the firearm and the host is the victim or the aggressor. The environment shapes the risks of gun injury and also the responses, which, for example, can be expressed in terms of the availability of emergency services.

Public health strategies focus on breaking the chain of the causes of an injury at the point where the link in the chain is weakest.[7] Interventions may also focus on reducing the severity of violence, through efforts to control exports or access to small arms. Finally, interventions may focus on "treatment," on trauma care, rehabilitation and reintegration. Measures that modify the potential vehicle or vector (firearm) or agent (ammunition) of injury, or the environment in which they occur, have proven more successful than measures in which individuals must make an effort or educate themselves.[8] The efficacy and use of control measures is inversely proportional to the individual effort required to implement them. For example, engineering changes to automobiles, such as air bags, are more effective than measures such as seat belts alone, which require human agency or education. As Harvard professor David Hemenway notes:

The public health approach broadens the policy options from an exclusive focus on holding individual citizens responsible for their actions (which they should be) to also consider ways to improve the physical and social environment 1) to reduce the likelihood of impulsive, imprudent, improper and immoral behaviour and 2) to reduce the harm done by such conduct.[9]

Factors Affecting the "Demand" for Firearms

Societal factors fuel both the supply and demand for firearms. Factors at the international level include the globalization of the arms trade, narcotics trafficking and organized crime, while factors at the national level include failures of states to provide security, failures to regulate and national cultural norms, as well as community factors.

Socioeconomic factors such as poverty, family disruptions (separation, death, divorce), alcoholism, mental illness, history of violence and illicit drug use all serve as predictors of individual and group violence in both industrialized and unindustrialized settings. Recently, much attention has focused on the creation of "demand" for weapons, the factors that fuel demand and the ways in which the cycle can be broken.

While socioeconomic conditions have long been regarded as a root cause of both conflict and violence, the relationship is not that simple. The poorest communities are not always the most violent. Perceptions of inequality or marginalization and the gap between rich and poor appear to be important considerations, rather than simply mean per capita income levels. In addition, suicide rates increase with development, independently of inequality. While homicide rates are inversely associated with development (more-developed countries typically have lower homicide rates than less-industrialized countries), this relationship disappears when controls are introduced for inequality. In other words, inequality is a stronger predictor of homicide than the lack of economic development alone.[10]

Lack of democracy, or political inequality, is also an important factor driving demand for firearms. Individuals and groups may see weapons as a means to gain access to political or economic control.

Another important factor is insecurity. Perceptions of insecurity or threats to safety can fuel persistent demand for weapons regardless of the level of regulation, particularly in instances where the state is unable to provide security for its citizens, or where state and police security are perceived to be corrupt and abusive. Although the evidence suggests that there is more peril than protection associated with firearm ownership, perceptions continue to fuel demand in high-crime and conflict-ridden settings.

Cultural factors are also important, and the socialization of boys and men strongly influences their potential for violence. The glorification of warriors and weapons through a variety of cultural practices—ranging from songs and legends in oral cultures to video games in industrialized cultures—also fuel demand. The links between firearms, masculinity and power are pervasive in many cultures around the world. Studies of cultural norms examine the role of national culture in shaping violence.[11] These are explored in more detail in Chapter 6.

Work to reduce demand for small arms may involve traditional humanitarian, social development and education projects but may also include a focus on understanding and addressing the specific reasons for weapons possession and use in a community or culture. Such efforts are aimed at reducing the overall levels of violence and include initiatives to address human insecurity, economic development, education, security sector reform, human rights protection, good governance and effective justice systems. Efforts to address social acceptability focus on education, stigmatization of weapons and countering the culture of violence.

Factors Affecting the "Supply" of Firearms

Regardless of the particular problem leading to firearm death and injury—conflict, domestic violence, "accidents," suicides or crime—what all these events have in common is access to firearms. Consequently, the firearm is an important focal point in public health strategies for preventive action.

Controlling availability is also fundamental to crime prevention approaches that identify firearms as a "facilitator" of crime and violence. Situational crime prevention suggests that limiting access to "facilitators" can reduce the occurrence and lethality associated with crime.[12]

Access to and availability of firearms is described by some as the "universal" risk factor. Many studies have suggested that access to firearms increases the lethality of violence, raising the probability that an act of violence will result in death. Others have shown that the "substitution" effect—the resort to alternate tools of violence in the event of blocked access to firearms—is inconsistent at best. These analysts suggest that controlling access to firearms can reduce the risk of death and injury. It can also prevent the diversion of weapons to those likely to use them for unlawful purposes.

Analysis of the relationship between firearms availability and death is hampered by limitations of data. Surveys, such as the International Crime Victim Survey,[13] provide estimates of the number and distribution of firearms in circulation, but the most reliable estimates come from comparing multiple sources. For example, in Canada, results from the International Crime Victim Survey and national surveys were closely aligned in 1989, 1992, 1996 and 2000.[14] Apart from surveys, it has been suggested that in industrialized countries one of the most reliable ways to estimate firearm ownership is to examine suicide data.[15] Measuring firearms illegally in circulation is a far more challenging task, and estimates vary widely. Again there are a variety of sources that can be employed, including the prices of firearms on illegal markets, the seizures of illegal firearms by police and customs officials and the rates of firearm death and injury, where other factors are common. In industrialized countries, for example, large supplies of illegal guns drive up homicide and suicide rates.

THE ACCESSIBILITY THESIS: AVAILABILITY OF FIREARMS AND LETHALITY

In conflict and postconflict contexts there are few ways to actually measure the firearms in circulation. In the absence of targeted disarmament, demobilization and reintegration programs, it is reasonable to assume that following many conflicts the arms remain in circulation. This is further supported by the mortality and morbidity data collected by hospitals in conflict zones. Often there is only limited change in the level of violence following the cessation of formal fighting, as interpersonal violence with firearms takes the place of violence between warring factions. One study compared the rate of weapons injury five years before the region came under uncontested control and one and a half years after. Weapons injury declined only 20 to 40 percent.[16]

Many working on peace building and disarmament argue that the link between violence levels and access to weapons is self-evident.[17] When firearms are not removed following conflicts, mortality rates remain high, as interpersonal violence substitutes for war. The proliferation of firearms also leads to an escalation of a domestic "arms race," with widespread criminality and the breakdown of legal norms. The International Committee of the Red Cross argued, "The proliferation of these weapons has facilitated an increase in the scale and duration of conflict in many states and in some cases has made the outbreak of armed violence more likely."[18]

A study of firearm death and legislation in ten southern African countries revealed that, in spite of data limitations, countries with strict firearm regulation and lower rates of ownership appeared to have lower rates of death. At the same time, illegal firearms tended to flow from unregulated countries with weak legislation (such as South Africa) to other countries (such as Botswana).[19] The pattern is also reflected in studies of regions within countries such as Afghanistan.[20]

To prevent an illness or injury, public health experts consider preventive action to control the agent and the vehicle to protect the host. In the case of injury due to gunshot wounds, the agent is the ammunition deployed by firing a gun, the vehicle is the gun and the human host is the victim. Access to firearms and ammunition constitutes the universal link—the one against which we can take action—in the chain of events leading to any injury with a firearm.[21]

A number of researchers have maintained that there is sufficient evidence to conclude that rates of firearm death and injury are linked to access to firearms.[22] Access to firearms may be defined in a number of ways, including the percentage of households where firearms are present (or various surrogate measures),[23] or the ease with which individuals can obtain firearms and ammunition in a given place at a given time.

While rates of violence per se are not directly affected by the availability of firearms, rates of lethal violence are. High levels of gun use in assault and robbery in the United States, for example, are strongly associated with elevated U.S. death rates from violence. A number of studies have examined the difference in outcomes between assaults with knives and assaults with firearms and have concluded that the objective dangerousness of the instrument used in violent assaults has a direct and measurable impact on the number of victims who will die in the attack, known as the "instrumentality effect." For street robberies and robberies of commercial establishments, the death rate for every 1,000 robberies in which firearms are used is roughly three times the death rate for robberies at knife point and about ten times the death rate for robberies involving physical force without the use of a weapon.[24] Not only has this been shown to be the case where guns are used instead of knives, but increased use of particular types of firearms, such as high-calibre handguns or military assault weapons, has also been linked to increases in death rates. Studies show 96 percent of suicides attempted with firearms result in death and suggest reducing access to them could save lives.[25] Similarly, when firearms are used in domestic violence, there is an increased likelihood of multiple victims (usually the children) and suicide of the perpetrator.

Many of the research projects examining the accessibility thesis have conducted comparisons of homes in which firearms are present to those in which they are not.[26] Kellermann and his colleagues concluded that the homicide of a family member was 2.7 times more likely to occur in a home with a firearm than in a home without a gun. After accounting for several independent risk factors, another study concluded that keeping one or more firearms was associated with a 4.8-fold higher risk of suicide in the home.[27] The risks are higher, particularly for adolescents, in homes in which the guns were kept loaded and unlocked.[28]

Studies have also compared the rates of death from firearms in Canada and the United States. One of the most well-known studies was a comparison of Seattle, Washington, and Vancouver, British Columbia.[29] This study showed that despite similarities in size and demographics, there are huge differences in the rate of firearm homicide as a result of the differences in the availability of firearms in the two countries.[30]

A study that examined the link between gun ownership rates and firearm death rates in Canada, the United States, England and Wales and Australia concluded that 92 percent of the variance in death rates was explained by differences in access to firearms.[31] The international experience with firearms regulation and comparative mortality statistics tends to reinforce the conclusion that there is a link between access to firearms and firearm death in industrialized nations, although there are issues around uniform reporting and other variables that must be addressed. For example, a review of thirteen countries showed a strong correlation between gun ownership and both homicide with a gun and overall homicide rates. In an analysis of fourteen countries, the correlation between gun ownership and gun suicide was also significant, as was the correlation of rate of gun ownership with overall suicide rates. Killias found no evidence of a substitution effect (whereby other means were substituted for firearms).[32]

In another study, based on a standardized survey of victimization in fifty-four countries, gun ownership was significantly related to both the level of robberies and the level of sexual assaults. Additionally, it was concluded that high levels of gun ownership, such as in the United States, the former Yugoslavia, South Africa and several Latin American countries, are strongly related to higher levels of violence generally.[33]

Other studies have examined correlates in specific populations. Studies in Finland have linked the high suicide rates among fifteen- to twenty-four-year-old males to firearm ownership. The annual suicide rate in this group was 51 per 100,000. Sixty-two percent of the suicides involved firearms, and 60 percent of the firearm suicides involved legal hunting guns stored in the homes of the victims.[34]

While more research could illuminate the interactions among the range of factors shaping the demand for firearms at the societal level and at the individual level (such as criminal activity, drug use and parental factors),[35] there is also a growing body of literature that reveals a relationships among access to firearms, firearm death rates and certain types of crime.[36] This finding underpins the notion that reducing access to firearms through regulation will reduce the lethality of assaults and suicide attempts.

Comparisons between Canada and the United States are also instructive. The United States has a higher rate of gun ownership, particularly handguns, per capita than any other industrialized country in the world. Approximately 40 percent of U.S. households have firearms.[37] Estimates of the rate of gun ownership and the number of guns, however, vary considerably. In the United States, a country with a population of 290 million, it is estimated that there are more than 200 million firearms owned,[38] a third of them handguns. One survey[39] found that 41 percent of adult respondents reported having a firearm in their home in 1994, and 35 percent did so in 1998. Rates of firearm ownership in the United States also exceed those of fourteen other nations for which data are available, with the exception of Finland. In 1994, it was estimated that there were 192 million firearms owned in the United States, including 65 million handguns, 70 million rifles; 49 million shotguns; the remainder was other guns.[40] One-sixth of the handguns owned were regularly carried by their owners, approximately half in the owners' cars and the other half on the owners' persons.

In contrast, in Canada, a country with 32 million people, it is estimated that there are approximately 7 million firearms, only about 500,000 of them handguns. Approximately 18 percent of Canadian households have firearms.[41] Handguns are strictly regulated, and few citizens (about fifty) have permits to carry them for self-protection.

The rate (per 100,000) of homicides committed *without* guns in the United States is only slightly higher (1.6 times) than the rate of murders *without* guns Canada.[42] However, the rate of murders with handguns in the United States is almost eight times higher than that in Canada. Therefore, the difference in the murder rate between Canada and the United States is accounted for, in large part, by the difference in the homicide rate due to firearms. We see a similar pattern with robbery: rates (per 100,000) of robbery *without* firearms in the two countries are comparable. The rate of robbery *with* firearms in the United States is much higher (see Figure 3.2).

Despite the challenges of measurement, there is significant evidence that among high-income countries, those with higher reported percentages of households with firearms tend to have higher intentional firearm death rates (homicide and suicide). (See Figure 3.3.)

The relationship continues for firearm death rates among children, with the United States, Finland, Canada and a number of European countries all presenting high rates. In contrast, countries such as Germany, England and Wales, which have low rates of gun ownership, have low rates of children killed with firearms.

This pattern holds for other countries such as Austria and Switzerland that are relatively similar. One of the very clear differences between these countries is the availability of firearms, particularly in rural areas. While many countries have higher firearm homicide rates, Austria has one of the highest firearm suicide rates in the industrialized world. The role of firearms in homicide is also seen if we compare Austria to other German-speaking regions. According to the United Nations International Study of Firearm Regulation, the mean (over five years) of nonfirearm homicide rates in Austria, Germany and Switzerland are roughly the same (1.61, 1.60 and 1.56 per 100,000, respectively). The overall homicide rates (2.14, 1.81 and 2.47 per 100,000, respectively) appear to be associated with differences in the rates of firearm homicide (0.53, 0.21 and 0.91 per 100,000, respectively).[43] This parallels the differences in firearm ownership rates in the three countries.

The pattern is also reflected in some regional studies. Within Canada, there is a fairly strong association between rates of firearm ownership in different regions in the country and rates of firearm death. The Yukon and the Northwest Territories, which have the highest rates of gun ownership in Canada (70 percent of households), have a rate of firearm death higher than that of the United States.[44]

Firearm possession is one of the highest risk factors for domestic homicide in the United States.[45] It also strongly correlates with levels of murder of women in a recent survey of twenty-six countries.[46] Countries with higher rates of firearm ownership tend to have higher rates of women killed with guns. This is because most women murdered in developing countries

Figure 3.2 Canada and the United States: Comparing Firearm-Related Deaths and Crimes

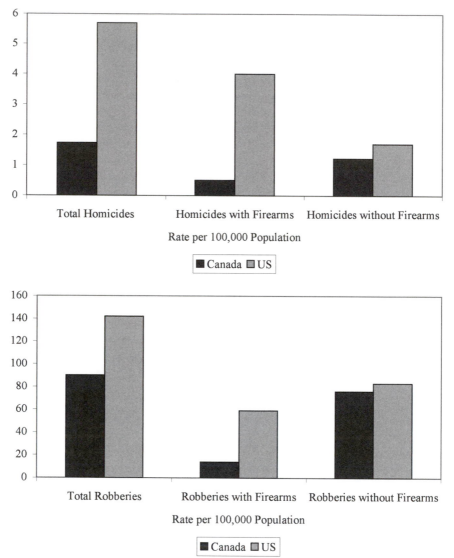

Source: Kwing Hung, Firearm Statistics: Updated Tables. Department of Justice Canada, Ottawa, January 2005.

Figure 3.3 Firearm Ownership and Intentional Firearm Death Rates in High-Income Countries

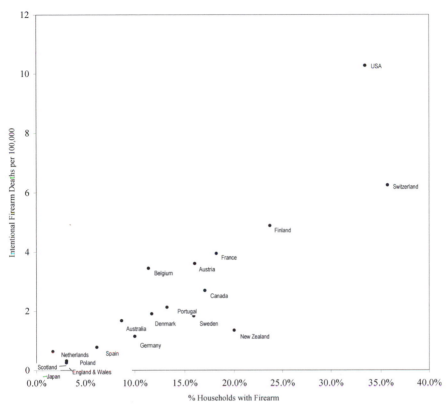

Source: *Global Firearm Deaths* (Toronto: Small Arms/Firearms Education and Research Network, 2005), www.ryerson.ca/SAFER-Net/issues/globalfirearmdeaths.html; also United Nations (UN), *The Eighth International Crime Victims Survey, 2000*. Prepared by the Interregional Crime and Justice Research Institute, 2003, http://www.unicri.it/wwd/analysis/icvs/data.php.

are killed in the home by their partners, and the availability of firearms has a direct impact on the lethality of violence against women.

DEVELOPING INTERVENTIONS

The public health approach focuses on developing interventions that address the causal factors which produce the death or injury. These interventions are often categorized into six groups:

- *Environment:* Interventions that are focused on shaping the environment in which the injury occurs. These might include strategies aimed at the social and cultural environment. For example, strategies to stig-matize smoking and drinking or counter the culture of violence would be considered environmental interventions. They would also include development efforts aimed at the root causes of violence; for example, providing opportunities for youth education and employment.

- *Enforcement:* Regulatory strategies coupled with enforcement efforts; for example, lowering acceptable blood alcohol levels combined with police spot checks; legislating sales of tobacco to minors combined with rigorous enforcement; establishing rules for gun sales coupled with inspections of gun dealers.

- *Engineering:* Interventions that focus on altering the product or its marketing to make the product itself less likely to cause harm; for ex-ample, airbags for automobiles and legislated nicotine levels for ciga-rettes; requirements for marking and record keeping by firearm manufacturers; safety features to reduce the risk of accidental or unau-thorized use.

- *Economics:* Interventions that focus on affecting the price and there-fore demand for the product; for example, regulatory schemes that raise the effective "price" of a product, thereby discouraging casual use, have been employed in efforts to reduce consumption of tobacco and alcohol.

- *Education:* Interventions that are focused on individuals to encourage them to consider the risks and make informed choices.

- *Control:* Interventions, designed to reduce the destructive impacts of an event after the fact, for example, emergency services.

Many injury prevention experts have maintained that more attention needs to be focused on the issues related to injury "control"; that is, to minimizing the effects of an event once it occurs. This would include rapid emergency responses to car crashes, for example, as well as appropriate hospital resources. It would include humanitarian assistance to conflict zones. Policing, courts and corrections for offenders arguably are part of an injury control strategy. Not only do these methods support general de-terrence, but removing potentially violent offenders from circulation may reduce their ability to reoffend.

Table 3.1 suggests ways in which current interventions to reduce firearm misuse might be categorized using this framework. Of course, no models are perfect, and some interventions could fit in different categories.

Limiting Access to Firearms

A driving principle, then, is the notion that if access to firearms is re-duced, then death through firearms will also be reduced. There is a strong theoretical basis for this principle, both in the injury prevention literature[47]

Table 3.1 Approaches to Preventing and Controlling Firearm Death and Injury

Prevention	Examples
Environment	Crime prevention through social development. Democracy building and security sector reform. Cultural change. Weapons collection.
Enforcement	International agreements for example, export controls, tracing, etc. National legislation related to access to firearms, safe storage, etc. Controls on media and marketing of firearms.
Engineering	Manufacturing controls and standards for example, marking, and tracing. Safety standards. Prohibitions on certain firearms for certain markets.
Economics	Regulatory schemes such as licensing dealers, individuals, etc. Disarmament, demobilization, and reintegration.
Education	General deterrence measures. Increased risk awareness. Safety training in the use of firearms.
Control	Hospital treatment. Incarceration and mandatory supervision.

Source: International Physicians for the Prevention of Nuclear War (IPPNW), Aiming for Prevention: International Medical Conference on Small Arms, Gun Violence and Injury (Helsinki, Finland, September 28–30, 2001), http://www.ippnw.org/Helsinki.html.

and in the situational crime prevention literature.[48] Firearm controls such as licensing and regulation in effect raise costs and discourage casual gun ownership.[49] Legislative interventions also aim at reducing the probability that those at risk to misuse guns will gain access to the licensing, training and screening processes that are in place in many countries. In addition, there are interventions that are focused on increasing the barriers between individuals and guns, for example, safe storage intended to reduce impulsive and unauthorized access to firearms.

The heart of the policy response to gun violence focuses on efforts to reduce access to guns that may be used in crime by restricting supply and thus making it more difficult, time-consuming or costly for individuals to obtain a gun.[50] The purpose of regulation is to decrease the ease with which individuals can obtain firearms and ammunition. Most industrialized countries license firearm owners and register firearms in an effort to reduce the risk that firearms will be misused or diverted to illegal markets. Generally, industrialized countries with strict regulations also have lower rates of civilian possession of firearms and lower rates of firearm injury and death.

Accessibility in terms of ease of acquisition may be measured by the rigour of the processes controlling the licensing of gun owners. An analogous situation exists with other forms of licensing in which processes are designed to allow only those considered well qualified to use potentially dangerous goods, such as automobiles. Licensing regimes may identify risk factors and raise the standards to reduce the risk of misuse. For example, in 1991, the minimum age required to obtain a Firearm Acquisition Certificate in Canada was raised to eighteen, although minors' permits were allowed under particular circumstances. More recent legislation, adopted in 1995, requires screening of all current owners of firearms for records of criminal behavior or other risk factors; in cases in which individuals wish to acquire guns, screening is more rigorous and includes notification of current and previous spouses to reduce the risks that individuals with a history of domestic violence will have access to firearms.

Other initiatives aim at reducing access in specific contexts. Gun-free zones, for example, which are included in the new firearms legislation in South Africa, aim at reducing access to guns in drinking establishments.[51] Initiatives in Cali and in Bogotá, Colombia, introduced temporary time-restricted bans on the carrying of handguns and were associated with a roughly 14 percent reduction in homicide.[52] Other studies in Latin America reinforce the notion that areas with stricter controls, such as Costa Rica, have lower rates of firearm violence, although many other factors are at play.[53]

Weapons collection and destruction programs may also reduce availability. For example, reforms in Australia and the United Kingdom not only tightened legislation, but also included a massive buy-back. Owners were paid an established amount to turn in their firearms for destruction.[54]

Research in the United States supports the notion that if controls on firearms at the state level are increased, the likelihood that the firearms originating in that state will be used in crime is reduced. However, because states in the United States have open borders, the guns used in crime tend to come from out of state. In cities where there was no gun licensing or registration requirement, 84 percent of the guns recovered in crime were from local markets, while in cities in states that had both licensing and registration requirements, very few of the guns originated from local markets.[55] There is some longitudinal research that links adoption of stronger regulations and declining death rates.[56] Of course, longitudinal studies are often inconclusive when examining complex phenomena such as crime and suicide. Because of the wide range of factors that come into play, it is difficult to isolate the impact of legislation on firearms availability. However, in Canada there is evidence that stricter controls have had some impact.

Firearm homicide and suicide are the lowest they have been in thirty-five years.[57] Similarly, in Australia, there is evidence that indicates that stricter controls have contributed to a reduction in firearm crime and death rates.[58] Similarly, the UK handgun ban appears to have had a demonstrable impact on female firearm homicide rates, which have declined significantly. Nonetheless, the effectiveness of national interventions is limited with the increased globalization of the illegal gun trade (discussed in Chapter 5) Firearms continue to come into Canada from the United States and into Great Britain from the rest of Europe, highlighting the importance of co-ordinated international action to address the illicit trade.

There are difficulties associated with evaluating the impact of legislative reforms on such complex problems as crime. Yet studies show that, even in very violent contexts, there may be evidence to suggest that restrictions on firearms can have an impact.[59] In South Africa, new legislation has attempted to create gun-free zones in high-risk contexts, such as drinking establishments, but the impacts of these interventions are not yet clear. (A wide range of interventions and their impacts are discussed further in Chapter 7.)

Measures to reduce access to small arms are focused on reducing the lethality of violence but not necessarily its frequency. Limitation of access is possible at several levels. (See Table 3.2.)

Table 3.2 Limiting Access to Firearms

Type of Limitation	Example
General access	Increase the cost of obtaining a weapon—licensing other forms of regulation increase costs.
Reduce at-risk access by risk group, time, or place	Safe storage (for the risk group of children). Restrictions on conditions under which firearms may be carried.
Reduce surplus	Weapons collection and destruction programs.
Prevent diversion to illicit market	Control primary and secondary sales. International efforts for controls on import/export/ transfer. License legal gun owners and register firearms.
Prevent supply to in-appropriate users	Criteria for restrictions on legal arms transfers and sales. Licensing firearms owners.

Source: International Physicians for the Prevention of Nuclear War (IPPNW), Aiming for Prevention: International Medical Conference on Small Arms, Gun Violence and Injury (Helsinki, Finland, September 28–30, 2001), http://www.ippnw.org/Helsinki.html.

Some have disputed the argument that stricter regulation of firearms reduces gun death and injury. Some have even suggested that increasing access to firearms through arming for self-protection saves lives and reduces injury. For example, Kleck and Goertz have conducted surveys in which respondents claim that they have protected themselves with firearms from animals or humans. The authors then extrapolate to the general population and claim that millions of self-defense occurrences a year prove that restricting access to firearms will reduce safety. For example, in 1992, Kleck and Gertz conducted a national random-digit-dial survey in the United States of five thousand dwelling units, asking detailed questions about self-defense gun use. They estimated that Americans use guns to defend themselves 2.5 million times a year, based on the fact that 1.33 percent of the individuals surveyed reported that they themselves used a gun in self-defense during the past year (about 66 people out of 5,000 respondents).[60]

A similar study was conducted in Canada, in which Mauser estimated that firearms were used between 62,500 and 80,000 times per year for self-defence. This estimate is based on a 1995 telephone survey of 1,505 Canadians, in which 2.1 percent (32) of respondents claimed that they or a member of their household had used a gun for self-protection (against either a person or an animal) over the last five years. Of those, 12.9 percent (5) claimed that they or a member of their household had used a gun for protection against a person within the past five years. Mauser extrapolates these figures to the Canadian population.[61]

Hemenway maintains, however, that these approaches are based on "incorrect assertions and misleading statements." The study fails to distinguish perception from reality—grabbing a gun in response to a bump in the night does not mean that anyone has actually defended him- or herself against a threat. "It is not appropriate to extrapolate the results of a simple, self-reported study of a rare event, particularly when there is the possibility of positive social desirability response or personal presentation bias. The results will be wild over-estimates." Hemenway compares these methodologies to a 1995 survey by NBC that asked 1,500 Americans, "Have you personally ever been in contact with aliens from another planet or not?" Extrapolating the results (0.6%) to the entire U.S. population would suggest that 1.2 million Americans have been in contact with aliens.[62]

In some U.S. states, "shall issue" laws ensure that permits to carry concealed weapons are readily available to citizens who want guns for personal protection. Some studies have compared crime rates in states with these laws to states without these laws.[63] These studies have been critiqued as well. For example, John Donahue argues, "There is much evidence to support the view that shall-issue laws (that is, a lack of gun control) tend to increase crime."[64] Evidence from other countries such as South Africa has suggested that armed citizens are more likely to be injured or killed during the course of a robbery than unarmed citizens.[65]

Other studies claim that countries without strong gun control laws are safer than countries with gun control, or suggest that gun control laws have made countries less safe. For example, Mauser claims that countries that have strengthened gun laws are less safe than countries that have not,[66] but this conclusion is based on overall rates of violent crime, which include assaults as well as lethal violence—notably, homicides. In addition, Mauser argues that lethal violence in the United States has declined more quickly than in Canada, but the graphs he uses to illustrate the point obscure the dramatic differences between the two countries by mixing scales. For example, on one graph he uses to show the trends, Canada's scale ranges from 0 to 3 deaths per 100,000 while the U.S. scale is 0 to 12 per 100,000.[67]

This argument has been countered by those who argue that while rates of "violent crime" in Canada, the United States, England and Australia are roughly comparable, what is dramatically different is the rate of *lethal* violence (homicide). As noted above, in 2002–2003, England, with a population of 52 million people, had 80 firearm murders (a rate of 0.15 per 100,000). In 2002, Australia had 47 firearm homicides, for a rate of 1.7 per 100,000. Canada had 148 in 2002, for a rate of 0.45 per 100,000 and the United States had 10,800, for a rate of 3.9 per 100,000.

The argument has also been made that countries such as Switzerland, with high rates of firearm ownership, have low rates of crime and violence and that cultural determinants of violence are more important than the availability of firearms.[68] While there is no doubt that cultural determinants are an important factor and that where there is strong demand for firearms, restricting availability has limited effect, where other factors are constant, the availability of firearms is associated with higher levels of firearm death. Switzerland has high rates of gun ownership but also has more controls over firearms than many claim.[69] In addition, while it may have lower rates of some violent crime, it also has the highest rate of firearm death (largely because of the high firearm suicide rate) in Europe,[70] and the highest rate of women killed with firearms (next to the United States) among twenty-five countries surveyed.[71] Both these forms of violence tend to be associated with rates of firearm ownership.

At the same time, there is no doubt that the availability of firearms is but one factor, albeit an important one. Zimring suggests that introducing 10,000 handguns into an environment where violent assault is a rare occurrence will not produce a large increase in homicide deaths unless it also produces an increase in the rate of assaults. On the other hand, introducing 10,000 handguns into an environment in which rates of attack and willingness to use guns are both high will likely produce a higher rate of deaths.[72] Firearms increase the lethality of violence whether against another or self-inflicted.

The Interaction Between Supply of and Demand for Guns

It is important to understand the complex interaction between supply and demand. Empirical research into attitudes toward killing in various contexts also reveals a strong link between laws and culture of violence.

There is a strong association between attitudes that include the willingness to kill to protect property, to kill to avenge the rape of a child or to lend support for capital punishment, on one hand, and homicide rates and attitudes to gun ownership, on the other.[73] In general, countries and regions with high scores on the "culture of violence" scale also have high rates of particular types of interpersonal violence. These countries and regions also tend to be resistant to laws that impose controls on firearms. This suggests that gun laws, rates of gun ownership and gun-related values are interactive and mutually influencing. Society shapes laws and laws shape societies.[74] Consequently, the availability of firearms not only has an instrumentality effect, but also has an impact on cultural norms and the willingness to resort to violence. Laws that control the availability of firearms are linked to both supply and demand. (See Chapter 6 for more detail.)

Integrated efforts at the community level that address both supply and demand are also important. One such program, Viva Rio, based in Rio de Janeiro, Brazil, combines efforts to address demand through stigmatizing firearm possession and building strong community-based policing in poor areas combined with legislation aimed at reducing supply.[75]

IMPLEMENTATION OF INTERVENTIONS

Without effective implementation, interventions are only words on paper. Often the best-laid plans do not achieve their potential because of inadequate attention to the organizational, technical, economic and political factors that will affect their feasibility and impact. Effective implementation rests on the coordination and cooperation of disparate stakeholders. For example, legislation to prevent potentially dangerous individuals from getting access to firearms requires that relevant information is available to the decision makers. Many countries, for example, have laws that prohibit people with a history of mental illness from owning firearms but do not actually have mechanisms in place (in part because of doctor-patient confidentiality) to provide information about mental health to licensing authorities. Attention to the processes, procedures and resources needed to make that happen is critical.

Legislation aimed at providing police with tools to take preventive action if firearms are registered to a particular address has value only if the police use the tools they are given to ascertain the presence of firearms and take appropriate action. Similarly, measures aimed at removing firearms from domestic violence situations require those in positions of authority to take action, to understand their responsibilities and to have access to the tools. Laws that impose stiffer sentences for illegal firearm possession work only if police are actually able to apprehend those with illegal guns, and this ability often depends less on the law than on the relationships between the police and the community. Measures aimed at encouraging people, whether in war zones or in inner cities, to surrender illegal guns work only if the reasons that led these people to possess the guns in the first place—insecurity, for example—are addressed by the provision of democratic and effective policing.

Internationally, we know, for example, that there are well-established embargoes on selling arms to countries in conflict, and yet arms continue to flow to those areas, as governments intent on buying and selling find ways of working around the rules. Similarly, we know in the United States that regulations regarding the sale of firearms were on the books for many years, but that stepped-up inspections were the key to controlling "dirty dealers." In Canada, many of the impediments to the application of more effective gun control legislation, which was passed in 1995, related to problems with political opposition, development of computer systems, noncompliance and delays in the implementation process. In Australia, the implementation of the scheme to buy back prohibited weapons rested entirely on a structured approach to implementation and enforcement. In Bogotá, Colombia, the ban on carrying handguns on weekends and paydays was coupled with a steep increase in patrols and enforcement.

Implementation of any intervention must rest on a careful assessment of the context and the factors that will affect its success and failure. A limitation of many evaluation studies is often that they focus on assessing the intervention as it is written rather than as it is actually applied. Understanding the implementation of interventions (and their limitations) can often provide an understanding of why a particular initiative did or did not deliver the results expected.

EVALUATION

A crucial component of public health interventions is the process of conducting an objective evaluation of their effectiveness. Given the complex web of causal factors associated with violence generally, it is no easy matter to evaluate the impact of interventions aimed specifically at reducing firearm death, injury, crime or conflict. Quite apart from the political controversies, the problems of evaluating the impact of legislative reforms on complex problems such as crime and violence or public health have been well documented.[76] Many factors influence crime rates: the proportion of young men in the population, social and economic inequity, culture and values, political environment, substance abuse and the presence of other high-risk behaviors.[77] It has been suggested, for example, that one of the most significant factors influencing declines in crime rates in many countries is the falling proportion of males between the ages of fifteen and twenty-four.[78]

Efforts at weapons collection may be ineffective where human insecurity and demand for arms are very high. Increasing resources for law enforcement may fail to have the desired effect if issues of corruption in the force and mistrust in the community are addressed. Strengthening firearm laws may prove futile without attention to implementation or in contexts where a new supply of guns flows over porous borders. In addition, holding one variable—changes to legislation, for example—may be difficult or impossible given changes to other variables. Still, following the implementation of an intervention, efforts should be made to develop evaluation measures. In general, countries have embarked on legislative changes to firearm regulation with a focus on addressing the misuse of firearms in crime. Although a number of these legislative changes are recent, some preliminary evaluations are reviewed in Chapter 7.

CONCLUSIONS

Applying a public health model to the global health problems caused by the misuse of firearms provides a useful, action-oriented perspective. The strategies employed for harm reduction of other legal but potentially dangerous products—automobiles, tobacco and alcohol—have parallels with respect to approaches to the global problems associated with firearms.[79]

Approaches to preventing firearm death, injury and crime are following similar trajectories. In the United States and in many other countries, regulatory agencies establish standards for products. While the United States applies some standards to firearms imported to the country, it applies few to those that are manufactured in the United States.[80] At the same time, there is evidence that the powerful gun lobby, like the tobacco lobby, will do whatever it can to discredit fact-based approaches and interventions.[81] Public health is, for the most part, focused on prevention rather than prohibition. While the gun lobby and its allies often draw parallels between "prohibitionists" and those advocating regulation of firearms, the more appropriate parallel is the regulation of other potentially dangerous commodities through the establishment of controls over use. The misuse of firearms endangers not only the users but those around them. While there may be some benefits associated with the use of firearms in some contexts, it is clear that the costs of firearm injury and death are borne by society and that firearm regulation is based on the need to reduce harm while allowing lawful possession and legitimate use. As Hemenway notes, the available evidence suggests that enforcement and education are not sufficient to reduce harm and that attention needs also to be focused on the product, the environment and the economics of use (pricing and access).[82]

The interactions among these factors are complex and are not easy to measure in longitudinal studies. While there is limited research suggesting that interventions focused on controlling access to firearms in countries such as Colombia[83] may have an impact, it is evident that other factors are strong determinants of overall rates of crime and violence, including criminal activity, drug use, parental factors, and that a number of factors may act as protective influences (for example, religious beliefs).[84] However, a number of studies have suggested that the decline in firearm-related deaths has been at least in part the result of stronger legislation. (See Chapter 7 for more detail.) Doing good research on the impact of legislative changes is notoriously difficult. As a recent review by the Centers for Disease Control recommended, more attention needs to be paid to multivariate analysis that controls for other variables, including the degree of enforcement, socioeconomic status and gang activity. Further problems with data collection include the fact that crime data are consistently underreported. Aggregated crime data obscure the specific ways in which laws do and do not work.[85]

At the same time, we must recognize that the burden of proof demanded for interventions related to firearms is far greater than that demanded for other policy interventions. Certainly there is far less rigorous empirical research evaluating the impact of arms embargoes; export controls; disarmament, demobilization, reintegration (DDR); global or regional conventions or codes of conduct; or education campaigns compared to what exists for domestic regulation of firearms, despite the widespread conviction by governments and others that this research is needed. In general the burden of proof placed on interventions related to firearms regulation is much higher than that applied to other criminal justice reforms, largely because of the political opposition. As criminologist Neil Boyd concluded, there is more evidence to support the efficacy of gun control legislation in reducing death and injury than for most other legislative interventions.[86]

We return to discussions of the interventions aimed at reducing the misuse of firearms in Chapter 7, but first, a better understanding of the legal and illegal markets for firearms is needed.

4

The Global Gun Trade

The international market for firearms is large and complex in terms of both the markets served and the players involved in various stages, from production through use. Some aspect of firearm manufacture takes place in almost 100 countries, but much of the production is concentrated in a few countries. In many cases, the production of firearms is state controlled in countries in which states are tied very closely to the defense industries. In other cases, manufacturers focus on consumer markets and are extremely diverse in their scale and products.

Although the manufacture of small arms and light weapons is widely dispersed, a dozen or so countries are responsible for the bulk of the arms sold on the international market. These include the five permanent members of the UN Security Council—the United States, Russia, China, the United Kingdom and France—plus a number of other European, Asian and Latin American countries. If these countries could agree to a common system of restraints on exports, the sale of arms to areas of instability is likely to fall substantially. Some weapons would still flow through clandestine channels, but most large-scale transactions would be subject to international oversight.[1]

The production and distribution chain for firearms is complex: guns often change hands many times before reaching their final destination, and the resale markets (legal and illegal) are substantial because of the durability of the product. As Senator Daniel Patrick Moynihan of New York noted, "The life of a handgun seems to be measured in decades, generations, and even centuries."[2] The same is true of military weapons, which move from conflict to conflict.

Manufacturers of firearms can be analyzed from the perspective of the primary customers they serve (state or civilian markets), the types of weapons produced and sold (handguns, rifles, shotguns, military assault weapons) or the region. In some cases, a manufacturer focuses on a single market; for example, Austria's Glock focuses primarily on handguns, and Canada's Deimaco serves only government markets and the military. But often the same manufacturer serves state and civilian markets with a wide range of products. The United States' Ruger, for example, manufactures tactical weapons for state markets as well hunting rifles and handguns. Heckler Koch of Germany supplies both government and civilian markets.

The basic production and distribution chain for small arms/firearms is shown in Figure 4.1. In civilian markets, firearms are often sold by manufacturers to wholesalers and resold through various channels before they reach civilians. Markets for government arms are served directly by manufacturers as well as by arms brokers, who arrange transfers.

TYPES OF FIREARMS

While the term *small arm* has historically been used in military contexts to describe weapons primarily made to military specifications, and *firearm* has been used to describe weapons primarily produced for civilian markets, these distinctions have become more and more blurred. In many contexts, efforts to distinguish military-specification "small arms" from other firearms have proved difficult, if not futile, as weapons originally intended for military use are often adapted to civilian markets. Indeed, many companies use their success in military and police markets as a selling point to civilians.

A number of international groups have suggested that the distinction between small arms and firearms is meaningless and have proposed that there be a focus on a single accepted definition. The term *firearm* encompasses the full range of these, including "revolvers and self-loading pistols; rifles and carbines; submachine guns; assault rifles; and light machine guns,"[3] regardless of their intended use.

Firearms can be further divided into types. Definitions vary considerably from jurisdiction to jurisdiction, but the markets for different types of firearms are relatively distinct. Often national laws distinguish among long guns, including rifles and shotguns; handguns, including revolvers and pistols; and military assault weapons:

- Long guns: principally rifles and shotguns, designed to be fired from the shoulder with two hands. The inside of a rifle barrel is grooved with spiral channels, thus giving the ball a rotary motion and insuring greater accuracy. Rifles are preferred by hunters and are equipped with a range of mechanisms (semiautomatic, fully automatic and selective fire). They can be extremely accurate, with a range of over a mile. A shotgun is a light, smooth-bored gun, often double-barreled,

Figure 4.1 U.S. Firearm Production by Category over Time

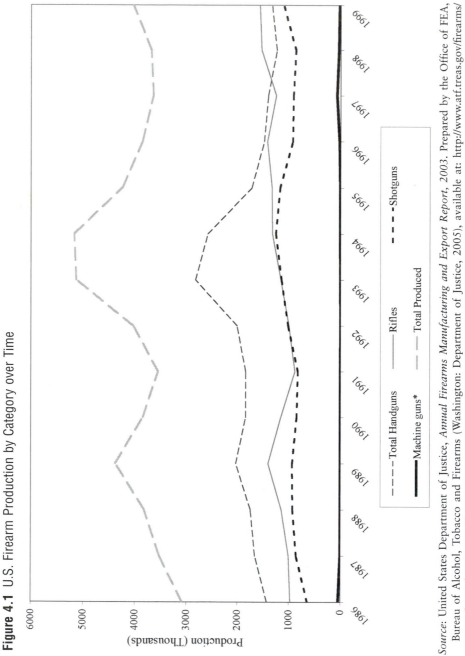

Source: United States Department of Justice, *Annual Firearms Manufacturing and Export Report, 2003.* Prepared by the Office of FEA, Bureau of Alcohol, Tobacco and Firearms (Washington: Department of Justice, 2005), available at: http://www.atf.treas.gov/firearms/stats/afmer/afmer2003.pdf.

especially designed for firing small shot at short range and killing small game.

- Handguns: principally pistols and revolvers, designed to be fired with a single hand. Handguns are classified as revolvers or pistols. Revolvers have a round cylinder, which is the magazine for holding bullets and acts as a chamber when properly aligned with the barrel. In double-action revolvers, each time the trigger is pulled the weapon fires and the cylinder advances to the next chamber. Single-action revolvers require that the hammer be manually cocked before each shot. A revolver's cylinder usually holds six cartridges. Instead of having a revolving cylinder, a semiautomatic handgun (also known as a pistol) carries its extra cartridges in an ammunition magazine, usually located in the handle of the handgun. Spring pressure forces the cartridges upward in the magazine. In the United States, it has become common to refer to a specific class of handguns, either pistols or revolvers, known as "Saturday night specials." These are small, short-barrelled handguns made of inexpensive and often inferior materials. Because of their low quality and lack of accuracy, these weapons have little or no use in sport but are used by criminals who care less about these criteria.
- Military assault weapons: principally designed to fire large quantities of ammunition quickly and have a range of specific features designed for combat conditions. Assault firearms may be semiautomatic (firing one bullet per trigger pull), fully automatic (firing more than one bullet per trigger pull), or selective fire (can be set to fire either as a semiautomatic or fully automatic weapon). This category includes rifles, shotguns and handguns that are designed primarily for military and law enforcement use and are not particularly suitable or readily adaptable for sporting purposes. Characteristics that are often present in assault weapons include the ability to accept a detachable ammunition magazine; folding stocks; flash suppressors; bipod mounts on pistol grips, rifles or shotguns; threaded barrels (allowing for the easy attachment of silencers on assault pistols); and concealability.[4]

Further distinctions may be made based on characteristics of the firearms; for example, fully automatic firearms (or machine guns) will fire repeatedly with one press of the trigger, while semiautomatic or self-loading firearms repeat the process of firing, ejecting, and reloading.

THE GLOBAL FIREARMS MARKET

Because reporting requirements vary from country to country, estimates of global firearm production vary. The global annual volume of small arms production is estimated to be between 7.5 million and 8 million firearms, according to the *Small Arms Survey 2004*.[5] Most of these firearms (5–7.5

million) are destined for commercial markets. Production of military-style weapons amounts to 500,000 to 1 million firearms per year.

There are thousands of firearm manufacturers in the world, with 1,700 in the United States alone.[6] The commercial market is dominated by the United States (which produces more than 3 million weapons annually), and the European Union and the Russian Federation (each producing 1 million weapons annually).[7] Very few national governments publish statistics on the sale or transfer of small arms and light weapons, and there are more weapons in the hands of civilians than in the possession of states. Efforts to tap new markets coupled with efforts to avoid high labor costs, regulatory regimes and other "costs of doing business" have been said to fuel the growth of "licensed" production in developing countries, where manufacturers, in effect, contract out to local providers.[8]

Military and State Markets

The major producers of small arms worldwide are governments, mainly for the armed forces and police. The principal suppliers of military weapons worldwide include China, Russia and the United States. Until the 1950s the major industrialized countries of the West and the Soviet bloc were the main producers of small arms and light weapons. In the 1960s and 1970s, an increasing number of these weapons were also produced under license by U.S. and Soviet cold war allies and by a few countries in the developing world. It is estimated that between 55 million and 72 million rapid-fire assault rifles were produced, many under license, in fifty-four countries in the post–World War II period (1945–1990).[9] Many of these weapons are still in circulation today, moving with relative ease from one conflict area to another. Starting in the 1980s, the number of manufacturers of small arms increased to three hundred companies in more than seventy countries.[10] At the end of the cold war, a survey of 147 countries found that 83 had the Belgium FN rifle, 61 had Russian AK-47s and 53 had German H&K rifles.[11]

Although the United States, the Russian Federation and China dominate the military small arms market, there are least twenty-seven other countries that must be considered as producers. They include: Austria, Belgium, Bulgaria, the Czech Republic, Finland, France, Germany, Italy, Poland, Portugal, Romania, Spain, Sweden, Switzerland and the United Kingdom in Europe; Canada and Brazil in the Americas; India, Japan, Singapore, South Korea and Taiwan in the Asia Pacific area; Iran, Israel and Turkey in the Middle East; and South Africa in sub-Saharan Africa.[12]

Statistics on production of firearms for government markets are murky.[13] The United States sold or transferred an estimated $463 million worth of small arms and ammunition to 124 countries in 1998. Of these countries, about 30 were at war or experiencing persistent civil violence in 1998.[14]

Table 4.1 Top Five Small Arms Producing Companies in Various Military Weapons Categories

Military Side Arms	Rifles	Submachine Guns	Machine Guns	Small Arms Ammunition
Beretta (Italy)	Norinco (China)	Norinco (China)	Norinco (China)	Sellier & Bellot (Czech Republic)
Heckler and Koch (United Kingdom/Germany)	Heckler and Koch (United Kingdom/Germany)	Heckler and Koch (United Kingdom/Germany)	Heckler and Koch (United Kingdom/Germany)	Winchester Olin (United States/Belgium)
Smith & Wesson (United States)	Izhmash (Russia)	Izhmash (Russia)	Izhmash (Russia)	Nammo (Finland/Sweden/Norway)
Colt (United States)	Colt (United States)	IMI (Israel)	IMI (Israel)	Giat (France)
FN Herstal (Belgium)	FN Herstal (Belgium)	KBP (Russia)	FN Herstal (Belgium)	FN Herstal (Belgium)

Source: T. Gander, "Small Arms Technologies," Background Paper, *Small Arms Survey 2002* (Geneva, 2002).

The U.S. Market

The United States is the largest civilian market in the world for firearms. The United States produced approximately 3 million firearms in 2001, the majority of which were sold in the United States. The United States imports more than $1 million worth of firearms annually. In 2000 U.S. exports were estimated to have a value of $2.39 billion.[15] There are more than 1,700 firearms manufacturers and 750 licensed firearm importers in the United States, according to Bureau of Alcohol, Tobacco, and Firearms (BATF) reports. In 2003, the most recent year of available data, manufacturers sold over 1 million handguns and more than 2 million rifles and shotguns. The United States also imports more than 1 million guns each year, while exporting an average of 400,000.[16] (See Table 4.2.)

The U.S. gun industry consists of a large of number of privately held manufacturing firms dispersed in many states in the country. Only three public companies are active in the manufacture of firearms, one owned by a conglomerate with headquarters in the United Kingdom. Another well-known brand, Beretta, is part of an Italian company. The competitive position of the companies differs by product category—pistol, revolver and shotgun. Manufacturing of shotguns and revolvers is concentrated in a few companies, while manufacturing of pistols is more competitive. There is a strong competition from foreign manufacturers: as domestic production decreases, imports increase.[17]

Because the industry consists mostly of privately held firms, it is difficult to obtain financial information about them. Based on the available data, the industry is mature, in decline and not attractive to investors. There are no new entrants to the market, and several firms have stop manufacturing firearms altogether. Stocks of the publicly held companies—Olin, Tomkins and Sturm, Ruger—have consistently declined over several years but production has begun to increase since 2001.[18] Figure 4.2 shows U.S. firearm production by type.

Since 1986, production in all segments has declined, although there was a slight upturn since 2001.

Although the domestic production and export of U.S.-manufactured guns have declined, imports of guns have increased. Despite their limited success in the courtrooms, lawsuits as well as public debate about gun control have created an unstable market, and at least one company—Lorcin, noted manufacturer of Saturday night specials—has ceased operations. Although few lawsuits against manufacturers have been successful, they have increased the cost of doing business and undermined the reputation of the industry. A Brooklyn, New York, jury held manufacturers liable for "negligent marketing" by dumping weapons on the market in such a way that any reasonable person could predict they would get into the hands of people who would misuse them.

Furthermore, testimony by industry insiders has not helped the industry. Robert Haas, a former vice president of marketing for Smith & Wesson,

Figure 4.2 U.S. Firearm Market Structure

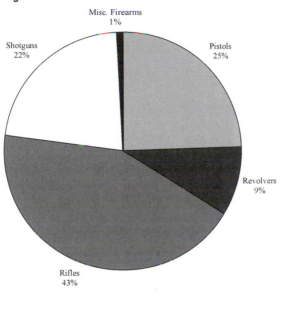

Source: United States Department of Justice, *Annual Firearms Manufacturing and Export Report, 2003*. Prepared by the Office of FEA, Bureau of Alcohol, Tobacco and Firearms (Washington: Department of Justice, 2005), available at: http://www.atf.treas.gov/firearms/stats/afmer/afmer2003.pdf.

testified that manufacturers could easily cut off retailers that repeatedly make multiple sales of guns or have crime guns traced to them "in the same way a retailer would be cut off who broke [price] agreements."[19] The judge agreed, maintaining, "It is the duty of manufacturers of a uniquely hazardous product, designed to kill and wound human beings, to take reasonable steps ... at the point of sale to primary distributors" to prevent their misuse.[20]

A growing number of cities have filed their own liability suits, demanding to be reimbursed for the cost of treating victims of shootings. Although pro-gun advocates retaliated with legislation intended to indemnify gun makers, it failed to secure passage. More than thirty-five major private suits have also been filed since 1998, and approximately thirty-three cities and the state of New York have brought lawsuits against gun makers and retailers seeking to hold the companies responsible for the misuse of their products. The legal costs for these suits have been funded primarily by

George Soros, the Brady Campaign and its predecessor, Handgun Control.[21] The outcomes of these suits have been varied. For instance, in September 2000, a Chicago lawsuit against gun manufacturers was initially dismissed by a Cook County judge. Recent federal legislation protects gun manufacturers from lawsuit by civilians.[22]

As weapons sales decline, as manufacturing standards rise and as lawsuits are filed, gun manufacturers across the United States are feeling pressure. Some have declared bankruptcy as a way of protecting themselves from lawsuits. Others have quietly closed down, for example, Lorcin, which is currently named in twenty-two lawsuits. Lorcin and other manufacturers of cheap handguns such as Davis and Bryco Arms, which depended on high volumes and low margins, are particularly hard-pressed.

Despite the large number of manufacturers, the industry is relatively concentrated, with a few firms dominating the market. The top manufacturers for the years 2003 are shown in Figure 4.3. In the handgun market, Sturm, Ruger dominates sales of pistols, while Smith & Wesson leads sales of revolvers. Sturm, Ruger also leads in rifle production, while Remington dominates the shotgun market. For example, data from 2003 show that Sturm, Ruger and Smith & Wesson account for 75 percent of total revolver production.

The pistol market is more diffuse, with thirty-two different producers. The four largest manufacturers—Sturm, Beretta, Beemiller and Springfield—accounted for 43.1 percent of total production in 2003. In the past, pistol production was dominated by the same firms, with the exception of Bryco Arms, which has replaced Lorcin. (See Figure 4.5.)

There are four major rifle manufacturers within the United States. The majority of the market is now controlled by Remington, which in 2003, the most recent year for which data are available, produced 290,873 rifles. Sturm, Ruger, formerly the dominant player has fallen to third place.

There are eleven shotgun manufacturers in the United States, but four firms—Remington, O.F. Mossberg, Harrington & Richardson and U.S. Repeating Arms—control more than 88 percent of the market. (See Figure 4.7.)

During the 1990s, between one-third and one-half of the guns sold on the U.S. market were imported. (See Figure 4.8.) Import restrictions are designed to filter out low-quality weapons and military weapons and require only that weapons meet a "sporting purposes test." Foreign imports fuel civilian markets. Foreign imports grew from 747,138 in 1978 to 2,239,460 in 1994. More than 20 million guns were imported into the U.S. civilian market between 1978 and 1996, and the share of the U.S. market held by foreign manufacturers has increased.[23] In 1999, foreign companies accounted for a third of all handguns on the market. Brazil, Austria, Italy, Germany and Spain remain the largest handgun exporters to the United States. Austria's Glock has become one of the biggest arms dealers, supplying U.S. law enforcement since the 1990s. But in 1995, when more than half a million Glocks were in circulation in the United States, 80 percent

Figure 4.3 Top U.S. Producers of Firearms Ranked by Weapon Type, 2003

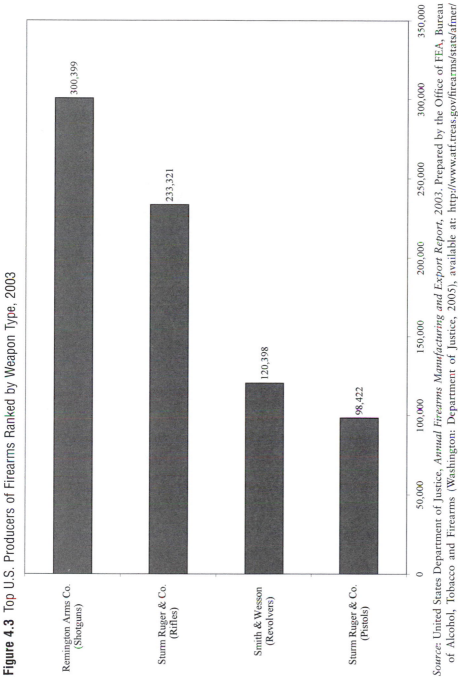

Source: United States Department of Justice, *Annual Firearms Manufacturing and Export Report, 2003.* Prepared by the Office of FEA, Bureau of Alcohol, Tobacco and Firearms (Washington: Department of Justice, 2005), available at: http://www.atf.treas.gov/firearms/stats/afmer/afmer2003.pdf.

Figure 4.4 Share of U.S. Revolver Production by Firm in 2003

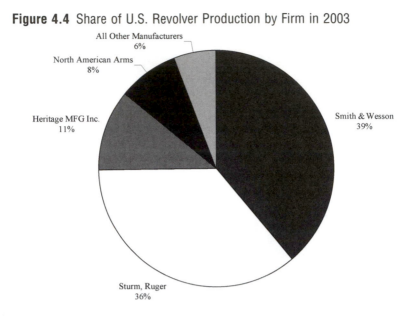

All Other Manufacturers
6%

North American Arms
8%

Heritage MFG Inc.
11%

Smith & Wesson
39%

Sturm, Ruger
36%

■ Smith & Wesson   □ Sturm, Ruger ■ Heritage MFG Inc. ■ North American Arms ▣ All Other Manufacturers

Source: United States Department of Justice, *Annual Firearms Manufacturing and Export Report, 2003*. Prepared by the Office of FEA, Bureau of Alcohol, Tobacco and Firearms (Washington: Department of Justice, 2005), available at: http://www.atf.treas.gov/firearms/stats/afmer/afmer2003.pdf.

were in civilian hands. The U.S. civilian market being more lucrative, Glock began by targeting both law enforcement and the civilian population.[24] See Figure 4.8 for the major exporters to the United States.

Russia

Although Russia is famed for the Kalashnikov rifle (called the AK-47) worldwide, it no longer produces the weapon in its original design. The Kalashnikov and its variants have been produced in Bulgaria, China, Cuba, East Germany, Egypt, Hungary, India, North Korea, Poland, Romania, Slovenia, Turkey and Yugoslavia. The breakup of the Soviet Union and the end of the cold war had a significant impact on small arms production in Russia, as its principal market for weapons—the Soviet military machine and its allies—collapsed. A recent comprehensive report on the Russian army reveals that in recent years the country has begun to shift its production of rifles and handguns from military to civilian markets. These are primarily for export purposes, and this area of production appears to be growing. The Russian industry produced more than 1 million commercial

Figure 4.5 Share of U.S. Pistol Production by Firm in 2003

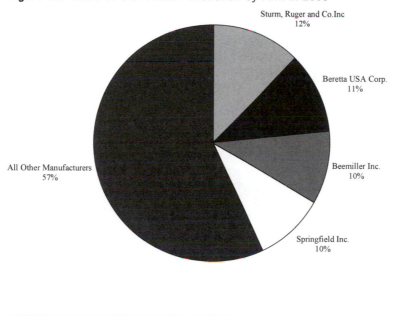

Source: United States Department of Justice, *Annual Firearms Manufacturing and Export Report, 2003*. Prepared by the Office of FEA, Bureau of Alcohol, Tobacco and Firearms (Washington: Department of Justice, 2005), available at: http://www.atf.treas.gov/firearms/stats/afmer/afmer2003.pdf.

firearms in 1999, 800,000 of them sporting and hunting rifles from the Izhevsky plant, up 30 percent from 1998. The total value of this production in Russia was calculated in 2001 to be US$250 million.[25] Exports are estimated at just over half that amount, US$130 million. The Russian industry is believed to employ more than 80,000 people. As part of government policy there has been increased consolidation in the sector, with the aim of merging all Russian developers and manufacturers into two major government-owned holding companies: the Small Arms and Cartidges Corporation (with JSC Izmash as its core company, along with twelve others) and the High Precision Weapons Corporation, which will focus on light weapons and missiles.[26]

After the fall of the Berlin Wall, arms from the former Soviet Union began to be exported in larger numbers to the United States. Between 1993 and 1994, the number grew from less than 3,000 annually to more than 250,000.[27]

Russia has in recent years increased the transparency surrounding the reporting of its small arms and firearms production. Although the government does not provide an annual arms report, data are available from

Figure 4.6 Share of U.S. Rifle Production by Firm in 2003

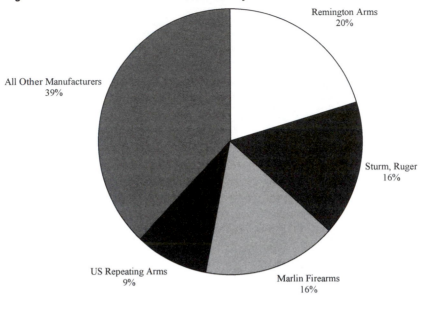

Remington Arms
20%

All Other Manufacturers
39%

Sturm, Ruger
16%

US Repeating Arms
9%

Marlin Firearms
16%

□ Remington Arms ■ Sturm, Ruger ▣ Marlin Firearms ■ US Repeating Arms ■ All Other Manufacturers

Source: United States Department of Justice, *Annual Firearms Manufacturing and Export Report, 2003*. Prepared by the Office of FEA, Bureau of Alcohol, Tobacco and Firearms (Washington: Department of Justice, 2005), available at: http://www.atf.treas.gov/firearms/stats/afmer/afmer2003.pdf.

Rosoboronexport, the major arms exporting agency, and others (see Table 4.2). Russia has standards for marking weapons at the point of production and export control processes in place, with control concentrated in the Russian executive branch.

Brazil

In Brazil, the major provider of military weapons is the state-owned Indústria de Material Bélico do Brasil (IMBEL), which produces the FN FAL rifle under license as well as .45-caliber pistols destined primarily for the U.S. market. There are more than eighteen small arms manufacturers, including large private companies such as Forjas Taurus SA and Companhia Brasileira de Cartuchos (CBC), which supply the civilian markets within Brazil as well as export markets in surrounding countries and the United States, South Africa and other countries. Forjas Taurus SA, for example, is the country's leading producer and exporter of handguns, with 60 percent

Figure 4.7 Share of U.S. Shotgun Production by Firm in 2003

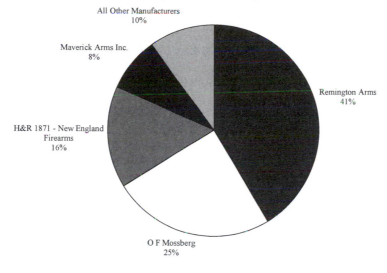

All Other Manufacturers
10%

Maverick Arms Inc.
8%

Remington Arms
41%

H&R 1871 - New England
Firearms
16%

O F Mossberg
25%

■ Remington Arms □ O F Mossberg ■ H&R 1871 - New England Firearms ■ Maverick Arms Inc. ▨ All Other Manufacturers

Source: United States Department of Justice, *Annual Firearms Manufacturing and Export Report, 2003*. Prepared by the Office of FEA, Bureau of Alcohol, Tobacco and Firearms (Washington: Department of Justice, 2005), available at: http://www.atf.treas.gov/firearms/stats/afmer/afmer2003.pdf.

Figure 4.8 Major Exporters of Firearms to United States

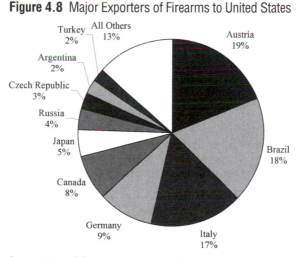

Turkey All Others
2% 13%

Argentina
2%

Czech Republic
3%

Russia
4%

Japan
5%

Canada
8%

Germany
9%

Austria
19%

Brazil
18%

Italy
17%

Source: United States Department of Justice, *Firearms Commerce in the United States, 2001/2002*. Prepared by the Office of FEA, Bureau of Alcohol, Tobacco and Firearms (Washington: Department of Justice).

Table 4.2 Russia's Small Arms Producers, Selected Financial Indicators, 1999–2001

Company	Total Sales			Employees		
	1999	2000	2001	1999	2000	2001
JSC Izhmash	90.0	170.7	199.5	22,900	25,400	27,300
VA Degtyarev (ZID)	51.9	59.7	84.3	n/a	15,368	15,000
JSC Izhevsky Mekanishesky Zavod (IMZ)	40.9	46.6	57.7	n/a	14,954	15,200
JSC Tulsky Oruzheiny Zavod	29.4	22.0	13.4	n/a	n/a	7,000
JSC Kovrov Mechanical Plant (KMP)	n/a	15.8	22.2	n/a	n/a	3,000
Vyatskiye Polyany Machine Building Plant Molot	24.7	25.6	21.2	n/a	n/a	7,430

Source: M. Pyadushkin, M. Haug, and A. Matveeva, "Beyond the Kalashnikov: Small Arms Production, Export, Stockpiles in the Russian Federation," *Small Arms Survey*: *Occasional Paper No. 19* (Geneva, August 2003).

of its production destined for foreign markets. Amadeo Rossi is much smaller but markets guns in the United States as well.[28] Brazil's Taurus also exports a substantial number of handguns to the United States. In 2003, it was estimated that Brazil's small arm and firearm exports were worth US $94.3 million.[29] (See Table 4.3.)

Germany

Germany has more than thirty companies producing small arms, primarily for military markets, but its precision, high-end firearms are also popular among civilians, and it is a leading exporter to the United States. Germany is one of the few countries without a large civilian gun market that has a sizable small arm manufacturing operation. In fact, Germany, while playing a major role in supplying small arms to other countries, has one of the strictest gun control regimes in the world. Its estimated sales for hunting and sporting markets is about US$157 million.[30] Heckler and Koch, Germany's dominant provider of military weapons worldwide, is the third leading exporter of handguns to the United States, with annual rates around 100,000 units.[31]

Table 4.3 Estimated Production in Brazil by Major Providers in Millions of U.S. Dollars

Year	Taurus Production of Handguns (Thousands)	Taurus Exports ($Mil)	Other Firearm Exports ($Mil)
1988	419	39	23
1989	369	33	22
1990	193	33	21
1991	291	35	25
1992	378	43	21
1993	385	46	35
1994	340	49	45
1995	273	39	20
1996	189	38	15
1997	179	27	12
1998	210	28	20
1999	254	34	25
2000	233	34	21
2001	242	34	20
2002	311	46	26
2003	224	36	20

Source: Rubem C. Fernandes, Benjamin Lessing, Carolina Iootty, Julio Cesar Purcena, Luciana Phebo, Marcelo de Souza Nascimento, Pablo Dreyfus, and Patricia Rivero, "Brazil: The Arms and the Victims," *Viva Rio*, 2005, http://www.vivario.org.br/publique/cgi/cgilua.exe/sys/start.htm?sid=28&infoid=962.

China

The most prominent producer of small arms in Asia is China. The major producing company in China is the state-owned China North Industries Group Corporation (also known as Norinco). In the 1990s, its combined sales of military and civilian products averaged about $2 billion annually. However, weapons account for only 20 to 30 percent of overall production. In July 1999, Norinco was divided into China South Industries Group Corporation (CSG) and China North Industries Group Corporation (CNGN). CSG refocused almost entirely on civil production while CNGN produces most of China's small arms, supplemented by supplies from a few small People's Liberation Army (PLA) factories. It is estimated that the Chinese military inventory totaled at least 27 million firearms at its height, probably the biggest stockpile in the world. On the other hand, civilian possession of firearms in China is severely limited.

China moved aggressively into U.S. markets in the 1980s. Between 1982 and 1986, Chinese exports to the United States had never exceeded 6 percent of total imports to the United States, but in 1987 that number surged to 22 percent of imports. Between 1988 and 1989, AK-47 variant imports to the United States reached 40,379, 90 percent of them Chinese.[32] (See Table 4.4.)

DISTRIBUTION NETWORKS

State-to-State Transfers and Brokers

The international transfer of a weapon may occur in several ways. It may begin, for example, as a legal transaction between states as part of bilateral sales or military assistance programmes. In the late 1990s, the state-to-state trade in major conventional weapons declined, while, as we have noted, the production of small arms and light weapons appears to have increased. Even the former Czechoslovakia, which made a political decision in the early 1990s to cease firearm exports, subsequently chose to reenter the business for economic and other reasons. In addition, large quantities of surplus weapons have been transferred to developing countries in the form of direct aid, subsidized sales or intra-alliance transfers. The effects of cold war–era firearm transfers have been felt in numerous intrastate con-

Table 4.4 Rifle Imports from China to the United States, 1987–1994

Year	Total Rifles Imported	Chinese Rifles Imported	Percent Chinese
1987	452,059	100,897	22
1988	484,976	182,935	38
1989	350,012	141,382	40
1990	273,102	31,370	11
1991	339,966	115,902	34
1992	420,085	164,271	39
1993	764,498	490,399	64
1994	698,907	344,648	49
Total	3,783,605	1,571,804	42

Source: Tom Diaz, *Making a Killing: The Business of Guns in America* (New York: The New Press, 1999).

flicts around the world. Some of the factors identified as driving the increased use of small arms in conflict include

- Simplicity and durability: Because of minimal need for maintenance and relative ease of use, including use by uneducated people and child combatants, assault rifles can remain operational for twenty to forty years.

- Portability and concealability: Small arms are easily concealed on the person or in vehicles, making them easy to transport and smuggle into areas of conflict with legitimate cargo.

- Military, police and civilian uses: Small arms are well suited to military, police and civilian use. Recycling weapons from conflict to conflict has dropped the price in many countries below the cost of manufacture. For example, a 1996 report indicated that in Mozambique and Angola, an assault rifle could be purchased for less than $15 or traded for a bag of maize. In Uganda, the price was reported to be the same as that of a chicken.[33]

- Lethality: Some machine guns (automatic weapons) are capable of firing up to 700 rounds a minute and require minimal skill to use.[34]

State-owned and multinational companies have dominated the global arms business through government-to-government contracts, even if government forces are not the final owners. The contacts between the supplying government and the client government would normally run through official though discreet meetings involving business representatives and high-ranking military or embassy officials in the countries involved in the transfer. The United States, for example, recently negotiated Plan Colombia, a $1.3 billion aid package, ostensibly to help the Colombian government to fight rebels and the illegal drug trade, in spite of Colombia's poor human rights record. During the cold war, governments interested in arming allies covertly began to rely on arms brokers, who acted as middlemen and arranged arms trades even to countries under embargo. These networks of brokers are generally unregulated and may undertake complex subcontracting arrangements across several countries.

While most national laws require international arms transfers to be initiated as a transaction only after an exporting agent has obtained the approval of the home government, this is seldom a requirement if arms have been procured in a foreign country and do not enter the country in which the broker or shipping agent resides. This means that the activities of arms brokers and their shipping agents can remain outside the arms-control laws and regulations of their own countries.[35]

Diversions from legal to illegal markets have emerged as a problem, as many states resorted to middlemen to supply weapons in support of covert operations. Often the weapons supplied to one-time "allies" are turned against the suppliers, often termed "blow back" or the "boomerang effect."

During the 1980s, for example, at least $2 billion worth of arms and military training were sent to Islamic rebel groups (the mujahideen) by the CIA in an effort to topple the Soviet-backed Afghanistan government. These weapons were then used by the Taliban and Al Qaeda against the United States.[36]

Distribution Networks in Civilian Markets

In terms of civilian markets, most countries supply both domestic and foreign markets but often focus more on one than on the other. Major providers of firearms internationally, for example, are often also dominant within their local markets. In the United States, the firearm distribution network includes wholesalers (about 1,700 licensed firearms manufacturers and nearly 750 licensed importers[37]) as well as retailers.[38] Increased regulation has led to significant consolidation in the U.S. retail distribution networks. In 1994, it was estimated that there were 284,000 licensed firearm retailers in the United States. Only 20,000 of those had legitimate stockpiles, and half of those were pawnbrokers.[39] Many dealers sold "guns out of car[s], over the kitchen table, or at gun shows and flea markets."[40] Because of stricter licensing requirements introduced in 1994, the number of federally licensed firearm distributors in the United States has decreased dramatically: by 2001 that number had shrunk to 102,913.[41] However, in addition to federally licensed firearm dealers, there are a wide range of less formal distribution networks, notably gun shows as well as secondary sales by individuals. Often the gun shows and secondary sales are not regulated except by state or local law. The BATF estimates that 7.5 million new and used firearms are sold at retail outlets each year. Approximately 4.5 million new firearms are sold, including 2 million handguns. In addition, estimates of annual secondhand firearm transactions (i.e., sales, trades, or gifts) range from 2 million to 4.5 million. Gun shows are held in communities across the United States, where dealers and individuals are able to hawk their wares without regulation. The BATF estimates that there are approximately 2,000 gun shows held each year, although the National Association of Arms Shows estimates more than 5,000 a year.[42] Diversion from legal markets to illegal markets is a major problem in the United States and many other countries and is discussed in the next chapter.

MARKETING AND PROMOTION

While the marketing of small arms to governments is based on high-level negotiations behind closed doors, the marketing of firearms to consumers is evident on a daily basis through advertising, associations and even entertainment media.[43] The wide and complex array of gun promoters in the United States includes the gun press, advertisers and the entertainment media. Product placements in movies and popular TV series have been tied to increased demand for certain makes and models of firearms. Furthermore, industry associations as well as lobby groups—such as the National Rifle Association (NRA)—claiming to represent the interests of gun owners, play an important role in fueling demand and eroding any controls on supply. While the NRA tries to position itself as the voice of firearm owners, "it also has had a long and intimate relationship with gun makers and sellers."[44] The NRA's advocacy reduced barriers, such as regulation to gun markets, for the industry. It has, for example, fought regulation by the Consumer Product Safety Commission as well as regulations over sales or possession of firearms. The NRA Institute for Legislative Action (ILA) is the NRA's direct lobbying arm, and its political action committee (PAC) channels millions of dollars into gun-friendly politicians' campaigns and into efforts to "punish" its opponents.

CONCLUSIONS

The global firearms industry is increasingly shifting its focus to civilian markets, which is much larger than the military market. It is little surprise that American firearm manufacturers dominate the world market, serving both domestic and international customers and state and civilian markets. But other countries also play a significant role. As Tom Diaz from the Washington-based Violence Policy Center noted, in many cases they have strict controls over civilian possession within their borders, but have huge export markets. The blurring of military and civilian and of domestic and foreign markets has implications for the regulation of imports, exports and transfers. The distribution networks for firearms are extremely complex and multilayered, with brokers, wholesalers and retailers playing significant roles. In many countries, such as the United States, resale markets through dealers, gun shows and secondhand sales are huge. In general, many segments of firearm markets are in decline and the mechanisms for creating and sustaining demand are also complex, involving a wide range of associations, firearm publications and the media. The demand for firearms is discussed in more detail in Chapter 6.

5

Globalization and Gun Running

The illegal trade in firearms parallels in some respects the legal markets described in the previous chapter. Illegal trade occurs both within and among countries. Globalization and the erosion of boundaries between states, coupled with the growing sophistication of international criminal organizations, have caused the illegal trade to go global. Just as manufacturers serve both civilians and states, the illegal gun runners serve criminals, states and nonstate actors (who may be labeled insurgents, freedom fighters or terrorists, depending on the political agenda).

Those focused on conflict prevention worldwide have tended to concentrate on illegal transfers to states, insurgents and nonstate actors in violation of international embargoes and increasingly in violation of international law. Conversely, those focused on crime prevention have tended to focus on the mechanisms used to provide firearms to urban gangs and organized crime. As we have noted in previous chapters, many of these efforts to demarcate boundaries are undermined by the fact that the firearms, the supply chain and the actors involved in the illegal gun trade simply follow the money; they are not likely to distinguish among their clients based on motive, whether political or criminal. In some contexts—Colombia, for example—the boundaries between political violence and criminal violence are not clear. Firearms that had been supplied to political groups in Afghanistan now figure prominently in both political and criminal violence throughout South Asia. Understanding the sources of illegal firearms is important in devising effective strategies to stem the flow of guns to those likely to misuse them.

One thing is very clear: virtually every illegal gun begins as a legal gun. The production of illegal weapons accounts for only a small part of the problem. Efforts to combat the illegal trade in guns must focus on preventing the diversion of guns from legal to illegal markets. The mechanisms that fuel the illegal gun market in the United States have created the largest pool of illegal guns in the world. That pool is the principal source of illegal guns in the surrounding regions of Canada, Mexico and the Caribbean and extends to other countries around the world as well. Not only do guns from the United States fuel criminal markets, but they are also used to arm terrorist and insurgent groups worldwide.

Availability of Data

One of the major challenges in undertaking any study of illicit gun trafficking is the absence of reliable data. A large number of countries do not appear to systematically track or trace the sources of all firearms recovered in crime. Others appear to maintain ongoing records of firearms recovered in crime, but more often than not these records are kept only at the local level, if at all. Still other countries periodically trace particular firearms back to the source in the aid of criminal investigations, often relying on the services of the Bureau of Alcohol Tobacco and Firearms (BATF) in the United States or Interpol. The results of these tracing efforts, while they may reveal the workings of criminal networks, are not necessarily representative of the firearms used in crime. In fact, most countries have reported problems with the consistency, ease and coordination of their efforts to track firearms to their sources within their own jurisdictions. Problems at an international level are even greater.

There is little empirical analysis of the problem of illicit trafficking on a national level and even less at the international level. Interpol collects and aggregates data annually through the Interpol Weapons Electronic Tracing System (IWeTS). Participation in IWeTS is voluntary, the number of incidents reported is relatively low, and the system does not provide much insight into overall levels of illicit trafficking, but IWeTS does provide a wealth of useful anecdotal information helpful to criminal investigations.

A surprisingly large proportion of studies of illicit trafficking conducted to date are based on secondary literature or anecdotal information. This qualitative research provides useful insights into the mechanisms that operate in illicit markets. While anecdotal evidence is valuable in the absence of wider empirical studies, it has at times proved to be at odds with the results of larger empirical studies. For example, in Canada, a 1995 study revealed that the majority of firearms actually recovered in crime were rifles and shotguns.[1] In Brazil, where it has been estimated that there are about 7 million legal firearms and even more illegal firearms, an analysis of firearms recovered in crime showed that most of the guns recovered were domestically manufactured.[2] A study of firearms recovered in crime in South Africa showed that postconflict military weapons were a relatively small part of the problem.[3]

Many countries keep records of firearms that are reported lost or stolen as well as of those seized by customs officials. Systematic empirical analyses of large samples of firearms recovered in crime in a particular region, country or locality have been undertaken in an effort to trace these arms to their sources. Detailed analyses of the total firearms recovered in crime have been conducted in an effort to understand the types of firearms used and the likely sources. In all these cases, however, the data are incomplete because only a small fraction of illegally trafficked or imported firearms are actually intercepted.

Theft of firearms is also underreported, particularly in countries without mandatory reporting requirements or accountability mechanisms. Some countries simply destroy seized firearms or, in the case of some Caribbean nations, dump them in the ocean without recording information about the weapons that might prove useful to understanding or investigating the illegal trade. Finally, only a portion of firearms used in crime are ever actually recovered. Consequently, the data available for quantitative analyses are limited.[4]

The largest study of the subject was undertaken in the United Nations International Study on Firearms Regulation, which surveyed countries to determine the seriousness of the problem of illicit trafficking. The study collected important data regarding:

- Levels of firearms death, injury and crime
- Firearms regulation and legislation
- Reported theft and losses of firearms
- Perceptions of problems with illicit sales and distribution, illegal importation and illegal manufacture
- Anecdotal evidence regarding incidents of illegal trafficking and methods used
- Initiatives focused on preventing smuggling and illicit trafficking

Very few countries had detailed information regarding the types or sources of firearms recovered in crime because of problems with data collection and consistency.[5]

In addition, some governments have sponsored specific research projects. For example, the Bureau of Alcohol, Tobacco and Firearms in the United States has funded large projects such as the Identification Patterns in Firearms Trafficking: Implications for Focused Enforcement Strategies Report to assist with enforcement and tracing.[6] Many of these studies suggest that in the United States illicit firearms often come from particular regions and indeed from particular dealers. These studies have also shed light on the various mechanisms involved in channeling firearms from licit to illicit markets. The BATF has also invested significantly in partnerships with academic institutions to develop rigorous methods for collecting, analyzing and applying intelligence about firearms trafficking.[7]

Some larger international research initiatives under way are focused on illicit trafficking in the context of conflict rather than crime, although increasingly these distinctions are less clear. Often these studies are qualitative in nature or rely on anecdotal information from, for example, the Federal Broadcast Information Service Daily Reports. In addition, many of the studies focus on particular regions.

UNDERSTANDING ILLICIT MARKETS

Overview of Patterns

The United Nations study surveyed more than sixty countries and solicited information on illicit trafficking. Of the countries that responded, twenty reported instances of illegal import of firearms and ammunition, while seven reported none. However, none of the countries could provide estimates of the volume of illegal sales. Conversely, seven countries reported instances of illegal export, while twenty reported none. Only twelve reported instances of illegal manufacturing of firearms, compared to thirty-one that reported none. The record-keeping and tracing capabilities of the respondents were uneven, and many countries reported problems with the completeness and accuracy of records. Countries also reported penalties for illegal firearm dealings. Most of these penalties included prison sentences, while others had capital punishment for arms trafficking.

More than thirty countries provided anecdotal examples of the mechanisms used to supply illicit markets. The evidence cited by these countries suggests that sources of illicit firearms vary considerably from region to region. In Canada, the Caribbean and parts of Latin America, for example, firearms diverted from legal American domestic markets appear to be the principal problem. Guns in Japan enter from the United States and China, but also from as far away as South Africa. One of the largest shipments of handguns ever seized by the Japanese police agency, for example, originated in South Africa. In Asia and parts of Europe, state-imported supplies from the former Soviet Union appear to be a major problem both in ethnic conflict and in crime.[8] The links are transnational, with examples of firearms being recovered after being transferred through many distribution networks that span the world. Regional perspectives on the illegal trade are discussed later in this chapter in more detail, but highlights include:

- Guns flow from unregulated to regulated civilian markets. The United States has one-third of the world's firearms in circulation, and the lack of regulation makes it the principal source of illegal guns worldwide. More than half the illegal handguns in Canada, 80 percent of the illegal guns in Mexico and most of the illegal guns in the Caribbean originate in the United States. Even as far away as Japan, one-third of firearms recovered by the national police agency originated in the United States in 1996. Similar patterns are seen in southern Africa, where illegal guns flow from South Africa to surrounding countries.

- Arms supplied through covert operations during the cold war have created a durable source of weapons for conflicts and crime world-wide. The CIA channelled weapons to Afghanis fighting the Soviets—the Afghan pipeline. Many of these weapons were later used to fight against the U.S. forces and have fuelled violence throughout the region. Air America, one of the largest private airlines in the 1960s, was secretly owned by the U.S. Central Intelligence Agency to camouflage its clandestine missions in Laos, Vietnam and Cambodia.[9] The agency's report on the U.S.-backed Contra guerrillas in Nicaragua revealed that at least ten privately operated airlines and crews were involved.[10] Clandestine arms deals involving officials in many countries attempting to defend their political and economic interests have been well documented, and complex transactions often involved many countries.[11] For example, in December 1989, a huge secret arms and ammunition depot was uncovered in Rostock, East Germany. This depot had been under the control of IMES GmbH, a little-known East German state company that was run by East Germany's deputy foreign trade minister, Alexander Schalck-Golodkowski. The East German company had been a key part of an international smuggling network with secret bank accounts and shell companies in West Germany, Switzerland and Liechtenstein. Western intelligence agencies, including the U.S. Iran-Contra arms and money networks, used IMES and the East German structure to secretly supply weapons to guerrilla movements in Central America.[12]

- Not only did the former Soviet Union arm its allies through similar mechanisms, but following the end of the cold war and the deterioration of the economic conditions in the region, firearms became a source of hard currency. The sale of weapons by former Soviet Union military and police personnel has fuelled violence throughout the region. With the expansion of the European Union and the erosion of trade and customs barriers, these weapons have flowed West as well as East.

- The interaction between illegal guns for criminal and political purposes is nowhere more evident than in an examination of the weapons sources of "terrorist" organizations. On September 10, 2001, Ali Boumelhem was convicted on a variety of weapons violations plus conspiracy to ship weapons to the terrorist organization Hezbollah in Lebanon. He and his brother Mohamed had purchased an arsenal of shotguns, hundreds of rounds of ammunition, flash suppressers and assault weapon parts from Michigan gun shows. Mohamed had a clean record, but Ali was legally prohibited from purchasing firearms as a result of a felony grand-theft conviction. An Al Qaeda manual recovered in Afghanistan entitled "How Can I Train Myself for Jihad" contained an entire section on firearms training. The United States was identified as a good source for illegal weapons, and Al Qaeda members living in the United States are instructed to "obtain an assault weapon legally, preferably AK-47 or [other] variations."[13] American gun shows were also a major source of firearms channeled to the Irish Republican Army during the conflict there.[14]

- Over the last few decades, high-profile scandals have shed light on the complex networks of brokers, many of them created during the cold war as agents for covert state security operations. Adnan Khashoggi, reputed to be one of the richest men in the world, was a key player in the Iran-Contra case as well as numerous smaller scandals involving the arming of dictatorships and of U.S.-favored guerrilla movements in the third world. Rakesh Saxena, an acquaintance of Khashoggi and a former adviser to the Bangkok Bank, is alleged to have financed the $10 million consignment of arms that were sent to UN-embargoed Sierra Leone by the British private military company Sandline International. Syrian dealer Monzer Al Kassar was under investigation in Switzerland for violating the arms embargo on Croatia and Bosnia-Herzegovina. He was involved in the illegal sale of weapons to Libya in 1983 and was sought by Interpol for swapping weapons supplied by the Italian mafia for drugs in 1977. He was suspected of supplying weapons to the commando group that hijacked the *Achille Lauro* in 1985, and was also named as a suspect in the 1991 terrorist attack on the passenger jet over Lockerbie, Scotland. Recently, he was named in political scandals involving the president of Argentina and the mayor of the coastal resort of Marbella in Spain, where Al Kassar—the "Prince of Marbella"—owned a large residence.[15]

Models of Illicit Markets

The complex structure of licit, illicit and "gray" markets, the links between civilian and military markets, and the interplay between domestic and international markets have been the subject of much analysis. Studies have examined Africa,[16] Central America,[17] South Asia,[18] and Canada.[19] Most large manufacturers and brokers serve domestic, international, civilian and military markets.[20] Links, interactions and dependencies among different networks suggest that there are no simple solutions to the problems of the proliferation and misuse of these weapons. Legal, covert and illicit networks for large-scale distribution of firearms and ammunition share various transportation, banking and personnel networks, thereby creating a complex global system. Changes in one network may result in changes in the global distribution pattern of firearms and ammunition and in the distribution of risk of death or injury. When one network is constrained, often by political forces, another network may assume some of the distribution function. When arms embargoes are instituted against legal transfers, for example, the covert and illicit networks become operative.

On the other hand, when a powerful state has an incentive to contribute to the arming of a particular faction or to facilitate internal instability, legal and covert channels become operative while the illicit networks are subdued or controlled by the powerful state's political agenda. The end of the cold war eliminated or lessened the political agendas of major powers that directed much of the firearms and ammunition trade and constrained the expansion of illicit forces, while leaving the transportation, storage, banking and personnel elements of the network intact for private entities to use.[21] Countries in dire need of foreign exchange and revenue, while caught in the tense transition to free trade, have often directly or indirectly facilitated the transnational movement of arms and ammunition.[22]

The efforts by individual states to constrain legal access to firearms may be undercut by the inadequacy of controls in other countries. Weapons bought in the United States are illegally imported to Canada, Japan and Mexico. Even within the United States, guns flow from unregulated states to regulated states. It is important to emphasize, however, that the evidence indicates that regulatory efforts are not futile, because the growth in informal or illegal markets seldom is large enough to offset the decline in legal or formal markets.[23]

Diversions of firearms from licit to illicit markets are a major contributor to the illegal trade in firearms and light weapons. It is estimated that as many as 500,000 firearms are stolen each year from the United States, by definition falling into the hands of criminals.[24] In many countries the majority of firearms recovered in crime appear to have been at one time legally owned by states or by civilians. Countries that establish strict controls on civilian possession of firearms are still vulnerable to weapons illegally imported from other countries. In regions where firearms are more readily available from legal sources without licensing or registration, civilian weapons are a significant source of supply to the illegal markets.[25]

Surplus weapons constitute another source for illicit trafficking. There are many documented cases of surplus military weapons, police weapons and weapons recovered in crime reentering the market. Weapons collection programs in postconflict areas are critical to the establishment of lasting peace; if these weapons are not collected, the risk of high levels of violence remains.[26]

There is a range of methods by which firearms held legally by states, organizations and civilians are diverted to illegal markets.[27] Misuse and diversion occur through a variety of mechanisms, but the evidence generally suggests that illegal firearms fall into three broad categories:

- Legally held firearms that are misused by their lawful owners, whether states, organizations or individuals;
- Legal firearms that are diverted by legal owners to unauthorized individuals—the "gray" market—illegally sold, stolen or diverted through other means; and

- Illegally manufactured and distributed firearms. These account for a small fraction of illegal firearms overall but are a particular problem in some regions.

Very limited empirical or theoretical work has been done that examines the interactions of supply and demand and licit and illicit national and international markets. Comparisons have been made between illicit drug and firearm markets largely because their users intersect, and they may share distribution networks at the local and international levels.[28] These links have been documented by a number of researchers and law enforcement agencies.[29] Narcotics trafficking generates a demand for illegal arms both directly and indirectly by developing an infrastructure that is also used for gun trafficking. This international infrastructure, particularly the distribution and money-laundering components, can also be used to support the illicit gun trade.

The networks used to distribute illicit drugs, stolen goods and other illegal products are often the same ones used to distribute illegal guns. Often guns are traded for drugs, and many of the people who are involved in the illegal drug trade are also involved in the trade in illicit firearms. Such links are well known and include shared transit routes, the use of weapons for protection by drug traffickers and the funding of gunrunning with drug trade profits. The links among drugs, guns and illicit activities such as credit card fraud have been made in other contexts as well.[30] Williams cites a case in Italy in which profits from drug sales were used by the Mafia to buy weapons that were subsequently sold to various Arab countries.[31]

At the same time, there are significant differences between drug and firearm trafficking. Illicit drugs are generally illegal from the point of production to the point of consumption. In contrast, most firearms are manufactured legally but become illegal by virtue of the conditions of their possession or their misuse. The problem with guns is further compounded by the fact that they are not consumed but are durable and are, therefore, resold and reused.[32] In addition, the firearm market has a dual structure, including substantial legal government and consumer markets as well as illicit markets. There are recognized legitimate purposes for firearms in most countries, which make dealing with the problem of misuse particularly difficult.

Regulation of the legal trade is essential. While other factors are important and the interplay between laws and values is complex, the rates of firearm death are positively correlated with levels of firearm ownership in high-income and industrialized countries.[33] Misuse of legal firearms and the leakage of legal firearms to illegal markets through various channels form the foundation of underlying efforts to apply regulations to legal use. The most extensive empirical research available on illicit firearm markets comes from the United States.[34] Leakage from legal to illegal markets is the principal source of firearms in criminal activity in the country.

Figure 5.1 Licit and Illicit Supplies of Firearms

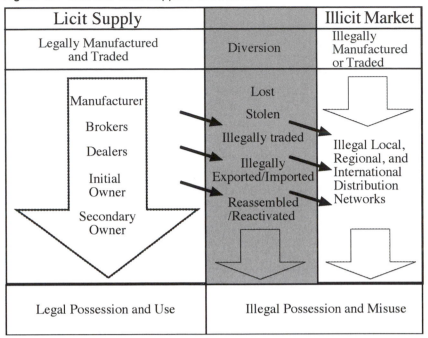

Licit Supply	Diversion	Illicit Market
Legally Manufactured and Traded	Diversion	Illegally Manufactured or Traded

Manufacturer
Brokers
Dealers
Initial Owner
Secondary Owner

Lost
Stolen
Illegally traded
Illegally Exported/Imported
Reassembled /Reactivated

Illegal Local, Regional, and International Distribution Networks

Legal Possession and Use	Illegal Possession and Misuse

Source: W. Cukier, "Vuurwapens: legale en illegale kanalen," *Tijdschrift voor—Criminologie* 43, no. 1 (2001): 27–41, translated as "Firearms: Licit/Illicit Links."

Models of Illicit Firearm Markets

Research into illicit markets suggests that the dynamics of international markets may be similar to the models of illegal gun markets in the United States. One of the effects of strict gun control is to raise the effective price of illegal guns. Collecting information about firearms and their manufactures, dealers and owners also helps focus enforcement efforts.

The complexity of the definition and interactions between licit and illicit, as explained by Cook, are enlightening. The distinction between licit and illicit gun sales is a function of the status of the buyer (entitled or proscribed), the status of the seller (licensed or unlicensed), the status of the weapon (legal or illegal model; legally acquired or stolen) and the details of the transaction (formal or informal). The primary and secondary markets are closely linked, as buyers choose their product based on price and other aspects of the transaction. The primary market is attractive to buyers who want the latest models, but regulations (including fees and waiting periods) raise the effective price of guns in primary markets and may either reduce demand or shift demand to secondary markets.

As demand for firearms in secondary markets increases, so do prices, and this presumably reduces casual demand. It would also follow that as the difficulty associated with legally obtaining firearms increases, so will the price of guns on the secondary market. This is confirmed by empirical evidence about the street prices of firearms. Where firearms are strictly regulated, as in New York, the street prices for firearms are higher than in other markets. Dealers consequently make profits buying in unregulated markets, such as Virginia, and selling in regulated markets, such as New York City.[35]

The relaxation of border controls and the growing scale of transnational organized crime are also believed to have contributed to the expansion of the illicit trafficking of firearms on a global basis.[36] Added to this is the globalization of finance, which enables money used in illicit firearms deals to be transfered to bank accounts and difficult to trace.[37] Globalization of supply and criminal infrastructure have been widely discussed.[38] With the globalization of crime, there is a need for the globalization of crime prevention strategies and in particular a need for harmonization and information sharing.[39]

Illegal Manufacture, Assembly and Reactivation

Overall, illegal manufacture accounts for a small percentage of the illegal firearm trade worldwide. Illegally manufactured firearms, components and ammunition are seldom seen in the United States but some regions have thriving firearm "cottage" industries. For example, in South Africa, of the firearms seized by the South African Police Service in 1998, approximately 15 percent were homemade.[40]

In some countries, the illegal or unauthorised manufacture of weapons is facilitated by the use of components that have been imported or stolen. The domestic manufacture and assembly of firearms from imported parts is a major source of illicit weapons in Australia.[41] There are similar Canadian examples as well. Employees of Para-Ordnance, Canada's only handgun manufacturer, based in Scarborough, were implicated in a trafficking ring when unmarked handguns reassembled from parts stolen from the plant were found on the streets of Toronto.

Canadian and U.S. law enforcement agencies have combined their efforts to conduct one of the largest seizures of illegal handguns in the past decade. Their investigation, dubbed Project TUG (Trace Unserialized Guns), has resulted in seven individuals being charged with weapons offences. The search efforts, coupled with undercover purchases, led to the seizure of ninety-five handguns and fourteen long guns. Also seized were hundreds of ammunition magazines and more than 500,000 rounds of ammunition. The seizures and resulting criminal charges are the culmination of a one-year investigation into a firearms trafficking network in the Greater Toronto area. Members of the U.S. BAT Firearms were sworn in as special constables with the Ontario Provincial Police during the investigation and took part in undercover purchases. Several of the firearms seized had no serial numbers, making them attractive weapons for use by criminals. In the past, weapons similar to those seized during this investigation have been recovered at murder and attempted murder crime scenes. Police believe that gun parts were stolen by employees from Para-Ordnance and assembled to produce these illegal handguns recovered in Toronto and the United States.[42]

A related problem is posed by the reactivation of firearms that had been legally owned at one time but that had been deactivated because of a change in laws. Loopholes in the law have sometimes allowed such weapons to be reactivated and resold.[43] As an example, up to 100 deactivated machine pistols were legally exported as collectors' items from the United States before being reactivated and sold to criminals in Britain.[44]

Illegal Sales

Firearms, whether for state or civilian markets, are sold and resold several times because of their durability. At each point in the distribution cycle there are many opportunities for diversion, as detailed below:

Illegal Sales by Dealers.   There is considerable evidence that some federally licensed firearm dealers in the United States are willing to violate national and local laws to provide guns to juveniles and adults otherwise prohibited from making legal gun purchases.[45] Recent evidence indicates that more than half the weapons submitted by local and state police to the BATF for tracing originated from less than one-half of 1 percent of the United States' 180,000 licensed dealers.[46] In some cases dishonest firearm dealers have engaged in legal firearm trade while diverting some of their firearms to illicit markets. Several instances of this type have been identified in Canada (Operation Pinball), the United States, and the United Kingdom (Operation ABONAR).[47]

"Straw Purchases" and Other Unregulated Resale.   "Straw purchases," in which firearms are bought legally by someone with a clean record and then sold or given to a second owner, are a major way in which legal firearms are diverted to illegal markets. Studies show that within countries that have diverse domestic regulatory standards, illegal guns flow from areas with weaker regulations. Within the United States, "straw purchases" and other mechanisms are used to move guns from states with lax controls to states with stricter controls. A study of guns recovered at crime scenes revealed that one-quarter of all weapons that came from outside the state in which they were recovered came from Georgia, South Carolina and Texas.[48] In one case, a Georgia resident purchased thirty-two semiautomatic pistols from a pawnshop in Jonesboro, Georgia. All the firearms were transported to Boston, where the Georgia resident sold them to an intermediary, who sold them to other individuals. Twelve of them were recovered from crime scenes, including a murder scene.[49]

Similarly, weapons flow from countries with weaker regulations to those with tighter gun ownership laws and practices. A high percentage of the handguns recovered in crime in Canada, for example, originate in the

United States, and investigations have revealed that "straw purchases" and gun shows are major sources of illegal guns.[50] Similar mechanisms have been documented for cross-border gunrunning from the United States to Mexico.[51]

There are many other examples of U.S. guns being diverted to illegal markets. For example, two hundred firearms were seized in Colombia from "drug lord" Ivan Urdinola. All the weapons had been legally purchased and imported from the United States and registered in Colombia before being used by paramilitary assassins to commit a series of murders.[52] In Jamaica, authorities confiscated 338 assorted firearms, mostly originating from the United States, including U.S. army standard issue M16 assault rifles. The weapons were intended for market distribution in Jamaica for robberies and drug-related crimes.[53]

In a number of countries, including the United States and South Africa, initial sales of firearms are regulated, but secondary sales are not. In addition, gun shows, which are largely unregulated, have proved to be a major source of illicit guns both within the United States and in international illegal markets. For example, an individual was arrested who purchased thirty Lorcin pistols at gun shows in Miami and Dallas. The weapons were destined for Romania.[54]

Theft

Governments participating in the International Study on Firearm Regulation conducted by the United Nations in 1998 reported more than 100,000 firearms lost or stolen annually. According to the UN study, the United States reported more than 12,000 stolen guns during a nine-month period in 1996. However, other sources have estimated that the number of guns stolen each year in the United States could be as high as half a million. The FBI compiles national data only on the value of the firearms reported to the police department, not on the actual number of firearms reported stolen. Depending on the assumptions about the average value of guns, the Police Foundation estimated that in 1991 between 300,000 and 600,000 guns were stolen. According to the U.S. National Crime Victimization Study, the mean number of incidents in which at least one gun was stolen during the period 1987–1992 was 340,700 per year.[55] South Africa reported to the UN study that nearly 17,500 guns are stolen annually. More recent studies indicate that the figure is at least twice this.[56] Canadian citizens annually report around 3,000 firearm thefts, but the actual number of thefts is likely much higher. Often crime guns are traced back to gun thefts.[57] Once in the illegal market, they travel the world.

Small-scale theft of firearms sent via mail order is a problem in several countries, including Canada, the United States and Australia.[58] A private delivery company in the United States, United Parcel Service (UPS), currently delivers approximately three-quarters of all firearm shipments in the

United States from manufacturers to distributors, as well as nearly 99 percent of all firearms sent from distributors to dealers. In 1998 alone, 941 firearms were reported stolen from UPS interstate shipments.[59] A single dealer reported that sixty of his guns had been stolen en route over eighteen months.[60] Mail-order distribution of prohibited components is a related problem. Cheap and anonymous gun advertising on the Internet has been identified as a contributing factor to the latter phenomenon. Early in 2004, a Canadian teenager received a semiautomatic variant of a military weapon from a Michigan teenager that had been sent through the mail labelled as an aluminium baseball bat.[61]

Reports from around the world illustrate the ways in which state-owned firearms leak into illicit markets through theft, corruption or other forms of diversion from military and police stockpiles. Military personnel in Australia falsified records to conceal the theft of firearms from national stockpiles.[62] Police have reported more than 14,000 firearms lost or stolen in South Africa.[63] Several police departments in the United States, in upgrading their firearms, came under widespread criticism for inadvertently supplying illicit markets when they sold their old guns rather than destroying them.[64] In addition, investigators from the U.S. General Accounting Office discovered that gun parts were routinely stolen from U.S. military bases and resold at gun shows or to gun dealers.[65] In 1997 undercover FBI agents arrested six U.S. Marines and seven civilians for weapons trafficking after recovering more than fifty machine guns, explosives, rockets and other military devices. These arrests were part of a larger investigation in the southeastern United States that focused on gun shows, military bases and dealers.[66] Russian servicemen have been charged with illegal sales.[67] In Mexico, 16,000 handguns and 6,000 rifles were seized by the police from drug gangs. The weapons had been meant for the exclusive use of the army.[68] More than 3,000 firearms recovered in crime or surrendered in amnesties to the Metropolitan Toronto Police Service in Canada were discovered to be missing. Officers and civilians working in the police unit were found to have sold them illegally.[69]

Illegal Import, Export and Transfers

Millions of firearms cross national borders annually. Some are imported for civilian use by dealers or individuals and some are imported and reexported by brokers. Record keeping on the levels of imports and exports of commercial firearm shipments is uneven. Controls over third-party brokers are also irregular, with many loopholes and gray areas that can be exploited. Arms brokering itself is not illegal, but arms brokers often exploit loopholes and weak regulation in order to bypass arms embargoes and to supply arms to regions where they are likely to be misused. Brokers are able to use agents and techniques developed in the modern international transport industry to conduct covert deliveries to sensitive destinations.

They arrange complex international banking transactions and company formations in many countries, which may include the use of tax havens. Typically they locate sources of cheap, easily transportable arms for customers in areas of violent conflict willing to pay inflated prices. They are able to succeed because of corruptible officials and weak law enforcement. Brokers are also often tempted to use fake documentation and bribery, which can lead to involvement with smuggling and organized crime.[70]

U.S. Customs agents intervened in an attempt by Colombian nationals to export fifty-three military rifles to Colombia without proper authorisation. In another instance, a former Venezuelan security officer attempted to ship 120 firearms from the United States to Venezuela illegally.[71] In 1991, the BATF reported that three Arizona residents had previously purchased ninety-three assault rifles and twenty-two handguns for resale to a Mexican drug baron who then smuggled the guns into Mexico.[72]

Smugglers have used false documentation, misreporting and concealment with other commodities to ship weapons commercially from the United States to Canada.[73] Similarly, a major consignment of parts for M2 automatic rifles originating in Vietnam and destined for Mexico was found in a sealed container in San Diego falsely labelled as hand tools and strap hangers.[74] In another instance, an effort was made to export shotguns, pistols and rifles to Ireland from the United States falsely labelling them as toys.[75]

Enforcement

The penalties associated with the illegal possession or trafficking of firearms vary considerably from jurisdiction to jurisdiction. While the evidence of wrongdoing is clear—certainty of conviction is generally more important than severity of sentence—there are many examples in which the costs and benefits of illegal trafficking are such that there are few disincentives. In Canada, for example, it was recently reported that an individual caught illegally importing a firearm into the country might face a fine of only $500. Often the street value of an illegal firearm is more than $1000.[76]

With freer trade aimed at facilitating the movement of goods and services, controls at many borders have been eroded. One of the best examples of this, of course, is the European Union. In the past, a firearm from a former Soviet-aligned country such as Czechoslovakia would have had to pass through several border points en route to the United Kingdom, potentially eluding officials at the Austrian, German, French and English borders. Now, once in the European Union, people and goods, both legal and illegal, can move relatively freely. With the expansion of the European Union to include more and more countries with high rates of illegal guns and limited enforcement resources, the problem will be exacerbated. One of the most consistent contributors to the problem is resource related. The principles of border controls rest on risk assessment and detection, and it is clear that only a small fraction of illegally imported shipments are ever intercepted. For example, in Canada, which shares the longest unprotected border in the world with the United States, a country with almost as many guns as people, fewer than 3 percent of shipments are actually checked.

As mentioned previously, the priority police assign to tracking illegal firearms varies considerably from jurisdiction to jurisdiction. Senior officials of many police services in many countries do not appear to understand the value of tracking illegal guns, and the priority assigned by rank-and-file officers also varies considerably. Even in highly developed countries, police pursuing criminal investigations related to robberies, drugs or homicides may not necessarily pay much attention to tracking illegal firearms. In Canada, for example, the members of the National Weapons Enforcement Support Team (NWEST) of the Royal Canadian Mounted Police undertake a trafficking course in an effort to sensitize police officers to the importance of collecting information about guns recovered in crime. Regardless of the offence being investigated, if a firearm is involved police are instructed to collect information that may assist in anti-trafficking efforts. (See Table 5.1.)

Criminal investigations related to illegal firearm trafficking are exceedingly complex and often involve violations of laws in several countries. Sophisticated arms traffickers are often skilled at covering their tracks, and even when charges are made, prosecutions do not always succeed, or lesser

Table 5.1 Firearms Investigation Guide

Where did you get the gun?

Who else bought guns from your supplier?

What other crime is your supplier into?

Does your supplier carry a gun?

Is your supplier violent?

Who else sells guns on the street?

Is this gun stolen?

Did you remove the serial number? If not then who did?

Did you cut down the gun? Who did?

Can you get more guns?

If given money, where would you buy guns right now?

Can you introduce a friend to a supplier?

Source: Canada, Royal Canadian Mounted Police, National Weapons Enforcement Support Team, *Investigation Guide* (Ottawa: Royal Canadian Mounted Police, 2003).

charges are pursued. Thus, international cooperation among police and prosecutors is often critical. For example, East Germany's former deputy foreign trade minister, Alexander Schalck-Golodkowski, had reportedly been involved in a massive, decade-long smuggling operation of weapons, antiques and even drugs. He was, however, charged with only the illicit import of military and dual-use items into East Germany between 1986 and 1989 and with the embezzlement of rather small amounts of foreign currency. He was sentenced in January 1996 to one year's imprisonment, and in 1997 to 16 months' imprisonment, respectively. In April 1999, a higher court acquitted him on the latter of the two charges.[77]

REGIONAL PERSPECTIVES

North America

United States. The extent and characteristics of illicit firearm markets have been studied at the national level in the United States. The U.S. Treasury Department's BATF is the agency responsible for investigating illegal arms dealing within the United States, and it also works with other countries to trace weapons of U.S. origin used in crimes abroad. The BATF funds research to assist its enforcement efforts. Many of these studies suggest that, within the United States, illicit firearms often originate in particular regions and from particular dealers.[78] For example, BATF data revealed that between 1996 and 1998, nearly 35,000 weapons recovered from crime scenes originated with 140 federally licensed firearm dealers (less than 1 percent of all licensed U.S. dealers). Of those guns, 87 percent were not in the hands of the original purchaser at the time they were used in a crime. This reinforces the notion that diversion from licit to illicit markets through secondary markets (resale) and theft is a critical issue.[79] Within the United States, illicit firearms often originate in particular regions and from particular dealers.[80] Theft is also a major source of illegal guns in the United States, as noted above. A study by the BATF between 1996 and 1998 showed that 11.1 percent of traces of firearms they conducted involved shipments across international borders.[81]

Canada. In Canada, studies undertaken in 1995 and 1997 in a number of jurisdictions revealed that the firearms most often recovered in crime were rifles and shotguns, most of which originated in domestic markets.[82] This finding contradicted previous claims, based on anecdotal studies, that handguns were most often used in crime.[83] In 2004 a study of firearms recovered in Canada's largest city revealed a similar pattern. Almost half the firearms recovered were long guns (rifles and shotguns). While guns smuggled in from the United States were a major source, so were firearms that had been diverted from Canadian gun owners and dealers, through illegal sale or theft.[84] Canada historically has had very strict controls on handguns, and only about 20 percent of the firearms recovered were handguns.

Of those handguns that could be traced, 40 percent were found to have been legally registered to owners in Canada, while the remainder was not.[85] While these other guns may have originated from a variety of sources, traces suggest that the United States is the principal source of illegally imported handguns in Canada. Canada and the United States share the world's largest undefended border, and there are many ways in which firearms can enter Canada illegally. Seizures capture only the tip of the iceberg of illegal shipments. Evidence suggest that many firearms enter through small shipments brought in by individuals, as well as large "commercial" shipments, and through criminal networks used to distribute other illegal commodities including drugs. According to Canadian customs officials, 820 handguns, 130 shotguns, 166 rifles and 13 antique firearms were seized in 2000. This, however, represents only a small percentage of illegal shipments, as customs officials check only 3 percent of traffic crossing the border.[86] The same mechanisms used to divert legal firearms to domestic illicit markets are used to supply international markets.

Mexico. An estimated 80 percent of the illegal guns in Mexico originate in the United States. Many of the guns originate in gun shops and pawn brokers in California, Texas, Arizona and New Mexico, as well as Florida.[87] Of the guns smuggled into Mexico, many travel through the "ant trade,"[88] small smugglers, typically moving just one to a few dozen weapons at a time. Anecdotal reports suggest that in Africa, this "ant trade" is increasingly common, facilitated by the lack of effective border controls and lubricated by corruption."[89]

South and Central America

In Brazil, there has also been some study of gun smuggling into the country through illicit markets. According to a recent analysis of guns recovered in Rio de Janeiro during 1994–1999, the vast majority (more than 44,000, or 83 percent) was manufactured in Brazil. Just over 1,000 guns (2.5 percent) were made in Argentina, and 3,000 (6.7 percent) were manufactured in the United States.[90] In Brazil[91] and Colombia, most of the weapons recovered are actually handguns, not military assault weapons.

The United States is the largest supplier of illegal firearms to Latin America. Much of the illicit trafficking, contrary to mythologies of large-scale crime circles, involves small-scale criminals, and the smugglers are able to take advantage of the availability of guns in the United States and its loose gun control policies. A 2002 investigation revealed that between the years 1998 and 1999, small operators, were able to channel more than 800 AK-47s to rebels in Columbia.[92] Argentina also has problems controlling its borders, which contributes to illicit gun trade. More than 3,000 illegal Argentine guns were found in Rio de Janeiro, and of those, 315 came from Argentine military arsenals.[93]

Illicit trafficking crosses international borders and often involves several countries. For example, dealers in Guatemala and Panama arranged for a shipment of 3,117 AK-47s and 2.5 million rounds of ammunition to be sent to an illegal group in Colombia.[94] The dealers claimed to be buying the weapons for police in Panama. Those brokering the deal were Israeli nationals who claimed to be official representatives of the Israeli government, and Nicaragua's officials did not verify the end use of the weapons. The ship carrying the weapons, described in shipping documents as children's plastic balls, managed to avoid detection, finally docking at a remote northern point in Colombia to deliver the weapons.[95]

Europe

The weapons that fuel Russia's illegal trade come from four main sources: theft from army depots and units, theft from production facilities, theft of arms in legal possession and the sale of found and restored World War II weapons.[96]

Eastern European countries such as the Czech Republic, Slovakia, Bulgaria, Romania and Poland, in the process of modernizing their systems, have been dumping weapons and old cold war tanks on the military market, thus increasing the number of weapons available in conflict areas.[97] In Europe, state supplies from the former Soviet Union appear to be a source of illegal weapons both in ethnic conflict and in crime,[98] but there are anecdotes concerning seizures of weapons from dealers in Austria, Finland, Estonia, Poland, the United States and elsewhere.[99]

Although evidence regarding illicit trafficking is limited, there is anecdotal evidence to suggest that a substantial portion of the firearms used in crime in the United Kingdom are illegally imported from other countries. Incidents have been reported involving firearms from the United States, from Austria and from the former Soviet Union.[100] There is also evidence to suggest that illegal trafficking has been facilitated with the relaxation of border controls and the construction of the Chunnel.[101]

Great Britain has also been plagued with firearms[102] that were deactivitated and illegally reactivated as well as starter pistols converted to fire bullets.[103] Gun runners from the former Soviet Union and Czech Republic are believed to play a major role.[104]

Africa

In South Africa, efforts by the South African Police Service to track the supply of firearms recovered in crime are relatively recent, but they have tended to undermine claims based on anecdotal information regarding the prevalence of postconflict military weapons.[105] While more information about the type of firearm (rifle, revolver, pistol, etc.) and the extent of homemade firearms has been obtained, the sources of illegal firearms (domestic versus illegally imported) are still the subject of some debate.[106]

However, detailed analyses of firearms recovered in crime have revealed that the bulk of the weapons used are actually handguns, many of them at one time legally owned. Military-style weapons, such as assault rifles, have represented a small proportion of guns used in crime.[107] Many states in southern Africa have strict domestic controls on firearms and correspondingly lower crime rates; the smuggling and legal purchase of firearms from South Africa, where controls are far less strict, affect Lesotho, Botswana and Malawi.[108]

Illicit gun transfers in South Africa are made that much easier by the lack of proper border controls. In 1996, a team of U.S. researchers conducted a study on South African borders and determined that illegal borders crossings, the smuggling of firearms, vehicles and drugs "seem to be the order of the day."[109] Compounding the problem is the lack of information sharing on weapons imported and exported in the country. Other problems include the lack of proper screening equipment in the Johannesburg International Airport, unscheduled flights and security loopholes and baggage problems in the Durban Airport, the Lanseria Airport and the Richards Bay Harbour, for example.[110]

In sub-Saharan Africa, data regarding the prevalence of illicit firearm trafficking are very incomplete; however, it is believed that the number of nondeclaring exporters (illicit trafficking) is greater than that of legal transfers. According to the *Small Arms Survey 2003*, "Embargoed governments and insurgent movements are so numerous that they create a market for illicit weapons possibly rivalling the scale of legal demand."[111] These countries tend to get their imports from Asia or central or eastern Europe, where guns are harder to trace. Much of the trade in the region is concealed, which makes gathering exact evidence on the extent of illicit trade difficult.

South Asia

Pakistan and Afghanistan continue to be the largest source of weapons for most militant and criminal groups in South Asia. Weapons previously supplied via the CIA during the cold war through the "Afghanistan pipeline" continue to plague the region. In India, all types of firearms are strictly regulated by the provisions of the Arms Act and other regulations, but illegal weapons proliferate due to porous borders and absence of controls in neighboring states.[112]

Southeast Asia

Although civilian possession of firearms is strongly regulated in many countries in Southeast Asia, the supply of illegal weapons is significant. Organized crime in the area, including Taiwanese, Japanese and America triads, is extensively involved in the illegal gun trade in China. One indication of the extent of the problem is that, according to the Chinese police,

600,000 guns were confiscated, including 8,800 military weapons, between March and June 2001 alone. Claims have been made that a staggering 2.4 million weapons have been confiscated over the past five years. Surplus weapons from the conflicts in Cambodia, Myanmar and in some cases China are trafficked along with drugs.[113]

In this region, Thailand is a major transshipment point, as firearms flow from postconflict zones such as Cambodia (and to a lesser extent Pakistan, China and North Korea) and are passed on to other destinations through well-established networks of brokers.[114] Thailand pays a heavy price for this—leakage from the shipments fuels violence in Thailand.

Japan, conversely, has very strict controls on handguns; nevertheless, police recover approximately 1,000 each year. According to the national police agency, most of these guns are illegally imported. An analysis of illegally imported firearms seized by police and customs indicated that 30 percent originated in the United States and 21 percent in mainland China.[115] They enter the countries through a variety of channels.

Singapore is an important producer of firearms in the region; weapons produced here are sold to countries such as Myanmar, Somalia, Sri Lanka and Papua New Guinea. Illicit weapons transfers are also driven by the numerous conflicts in Southeast Asia. In this region, the acquisition of military firearms is easy as a result of past conflicts. The illegal movement of firearms is made worse by the fact that the area is home to several weak nations that have difficulty controlling their borders.[116]

Cambodia is the largest supplier of used firearms in Southeast Asia. The illicit transfer of weapons often involves criminals, and the weapons are sent to conflict areas. Though these transfers are not officially sanctioned by government officials, in some cases, high-level government personnel have been implicated in black market transfers.[117]

Australia and New Zealand

The origins of smuggled guns into Australia remain uncertain; rumours suggest that guns are smuggled from China, but evidence does not tend to support this theory. Instead, theft of legally owned guns from their owners accounts for many of the illegal weapons.[118]

Borders in Papua New Guinea are hard to monitor, resulting in a flow of illegal weapons. Most of the illegal guns come from state or police leakage. Those guns that come from other countries typically follow one of three routes: (1) across the Torres Strait, where the large number of islands makes it difficult for strict border control; (2) from Asia to Papua New Guinea, where the coastal entry points from cargo vessels are hard to control and anecdotal evidence suggests that Malaysian, Philippine and Singaporean logging companies may be involved in trafficking; and (3) between Papua New Guinea and West Papua, where,

again, insufficient border control is the main reason for illicit transfers.[119]

CONCLUSION

Given the enormity of the problem of illicit trafficking in firearms, from
the perspective of both crime and conflict, it is surprising that there has
been so little research on its dimensions and effects. One of the major challenges in understanding the problem, quite apart from the limited availability of empirical evidence, results from the inherent complexity, diversity
and political sensitivity of the issue in many contexts. The dynamics of the
problem, the types of firearms and the sources of firearms vary considerably from region to region. At the same time, there is enough empirical and
anecdotal evidence to draw some broad conclusions. First, while firearm
trafficking and drug trafficking share common distribution networks and
are both forms of currency, there are significant differences. The vast majority of firearms recovered in crime were at one time legally owned. Consequently, the interplay between licit and illicit markets coupled with the
durability of firearms and uneven national regulatory standards result in
very different market dynamics. While the means of diversion vary, there
is no question that the majority of illegal firearms, worldwide, began as
legal firearms. Given the sheer volume of firearms in the United States—
one third of the world's guns and the limited controls over these weapons—
it is a major source of illegal weapons worldwide. Every year in the United
States it is estimated that as many as 500,000 firearms are stolen, by definition entering the illegal market. In addition, there is ample documentation of diversion through "straw purchases," illegal sales and gun shows.
Not only do U.S. guns account for half the handguns recovered in crime
in Canada, and 80 percent of the guns recovered in crime in Mexico but
of the guns seized in Japan, as many as one third have originated in the
United States. American gun shows have also provided weapons which
have fueled conflicts in Eastern Europe and Northern Ireland as well as in
Latin America. Similar patterns of firearms moving from unregulated areas
to regulated areas are seen when we examine the flow of illegal weapons
in Europe or southern Africa. In recent years, growing concern over the
globalization of the illegal gun trade has led countries to attempt to establish international standards and mechanisms at the global and regional level
to reduce the diversion of legal guns to illegal markets. Attention has also
focused on efforts to improve import/export controls, marking and tracing
as well as coordination of international law enforcement efforts to share
intelligence, track and prosecute illegal gun traders.

6

"Gun Culture" and the Demand for Firearms

This chapter examines the legal ownership of firearms, the marketing of firearms, and the role of gender and culture in shaping demand. There is little doubt that there are huge differences among nations in terms of the rate and purposes of firearm ownership as well as attitudes to firearms. Firearm ownership rates range from less than 1 percent of households in countries such as England, Wales, Germany and Japan to more than 40 percent in countries such as the United States and Yemen. The purposes for owning firearms vary considerably—some countries such as Canada, Austria and the United States have extensive recreational hunting. Others such as Kenya use firearms to protect herds from predators. Many permit sporting uses of firearms for target shooting and collecting. Relatively few allow civilians to carry firearms for personal protection. In many contexts firearms are possessed, legally or illegally, as a means of promoting a sense of security in the face of crime or political instability.

In many countries, gun manufacturers and sellers work closely with firearm user groups to promote and preserve firearm ownership and to build markets. The activities of the gun lobby nationally and internationally are evident in the resistance to stronger regulation, which would increase effective costs to both buyers and sellers and which would erode markets.

Regardless of the differences among cultures, one factor is constant: Firearm possession is a predominantly male activity, whether for lawful employment or for recreation. Worldwide, the vast majority of those in possession of legal and illegal firearms are men and boys. There is strong evidence that the link between masculinity and firearms permeates many cultures—both industrialized and developing. A range of cultural carriers, from traditional practices through electronic media, reinforces these links and promotes demand. Firearm sellers exploit many of these beliefs and values in their efforts to sell more guns.

Fear and insecurity drive the demand for firearms in many contexts. More weapons tend to promote armed violence, which in turn promotes fear, which drives demand. Consequently, it is not surprising that countries and regions with the highest levels of firearm violence and ownership are less able to address them than countries with low rates of firearm violence and ownership. The relationship between the demand for weapons is also strongly influenced by culture, values and definitions of masculinity. In this context, firearms legislation plays a multifaceted role—it both reflects and shapes culture and values.[1]

FIREARM OWNERSHIP AROUND THE WORLD

The information about firearm ownership is derived from a range of sources. (See Table 6.1 for gun ownership rates in selected countries.) Government statistics provide one indication of legal ownership in countries in which firearms are strongly regulated and regulations are well enforced. But even they vary dramatically; for example, in Finland, official sources reported 50 percent of households,[2] while others reported 25.2 percent.[3] In other contexts, such as the United States, where guns are not well regulated, estimates are derived in large part from surveys. These too have been criticized for reporting errors. However, the International Crime Victimization Survey estimates correspond closely with national survey. (See Table 6.1.)

Estimates of illegal firearms are even more problematic. Most of the estimates are based on anecdotal evidence or on assumptions derived from crime and death rates. For example, in Brazil and South Africa, it is estimated that there are as many or more illegal weapons in circulation than there are legal firearms.

Sometimes efforts are made to estimate the firearms in circulation based on manufacturing and sales data. In the United States, for example, approximately 4.5 million firearms were produced each year between 1973 and 1999.[4] During these years, the average number of exports was less than 400,000 a year, while imports averaged close to 1 million. Consequently, over the period, a total of more than 125 million new firearms were introduced into the domestic U.S. market.

It is estimated that there are approximately 230 million legal firearms in U.S. households, almost as many as in the rest of the world's civilian markets combined.[5] At least one-third of these are handguns. Estimates are difficult to obtain because of the poor records kept in many countries, but according to estimates by the *Small Arms Survey*, the United States may have almost one-third of the world's 700 million guns. A 1993 U.S. Department of Justice survey reported that one-half of American homes own a firearm.[6] The mean number of firearms in these homes is reported to be 4.1.[7] This percentage has remained relatively constant since 1959.[8] Other

Table 6.1 International Comparisons of Firearm Ownership and Purposes

	Percent Household with Firearms	Percent Handgun	Percent Self-Protection
Asia			
India	0.9	0.4	0.20
Indonesia	4.7	2.8	1.40
China	0.2	0.0	
Hong Kong			
Japan	0.6		
Philippines	5.0	4.1	3.50
Africa			
Uganda	1.7	0.7	1.60
Egypt	8.3	7.4	5.20
South Africa	12.4	10.5	10.60
Tanzania	10.1		
Tunisia	3.5	1.3	
Zimbabwe	2.8	0.6	2.10
Botswana	6.3	0.7	0.50
Europe			
Austria	16.0		4.10
Belgium	11.4		
Denmark	11.7		
England and Wales	3.1		0.06
Finland	23.7		
France	18.2		4.03
Netherlands	1.7		0.13
Poland	3.7		
Portugal	13.2		
Scotland	3.1		0.10
Spain	6.2		
Sweden	15.9		0.08
Switzerland	35.7		2.58

Table 6.1 (continued)

	Percent Household with Firearms	Percent Handgun	Percent Self-Protection
Latin America			
Costa Rica	19.1	14.6	16.60
Brazil	12.5	12.3	10.30
Argentina	29.5	23.6	18.60
Bolivia	8.8	4.3	3.90
Paraguay	31.9	29.9	27.40
Colombia	19.1	14.8	13.60
North America			
Canada	17.0		0.78
USA	33.5		13.00
Australasia			
Australia	8.70		
New Zealand	20.0		

Source: United Nations (UN), *The Eighth International Crime Victims Survey, 2000*. Prepared by the Interregional Crime and Justice Research Institute, 2003, http://www.unicri.it/wwd/analysis/icvs/data.php; Richard Block, *Firearms in Canada and Eight Other Western Countries: Selected Findings of the 1996 International Crime (Victim) Survey* (Ottawa, Canada: Department of Justice, 1998).

studies estimate that 40 percent of homes in the United States have firearms[9] and this was also reported in the UN Survey in 1998.[10] In the United States and indeed in most industrialized countries, the demand for sporting-use firearms has been decreasing with changes in demographics, urbanization and lifestyle. In the United States in 1994, adults in 20 percent of American households identified themselves as hunters, down from 29 percent in 1977.[11] Also unique in the United States is the high percentage of handguns, which account for approximately 30 percent of the guns in circulation in the United States. In contrast, in Canada, surveys have put household ownership rates at 18 percent[12] to 26 percent.[13] Of the estimated 7 million firearms in circulation, only about 500,000 of them are handguns.

Rates of firearm ownership in Latin American countries tend to be higher than in many other regions—in part a legacy of political conflict and high rates of crime. Firearm carrying in countries such as Colombia, for example, is widespread. Most Caribbean countries, in contrast, have laws more in keeping with the rest of the United Kingdom, where legal firearm carrying is restricted. The *Small Arms Survey* has estimated that eleven Latin American countries have roughly 45 to 80 million firearms.[14]

The total number of guns in public hands in Europe has been difficult to determine. Among the fifteen formal European Union member countries, estimates of firearms are made from a variety of sources, often with widely disparate results.[15] Hunting with firearms is well established in some European countries, such as Finland, France, Austria, Greece and Italy, but is much less widespread in England, Wales, Germany and the Netherlands. Few countries (Austria is the exception) allow widespread carrying of firearms for personal protection. Depending on the sources, Switzerland or Finland is estimated to have the highest rate of firearm ownership in Europe, with firearms in between 30 and 40 percent of homes. Switzerland's high ownership rate is in large part a function of its large standing army—most adult males in Switzerland must perform military service and possess a military weapon in their household. The victimization survey indicated that this was the reason cited for gun ownership by 64.3 percent of respondents in Switzerland. Hunting is well established in countries such as Russia, and postconflict weapons are said to flow across borders, but overall rates of firearm possession are comparable to those in the rest of Europe.

Most countries in Africa have relatively restrictive laws concerning possession of firearms. South Africa is a notable exception but still has only about 2 million legal firearms for 40 million people. In some parts of the countries, firearms are used for hunting, but in urban centers, handgun carrying is primarily driven by the perception of a need for protection. In north Africa, carrying firearms is relatively restricted. In countries such as Kenya, firearm possession is said to be high in rural areas, where guns are used to protect herds from rustlers. However, actual data on rates of firearm ownership are limited.

"Gun cultures," discussed below, are said to exist in a number of Middle Eastern countries, leading to high rates of firearm possession. It has been widely reported, for example, that Yemen has a higher percentage of households with guns than any other country, but recent studies suggest the rates are comparable to those in the United States.[16] It has been suggested that firearm ownership is considered a legal right of the citizen in Yemen, under the law.[17] However, recently Yemen has banned civilians from carrying guns on all city streets in urban areas.[18] In postconflict environments in the region—for example, Iraq—high rates of gun ownership have persisted in spite of weapon-collection efforts. In Iraq, for example, it is estimated that there are about 7 million firearms in the hands of 24 million people, a firearm ownership rate slightly higher than Canada's. In 2003, an attempt was made to prohibit civilian possession of firearms in Iraq with little success. Thinly staffed police stations were supposed to serve as collection points, but with citizens feeling a lack of security in the country, there was little incentive to hand in the firearms, which were considered important assets.[19]

In South Asia, legal ownership of firearms is low in India, Sri Lanka and Bangladesh but higher in Pakistan than in other parts of the region. In the Far East, legal gun ownership is extremely low in countries such as Japan, China, Singapore and Thailand, which have strict laws regulating use. However, postconflict weapon flows affect the illegal supply of firearms in the region.

In Australia and New Zealand, hunters and farmers are the principal firearm owners. In the rest of the Asia-Pacific region, rates of gun ownership are believed to be relatively low.

THE ROLE OF THE GUN LOBBY

In the United States, the gun lobby and in particular the National Rifle Association (NRA) play a significant role in opposition to gun registration policies and in their endorsement of "gun culture." The NRA's gun ideology is linked closely to American nationalism and conventional notions of masculinity.[20] There have also been studies of the NRA's use of advertising as well as the discourse that pervades its magazines.[21] O'Neill argues that the NRA deliberately invokes a faceless and nameless threat, one that threatens people's homes, in an effort to defend gun ownership rights and reinforce a particular notion of masculinity.[22] Gun advertisements offering a choice of a gun or calling 911 for emergency assistance reinforce this. The famous picture of Charleton Heston, who was president of the NRA and known for his film role as Moses, with rifle raised, proclaiming "out of my cold dead hands," linked heroism with the defense of "gun rights." The NRA invokes history (the founding fathers and the Constitution), family values, honor and self reliance, linking heroic myth to the struggles of the gun lobby.

Manufacturers advertise extensively in NRA publications, *American Rifleman* and *American Hunter*, providing about 8 percent of the NRA's overall revenues.[23] Other reciprocal relationships exist; for example, manufacturers distribute NRA membership materials in their packaging and the NRA provides discount gun purchase offers as well as publicity and advertising.

Fear for personal safety at home and on the streets is a significant factor influencing firearm demand in countries that allow carrying guns for personal protection.[24] As the former NRA president Wayne Lapierre put it, "The market's being driven by fear."[25] Growth in handgun sales in the United States, for example, has been linked to the Watts riots in 1965 and the Detroit riots in 1967. Advertisements placed by gun dealers and the NRA following the riots used fear to promote sales.[26] Concern for personal safety is also exploited in the promotion of laws that permit civilians to carry concealed weapons in the United States.[27] Several states have enacted statutes permitting individuals to carry a concealed firearm.[28] These laws are seen by the firearm industry as expanding the market for handguns in spite of conclusive evidence of their lack of benefit in terms of self-protection.[29]

Concern for personal safety is the principal desire that the gun industry attempts to exploit in selling guns, particularly in the United States. Although its success is unclear, there is ample evidence of efforts to compensate for declining markets by targeting new segments, such as women.[30] In 1996, Glock, an Austrian handgun manufacturer, boasted that since an increasing number of women now are head of households, including single mothers who are responsible for home safety, they have become an exploitable market.[31]

Appeals to concerns for safety are evident in other countries as well. For example, the South African Gunowners Association (SAGA) writes:

A misinformed public fears firearms because they do not understand either them or their legitimate use. This public is increasingly exposed to sensational media coverage of the misuse of firearms and the false claim that gun control equals crime control. As violent crime increases, more people arm themselves for protection. As the number of firearms in circulation increases, so too does the number of "incidents"—thefts accidents, shootings. . . . As more incidents are reported, this uninvolved, well-intentioned and concerned public grows even more fearful of firearms, bringing more pressure to bear on the State for tighter controls. Unchecked, this pressure can become a serious threat not only to YOUR FREEDOM TO CHOOSE your sport or hobby, but to a viable means of protecting yourself, your family and property against unlawful attacks and violence.[32]

Even though Australia, like Canada, has no tradition of arming for self-protection, much of the rhetoric is the same. The Australian Sporting Shooters Association Web site contains extensive links to firearm suppliers as well as a range of advocacy materials. The association also publishes four different magazines—*Australian Shooter*, *Australian Handguns*, *Australian Hunter* and the *Australian Shooters Journal*—which contain extensive advertising by manufacturers. The association also works closely with the National Firearm Dealers and Traders Council of Australia on international advocacy. Table 6.2 provides a partial list of the gun organizations working internationally.

The links between the Australian gun lobby and its American counterparts are clear, as can be seen in their familiar rhetoric:

Rather than outlawing private ownership for self-defence, the sensible alternative might be to initiate a licensing system in Australia which allows fit and proper people to keep firearms for protection in their own home. . . . The fundamental freedom to protect one's life and property has been replaced by a policy which ignores the fact that no matter how well resourced a police ser-

Table 6.2 Some of the Major Organizations Promoting Firearm Ownership around the World

Country	Organization	Description
Global	World Forum of the Future of Sports Shooting Activities (WFSA)	Forty member organizations in some twenty nations around the world. In the United States members include the NRA, SCI, the Single Action Shooting Society, and several industry groups.
	World Shooting Federation	
North American		
United States	American Shooting Sports Council	Includes a wide range of gun magazine publishers. Funded by manufacturers. Offers a joint programme with the NRA.
	ILA Institute for Legislative Action	NRA legislative action arm.
	FireArms Importers Roundtable Trade Group (FAIR)	Established in 1994 in response to ban on Chinese imports.
	National Rifle Association (NRA)	Arguably the most powerful lobby of any kind in the world with annual budget of approximately $100 million and 2.9 million members. Has NGO status at the United Nations. Is a major participant in the WFSA. Supports gun lobby groups in other countries.
	National Shooting Sports Foundation (NSSF)	Trade association for the recreational shooting industry since 1961. More than 2,500 member companies including gun associations, publishing companies, as well as manufacturers, distributors, and retailers of sport firearms, ammunition, and associated products. www.nssf.org

Table 6.2 (continued)

Country	Organization	Description
	Sporting Arms and Ammunition Manufacturers Institute (SAAMI)	Founded in 1926 as an association of manufacturers of sporting firearms, ammunition, and components. SAAMI is involved in the publication of industry standards, coordination of technical data, and promotion of gun safety. The twenty-six member companies include major firearms manufacturers such as Baretta USA, Colt Inc., and Glock Inc.
	Wildlife Management Institute (WMI)	Established in 1911 as a conservancy agency WMI is a lobby group for hunters and outdoors businesses. They lobby the government on legislative issues, publish studies on wildlife issues, and review other conservancy organizations. http://www.wildlifemanagement institute.org
	Other	Range of niche groups such as Jews for the Preservation of Firearm Ownership Organization that promotes and maintains the right for citizens to bear arms. Producing pamphlets, videos, and occasional papers that decry gun control as a tool of tyranny. http://www.jpfo. org/
Canada	Canadian Wildlife Federation	A wildlife conservancy group since 1962. Promotes understanding human impact on the environment and the sustainable use of natural resources. CFW conducts research relating to wildlife and the environment, as well as lobbying the government to protect wildlife and its habitats.

Table 6.2 (continued)

Country	Organization	Description
	National Firearms Association	A largely conservative organization of firearm owners. They promote safe and responsible use of firearms while lobbying the government for more lax control on firearms. They also produce their own article and legal commentary. http://www.nfa.ca/index.html
	Sporting Arms and Ammunition	Forty member organizations in some twenty nations around the world. In the United States members include the NRA, SCI, the Single Action Shooting Society, and several industry groups.
South America		
Brazil		
	BVS e.V Federal Association of Shooting Ranges	Includes a wide range of gun magazine publishers. Funded by manufacturers. Offers a joint programme with the NRA.
	Imbel	http://www.imbel.gov.br/
Europe	AECAC European Association of the Civil Commerce of Weapons	
	Association of European Manufacturers of Sporting Ammunition (AFEMS)	An international NGO that lobbies on behalf of its members, establishes dialogue with decision-making bodies and acts as a forum where members can exchange technical and business information. Fifteen countries are represented by forty companies that produce sporting ammunition and component parts. http://www.afems.org/

Table 6.2 (continued)

Country	Organization	Description
	IEACS Institut Europeén des Armes de Chasse et de Sport	Secretariat—6, Cap de Bos Gaiac F-33430 FRANCE E-Mail: Eldwynn@aol.com (no Website; just contact info) Found at: http://www.afems.org/Test/coop.htm (In French)
Austria	Interessengemeinschaft Liberales Waffenrecht in Osterreich	http://www.iwoe.at (In German)
	IPSC (International Practical Shooting Confederation)	Association of shooters that run firearms "courses" at the competitive level. The Confederation includes members in sixty-nine countries all over the world. http://www.ipsc.org
Denmark	Danish Sport Shooters Association (DSSA)	http://www.dsf.dk (In Danish)
France	Fédération Française de Tir (FFdT)	http://www.fftir.asso.fr (In French)
	Federation Internationale de Tir aux Armes Sportives de Chasse (FITASC)	http://www.fitasc.com/public/accueil.asp (In French)
Germany	BDMP (Bund der Militärund Polizeischützen e. V.)	http://www.bdmp.de (In German)
	Forum Waffenrecht-Deutschland	http://www.fwr.de (In German)
Great Britain	British Shooting Sports Council (BSSC)	An umbrella association comprising all major sport shooting organizations in the United Kingdom. It also serves as an exchange of information between the Home Office and other Government Departments on the issue of sport shooting.

Table 6.2 (continued)

Country	Organization	Description
		Organizations represented: British Association for Shooting & Conservation, Association of Professional Clay Target Shooting Grounds, Countryside Alliance, Clay Pigeon Shooting Association, Gun Trade Association, Muzzle Loaders Association, Sportsman's Association of Great Britain & Northern Ireland, National Rifle Association, National Smallbore Rifle Association, Shooting Sports Trust, United Kingdom Practical Shooting Association, Institute of Clay Shooting Instructors, Association of Professional Shooting Instructors. http://www.bssc.org.uk
	Countryside Alliance	An English association that promotes rural issues such as wildlife conservancy, hunting, jobs, and land issues. It has over 400,000 full and affiliate members all over rural Britain. http://www.countryside-alliance.org
Italy	Association Nationale de Défense des Tireurs, Amateurs d'Armes et Collectionneurs (ANTAC)	http://www.antac.org (In French)
	Associazione Nazionale Produttori Armi e Munizioni (ANPAM)	http://www.anpam.it (In Italian)
	Consorzio Armaioli Bresciani (CAB)	http://www.armaiolibresciani.org (English pages not working)
	Federazione Italiana Tiro a Volo (FITAV)	http://www.fitav.it (In Italian)

Table 6.2 (continued)

Country	Organization	Description
	Federazione Italiana Tiro Dinamico Sportivo (FITDS)	http://www.fitds.it (In Italian)
	Unione Nazionale Associazioni Venatorie Italiane (UNAVI)	http://www.unavi.it (In Italian; Web site is down)
Portugal	Federaçào Portuguesa de Tiro com Armasde Caça (FPTAC)	
Other		
Australia	Sporting Shooters Association of Australia (SSAA)	The Sporting Shooters Association was established in 1948. It promotes shooting sports and represents licensed firearm owners. There are more than 120,000 members. http://www.ssaa.org.au
South Africa	South African Gunowners' Association (SAGA)	SAGA is an association of gun owners that lobbies the government for less strict control of gun laws and promotes a more positive image of guns and gun owners. http://www.saga.org.za

Source: World Forum on the Future of Sport Shooting Activities: Members and Links, 2001 (last update), http://www.wfsa.net/Links.htm.

vice may be, it cannot prevent violent home invasions. Drawing on the US experience, we know that firearms in the home have an important deterrent effect and we know that properly trained, responsible owners holding firearms for self-defence pose no threat other than to the criminal element. . . .[33]

As Tom Diaz of the Violence Policy Center suggests, "Lethality in guns is like nicotine in cigarettes—an addictive hook set deep into the irrational side of its customers."[34] The gun industry links its advertising and promotional efforts to the fantasies of its customers. Assault weapon sales got a huge boost from the film *Rambo*, and the Austrian-made Glock got a push from product placements in the films of Arnold Schwarzenegger (now governor of California). For example, when told in the film *End of Days* to trust in God, Schwarzenegger's character says he would rather trust in his Glock. Companies with strong links to military and policing markets exploited this relationship in their marketing efforts. For example, Heckler and Koch published advertisements aimed at civilians that emphasized the military lineage of its weapons.

Other factors also appear to shape demand. For example, dealers claim that the assault weapons ban increased the value of assault weapons in circulation and drove up demand. The terrorist attacks of September 11, 2001, also appear to have caused a spike in American gun sales, although the link between carrying a handgun and preventing terrorist attacks is unclear.

Manufacturers received considerable reinforcement in their efforts from the wide range of firearms magazine publishers and associations that reinforced the "fear factor" and promoted arming. As one gun industry publication noted, "While you may not have an overwhelming number of customers who would carry two firearms, it does open a new market; each backup gun you sell brings with it ancillary sales of ankle holsters, pocket holsters or belly bands, perhaps some Speed Strips for spare ammo and of course, ammo itself."[35]

GENDER, EXPERIENCE AND ATTITUDES TO FIREARMS

Manufacturers are constantly exploring ways to expand civilian markets by targeting specific market segments, such as women. In the United States, gun ownership among women has stayed relatively constant at about 8 percent of women over the last two decades but that has not stopped the gun makers and their allies from focusing on women as a market. Smith & Wesson's "Ladysmith" campaign and the NRA's "Refuse to be a victim" campaign are examples.[36] Similar strategies have been adopted in other countries. In Canada, where carrying firearms for self-protection is limited to police officers, security guards and citizens who can prove that their lives are in danger and the police cannot protect them, the National Firearms Association has promoted the "Lioness method of rape protection." The pamphlet, playing on women's fears, describes in graphic detail the consequences of rape and includes carrying guns as one means of prevention. "When a rape begins, there is no one there but you and the rapist. When it ends, there is still no one there but you and the rapist. When it ends, you will be dead or alive, but physically and emotionally shattered, probably permanently. You may also be pregnant, or under sentence of death from the AIDS infection he just gave you. Rapists don't use condoms."[37]

In the United States, new organizations such as Women Against Gun Control have launched campaigns reminiscent of the NRA's "Refuse to be a victim" campaign, intended to invoke women's fears about safety, thereby creating a new market for firearm sales and adding strength to the gun lobby campaign. In addition, the NRA developed a column in the *Rifleman* specifically aimed at women.[38] To date, there is limited evidence that efforts to increase gun ownership among women have been successful. In fact, *Ms* magazine has criticized this new "power feminism," and most women's organizations have reinforced the fact that where there are more guns, more women are likely to be killed by their partners.[39]

Worldwide, most firearm owners and users are male. Men dominate the military and the police. Men also dominate civilian firearm ownership in the United States and Canada.[40] Women represent a very small proportion of gun owners but tend to be victims of gun violence in greater proportions. This imbalance has been one of the arguments advanced for positioning this debate in the context of human rights and equity.[41]

Because women are more likely than men to fear guns, gender attitudes to guns are important in definitions of human security and human rights. While more than half of Americans indicated that recent shootings in the news have made them worry about their own safety, almost two-thirds of women said they are likely to feel that way.[42] Indeed, there have been efforts to exploit this fear in marketing guns to women.

Women generally have more negative attitudes toward weapons than men do, and are generally more committed to measures to reduce their misuse and proliferation. This is an important factor in terms of mobilization for and resistance to policy change. Recent polls conducted in Canada illustrate a significant gender split in attitudes toward firearms. In one poll, 84 percent of women and 65 percent of men favored restricting access to ammunition; support for mandatory firearm registration showed a much wider gap between men and women.[43] In another recent poll, 50 percent of gun owners opposed gun control legislation and 77 percent of people *living with gun owners* supported it.[44]

Polls in the United States show similar gender splits; a 1999 poll showed that 45 percent of men and 66 percent of women wanted stricter controls.[45] These gender splits are observed in the voting behavior of U.S. politicians as well. In the final vote on the Brady Bill, in the House of Representatives, 51 percent of men voted for adoption compared to 81 percent of women. In the Senate, the split was 60 percent of men and 100 percent of women in favor.[46] Polls in industrialized countries also show that women are less likely to own guns and more likely to support stricter regulations. Indeed, women have played a critical role worldwide in movements for stricter regulation (discussed in Chapter 8).

In a study of three high-crime communities in South Africa, for example, 34.4 percent of women wanted to own firearms compared to 44.9 percent of men.[47] Similarly, a recent survey conducted in Phnom Penh, Cambodia, an area with high rates of firearm injuries, found that 43 percent of men would own a gun if it were legal to do so compared to 31 percent of women.[48]

YOUTH AND GUNS

There is evidence that some gun manufacturers, like tobacco companies, are targeting youth in order to sustain markets.[49] There have been parallels between the effects of the gun lobby and those of the tobacco lobby to shape the research agenda and to block regulatory efforts.[50] Firearm associations have also been accused of marketing guns to teens and children under the guise of teaching firearm safety. A U.S. study from the Violence Policy Center entitled "Eddie the Eagle: Joe Camel with Feathers" documented the technique of luring children into the gun culture at a very young age under the pretext of teaching them firearm safety. Parallel efforts have been documented in other countries. In Canada, for example, the National Firearms Association advises against storing firearms safely (required under Canadian law) and in favor of "gunproofing children," a strategy that involves teaching them how to load, aim and fire guns.[51] Hunters in Canada have also targeted schools for their "firearm safety programs," despite vehement opposition from child safety groups such as the Canadian Paediatric Association.[52]

GUNS AND MASCULINITY

Most of the existing work exploring demand for firearms is silent on one of the factors found across nations, both in times of war and in times of peace: the majority of those who use and misuse firearms are men. Traditional male roles as providers, warriors or police officers often entail the use of firearms, but even among civilian populations demand for both legal and illegal guns is much higher among men than among women. This would appear to suggest that in order to develop effective strategies to stem the misuse and proliferation of firearms we must understand the ways in which concepts of masculinity affect demand. Conventional notions of masculinity ascribe the role of protector and defender to men, and for many, gun ownership is a symbol of masculine power and status.

While violence is not an exclusively male practice, it is linked, along with guns, to masculine identity. The values, social practices and institutions that together constitute this gun culture include "consumerist militarism," which can be defined as the normalization and even glorification of war, weaponry, military force and violence through television, films, books, songs, dances, games, sports and toys. In South Africa, for example, Jacklyn Cock argues that the demand for guns is a socially constructed concept that is embedded in culture.[53] Dealing with the culture of violence is, therefore, an essential part of a strategy to counter violence.

A recent report by Oxfam International and Amnesty International highlights the ways in which firearms are linked to male identity in a number of countries, including Albania, Afghanistan, Uganda, Somalia, Papua New

Guinea and Iraq.[54] In such countries, gun possession is widespread and strongly linked to notions of masculinity: At the birth of a boy, guns are fired into the air and people exclaim, "We have increased by one gun!"[55] There are many examples of gun culture in nations from around the world.

- At the Acholi coming-of-age ceremony in Uganda, a boy receives his first gun as a symbol of the passage to manhood. Everyone blesses the gun.
- In Somalia, arms are so central to everyday life that parents have in some cases named their male infants "Uzi" or "AK-47."
- An Iraqi saying is, "Give everything to your friend, except your car, your wife and your gun."
- A resident of Papua New Guinea stated, "In my village, every man has a gun, a gun of his own. Now, if you don't have one for yourself, then you don't have a name in the village. Your wife can be raped. They can steal. They can do anything to you."[56]

Similar examples have been documented in South Africa, where weapons are emblematic of manliness across South African cultures; for example, "A Boer and his gun are inseparable"; "I joined the South African police so I could get a gun and feel like a proper man"; "The call to a ban on weapons is an insult to my manhood. It is an insult to the manhood of every Zulu man."[57]

Among industrialized societies, nowhere is the association of guns and masculinity stronger than in U.S. culture. The symbolic significance of guns has been made explicit in many ways.[58] For example, guns are essential equipment for cowboys, police officers and warriors, which play a significant role in the mythological history in the United States.

Scholars have analyzed American gun culture from a number of vantage points often arguing that gun ownership is strongly tied to American identity. "It is that of the independent frontiersman who takes care of himself and his family with no interference from the state."[59] "Just to hold [a Colt Model 'P'] in your hand produces a feeling of kinship with our western heritage—an appreciation of things like courage and honor and chivalry and the sanctity of a man's world."[60] These linkages are reinforces at many levels—through entertainment media, through advertising and by the gun lobby. The connection between masculinity and firearms is reinforced by many iconic images in American culture—John Wayne, Clint Eastwood, Bruce Willis, Sylvestor Stallone. It is not without irony that the United Nations Special Rapporteur on the prevention of human rights violations committed with small arms and light weapons notes, "While male-dominated societies often justify small arms possession through the alleged need to protect vulnerable women, women actually face greater danger of violence when their families and communities are armed."[61] It is worth noting that while gun ownership and legitimate firearms activities are well established in many industrialized nations, the possession of firearms for "self-protection" is common primarily in developing nations like South Africa and Paraguay, as well as the United States. (See Table 6.1.)

Some criminologists, such as Rosemary Gartner, have argued that empirical evidence indicates that cultural factors are stronger predictors of violence than economic factors. Societies that are frequently at war consistently have higher rates of interpersonal and within-group violence. Homicide rates within participant nations have consistently increased after wars whether the nation has won or lost. Similarly, societies with violent sports and those that permit corporal and capital punishments tend to have higher levels of interpersonal violence. In such societies, male children are typically socialized for aggression, in part to equip them for adult roles as warriors.[62] Empirical research into attitudes toward killing in various contexts also reveals a strong association between homicide rates and attitudes that include the willingness to kill to protect property, to kill to avenge the rape of a child, support for capital punishment and attitudes to gun ownership.[63] The relationships among gun laws, rates of gun ownership and societal values are complex and mutually influencing. Society shapes its laws and its laws shape society.[64]

The (re)production of notions of masculinity is critical to understanding the demand for firearms, an often neglected area of research. There is an important need to examine notions of masculinity, the roles that guns play in male culture, and ways to decouple these. To date most discussions of the role of gender are relegated to "gender studies" rather than addressed in the dominant literatures.

CULTURE AND THE DEMAND FOR FIREARMS

What drives the demand for firearms? Extensive work has been done to address the root causes of violence, including economic and political inequality and a sense of insecurity. Factors often considered in the gun control debate include disparity in social and economic status; lack of basic necessities such as work and shelter; lack of protection from threats; lack of effective policing; lack of access to influence and lack of prestige goods.[65] There is extensive literature on this which reinforces the importance of primary prevention. Suffice it to say that gang members are not born they are bred. While much attention has been focused on measures to stem the flow of firearms, attention is increasingly being paid to understanding the root causes of violence and the factors that shape demand.

Opponents of gun control such as David Kopel have taken a cultural determinism view maintaining that firearms are intricately woven into American culture and history, making "gun control" not only a violation of the

U.S. constitution but also foreign to U.S. history and culture.[66] Cultural differences have been used as an excuse for resisting the development of international norms for weapons controls. For example, Kopel maintains that history and culture in places such as Japan and Canada are so distinct from the history and culture of the United States that their experience with gun control is not transferable.[67] Others have maintained that while history and culture are useful explanatory frameworks, they should not be used as excuses for inaction.

It is certainly true that in many countries around the world firearms are strongly tied to notions of freedom and independence as well as to masculinity. Yet politicians from countries such as Australia have noted that while firearms were part of its heritage and history, it is time for change. In Britain, a former cabinet minister who supported the handgun ban said, "If we want to import the American way of life, we've got to come to terms with the American way of death."[68] Relatively little has been written about ways to strike at the cultural roots of violence. Although the recent World Health Organization report recognizes the importance of the cultural environment as a root cause of violence, it has limited suggestions for ways to address this. To date, suggestions focus on school programs intended to explore relationships and gender roles or on legal and community interventions to stigmatize abusive behavior. Or they focus on broader issues such as violence in the media, videogames, etc. In general, there is limited exploration of the role of culture or ways in which it can be shaped.

GENDER VERSUS CULTURE

While gender is an important construct in understanding the use and misuse of guns, we also must recognize its limitations. It is absolutely true that the vast majority of those who own firearms worldwide are men; we find, however, that on many of the dimensions explored, particularly in attitudes to weapons and regulation of weapons, the cultural disparities, even within the same region, are greater than the gender differences. For example, an Associated Press poll, conducted in 1999 also showed that 83 percent of black Americans compared to 52 percent of white American's supported tougher gun controls. The gender split was 21 points of difference (45 percent of men and 66 percent of women) while the cultural split was 31 points (83 percent for African Americans and 52 percent for white Americans).[69] This is particularly interesting given that young black men are a disproportionate number of firearm victims in the United States.

As noted above, a survey of South Africans' attitudes to firearms showed that among the respondents, 46 percent of men compared to 38 percent of women believed "any adult should be allowed to own a gun." The gap between whites and blacks was far greater: 62 percent of white Africans believed anyone should be allowed to own a gun compared to only 29 percent of black Africans and 29 percent of Indian South Africans.[70] While class may be an issue, the differences in attitudes based on culture are much greater than the differences based on gender.

A similar phenomenon is found in the contrast between the gender split and the cultural split between French and English Canadians. There are often rural/urban splits and regional differences that are greater than the differences between men and women. While 82 percent of women compared to 65 percent of men nationwide support gun control, in Quebec, a predominantly Francophone province, support of gun control is consistently around 90 percent, compared to only 45 percent support in Saskatchewan, a rural Anglo province.[71]

Studies of the United States also show distinct differences in attitudes to guns in regions characterized by "the frontier mentality" of the West and the South. These regions also have what has been termed "a culture of honor." Southerners and westerners are likely to voice stronger support than northerners for honor-related violence, similar to what is seen in many southern countries.[72] The same study showed that states in the South were less likely to address domestic violence in the first place, for example, through mandatory arrest.[73]

Distinctions need to be made between symbolic and actual violence. Social psychologists have repeatedly demonstrated that attitudes are often poor predictors of behavior. While one study showed huge differences in the approval of symbolic violence in the South and West of the United States, these statistics did not correlate with rates of all types of actual violence. They did, however, correlate with homicides committed in the course of an argument, but not with those committed during the course of another crime.

GUNS AND THE MEDIA

In Western industrialized societies, the media is one of the principal conduits of culture. American media in particular tends to portray heroes using violence as a justified means of resolving conflict.[74] Some research suggests links among gender, media violence and behavior, although the definitions, analysis and explanatory frameworks differ. Research has tended to focus on exposure in the media to guns and violence. Content analyses, for example, have focused on violent acts, on how the protagonists are depicted, as well as on the association between exposure to violence in the media with a variety of physical and/or mental health problems among children and adolescents. Some of the disorders studied include aggressive behavior and desensitization to violence and fear. It has been noted that "titillating violence in sexual contexts and comic violence are particularly dangerous, because they associate positive feelings with hurting others."[75] These studies have considered violent entertainment as well as video games. Lynch and colleagues, for example, found that exposure to video game violence was positively correlated with hostile attitudes, arguments and fights, and hostility, and negatively correlated with positive school performance.[76] Sherry suggested that the effect of video games on aggression is smaller than the effect of television.[77] A broad-based study for the United Nations Educational, Scientific, and Cultural Organization concluded that there were not simple causal relations but broader effects on psychology and behavior as a result of video game violence.[78]

Another intersection of gun culture, the media and gender can be found in entertainment media. Studies of U.S. television and film have illuminated the relationships among guns, firearms and masculinity in the United States as revealed in Hollywood action films. Scholars have noted the rise of white, violent characters played by men such as Sylvester Stallone, Arnold Schwarzenegger and Bruce Willis as cinematic heroes for whom guns are iconic and suggested that the appeal of these stereotypes is particularly strong among disempowered white working-class men.[79] Furthermore, it has been noted that the depiction of gun use in films, particularly the use of guns for self-protection, is very much at odds with the reality of gun use by U.S. men. The masculine discourse of self-protection is pervasive, even though it flies in the face of reality. Moreover, critics have also discussed the "mythic" constructions of gunplay in U.S. movies.[80]

It is critical in exploring the media-culture-violence link that one understand that it is only one factor among many. Often it is used to minimize other factors such as socioeconomic disparity, inequity or access to firearms. Following the Columbine school shootings in the United States, National Rifle Association president Charlton Heston maintained that it was not the availability of guns that was an issue but rather violent video games. This thesis has been advanced by some researchers who explicitly oppose gun control.[81] Even Michael Moore's recent documentary *Bowling for Columbine,* which suggested that the U.S. culture of violence was the principal differentiator between the United States and Canada, downplayed the availability of guns as a factor.

The analysis of empirical studies must consequently be carefully nuanced. Some researchers frame their analysis in terms of gender stereotypes and role models in order to examine how violence affects girls and boys in different ways. Still others suggest that extensive exposure to violent media is symptomatic of other problems such as a lack of parental care and supervision, while others examine it in terms of violent media's contribution to a broader "culture of violence." The perspectives that focus on "cultures of violence" rather than on simple cause-and-effect relationships appear to be the most promising.[82]

ADVERTISING AND MARKETING MEDIA

The power of advertising is well understood. Studies have explored the ways in which gun manufacturers exploit traditional notions of masculinity in their advertisements by invoking the needs for self-protection and "awesome power beyond belief," and occasionally relying on scantily clad female models like those who populate car advertisements.[83] A semiotic analysis of hunting and gun magazines shows a number of common elements that are designed to invoke rugged individualism overlain with American nationalism.[84] Invocations of media heroes like Clint Eastwood's Dirty Harry are also found.

There have also been studies of the National Rifle Association's discourse and the use of advertising that pervades its magazines.[85] O'Neill argues that the National Rifle Association's production of a "faceless and nameless threat, one which terrorizes us in our most intimate spaces . . . is not intended exclusively to demonstrate that Americans must have the right to keep and bear arms. Instead the NRA also uses the Armed Citizen to manufacture its own politically potent mode of masculinity by way of a strategically constructed threat."[86]

There have also been studies of the construction of violent white masculinity in advertising.[87] One area of research, for example, has looked at the creation of modern masculine archetypes such as the Marlboro Man. Katz writes, "Guns are an important signifier of virility and power and hence an important way violent masculinity is constructed and then sold to an audience. In fact, the presence of guns in magazine and newspaper ads is crucial to communicating the extent of a movie's violent content. . . . Images of gun-toting macho males pervade the visual landscape."[88]

CONCLUSION

Reasons for owning guns and levels of gun ownership vary widely around the world. Addressing the factors that influence the demand for firearms is essential but also very difficult. Correcting deep-root structural problems—economic disparity, inequality and insecurity—requires systemic change and long-term investment. The link between masculinity and firearms is very strong in many cultures, and understanding ways in which this link is constructed (and potentially deconstructed) is essential to formulating change. While gender is one of the strongest predictors of gun use and misuse, there are many cultures where masculinity and guns are not strongly linked, where there seems to be evidence that national cultures exert stronger influence than the construction of gender. Work on these issues is only beginning, and more needs to be done.

7

The Regulation of Firearms

While gun control is extremely controversial in the United States, with opposition to even basic regulation such as licensing and registration, a review of legislation around the world shows that the norms in most countries, both industrialized and developing, are to strictly regulate civilian possession of firearms. In addition, a number of international agreements and resolutions provide support for regulating firearms in both postconflict and peaceful settings. This chapter reviews the principles and limitations of the regulation of firearms, components of firearm regulation, case studies of selected countries and existing international agreements and resolutions.

PRINCIPLES AND LIMITATIONS OF REGULATION

Regulation of civilian possession of firearms is intended to reduce the risk that legally acquired firearms will be misused or diverted to illegal markets. The effectiveness of laws in shaping behavior is always a result of a complex interaction of factors. Although the levels of firearm violence in a country are in general linked to the restrictiveness of the country's laws, there are exceptions. Some countries with relatively permissive laws have rates of violence lower than countries with restrictive laws.

The success of efforts to regulate civilian possession of firearms is influenced by many factors. Extensive voluntary compliance is generally essential for effective firearm regulation, particularly when a large percentage of the population is in possession of firearms. Voluntary compliance is generally seen in contexts where the majority of the population is law-abiding and regards the law as appropriate and fair. Although strenuous opposition from a vocal minority commonly accompanies efforts to strengthen controls over civilian possession of guns, and while attitudes to legislation change significantly over time, the laws generally need to be in line with what a substantial proportion of the population regards as reasonable. In the United States, polling suggests strong support for licensing and registration of handguns but rejects an outright ban.[1] In Canada, in contrast, the proportion of the population that supports licensing and registration is about the same as the proportion that supports a total ban on firearms.[2]

Within a society there can be significant differences in attitudes and norms. As noted in Chapter 6, there are huge splits in opinion based on gender,[3] age, education, region and residence in rural or urban areas.[4] Legislation to control access to firearms is only one piece of a comprehensive strategy to prevent violence. As discussed in Chapter 3, the public health approach focuses on analyzing the problem, determining the factors that contribute to the problem, developing interventions that address these factors, implementing these interventions and evaluating them. One way of understanding the ways in which we can prevent firearm violence is to think of it in the same way we think of cancer. While all cancers have some common elements—the reproduction of diseased cells—there are significant differences between lung cancer, breast cancer and prostate cancer, such as the risk factors and interventions to prevent and treat them. Firearm violence takes many forms—domestic violence, suicide, gang violence, unintentional injuries and conflict. These may have some common elements (the firearm), but they are also distinct in terms of the risk factors and interventions likely to be effective. Some are highly linked—for example, risk factors for suicide and homicide in the context of domestic violence are similar. But the factors linked to urban gang violence may be very different than those associated with violence in the home.

Integrated approaches to reducing firearm violence must take into account the differences as well as the similarities among its different forms of violence. With cancer, we know that primary prevention interventions (healthy diet, exercise, not smoking) are most effective in reducing the risks of certain forms of cancer. Screening and early detection for individuals at risk are also important. Treatments may also be effective although some cancers are less receptive to interventions. As with cancer there is no "one size fits all" solution to the problem of gun violence. We know that primary prevention that has a long term focus on the root causes is most effective. We also have evidence that reducing access to firearms can reduce the risk and lethality of certain forms of violence. There is also some evidence that enforcement measures can help contain the problem and that control measures—appropriate medical treatment, etc.—can somewhat alleviate the effects.

Firearm legislation plays a role at all three levels. First, as discussed previously, legislation not only reflects but also shapes values and culture. Legislation also reduces the ease with which guns may be obtained and reduces the risks that firearms will be easily acquired by individuals who pose a threat to themselves or others. It also reduces the likelihood that legal firearms will be diverted for illegal purposes. In crime prevention parlance, legislative controls on firearms constitute "target hardening."[5] While highly motivated individuals with suicidal or criminal intent may find ways to acquire firearms, regardless of the laws or other measures in place to reduce access, some individuals will be prevented from gaining access. This is particularly important with respect to the forms of firearm violence where impulsivity and access play major roles—for example in many suicides among youth, domestic homicides, school shootings, and in "accidents" involving children. There is also evidence to suggest that raising the effective price of firearms through regulation and increasing the accountability of firearm owners can reduce the diversion of legal guns to illegal markets and may have an impact on "crime guns" and related activies. It may be true some people will get guns regardless of these impediments, but that is not an argument for making it easier for them to get them. As entertainer Ozzy Osbourne said, "I keep hearing this thing that guns don't kill people, but people kill people. If that's the case, why do we give people guns when they go to war? Why not just send the people?"[6] Controls on firearms will not generally reduce violent crime or suicide attempts but will reduce the use of guns in violence and crime and therefore, reduce the lethal consequences.

At the same time, it is important to understand the limitations of legislative interventions. First, measures to address the root causes are essential. As noted earlier, a range of factors influence the demand for firearms. In conflicts, these factors may include a combination of socioeconomic, political and cultural forces. If these are not addressed there cannot be lasting peace. With violence against women, efforts must focus on the underlying values and power relationships that shape this crime. Suicides, particularly involving youth, are also a result of a combination of forces—early interventions are key. Urban violence is also often linked to a variety of factors that produce large numbers of disenfranchised young men. Gang members are not born but bred and a host of factors contribute. Guns are just one part of the mix.

The context into which laws are introduced has a significant impact on the extent to which they will be effective. In areas where the forces driving demand are particularly strong, laws may not have much impact. Also, laws are only words on paper if they are not accompanied by careful attention to implementation. Given the limitations of law enforcement and justice systems, most laws depend on high levels of voluntary compliance. Often, whether they agree with them or not, "law-abiding citizens" will comply with laws. In fact, it has been said that deterrence measures are most effective with law abiding citizens. In some contexts, however, given the politicization of gun laws, noncompliance is actively promoted with gun lobby groups and this needs to be taken into account when laws are developed and implemented. If laws cannot be enforced, their impact is weakened.

Effective enforcement of laws often requires substantial resources for training, policies, procedures and technology to allow citizens to easily comply with the laws and to ensure that police are able to enforce the laws. Careful attention to these issues is critical to ensure that the laws achieve their intended effects.

Severe penalties for gun crimes are not particularly meaningful if police cannot apprehend criminals or if courts do not apply the sentences. For some forms of violence—particularly urban, gang relative violence—police may have difficulty proceeding with their investigations because of a lack of information or cooperative witnesses. In many cases, the clearance rates, that is, the rate at which the crimes are "solved," is very low. Moreover, it is generally understood that effective strategies to address violence need community involvement. There are many examples of successful cross-sectoral projects where firearm laws have been supported with targeted policing and community participation.

A project in Pittsburgh targeted high crime neighborhoods with increased police patrols. High risk times and locations were identified through detailed analysis of shots-fired activity. Police used pedestrian and traffic stops to focus on suspicious people but also to engage in information collection discussions with other citizens. Studies have concluded that the efforts produced significant reductions in shots fired and injuries and that the increase in police resources was a good investment, given the costs of gun violence.[7] The Chicago Gun Project (1992–1997) used an integrated project team of police, street workers, probation officers and others to focus on community mobilization, social intervention (including outreach), providing opportunities for at-risk youth, suppression and accountability. The evaluation of the five-year project demonstrated that the program had a positive effect on reducing gang violence and on the community's perception of the gang problem and the police response to gangs. "Operation Ceasefire," the Boston Gun Project, used similar principles. Although the State of Massachusetts had some of the strongest firearm laws in the country it experienced an increase in youth homicide between the late 1980s and early 1990s. A Boston Gun Project Working Group was established that included the Boston Police Department, the Massachusetts Departments of Probation and Parole, the office of the Suffolk County District Attorney, the office of the United States Attorney, the Bureau of Alcohol, Tobacco, and Firearms, the Massachusetts Department of Youth Services (juvenile corrections), Boston School Police, and gang outreach and prevention "streetworkers" attached to the Boston Community Centers program. Other important participants included the Ten Point Coalition of activist black clergy, the Drug Enforcement Administration, the Massachusetts State Police, and the office of the Massachusetts Attorney General. The Project focused on a small number of chronically offending gang-involved youth responsible for much of Boston's youth homicide problem. The results of the project included significant reductions in youth homicide victimization, shots fired, calls for service, and gun assault incidents in Boston. Project Trident in London focused on strengthening links between the police and community in order to build community ownership of the gun problem through aggressive publicity and outreach, and "gun stopper" information lines to collect information. Although a full evaluation is in progress gun crime clearance rates increased.[8]

Even in developing countries with limited infrastructure, targeted policing may have an impact—limited bans on carrying handguns in Cali and Bogota coupled with aggressive enforcement are believed to have reduced the homicide rates during the period of the intervention. However, challenges remain in contexts that lack effective policing and justice systems.[9] All of this can have an impact on the effectiveness of legislation. For example, in Canada, only 45 percent of gunowners supported the law making it more difficult to encourage compliance. The two-way interaction between legislation on the one hand and normative values on the other means that legislation not only has a practical effect on limiting supply but may shape values and in turn shape demand. Apart from the factors of norm building and voluntary compliance, there is also a need to reinforce legislation. Successful legislative interventions must always be accompanied by careful attention to implementation issues, including policies and procedures, resources, training and technology. Laws alone are not effective if they are not coupled with appropriate levels of enforcement or where the factors fuelling demand are particularly strong. The regulation of firearms is only one part of an integrated crime prevention strategy.

Penalties for not complying with laws differ dramatically from country to country. Some have implemented draconian penalties for illegal activities, including capital punishment for firearms trafficking. The impact of deterrence measures is affected, however, by many factors. Generally it is believed that the certainty of apprehension is more significant than the severity of punishment, which is why effective policing and justice systems are critically important. Moreover, most deterrence measures are based on models of rational choice; they assume that an individual makes a decision to obey or disobey a law after carefully weighing the costs and benefits of breaking the law. However, where fear of the consequences of being disarmed surpasses fear of the consequences of being apprehended, regulatory regimes may be less effective. In Central America, for example, weak governance and lack of state authority may lead individuals to arm themselves or rely on private security companies for protection. This is one of the reasons implementation issues are a critically important and security-sector reform must go hand in hand with stronger laws, particularly in countries with high levels of violence. Once again, laws are only words on paper unless the technological, operational and financial resources required are in place to support them.

ELEMENTS OF FIREARM REGULATION

Overview

Despite continued opposition by the United States, it is clear that strong domestic regulation of civilian possession and use is regarded as critical to reducing weapons misuse and potential diversion to illegal markets in most countries in the world.[10] Regulation is intended to reduce harm by reducing risk: the risk that firearms will be diverted from legal to illegal markets and the risk that firearms will be misused.

Most initiatives that have been proposed are aimed at reducing the availability of illicit firearms and aiding the enforcement of laws against illicit trafficking. In theory, the notion is that by reducing the availability of illicit firearms, it will be possible to reduce certain types of criminal activity and reduce the lethality of violent encounters. The theory also assumes that improved enforcement will both remove incentives and deter criminal behaviors by increasing the likelihood of apprehension. Just as there has been limited research on the extent of the problem of illicit trafficking, there has been little evaluation of the effects of various deterrence measures. Improved data collection and sharing would assist in benchmarking and evaluation.

Various interventions to restrict supply aim at making it more difficult, time-consuming or costly for a potentially violent individual or a suicidal individual to obtain a gun. As Cook and Ludwig emphasize, the intention of legislative controls is to reduce gun use in crime by restricting supply and thus making it more difficult, time consuming or costly for a violent individual to obtain a gun."[11] Firearm controls such as licensing and regulation are intended to raise costs and discourage casual gun ownership.[12]

Legislative interventions—licensing, training and screening processes, for example—also aim at reducing the chances that dangerous individuals or arms traffickers will gain access to firearms. Research in the United States supports the view that if controls on firearms at the state level are strengthened, the likelihood that firearms originating in that state will be used in crime is reduced. One study showed that in cities in which there was no licensing or registration, 84 percent of the guns recovered from crime scenes were from local markets, while in cities that had both licensing and registration, very few of the guns recovered actually originated from local markets.[13] There are also interventions focused on increasing the barriers between individuals and guns, particularly individuals who may be at risk for gun use, including children; safe storage requirements fall into that category.

International efforts to establish norms for domestic regulation, most recently at the 2001 UN Conference on the Illicit Trade in Small Arms, but also at meetings of the Organization of Security and Co-operation in Europe and the Organization of American States (OAS), have been blocked by some countries, most notably the United States. At the UN conference, for example, the United States forced the removal of any reference to the responsibility of nations to regulate civilian possession of firearms adequately.[14]

According to the United Nation's *International Study on Firearm Regulation*, approximately half the nations in the study reported that the administration of their database detailing civilian ownership of firearms was maintained at the national level, with nine nations reporting it at the regional level and ten at the local. In two nations, the administrative level depended on the type of firearm. Only eighteen nations reported having a computerized record of firearm owners in 1997, and only Norway reported that this information was available to the public.[15] Since that initial survey, more than half the participating nations have reported that they have amended their legislation and strengthened the regulation of civilian firearm ownership. More recent studies have shown nuanced differences in the approaches to firearm regulation and have highlighted the challenges of establishing international norms and harmonizing regional laws.[16]

The legislative approaches attempt to regulate firearms at various stages in the supply chain, from production to use—or misuse. The purpose of regulation of firearms is to keep legal guns in the hands of law-abiding gun owners for legitimate purposes. A wide range of measures are intended to reduce the potential for misuse of legal firearms as well as the diversion of firearms through illegal sale, gun theft, straw purchases and other methods to illegal markets.

Manufacturing

The defense industry, which manufactures firearms for military purposes, is often tightly linked to national defense strategy and employment. Generally, gun industries are regulated in terms of what they can manufacture, who they can sell to and reporting requirements. Some countries have substantial government investments, direct and indirect, in the defense industry and explicitly recognize its importance to the economy. The manufacture of firearms for civilian markets is generally regulated separately, again with licensing and reporting requirements. In some countries, such as South Africa, there is a recognition that the two sectors of the market are tightly linked.

Virtually all countries require licenses for the manufacture of firearms, although standards vary. The Organization for Security and Co-operation in Europe, for example, established best practices for licensing requirements and conditions, including appropriate standard specifications and compliance, appropriately qualified personnel, structural subunits, premises, equipment, testing and measuring apparatus, the protection of state secrets (where appropriate), maintenance of records and safe storage of documentation, weapons and components, protection of the production and storage of weapons and their components, quality control and a commission to monitor compliance. It also recommends the establishment of a single state authority to authorize manufacture.[17] Record keeping is critical in manufacturing for both military and civilian markets, but the extent to which this information is made public varies considerably.

While there are some controls in most countries over who is allowed to manufacture guns and there are requirements for record keeping, the standards for the products themselves in some countries, such as the United States, are much lower than for other consumer products, such as sleepwear, toys, automobiles or vitamins. Some firearms are poorly made, but protectionist policies often protect domestic manufacturers while applying rigorous standards to foreign gun makers. One study found that handguns manufactured in the United States are subject to much lower standards than are foreign-made, imported handguns.[18] Although studies have shown that built-in safety devices on firearms can have a significant effect on preventing unintentional gun deaths, the U.S. Consumer Product Safety Commission is explicitly prohibited from imposing controls on guns or munitions. Consumer safety and public health experts have argued for strengthening controls over the manufacture of firearms to facilitate law enforcement efforts, to reduce the likelihood of injury and to develop new products responsibly.[19] However, the U.S. government has moved in the opposite direction, recently taking steps to protect gun manufacturers from litigation by consumers.

Marking and Tracing

Most industrialized countries require privately owned guns to be permanently marked, with records kept of guns manufactured and sold. In the United States, for example, all firearm manufacturers must maintain records of sales to wholesalers and licensed dealers. Record keeping of secondary sales—from dealers to individuals and from one individual to another is where the loophole lies.

With the adoption of a number of international agreements, such as the 1997 OAS Inter-American Convention against the Illicit Manufacturing of and Trafficking in Firearms and the 2001 UN Firearms Protocol (ratified in 2005), many countries have moved to define the requirements for marking firearms. The requirements for marking are at manufacture, at import, at export and at destruction. Many issues surrounding marking are yet to be resolved, For example, the precise contents of the marks, the record-keeping standards and the acceptable technologies for marking. Manufacturers could be compelled to make it more difficult to remove serial numbers with new marking technologies, but costs remain an issue. For example, in the United States the Bureau of Alcohol, Tobacco, and Firearms noted that one in five guns recovered in Boston, Massachusetts, between 1991 and 1994 had the serial number removed. The state of Massachusetts responded by requiring manufacturers to sell guns that are tamper resistant.[20]

Canada requires that all civilian firearms be engraved with serial numbers, but military arms are exempt. Firearms imported without serial numbers are assigned a serial number and affixed with a sticker. Gun organizations successfully argued that forcing guns to be marked on import with more permanent solutions (such as metal stamping) would be too costly. Switzerland's law is similar but has the additional requirement that explosives must be marked as well. South Africa also makes the distinction between civilian and military firearms, requiring only civilian firearms to be engraved with a number by the Central Firearms Register. This system has not been very effective in practice, since the marking is often rendered illegible by the gun user. There is no requirement for ammunition to be marked, but cartridges are typically stamped with the manufacturer's initials.[21] Given the importance of standardized marking to law enforcement, the development of rigorous international standards is critical. The UN Firearms Protocol is now in force, but only forty countries have ratified it. Negotiations of a binding international instrument on marking and tracing as part of the UN Programme of Action on the Illicit Trade in Small Arms in All Its Aspects is proceeding but not expected to produce a rigorous standard.

Import and Export of Firearms

Most nations regulate the import and export of firearms, and many nations are changing their domestic laws to conform to the international standards outlined in the OAS Inter-American Convention against the Illicit Manufacturing of and Trafficking in Firearms and in the Firearms Protocol of the United Nations. The UN Firearms Protocol sets out procedures for import, export and transfers, including systems of government authorization and marking and tracing. These standards apply only to commercial shipments of firearms but do establish standards for documentation of imports, exports and in-transit shipments in an effort to reduce the opportunities for the illicit trade. For example, the standards require that an exporting country receive authorization from an importing country before allowing shipments of weapons to proceed and require more detailed standards for tracking the shipments, including a comprehensive record of the firearms contained in the shipment and their serial numbers. Many countries are updating their legislation to be more rigorous. For example, under South Africa's new law, firearms and ammunition may be imported or exported only if an import or export permit has been issued. The issuing of such permits is to be controlled at the South African Police Service's Central Firearm Register. An in-transit permit is required for anyone carrying a firearm or ammunition through South Africa. Both old and new acts stipulate that no permit (export, import or in-transit) will be issued for any firearm or ammunition that lacks the required identification marks. Diversions from in-transit shipments had been identified as a particular problem not just in South Africa but also in Canada and other states. The strengthening of in-transit controls is considered an important provision of the new firearms protocol. However, concerns remain about the level of control in place on brokers and the inconsistencies between the controls over commercial shipments and state-to-state transfers.

The standards set by United Nations Programme of Action on the Illicit Trade in Small Arms in All Its Aspects that deal with state-to-state transfers do not prevent countries from transferring small arms to countries likely to misuse them. Consequently, work is under way outside the United Nations to develop an arms trade treaty that will improve standards.

Regulating the Sale of Weapons

Most countries regulate the sale of weapons to civilians. Some regulate gun dealers and sellers and have significant record-keeping and reporting requirements. In Poland, for example, a gun seller is obliged to provide the police with information about every firearm sold. This includes the type of firearm, name, bore, kind, serial number and year of production. Since 1990, firearm dealers have been obligated to fire three shots from the weapon to be sold in the presence of a police official. The cartridge cases are kept in police headquarters for forensic purposes.[22] Few other jurisdictions go to these lengths, although the state of Maryland in the United States also retains ballistics records of all firearms manufactured.[23]

There are varying degrees of regulation governing resale. In Switzerland, individuals must keep a record of private sales but need not report them to the authorities. In the French Pacific territories, information on every firearm sale must be provided by gunsmiths to the police on a monthly basis. In Samoa, Niue and New Zealand, at the other end of the spectrum, long guns may be transferred to anyone with a valid licence, and no report of the transfer to the authorities is required.[24] Brazil has recently adopted a law that calls for a national referendum to decide whether civilian gun sales should be banned. A national poll published in October 2003 indicated that 74.1 percent of civilians would support such a ban.[25] While most U.S. states conduct checks on initial sales, secondary sales among individuals escape control even though they account for a substantial proportion of diversions from legal to illicit markets. Gun shows, where individuals sell firearms, are unregulated. Among those countries surveyed in the UN study, virtually all countries reported some regulation on the purchase of firearms.[26]

Defining Lawful Purposes and "Legitimate" Firearms

Countries differ in the reasons they allow civilians to have firearms. In general, countries prohibit possession of weapons in situations in which they believe the risks of illegal use outweigh the utility of lawful use, but this calculation varies considerably. The majority of nations sampled in the

1997 UN study, for example, restricted the ownership of long guns and handguns and prohibited the ownership of certain types of long guns and handguns. Indeed, only twelve of the sixty-nine participating nations had no prohibitions on either long guns or handguns.[27] Conversely, three countries—Brunei Darussalam, Luxembourg and Malaysia—reported a total prohibition on civilian gun ownership.[28] Some countries, such as Japan, China and Great Britain, severely restrict civilian possession and have very low rates of firearm ownership. Germany has a low rate of firearm possession; a legitimate requirement must be proven and a firearm license usually applies exclusively to the home of the applicant. Some countries allow possession of certain types of firearms for target shooting. Two-thirds of nations recognize the "collection" of handguns as a basis for obtaining a permit to own one. Most countries allow firearm possession for hunting or predator control on farms. In Vietnam, for example, hunting is the only reason for which an individual can be granted a firearm license.[29]

Prohibitions of Weapons

Most countries prohibit the civilian possession of firearms when the risk of ownership outweighs the utility. This determination is often shaped by history and culture. While only three of the sixty-nine countries involved in the UN survey have an outright prohibition on the civilian possession of any firearms, most countries worldwide prohibit civilian possession of fully automatic military-style rifles. (See Table 7.1.) Many also prohibit possession of semiautomatic or convertible versions of such weapons. Definitions of "military weapons" vary considerably from jurisdiction to jurisdiction.[30]

In the United States, ownership of machine guns has been tightly controlled since passage of the National Firearms Act of 1934, and their manufacture for the civilian market was halted in 1986. However, semiautomatic versions of those same guns were still being produced until the federal assault weapons ban was enacted in 1994; this ban expired in 2004. The assault weapons ban regulated domestic manufacture of semiautomatic assault weapons and large-capacity magazines. President Clinton signed the Violent Crime Control and Law Enforcement Act into law on September 13, 1994. Domestic gun manufacturers were required to stop production of semiautomatic assault weapons and ammunition clips holding more than ten rounds except for military or police use. Imports of assault weapons not already banned by administrative action under Presidents Reagan and George H. W. Bush were also halted. Assault weapons and ammunition clips holding more than ten rounds produced prior to September 13, 1994, were grandfathered in under the law and could still be possessed and sold.

The bill banned, by name, the manufacture of nineteen different weapons, including:

- Norinco, Mitchell and Poly Technologies Avtomat Kalashnikovs (all models);

Table 7.1 Overview of Weapons Prohibited in National Legislation

Issue	All		Some		None		Total Responses
	Number of Countries	Percent	Number of Countries	Percent	Number of Countries	Percent	Number of Countries
Prohibits ownership of military assault weapons	34[a]	42	39[b]	48	8	19.3	81
Prohibits ownership of handguns	16	19.2	49	59.1	18	21.7	83

[a] (including semiautomatic variants)
[b] (fully automatic versions)

Source: W. Cukier, "The Feasibility of Increased Restrictions on the Civilian Possession of Military Assault Weapons at the Global Level," Research Report, The Peacebuilding and Human Security: Development of Policy Capacity of the Voluntary Sector Project for the Canadian Peacebuilding Coordinating Committee (CPCC), 2005.

- Action Arms Israeli Military Industries UZI and Galil;
- Beretta Ar70 (SC-70);
- Colt AR-15;
- Fabrique National FN/FAL, FN/LAR and FNC;
- SWD M-10, M-11, M-11/9 and M-12;
- Steyr AUG;
- INTRATEC TEC-9, TEC-DC9 and TEC-22; and
- revolving cylinder shotguns such as (or similar to) the Street Sweeper and Striker 12.

The bill also banned "copies" or "duplicates" of any of these weapons. Several states have legislation, still in effect, banning possession of assault weapons.[31] In addition, the U.S. law prohibits manufacturers from producing firearms with more than one of the following assault weapon features:

Rifles

- Folding/telescoping stock
- Protruding pistol grip
- Bayonet mount
- Threaded muzzle or flash suppressor
- Grenade launcher

Pistols

- Magazine outside grip
- Threaded muzzle
- Barrel shroud
- Unloaded weight of fifty ounces or more
- Semiautomatic version of a fully automatic weapon

Shotguns

- Folding/telescoping stock
- Protruding pistol grip
- Detachable magazine capacity
- Fixed magazine capacity greater than five rounds

In Canada, there has been a progressive ban on military weapons. In 1977, fully automatic weapons were prohibited. In 1991, large-capacity magazines were prohibited along with semiautomatics that could be converted to fully automatic fire, and in 1995, additional semiautomatic variants of fully automatic weapons were prohibited. Under Canadian law, however, existing owners were grandfathered, meaning that current owners could keep their firearms. There were also anomalies; for example, the AR-15 is still sold to civilians as a restricted firearm (for collectors or target shooting), and the Ruger Mini-14 is sold as an unrestricted hunting rifle.[32]

Handguns. Access to handguns is frequently outlawed or severely restricted, given their concealable nature and consequent utility in crime. Six countries involved in the UN survey, aside from the three that have a ban on all types of firearms, reported a complete ban on handgun ownership.[33] Botswana, for example, presently has a total prohibition on issuing handgun licenses to individuals. Great Britain also banned civilian possession of handguns in 1997,[34] and Canada banned possession of short-barrelled and .22-caliber handguns in 1995 (with a grandfather clause for existing owners).

While fifty of the sixty-nine countries included in the UN study do allow handgun ownership for the purpose of protection of person or property, most industrialized countries strictly control civilian access to handguns and allow the carrying of handguns for personal protection only under very restrictive conditions, in an effort to reduce the risk that firearms will be misused or diverted to illegal markets.[35] In Canada, for example, reasons for owning handguns are strictly defined as (1) for lawful occupation as a police officer or security guard; (2) for target shooting, supported with evidence of membership in a gun club; (3) as part of a bona fide collection and (4) on rare (about fifty in the country) occasions where an individual can (a) prove his or her life is in danger and (b) prove that the police cannot protect him or her.[36]

The United States is the notable exception, where approximately 35 percent[37] of households own handguns and almost 40 percent of gun owners report having them for protection. In the United States, most firearm regulation is at the state level and is very diverse. Despite its present international stance on the matter, the United States does not have a unified national policy. Hawaii, New York, Massachusetts and the District of Columbia, for example, have laws comparable to those in most European countries.[38] However, other states have extremely permissive laws. Permits to carry concealed handguns are easily obtained in many states. Shall-issue concealed-weapon carry laws (shall-issue laws) require the issuing of a concealed-weapon carry permit to all applicants not disqualified by specified criteria. Shall-issue laws are usually implemented in place of may-issue laws, in which the issuing of a concealed-weapon carry permit is discretionary (based on criteria such as the perceived need or moral character of the applicant). A third alternative, total prohibition of the carrying of concealed weapons, was in effect in six states in 2001.[39]

Many countries in Central America also have permissive laws regarding the carrying of concealed handguns, although typically these weapons are licensed and registered. For example, in El Salvador, a country with 170,000 legally registered firearms, authorities have issued 143,125 licenses to carry a concealed weapon. This ratio of registered firearms to concealed-weapon carry permits is typical in Central America.[40] Obtaining permission to carry firearms is also relatively easy in Austria, where 8.1 percent of households have handguns and 26 percent of firearm owners have their guns for protection.[41]

In January 2002, the Somali Transitional National Government issued a proclamation prohibiting Mogadishu residents from carrying weapons in the streets of the capital. The police have been given a mandate to confiscate weapons, including assault rifles. Two thousand police have been deployed in Mogadishu to tackle rampant banditry. The government has cautioned rival warlords not to contest the ban, warning them to refrain from actions that might lead to what they called the "creation of a sensitive military situation." Somali women's organizations and female parliamentarians have been raising funds to support this initiative, to which the government has allocated $5,000.[42]

Following the shooting incident at Monash University in Melbourne, on October 21, 2002, the federal and state governments of Australia agreed on further measures to limit the types of handguns that may be owned and used by sporting shooters. Semiautomatic handguns with a barrel length of less than 120 millimeters, and revolvers and single-shot handguns with a barrel length of less than 100 millimeters are now prohibited.[43]

According to a 1998 national study on crime and violence in El Salvador, 73 percent of firearm owners surveyed stated that they held weapons for the purpose of self-protection, while only 13.5 percent held them for work and 9 percent for sport.[44] Conversely, in order to obtain a permit on the basis of self-protection in Myanmar and Singapore, proof must be provided by the individual that there are credible reasons to fear that his or her security is at risk.[45] Among Pacific nations, only Papua New Guinea and the French territories allow ownership of firearms for the expressed reason of self-defence, with most nations limiting lawful possession to those licensing firearms for the purposes of hunting, farming and fishing.[46] Similarly, in Tanzania a firearm license may be obtained from the police for the purposes of security, hunting and protection of crops from wild pigs and monkeys.[47] In South Africa, since the adoption of the Firearms Control Bill in 2000, an individual seeking to obtain a firearm license for the purpose of self-defence must demonstrate that he or she "cannot reasonably satisfy that need by means other than the possession of a firearm."[48]

Rifles and Shotguns. Many countries allow access to rifles and shotguns for hunting and pest control (see Table 7.2), although some prohibit possession of specific types. For example, in 1997, Australia banned possession of semiautomatic rifles. Furthermore, Great Britain banned the use of

Table 7.2 Legal Purposes for Owning Firearms

| Issue | Yes | | No | | Total Responses |
	Number	Percentage	Number	Percentage	Number
Private security	59	76.6	18	23.4	77
Protection of person or property	63	81.8	14	18.2	77
Collection	59	78.7	16	21.3	75
Target shooting	74	97.4	2	2.6	76
Hunting of game for sport or food	71	93.4	5	6.58	76

Source: Wendy Cukier, David Lochhead, J. Susla, and A. Kooistra, "Emerging Global Norms in the Regulation of Civilian Possession of Small Arms," updated (Toronto: SAFER-Net, July 2005).

pump-action shotguns over .22-caliber as well as short-barreled shotguns.[49] Lesotho's Internal Security Arms and Ammunition Act requires firearm owners to be licensed and registration certificates to be issued by local police. Rifles were banned in 1999.[50]

REGULATING POSSESSION: SCREENING AND LICENSING

Legally held firearms are frequently misused, particularly in suicides and domestic violence. In order to prevent this, and for purposes of tracking legal possession, most countries screen and license firearm owners. (See Table 7.3.) Requiring a firearm license increases the effective cost of possession, making the purchase of a gun different from the purchase of other consumer items. This discourages casual ownership, which, given the link between accessibility and misuse, also reduces risk. Three quarters of countries surveyed require a license for all firearms.

However, there are significant differences. Most countries impose age restrictions and check criminal records. Some require formal safety training. Certain categories of firearms may be restricted to those with a proven need for having them. Nations may also require the provision of references, self-identification, training certification, background checks and the payment of fees as part of the purchasing process. Of these requirements, self-identification and background checks are reportedly the most common, fol-

Table 7.3 Firearm Purchasing Process

Requirement	Yes Number	Yes Percentage	No Number	No Percentage	Total Responses Number
Provides information on proposed storage	32	71.1	13	28.9	45
Varies process with type/class of weapon	41	75.9	13	24.1	54
Requires a CV	11	30.6	25	69.4	36
Requires a photograph	27	57.4	20	42.6	47
Requires acquisition certificate/ permit to acquire	37	77.1	11	22.9	48
Requests genuine reason/aim of use	43	87.8	6	12.2	49
Performs background check	55	91.7	5	8.3	60
Requires payment of a fee	50	89.3	6	10.7	56
Requires training certification	32	66.7	16	33.3	48
Requires references	14	37.8	23	62.2	37
Requires self-identification	45	91.8	4	8.1	49

Source: Wendy Cukier, David Lochhead, J. Susla, and A. Kooistra, "Emerging Global Norms in the Regulation of Civilian Possession of Small Arms," updated (Toronto: SAFER-Net, July 2003).

lowed by payment of fees. Nations rarely identify the provision of references as part of their domestic purchasing process.

A number of countries have specific mechanisms in place, such as spousal notification, to limit the risks of firearm use in domestic violence. The vast majority of nations surveyed restrict or prohibit ownership where the applicant has a history of domestic violence; however, the rigor of screening varies.[51] Some rely on information about convictions for domestic violence. For example, in Australia, a person who is subject to a restraining order

Table 7.4 Regulation of Firearm Possession

Issue	Yes Number	Yes Percentage	No Number	No Percentage	Total Responses Number
Domestic violence	53	73.6	19	26.4	72
Mental illness	74	96.1	3	3.9	77
Criminal record	76	98.7	1	1.3	77
Citizenship	36	47.4	40	52.3	76
Regulates carrying firearms	63	79.7	16	20.3	79
Regulates transport of firearms	91	87.5	13	12/5	104
Regulates storage of firearms	57	72.2	22	27.8	79

Source: Wendy Cukier, David Lochhead, J. Susla, and A. Kooistra, "Emerging Global Norms in the Regulation of Civilian Possession of Small Arms," updated (Toronto: SAFER-Net, July 2003).

or who has been charged with or convicted of domestic violence faces a five-year prohibition on obtaining a firearm license. Australia and New Zealand require a spousal reference in order to obtain a license.[52] Other nations, such as Canada, require that current and former spouses (within the last two years) be notified of a license application.[53]

Virtually all nations place prohibitions or restrictions on the ownership of firearms by persons with a mental illness. However, as medical records are confidential, the mechanisms for identifying a history of mental illness vary considerably. In Pacific nations, a history of mental illness will in some cases disqualify an individual from firearm ownership, while in others it will be merely "taken into consideration."[54] In Canada, applicants must complete a detailed questionnaire and have references sign who will certify that they know of no good reason why the applicant should not have access to a firearm. In developed countries, where the risk of suicide outweighs the risk of other forms of violence, screening for potential suicide is often considered key. In addition, risk factors for suicide are often similar to the risk factors for homicide and may include precipitants such as job loss or marital breakdown, as well a history of mental illness or depression. Austria, for example, requires a psychological test for handgun owners, although the rigor of this test has been questioned.

In some cases, while there may not be statutes requiring them, police may still carry out background checks. The majority of nations also indicated restrictions for other reasons, including drug or alcohol addiction. While few countries restrict or prohibit ownership on the basis of citizenship, all restrict ownership on the basis of age, although the age at which individuals can acquire firearms varies.[55] (See Table 7.4.)

North America

In the United States, there are regulations at the federal and state levels to restrict the acquisition and use of firearms by individuals on the basis of their personal history. Reasons for restriction can include prior felony conviction, conviction of misdemeanor, intimate partner violence, drug abuse, adjudication as "mentally defective" and other characteristics (e.g., specified young age). The Brady Law established national restrictions on acquisition of firearms and ammunition from federal firearms licensees. The interim Brady Law (1994–1998) mandated a five-day waiting period to allow for background checks. The permanent Brady Law, enacted in 1998, eliminated the required waiting period. It normally allows three days for a background check, after which, if no evidence of a prohibited characteristic is found, the purchase may proceed. Certain states have established additional restrictions, and some require background checks of all firearm transactions, not only those conducted by federal firearms licensees. The permanent Brady Law depends on the National Instant Criminal Background Check System. However, this system lacks much of the required background information, particularly on certain restriction categories. Efforts to improve the availability of background information have been supported by the National Criminal History Improvement Program. Approximately 689,000 applications to acquire a firearm (2.3 percent of 30 million applications) were denied under the Brady Law from its first implementation in 1994 through 2000; the majority of denials were based on the applicant's criminal history.[56]

In October 2001, then-governor Gray Davis signed into law two bills requiring licenses for all new handgun purchasers in the state of California. The measures, AB 35 and SB 52, came into effect in January 2003. The signing of the bills makes California the thirteenth state to enact handgun licensing, and the sixth state to establish a comprehensive system of both handgun licensing and registration. Davis also signed SB 950, a bill that authorizes the California Department of Justice to run the conviction records of felons against the state's existing gun records of sale database.[57]

Waiting periods for firearm acquisition require a specified delay between application for and acquisition of a firearm. Waiting periods have been established by the federal government and by states to allow time to check the applicant's background or to provide a cooling-off period for persons at risk of committing suicide or impulsive acts against others. In Canada the waiting period is twenty-eight days; in the United States it is five days, although this is not applicable to all states.

South America

Most Latin American countries have relatively strict licensing requirements. For example, in order to obtain a licence in Argentina, the following must be shown to the National Firearms Registry: proof of identity, address, age of majority (twenty-one years for military firearms in civilian use, eighteen years for civilian firearms), absence of criminal record, good physical and mental health and the ability to handle firearms. An additional requirement is evidence of an honest way of life. While good mental health and aptitude in handling firearms are both conditions for licensing, submission of documents certifying this is required, in practice, only in cases in which the legitimate user license is being sought for a military weapon for conditional civilian use, or when an existing legitimate user applies for a permit to carry (right to use).[58]

Europe

European counties also have relatively stringent screening processes before allowing access to firearms. In France, applicants must pass a medical and psychological check. Owners must be members of a gun club (training may be required). Firearms in classes 5 to 7 require a valid hunting permit and a valid hunting license. Firearms in classes 1 to 4 (military/security weapons) may be used or granted to be used only in specific conditions approved by the government. Minors (under sixteen years old) must be authorized by their parents.[59] Germany requires applicants to be residents of the country for at least three years. Persons under the age of eighteen years are prohibited from possessing firearms, and a criminal record deems an applicant unfit to possess a firearm. To be entitled to carry a firearm permanently for personal security, the applicant has to prove that he or she is genuinely threatened and that carrying a firearm would improve his or her security. Permission for a license to carry a firearm for personal security is granted for a maximum period of three years and can be renewed only twice.[60]

In Austria, no one under the age of eighteen is allowed to possess firearms. Handguns are allowed only to those above the age of twenty-one. Furthermore, no one convicted of a "serious crime" can be given a license to own firearms, although discretion is left to the licensing authority. No one with mental disability or defect may possess firearms.[61] In Greece, according to the existing legislation, the prerequisites for firearm ownership licences are the same for any citizen staying legally in Greece, irrespective of citizenship: No firearm licence is issued to persons under the age of eighteen; firearm ownership and possession are not granted to persons who have been convicted of criminal offences; no firearm licence is issued to psychopathic persons or to persons who have been under treatment for mental disease and no firearm licence is issued to persons who have evidently shown violent behavior.[62]

Africa

South Africa has long had licensing and registration but has recently strengthened the screening requirements: According to South Africa's 2000 Firearms Control Bill, a person is ineligible to possess firearms if the person:

- Has been the subject of a restraining order in terms of the Domestic Violence Act, 1988;
- Has expressed the intention to kill or injure his- or herself or others;
- Has demonstrated an inclination to violence due to a mental condition;
- Is dependent on any substances having intoxicating effects; or
- Has provided information required under the Bill that is false.

In general, a court may declare a person unfit to possess a firearm if such person has been convicted of any offence involving firearms in transgression of the bill for which he or she had been sentenced to a period of imprisonment without the option of a fine, or any offence involving violence, sexual assault, dishonesty, abuse of alcohol or drugs or dealing in drugs.[63] Applicants for licenses in South Africa are also required to provide fingerprints.

Many countries include, as part of their licensing provisions, restrictions on the number of weapons individuals may possess. South Africa has recently passed new domestic legislation strengthening licensing requirements, reducing the number of firearms an individual may possess and closing loopholes identified in the existing legislation.[64] Namibia's domestic firearm policy allows licenses to be issued for up to four firearms, all of which must be registered; furthermore, owners must be fingerprinted and a photograph issued with the license.[65] Similarly, Malawi's Firearms Act allows annual firearm licenses to be issued.[66] Mozambique's domestic firearm legislation was created with the Regulamento de Armas e Municoes of 1973 and also requires that all firearm owners be licensed. Each license must be individually confirmed by the minister of the interior and accompanied by letters explaining the need for the firearm. Applicants are fingerprinted and ownership is restricted to three hunting rifles and one handgun per person. It is estimated that there are only about 3,000 legal firearm owners in the country.[67] Swaziland's Arms and Ammunition Act No. 24 of 1964 requires that licenses to possess firearms and purchase ammunition be renewed annually.[68] Zambia's Firearms Act of 1969 requires both licensing and registration and restricts ownership to individuals of twenty-one years and older.[69]

In the North African countries of Morocco, Algeria and Egypt, standards for the regulation of firearms are comparable to what is in place in most

European nations. There are strict provisions for licensing, registration and storage.[70]

South Asia

Many countries in South Asia were formerly part of the Commonwealth; their regulatory regimes governing firearms are similar to those in Great Britain. For example, in Bangladesh, all firearm owners must have a licence (renewable every year) to possess or acquire a firearm. Standard safety verifications are supposed to be performed to ensure that the individual does not pose a risk to public safety. If someone with a license becomes violent or commits a crime, he or she becomes ineligible to own firearms, and the deputy commissioner or the authorities in the Ministry of Home Affairs can revoke the licence. A judicial court may also revoke a license if the licensee is found to be a threat to public safety.[71] The government of Bangladesh has formed 102 committees to investigate whether licensing and arms collection are accomplished in compliance with the law.[72]

Licensing provisions not only establish standards for civilian possession but also allow police to take preventive action where risks become apparent. For example, in Canada, eligibility for firearm ownership is continuously monitored, and if a firearm owner is the subject of a complaint or a charge, his or her license may be reviewed and potentially revoked.

REGULATING THE SALE AND POSSESSION OF AMMUNITION

Firearms without ammunition are not useful and do not pose a risk to the public, and while ammunition is not terribly difficult to make, most countries regulate the sale of ammunition and many require that it be securely stored. Many countries define the conditions under which ammunition may be held, often making its purchase conditional on possession of the appropriate license. This is true, for example, in countries such as Canada, Great Britain, Australia, South Africa, Japan, France and New Zealand. Russia and India, on the other hand, require proof of ammunition storage standards.[73] Others, like the United States, leave retail trade in ammunition essentially unregulated. The majority of nations, however, do regulate the unloaded storage of ammunition. Those that do not are predominantly developing countries, with the notable exceptions of the United States, Germany and Finland.[74] Some nations, such as South Africa, limit the amount and type of ammunition that an individual may purchase or possess. Approximately half of Southeast Asian countries, for example, limit the amount of ammunition that an individual may possess, while Thailand restricts the purchase of ammunition to that used by the specific weapon licensed to the purchaser. The Philippines requires a separate license to purchase ammunition and limits the amount of ammunition that an individual can purchase based on the caliber of the ammunition. For example, an individual may possess only 100 rounds of high-powered ammunition.[75] Similarly, among Pacific Nations, only New Zealand, the Cook Islands and the state of Queensland in Australia allow an individual to purchase ammunition that is of a caliber different from that of the weapon licensed to the individual.[76]

RECORD KEEPING AND REGISTRATION OF FIREARMS

Record keeping and registration of firearms refer to keeping track of specific firearms. The registration of firearms and maintenance of records is principally aimed at preventing the diversion of legal guns to illegal markets and at facilitating law enforcement and tracing. In addition, the supreme court of Canada maintains that registration of firearms is essential to support the enforcement of the firearm licensing provisions. If firearms are not registered, it is difficult to prevent licensed firearm owners from selling firearms to unlicensed owners. If the firearms are registered, however, and can be traced to their source, diversion will be deterred and it will be possible to enforce the law prohibiting sales to unlicensed owners. It has also been suggested that the registration of firearms is essential to the enforcement of prohibition orders: It is necessary to know what guns an individual owns if they are to be confiscated because of infractions of the law.

At the same time, the registration of firearms arguably is one of the most contentious elements of firearm regulation, particularly in the United States, where the gun lobby paints registration as the first step toward confiscation. Hunting organizations, which may support other regulations such as licensing and safe storage, remain adamantly opposed to registration. On the other hand, law enforcement agencies worldwide have maintained that the registration of firearms is critical to combating the illegal gun trade, as it allows firearms to be traced to their source.[77]

Most industrialized countries register all guns. Some register only handguns and have looser controls over rifles and shotguns. Brazil, Australia and Japan, for example, require the registration of all weapons, while India registers all firearms at their point of manufacture or importation. Germany too requires the registry of all licensed firearms, while Austria requires the registration only of handguns; rifles and shotguns are largely unregistered.[78]

The United States does not have a federal registry, and state laws on registration vary widely. Certain states require a full central registry while others depend on a dealer-based registry system. Only Massachusetts and Hawaii demand registry of all firearms. California, Connecticut, Maryland, New Jersey, New York, North Carolina, South Carolina, Minnesota, Michigan, Missouri, Oregon and New Hampshire require, at least, the partial registry of handguns. Connecticut requires informal registration for rifles and shotguns.[79]

Since implementing its new law, Canada has registered over 7 million firearms.[80] France[81] and New Zealand[82] require the registration of all firearms except sporting rifles. Mexico requires that all firearm owners be licensed and all firearms registered.[83]

Only four of the ten members of the Association of Southeast Asean Nations (ASEAN) (Indonesia, Malaysia, Singapore and Thailand) require a unique distinguishing mark to identify each firearm as a part of the licensing process.[84] Thailand surpasses the marking requirements of industrialized nations by requiring that the firearm itself be marked to indicate the province of registration and a registration number.[85] Among Pacific nations, only New Zealand does not practice the registration of all types of firearms, requiring only handguns, military-style semiautomatics and machine guns in civilian possession to be registered. Only five Pacific nations have computerized registries. Differences in standards in terms of the specific type of information to be captured by firearm registries, as well as a lack of resources and training for armourers and police, make the accuracy and utility of registries uneven in this region. In Tanzania, the lack of a computer network is the main hindrance to maintaining an up-to-date firearms registry.[86]

The Ugandan government announced in June 2002 that it would inventory and register all arms in the hands of the military, police and intelligence services. When completed, the registration will be computerized.[87] Firearms held by local government administration and private security organizations will also be registered.[88] In Bangladesh, firearm registration is carried out by the Ministry of Home Affairs, which issues permission in favor of an applicant after proper verification. Based on this permission, the deputy commissioner issues the license. This license allows the holder to purchase the gun that is categorized in the license. Once the gun is purchased, it must then be registered and the identification number must be noted on the license. Every license holder is compelled to buy the gun from an arms dealer who is authorized by the government.[89]

SAFE STORAGE

Weapons stolen from armories, from dealers, from police and from civilians make up a substantial portion of the illegal market. Every year, approximately 7 million newly manufactured guns enter civilian hands and, in the United States alone, 500,000 are stolen, by definition entering illegal markets, as noted in Chapter 5. Safe-storage requirements are designed to reduce the risk that firearms will be acquired illegally or used impulsively. Perhaps their most important function is keeping loaded firearms away from children in the home. Safe-storage measures include the disablement of firearms, their separation from ammunition, and the use of locked containers and trigger locks. In most industrialized countries, firearms must be stored unloaded in a secure container, separate from ammunition.

Notable exceptions include Liechtenstein, Finland and the United States. While the United States does not have national regulations establishing safe-storage requirements, there are state-level controls. Child access prevention (CAP) laws are designed to limit children's access to and use of firearms in homes. The laws require firearm owners to store their firearms locked, unloaded or both, and make the firearm owners liable when children use a household firearm to threaten or harm themselves or others. In three states with CAP laws (Florida, Connecticut, California), this crime is a felony; in several others it is a misdemeanor. An American study analyzing the safe storage of firearms revealed that when guns are kept unlocked and loaded, the likelihood of them being used in suicide or causing unintentional injury increases greatly. Compared to households without firearms, the risk of suicide was found to increase ninefold in homes where weapons were stored loaded. The risk of suicide increased only threefold where firearms were locked or otherwise kept inoperable.[90]

All other nations that do not have regulations relating to the storage of firearms are in the developing world.[91] Seven of the ten ASEAN members have laws regulating the safe storage of arms and ammunition, while in that region, only Cambodia prohibits the storage of arms and ammunition by civilians.[92] In Indonesia, all weapons licensed for shooting and hunting must be stored at, and checked out of, a shooting club.[93]

In the Czech Republic, a person who keeps more than five weapons or more than 2,500 pieces of ammunition must take measures to secure the buildings or rooms where the weapons and ammunition are kept. Furthermore, the weapons "must be in such a condition precluding their immediate use," meaning that the "weapon is not loaded with cartridges in a magazine, a cartridge clip, the cartridge receptacle of the barrel or in a revolver cylinder, and the magazines are empty."[94] Estonia restricts the number of firearms and amount of ammunition a civilian may possess and has strict storage requirements:

> Firearm(s) should be kept unloaded [when] not in use. A private person is permitted to keep in his/her apartment not more than eight firearms and their ammunition, in [a] steel safe which [has] two strong locks and which is fixed to [the] wall or floor. Guns for hunting can also be kept using locked steel hook[s], if the room is equipped with [a] technical alarm system. A single firearm and its ammunition can be kept ignoring these requirements, but it should be kept hidden from strangers. More than eight firearms and their ammunition should be kept in special storage, which is situated outside the flat or dwelling house of [the] firearm owner.[95]

In Greece, "individuals possessing firearms are obliged to keep them in a safety closet, and those possessing more than three firearms are obliged to have an alarm system."[96] Japanese laws relating to storage state, "Licensed firearms may be transported or carried only while in use for the purposes for which they were licensed or other justifiable reasons. Licensed shotguns and hunting-rifles must be stored in a locked, metal strong safe by the owner. Licensed handguns must be entrusted to a law enforcement agency for safe storage."[97] As with other regulatory measures, however, mechanisms for enforcing safe storage are essential. The ability to trace weapons back to their owners certainly reinforces accountability, as do training and penalties for noncompliance.

WEAPONS COLLECTION AND DESTRUCTION

Measures have also been taken to reduce demand for firearms by publicizing the risks they pose, particularly in the home, and by offering amnesties and buybacks to encourage people to get rid of guns they do not want or need. These programs have been carried out, with and without compensation, in postconflict situations, in areas with high levels of illicit ownership or crime or both and as a result of changes in legislation. Weapons-collection programs have been carried out in Europe, North America, Africa, Latin America, Australia and Asia.

Some countries, notably Great Britain and Australia, have outlawed certain types of weapons and accompanied the new restrictions with buyback programs designed to remove banned weapons from circulation and have removed substantial numbers of firearms from circulation. In Australia's buyback program alone, 643,764 weapons that new legislation had recently prohibited were collected and destroyed.[98] Other countries, such as Canada, Brazil and South Africa, have used voluntary programs to encourage firearm owners to reassess the need for firearms in their homes. In several countries, educational programs have also focused on increasing awareness of safe practices and compliance with them.

Thailand, for example, has offered five amnesties since 1948, guaranteeing immunity from prosecution for individuals who turn in unlicensed firearms.[99] According to Alpers and Twyford, in their study of firearms in the Pacific, Fiji, Kiribati, the Solomon Islands, Tonga and Tuvalu have provisions for temporary weapons-surrender programs whereby firearms would be returned to their owners after the prohibition is revoked. In Palau and the Marshall Islands, "compulsory surrender orders" have been used to cancel all existing licenses.[100] The impact of these programs has been uneven, but even where the raw number of guns recovered is low, the effect on individual households appears to be considerable.

It has been suggested that in postconflict situations, disarmament must be linked to a lasting political solution, community and civil society involvement, destruction of weapons to instill public confidence and security-sector reform.[101] In Cambodia, the government has established the

Commission on the Control and Confiscation of Weapons to operational-ize a mobile arms collection and confiscation program.[102] Private-sector-run Goods for Guns programs in El Salvador, which were implemented between 1996 and 2000, while collecting more than 10,000 weapons, have not sig-nificantly reduced the overall quantity of weapons circulating in the area.[103]

In Costa Rica, in January 2000, a one-year amnesty was instituted, dur-ing which time citizens in possession of nonregistered legal weapons could have them registered without penalty, and citizens in possession of illegal weapons could surrender them without penalty.[104] In the northern states of Chihuahua and Nuevo Leon, home to some of Mexico's most notorious drug traffickers, a guns-for-food program in which people can hand over illegal arms in exchange for food vouchers has been launched. They also receive amnesty from prosecution for handing over illegal arms. The guns-for-food-vouchers programs were authorized by the Defense Ministry and are financed by local chambers of commerce.[105] In New Zealand, the re-sults of regular arms amnesties undertaken by the New Zealand police tend to support concerns regarding "gray" and illegal weapons. In 1993 alone, amnesties yielded over 3,000 illegal weapons, including 159 semiautomatic assault rifles.[106]

DETERRENCE MEASURES AND LAW ENFORCEMENT

The criminology literature tends to downplay the value of deterrence, or tertiary prevention, compared to primary prevention (focusing on root causes) or secondary crime prevention (target-hardening efforts and reduc-ing access to firearms). Deterrence is defined as "influencing by fear." Po-tential offenders are thought to refrain from criminal acts due to fear of apprehension, and the likelihood of deterrence increases with the risk of punishment, which in turn depends on strong enforcement capacity along the axes of severity, certainty and celerity. Specific deterrence initiatives focus on efforts to change the behavior of individuals, whereas general de-terrence initiatives involve a broader educative effect. Both types of deter-rence assume a rational offender and assume that crime is not rational. However, in many contexts, for example, in the case of drugs or prostitu-tion and in some instances of gun possession, the effectiveness of deterrence measures also depends on the individual's assessment of risk versus reward. Some criminal behavior seems largely unaffected by deterrence measures because of the demand factors or the "drivers" to illegal behavior.[107] For example, the famed U.S. "war on drugs" has been judged to be largely in-effective because of the strength of demand factors.[108]

Certainly, interventions aimed at reducing demand factors, as well as re-ducing opportunities or access to facilitators, are generally regarded as more effective than deterrence measures. Nevertheless, penalties for firearm offences—such as the use of a firearm in a crime, illegal possession or illicit trafficking of firearms—have recently been increased in many countries. Enforcement efforts have focused on problem areas in the illegal trade, such as the small number of firearm dealers who account for the largest percentage of illegal firearm transactions. Increased enforcement may act to deter some behavior by increasing the potential cost of illegal firearm possession or trafficking.[109] Measures such as licensing and registration also assist enforcement efforts, specifically in criminal investigations.

Penalties for illegal possession, theft and trafficking in firearms range dramatically within regions and even within countries. Some examples include:

- *Australia.* Owners of prohibited firearms had twelve months from the initiation of the new law to surrender them for compensation. After the close of the government-sponsored buyback, semiautomatic assault weapons and pump-action shotguns became banned firearms. Depending on the gun and the individual, violations are punishable by fines of up to $12,000 and two years in jail.[110]

- *Brazil.* A 1997 law put in place a registration system that established the conditions to register or carry firearms. The law also criminalized the possession of nonregistered firearms. Penalties may be up to a two-year jail sentence.

- *Canada.* Canada has a mandatory one-year sentence for possession of a stolen weapon.[111]

- *Estonia.* Penalties in Estonia for illegal possession, use, transport or dealing of firearms, ammunition or explosives will be punished with fine or imprisonment from one to five years. An ongoing national amnesty for illegal weapons allows that "a person who deliberately gives up illegally kept firearm, ammunition or explosives, will be discharged from criminal responsibility."[112]

- *Greece.* Penalties in Greece for smuggling, illegal dealing or both range from one month to twenty years' imprisonment, depending on the seriousness of the offence.[113]

- *New Zealand.* The illegal importation of a firearm is punishable by up to one year's imprisonment or a $2,000 fine. Illegally imported firearms may be seized. Illegal possession (without license or proper registration certificate) is punishable by up to three years' imprisonment or a $4,000 fine, as is illegal supply of weaponry. Those possessing military-style assault weapons without the requisite special endorsements on their firearm license are subject to a fine of $4,000, three years' imprisonment, and the potential forfeiture of the firearm.[114]

- *Russia.* Penalties in Russia for the illegal acquisition, transfer, sale, storage, manufacture, transportation or carrying of firearms, ammunition, explosives and explosive devices include the deprivation of liberty for a term from two to eight years. Embezzlement or extortion of firearms, ammunition, explosives and explosive devices results in the deprivation of liberty for a term of three to fifteen years.[115]

- *South Africa.* The 2000 Firearms Control Bill provides for very severe penalties for contravention of the act. It includes a system of punitive fines for administrative transgressions as well as maximum sentences for criminal offences following due legal process in court. Sentences range from one to twenty-five years, depending on the severity of the offence.

Inconsistencies between nations and even within nations abound, and these inconsistencies result in firearms tending to move from unregulated areas to regulated areas. This may also lead to "jurisdiction shopping." For example, the penalty for unlawful possession of a firearm in Palau is no less than fifteen years in prison and a fine of up to $5,000, while in New Caledonia, one would be subject to only up to ten days in jail and a fine of approximately $40. Similarly minimal penalties exist in Nauru ($40 and no jail sentence), the Cook Islands ($100 and no jail sentence) and Niue ($400 and up to three months in jail). However, typical penalties for this crime in the Pacific region range from six months to five years.[116]

Substantial differences in penalties for the same crime can also exist within a given state. For example, in the Australian state of New South Wales, penalties for unlawful firearm possession vary between five and fourteen years of imprisonment, depending on the type of firearm. In the state of Queensland, however, the same crime is punishable by six months' to two years' imprisonment. As well, many countries in the Pacific do not have defined penalties for one or more of a number of offences, including unlicensed firearm dealing, illegal manufacture, illegal import and illegal export.[117] In December 2002, the Australian government passed new legislation, raising the penalties for certain types of firearm infractions. Under the new legislation, anyone caught crossing state boundaries with an illegal firearm could be sentenced to ten years in prison and fined up to $250,000.[118]

In the Philippines, stiff new penalties for firearm violations were proposed in February 2003 to support the new limitations of firearm ownership. Senate Bill 2480 outlines punishment of six to ten years of imprisonment and penalties of between P20 and P100,000 for the carrying of firearms outside a residence. Additional penalties could be applied to members of the armed forces, public officials and police, including disqualification from holding public office, dishonorable discharge and forfeiture of all retirement privileges and benefits.[119]

Some recent examples of targeted enforcement efforts include the following:

- *China.* The Chinese police have been pursuing a weapons-collection campaign since 1996, claiming to have confiscated a total of 3.8 million firearms by mid-2002. These seizures included approximately 30,000 military firearms. According to the Chinese press, the rate of firearm crime has dropped substantially.[120]

- *Bangladesh.* An illegal arms–collection program carried out in 2002–2003 as part of Bangladesh's controversial crackdown on criminals, Operation Clean Heart, has netted 4,700 firearms. Of these, 55 were modern automatic weapons. As many as 34,000 weapons became illegal in November 2002 when their owners failed to renew their licenses.[121]

- *Sri Lanka.* A two-week-long weapons-collection amnesty program failed when Sri Lankan police managed to collect only a few unusable shotguns. According to police estimates, there are 20,000 illegal weapons held in Sri Lanka in spite of the fact that the penalty for illegal possession is seven years in prison. The police are setting up a special squad to arrest those in possession of illegal weapons. The government claims that firearms are being illegally held by gangsters and politicians who have not renewed their licenses.[122]

- *United Kingdom.* A gun amnesty program in the United Kingdom that ran until the end of April 2003 aimed to improve public safety by removing as many firearms as possible, including replica guns and air guns. This amnesty came ahead of the implementation of tougher new gun laws, which would impose a minimum sentence of five years of imprisonment for the illegal possession or use of a prohibited firearm.

FIREARM REGULATION AND "RIGHTS"

Controlling the international trafficking in firearms is not the only aim of domestic legislative schemes. No matter what the context, the misuse of firearms results in death, injury and psychological harm to human beings. What is common, either explicitly or implicitly, to legislative approaches to firearm control in various nations is a focus on protecting citizens' core human rights. This focus encompasses both constitutional rights belonging to the citizens of those nations and internationally recognized rights that accrue to the citizens of all countries that have become signatories to international covenants, treaties and agreements that recognize such rights. Rights arguments have certainly been prominent in the ongoing debate over firearm controls in Canada and in other jurisdictions. However, rather than any notion of a collective right to safety, the rights that tend to be emphasized are the purported rights of individual citizens to keep and bear arms free from state intervention. The principal source of this argument is, of course, the powerful gun lobby in the United States. On a visit to Canada in 2000, the former president of the National Rifle Association, actor Charlton Heston, referred to the right to bear arms as "God-given," telling a group of supporters, "You may not be absolutely free by owning a firearm . . . but I guarantee that you will never be free when you can't."[123] This conception of rights and freedom is generally propounded by those opposing restrictions on firearm ownership and use.

There is no civilian right to bear arms under any international human rights instrument. In terms of domestic rights guarantees, the United States appears to be the only jurisdiction in which such a right may have any semblance of a legal or constitutional basis. Even in that country, the existence of such a right is contested. A literal reading of the Second Amendment to the U.S. Constitution reveals that the provision relates to the possession of arms by the military, not individuals: "A well regulated Militia, being necessary to the security of a free State, the right of the people to keep and bear Arms, shall not be infringed."[124] In addition to this, U.S. courts have repeatedly and unanimously held that the U.S. Constitution does not guarantee individuals the right to possess or carry guns; the Second Amendment protects only the right of the states to maintain organized military forces.[125] It does not impede local, state or national legislatures from enacting or enforcing gun control laws.[126]

While controversy may remain over the interpretation of the U.S. Second Amendment, the notion that a right to bear arms exists has been dismissed in many other jurisdictions. Many other jurisdictions, including South Africa, the United Kingdom, New Zealand, Canada and the Philippines have explicitly rejected the notion that such a right exists, arguing that the right to life, liberty and security of the person under Article 3 of the Universal Declaration of Human Rights supports efforts to reduce access to arms. The issue of gun control was comprehensively revisited in the United Kingdom in the public inquiry following the Dunblane massacre. In the inquiry report, Lord Cullen declared that "the right to bear arms is not a live issue in the United Kingdom."[127] The New Zealand High Court has declared that "it should be emphasized, that there is no general right to bear arms in this country such as is safeguarded—if that is the appropriate term for it—under the United States Constitution."[128] In Canada, the Supreme Court, in a case dealing with legislative controls on automatic weapons, has stated that Canadians "do not have a constitutional right to bear arms. Indeed, most Canadians prefer the peace of mind and sense of security derived from the knowledge that the possession of automatic weapons is prohibited."[129]

Internationally, there is little legal basis for individuals to own or use firearms as a right. While recognizing this, it is important to consider the rights of those who are adversely affected by the use and presence of firearms. As firearms cause death, injury and fear to human beings, their unregulated presence in society affects the most fundamental of human rights. All human beings have the right to life, liberty and security of per-

Table 7.5 Firearm Legislation in High Income Countries

Country	Licensing of Owners?	Registration of All Firearms?	Other
Japan	Yes	Yes	Prohibits handguns with few exceptions.
Singapore	Yes	Yes	Most handguns and rifles prohibited.
Netherlands	Yes	Yes	
England/Wales	Yes	Yes	Prohibits handguns.
Scotland	Yes	Yes	Identical legislation to England and Wales though made separately.
Ireland	Yes	Yes	Severely restricts handguns.
Denmark	Yes	Partial	Records maintained for long guns only.
Northern Ireland	Yes	Yes	United Kingdom legislation applies except for right to possess for self defense.
Germany	Yes	Yes	Restrictive laws.
Spain	Yes	Yes	Some handguns and rifles are prohibited.
Austria	Handguns	Handguns	Certain handguns and rifles are prohibited.
Australia	Yes	Yes	Banned semiautomatics unless good reason is shown; banned many handguns.
Belgium	Yes	Yes	Some rifles are prohibited.
Sweden	Yes	Yes	Restrictions in some regions.
New Zealand	Yes	Partial	Hunting rifles are excluded.
France	Yes	Partial	Some hunting rifles excluded.
Canada	Yes	Yes	Automatic, converted, and semiautomatic assault weapons and some handguns.
Italy	Yes	Yes	

Table 7.5 (continued)

Country	Licensing of Owners?	Registration of All Firearms?	Other
Switzerland	Yes	Partial	Some hunting guns and secondary sales excluded. Variations among cantons (provinces).
Israel	Yes	Yes	
Norway	Yes	NA	
United States of America	Limited	Limited	Some states have licensing, some have registration, some have both. Many have neither. Fully automatics are prohibited.
Finland	Yes	Yes	Fully automatics are prohibited.

Source: Wendy Cukier, David Lochhead, J. Susla, and A. Kooistra, "Emerging Global Norms in the Regulation of Civilian Possession of Small Arms," revised (Toronto: SAFER-Net, July 2003).

son under Article 3 of the Universal Declaration of Human Rights. Furthermore, the preamble of the Universal Declaration states that freedom from fear is one of the highest aspirations of the common person.

Efforts to regulate civilian possession of firearms often raise questions of rights. In the past, the UN special rapporteur on violence against women has raised this issue in the context of the Declaration of the Elimination of Violence Against Women. More recently, the UN special rapporteur on human rights has added impetus to the movement by suggesting that states that fail to enact reasonable regulations to limit the availability and misuse of small arms by individuals within their borders may be failing in their obligations under international law. She argues that while rights for legitimate national security, self-determination, and national sovereignty have been reaffirmed several times, there is no evidence of a general right to unrestricted civilian access to arms under any international human rights instrument.[130]

Indeed the United Nations recently issued a working paper on small arms that reinforced the responsibility of states under international human rights law to address the problems associated with misuse of firearms by civilians generally and particularly from the perspective of the rights of women. In her recent report, the special rapporteur on Human Rights has issued a report that adds further impetus to international efforts to develop norms around civilian possession of small arms:[131]

> Under international human rights law, the State is responsible for violations committed with small arms by private persons who, because they are operating with the express or implicit permission of authorities, are considered to be State agents. Under this theory, the State would be responsible for failing to prevent, investigate or prosecute vigilante groups or private militias that carry out ethnic or religious massacres, or "social cleansing" of street children. There is also growing pressure to hold States accountable for patterns of abuses, such as the State's failure to establish reasonable regulation regarding the private ownership of small arms that are likely to be used in homicides, suicides and accidents; its failure to protect individuals from a pattern of domestic violence; and its failure to protect individuals from organized crimes including kidnapping and killing for ransom.

By rereading the discussion on regulation of civilian possession of small arms in the context of the right of civilians to be protected from small arms violence, the special rapporteur has provided new and important support for efforts to move in this direction that counter claims that have cast opposition to regulation of civilian possession of firearms as an exercise of rights.

EMERGING GLOBAL NORMS

Not only do we see evidence of norms emerging from the practices of nations but there have been attempts to establish minimum standards at the global and regional level. Over the past decade, increased attention has been focused on the need to establish international standards for firearms control as part of post-conflict peace processes, and efforts to prevent conflict and crime.

United Nations Disarmament Commission (1999)

The importance of firearm control in postconflict situations has been well established and it is an essential part of postconflict Disarmament, Demobilization and Reintegration (DDR) efforts. The report of the UN Disarmament Commission, reviewed at the UN General Assembly in December 1999 states:

> 36. States should work towards the introduction of appropriate national legislation, administrative regulations and licensing requirements that define the conditions under which firearms can be acquired, used and traded by private persons. In particular they should consider the prohibition of the unrestricted

trade and private ownership of small arms specifically designed for military purposes, such as automatic guns (e.g. assault rifles and machine guns).

UN Commission on Crime Prevention and Criminal Justice Resolution (1997)

At the United Nations Commission on Crime Prevention and Criminal Justice in 1997, a resolution was signed by more than thirty countries that specifically linked access to weapons availability to increased levels of death and injury, and acknowledged the important role of national legislation in controlling the flow of guns from less regulated to more regulated areas.[132] The resolution "Requests the Secretary-General to promote, within existing resources, technical cooperation projects that recognize the relevance of firearm regulation in addressing violence against women, in promoting justice for victims of crime and in addressing the problem of children and youth as victims and perpetrators of crime and in reestablishing or strengthening the rule of law in post-conflict peace-keeping projects."[133] Specifically, it:

Encourages Member States to consider, where they have not yet done so, regulatory approaches to the civilian use of firearms that include the following common elements:

(a) Regulations relating to firearm safety and storage;

(b) Appropriate penalties and/or administrative sanctions for offences involving the misuse or unlawful possession of firearms;

(c) Mitigation of, or exemption from, criminal responsibility, amnesty or similar programmes that individual Member States determine to be appropriate to encourage citizens to surrender illegal, unsafe or unwanted firearms;

(d) A licensing system, inter alia, including the licensing of firearm businesses, to ensure that firearms are not distributed to persons convicted of serious crimes or other persons who are prohibited under the laws of respective Member States from owning or possessing firearms;

(e) A record-keeping system for firearms, inter alia, including a system for the commercial distribution of firearms and a requirement for appropriate marking of firearms at manufacture and at import, to assist criminal investigations, discourage theft and ensure that firearms are distributed only to persons who may lawfully own or possess firearms under the laws of the respective Member States.

The resolution sponsored by Angola, Australia, Botswana, Brazil, Brunei, Burundi, Canada, Columbia, Croatia, Fiji, France, Gambia, Germany, Greece, Haiti, Italy, Japan, Lesotho, Malaysia, Mexico, Morocco, Netherlands, Philippines, Poland, Qatar, Republic of Korea, Romania, Saudi Arabia, Sweden, Thailand, Tunisia, Tanzania, and the Russian Federation emphasized the importance of state responsibility for effective regulation of civilian possession of firearms. It was never adopted, in large part because of opposition by the United States. The Firearms Protocol of the United Nations Convention on Transnational Organized Crime addressed only the issues associated with import, export, transit and marking of firearms and ammunition and dropped any reference to national legislation.

The Firearms Protocol of the United Nations Convention on Transnational Organized Crime

The United Nations Protocol against the Illicit Manufacturing of and Trafficking in Firearms, Their Parts and Components and Ammunition, supplementing the United Nations Convention against Transnational Organized Crime[134] represents the first legally binding international instrument aimed at tackling the illicit trade in firearms. While it falls short of addressing the full range of issues identified in the 1997 Commission on Crime Prevention and Criminal Justice, it nevertheless represents significant progress. The draft agreement seeks to combat and criminalize trafficking in firearms, through the development of harmonized international standards governing the manufacture, possession and transfer of commercial shipments of firearms. Among other things, its provisions commit states to:

- Adopt legislative measures to criminalize the illicit manufacture, trafficking, possession and use of firearms;
- Maintain detailed records on the import, export and in-transit movements of firearms;
- Adopt an international system for marking firearms at the time of manufacture and each time they are imported;
- Establish a licensing system governing the import, export, in-transit movement and re-export of firearms;
- Exchange information regarding authorized producers, dealers, importers and exporters, the routes used by illicit traffickers, best practice in combating trafficking in order to enhance states ability to prevent, detect and investigate illicit trafficking;
- Cooperate at the bilateral, regional and international level to prevent, combat and eradicate the illicit manufacturing of and trafficking in firearms.

The Protocol emphasizes the importance of international cooperation, information exchange and transparency. Core to the Firearms Protocol is the agreement to establish an international standard for marking firearms at the point of manufacture and at the point of import to assist in tracing and criminal investigations relating to crimes committed with firearms. The UN Protocol requires that records should be kept for not less than ten years. In July 2005, more than fifty countries had ratified the Protocol bringing it into force as an international standard.

United Nations Programme of Action Against the Illicit Trade in Small Arms in All Its Aspects (2001)

While the focus of the Programme of Action, developed in 2001, is on preventing the flow of arms to conflict zones, it became rapidly apparent to many participants that it was not possible to address this problem without addressing the problem of civilian firearms given that almost 60 percent of the world's guns are in the hands of civilians. Moreover, as almost all illegal small arms begin as legal small arms, preventing diversion of legal guns to illegal markets requires controls on civilian guns. Initial versions of the programme of action made explicit reference to the need for states to regulate civilian possession and use, highlighted below:

> To put in place adequate laws, regulations and administrative procedures to exercise effective control over the legal manufacture, stockpiling, transfer and possession of small arms and light weapons within their areas of jurisdiction. To ensure that those engaged in illegal manufacture, stockpiling, transfer and possession, can and will be prosecuted under appropriate penal codes.

> To seriously consider the prohibition of unrestricted trade and private ownership of small arms and light weapons specifically designed for military purposes.[135]

These references were dropped in the final version under pressure from the United States.[136] In spite of this, it has been suggested that the Programme implicitly requires national regulations over firearms in order to fulfil the obligations contained within the Programme of Action cannot be easily fulfilled without appropriate controls over the sale, possession and use of civilian weapons.[137] This is particularly true with respect to obligations for record-keeping and tracing. At the review conferences in both 2003 and 2005, most countries in reporting on their progress towards meeting the commitments of the describe changes to their national gun laws. Since 2001 more than fifty countries have strengthened their gun laws, among them: Canada, Poland, Somalia, Kenya, Uganda, France, Belgium, China, Australia, South Africa, Cambodia, United Kingdom, East Timor, Thailand, Afghanistan, Germany, Bahrain, Malaysia, Jordan and Israel. Only one, the United States, has relaxed them. The process associated with the development of the Programme of Action is discussed in more detail in Chapter 9.

Regional Measures

While efforts to establish global standards for the regulation of firearms have been slow, significant progress has been made in the establishment of regional standards. Again these initiatives have emerged from the recognition that countries with weak laws endanger the security of their neighbors as guns, once in illegal markets, easily move across borders. These agreements have also started to address standards for regulating weapons in the hands of civilians. For example the Joint Action of the European Communities Council (1998), the Bamako Declaration (2000), the Nadi Framework (2000), Southern African Development Community Protocol (2001), the Andean Plan (2003) and the Nairobi Protocol (2004) all have implications for the regulation of firearms.

1. The Report of the first continental meeting of African Experts on the Illicit Proliferation, Circulation and Trafficking of Small Arms and Light Weapons 17–19, 2000, emphasized that, "the civilian possession of military style arms (automatic and semiautomatic, etc.) was unacceptable."[138]

2. The Bamako Declaration on an African Common Position on the Illicit Proliferation, Circulation and Trafficking of Small Arms and Light Weapons, December 1, 2000, recommended that Member States should, "adopt, as soon as possible, where they do not exist, the necessary legislative and other measures to establish as a criminal offence under national law, the illicit manufacturing of, trafficking in, and illegal possession and use of small arms and light weapons, ammunition and other related materials" and At the regional level, "Encourage the codification and harmonization of legislation governing the manufacture, trading, brokering, possession and use of small arms and ammunition. Common standards include, but not be limited to, marking, record keeping and control governing imports, exports and the licit trade."[139]

3. The Nairobi Declaration on the Problem of the Proliferation of Illicit Small Arms and Light Weapons in the Great Lakes Region and the Horn of Africa, March 15, 2000, decided to, "Encourage the concrete and co-ordinated agenda for action for the sub-region to promote human security and ensure that states have in place adequate laws, regulations and administrative procedures to exercise effective control over the possession and transfer of small arms and light weapons, through measures, inter alia to. . . . Urge the strengthening and where they do not exist, the adoption of national laws, regulations and control mechanisms to govern civilian possession of arms."[140]

4. In May 1998 officials from the Southern African Development Community (SADC), the European Union and its member states came together to negotiate a SALW action plan for the Southern African sub-region. The resulting *Southern Africa Regional Action Programme on Light Arms and Illicit Arms Trafficking* was formally adopted at an EU-SADC Ministerial Conference later that year. In March 2001, SADC Heads of State or Gov-

ernment issued a *Declaration Concerning Firearms, Ammunition and Other Related Materials in the Southern African Development Community*. The *Declaration* formally expressed the political will to address the proliferation of SALWs in Southern Africa and commits the member states to review national legislation. The *Draft Protocol on Firearms*, an instrument drafted by the Southern African Regional Police Chiefs Cooperation Organization (SARPCCO) in 2000 at the behest of SADC, was endorsed at the Maputo Ministerial meeting in June 2001, and signed at the SADC Heads of State Summit in August of that year. The Protocol includes commitments such as:

- strengthening national controls over firearms;
- marking and record-keeping;
- collection and destruction of surplus or confiscated weapons;
- improved law enforcement; and
- transparency measures.[141]

5. The Andean Plan to Prevent, Combat and Eradicate Illicit Trade in Small Arms and Light Weapons in all its aspects, Columbia, June 25, 2003, also highlighted the importance of controls over civilian possession noting, "that the problem of proliferation of illicit arms may only be resolved extensively, broadly and in an integrated manner by reinforcing the capacity to regulate and comply with all aspects that govern the lawful manufacture, import, export, transfer, sale, brokerage, transport, possession, concealment, usurpation, carrying and use of arms of this kind, as well as establishing cooperative community mechanisms for this purpose." It states, "Member Countries shall, based on their national legislation and on administrative and operational provisions, regulations and procedures, control the illegal manufacture, import, export, transfer, sale, brokering, transport, possession, concealment, usurpation, carrying and use of small arms and light weapons and shall take the following measures, inter alia, that are within their possibilities: "Recommend the adoption, as promptly as possible and whenever appropriate, of the legislative and other measures that are needed to classify as a criminal offence under national law the illicit manufacture, import, export, transfer, sale, brokerage, transport, possession, concealment, usurpation, carrying and use of small arms and light weapons." It also recommends that countries, "Prepare and implement, as appropriate, domestic programs for . . . The adoption of appropriate national rules or regulations for improving and reinforcing laws that regulate the legal possession by civilians of firearms, ammunition, explosives and other related materials."[142]

6. The Nadi Framework—Legal Framework for a Common Approach to Weapons Control (Nadi, Fiji, March 10, 2000) also focused on the need,

"To confirm that the possession, and use of firearms, ammunition and related materials is a privilege that is conditional on the overriding need to ensure public safety; and To improve public safety by imposing strict controls on the possession and use of firearms, ammunition, other related materials and prohibited weapons."[143]

7. The Joint Action of the European Communities Council adopted by the Council on the basis of Article J.3 of the treaty on the European Union's contribution to combating the destabilizing accumulation and spread of small arms and light weapons (December 1998) also emphasized the importance of civilian controls when it states, "in order to ensure control, the establishment and maintenance of national inventories of legal weapons owned by the country's authorities including the establishment of restrictive national weapons regulation for small arms including penal sanctions and effective administrative control."[144]

CONCLUSION

Civilian gun ownership occurs in many different contexts and is largely influenced by history, culture, political and social conditions. Only a few countries, such as Brunei Darussalam, Luxembourg and Malaysia, have a total prohibition on civilian gun ownership and others, like Japan, China and Great Britain, severely restrict civilian possession. Most countries allow ownership for hunting or pest control on farms, and some allow possession of certain types of weapons for target shooting or "collection." There are significant differences in the historical and cultural evolution of firearm regulations in different countries, yet a surprising level of commonality emerges in a review of laws worldwide. Most countries have measures in place to prohibit possession of some firearms although the range of firearms considered legitimate varies by context. Most countries prohibit civilians from possessing military weapons by civilians, although again definitions vary. Most countries require some level of screening and licensing in order for civilians to own firearms although the criteria and standards differ considerably. Many also control the sale and possession of ammunition. Most countries maintain some form of record keeping or registration of the firearms in circulation. (See Table 7.5.) Most countries require some level of safe storage and relatively few encourage the carrying of firearms by civilians for "self-protection." Most countries have laws that penalize illegal possession and misuse of firearms and in recent years these penalties have been increased in many countries. In addition, there are a wide range of unique approaches such as gun-free zones, bans on carrying guns at certain times, child access protection laws, etc. Clearly firearms regulations are the norm, not the exception internationally.

8

National Approaches to Regulation

While there is evidence of emerging norms regarding firearm legislation, the approaches in various countries are wide ranging. Between 2001 and 2005, more than fifty countries introduced stronger gun laws. Only one—the United States—relaxed its controls. The following pages provide some snapshots of approaches to regulating firearms in countries from around the world.

As discussed previously, while there is evidence of emerging global norms concerning minimal standards for firearm regulation, an examination of national approaches reveals significant variations in the laws which have evolved in particular contexts. History, culture, politics and legal traditions all play a role in shaping the evolution of laws. Socioeconomic conditions, governance, policing and justice systems often play a role in shaping the ways in which laws are implemented.

The evaluation of the impact of policy changes in any context is difficult because of the interplay of multiple factors—particularly when longitudinal analysis is being undertaken. Even where policy interventions can in some ways be isolated and measured, the way in which they are implemented often shapes the outcomes. Another factor is the gap between laws as they are intended and laws as they are implemented. Often there are loopholes that undermine their effectiveness. Sometimes laws are passed without the resources, political will or ability to implement them appropriately. Moreover, in many contexts—for example the United States—the potential impact of strong laws in one jurisdiction is undermined by weaker laws in other jurisdictions as guns move across state borders. This phenomenon is also seen internationally where one country's efforts to implement stronger laws may be undermined by the flow of guns from countries without effective controls. The reality is that outside of the United States, there is relatively limited peer-reviewed literature even describing gun laws let alone evaluating their impact. In most countries they are accepted as part of the legislative and political fabric and do not attract the same attention that they do in the United States. In the same way, for example, there is very limited research examining the impact of licensing drivers and registering cars although there is certainly considerable research on the impact of particular interventions within this framework. Many regulatory schemes are not subjected to the level of scrutiny we see applied to firearms laws, particularly in the United States. Given the politicization of the firearms, any discussion of the evaluation of the impact of firearms laws is particularly charged. At the same time, the burden of proof demanded of gun policy is much higher than for other interventions. There is far less proof, for example that strong deterrence measures work, yet they are seldom scrutinized, costed or evaluated. In the United States, with its patchwork of local, state and federal laws, it is extremely difficult to isolate and assess individual interventions although some projects in some contexts appear to have produced reductions in particular forms of violence.

UNITED STATES OF AMERICA

Legislation

The United States has the highest rate of firearm death among industrialized countries. The United States is estimated to have almost as many guns as people.[1] In the United States, firearm regulation, along with criminal law, is, for the most part, a state responsibility, and there are also a variety of local ordinances related to firearms. The Brady Bill attempted to establish national standards, but some states were exempt from the provisions. Under the act, states were exempt from the five-day waiting period if their laws require law enforcement officials to conduct records checks to verify that prospective handgun purchasers are eligible to possess handguns. When President Clinton signed the act into law in 1993, eighteen states and the District of Columbia were automatically "Brady exempt." In 1997, key provisions—the background checks—were struck down by the courts and reverted to state responsibility. Consequently, firearm regulation in the United States cannot easily be summarized and ranges widely from state to state. This situation also poses significant challenges for evaluation, as guns easily travel across state borders from unregulated states to more regulated states.

Hawaii and the District of Columbia require the registration of handguns or firearms, while twenty-one states have record-of-sales laws. Fourteen states require the licensing of handgun owners, although the process is not uniformly rigorous across all states. Eleven of these fourteen states also have record-of-sale or registration requirements. It should be noted that not all record-of-sale laws are equally stringent. Some require information to be centrally stored by state authorities, while others simply require the information to be held for a time-limited period by local authorities.[2] After background checks, a key provision in the Brady Bill, were struck down in 1997, the issue has become a state responsibility. As of 2000, twenty-three states required only basic federal background checks when a handgun is purchased from a dealer, while twenty-seven states required checks of state police records as well. Most states do not require a waiting period for handgun purchases. A number of states have shall-issue laws, facilitating access to carry permits for handguns.[3] Seven states prohibit the carrying of concealed weapons, while in twenty-nine states almost anyone who does not have a criminal record can obtain a carrying-concealed-weapon (CCW) license.[4] Only four states (South Carolina, Virginia, Maryland and California) have one-handgun-per-month laws to restrict the number of firearms an individual can purchase in a one-month period.[5] A total of thirteen states have passed laws protecting the gun industry from being sued by local governments for negligent design or distribution of its products.[6]

Seven states have state assault weapons bans.[7] Currently there is a federal ban on assault weapons. The ban, however, is being circumvented by companies who are producing "sporterized versions" of the prohibited weapons, which are adapted to get around the ban. The legislation expired on September 13, 2004.[8]

Currently, federal law prohibits federally licensed firearm dealers from selling handguns to persons under age twenty-one. However, a loophole in federal law allows the private sale of handguns to persons between the ages of eighteen and twenty. Only twelve states prohibit such sales to juveniles. Most states do not even require a background check for private sales to people under twenty-one.[9] Further, in contrast to most other countries, ammunition sales are not regulated. However, the United States has recently increased its regulation of arms brokers by requiring them to obtain authorization from the State Department before buying or selling arms internationally.[10]

Evaluations

Most of the research performed on the impact of measures to reduce the misuse of firearms has been done in the United States. Given that the United States has a patchwork of legislation and that guns flow freely from one state to another, it is not an easy task to assess the impact of legislation. A recent meta analysis of evaluations of firearms legislation by the Centers for Disease Control has criticized many of these studies for their serious analytical and methodological flaws. The study noted that all such efforts have been impaired by research designs that fail to take into account all the variables. There is, for example, no linear relationship between firearm laws and firearm death rates. Issues related to implementation are often not considered—for example, while the assault weapons ban prohibited the sale and possession of semiautomatic weapons on paper, huge problems with its implementation, such as the grandfather clauses, have been identified. Consequently, it is difficult to determine whether the evaluations of the ban are evaluations of the principle or evaluations of the implementation. The level of police and judicial enforcement of new laws is rarely taken into account, yet it significantly affects the laws' effectiveness. It is also difficult to measure interventions at the state level because guns flow from states with lax regulations to states with more stringent regulations. This is one of the main arguments for national and international standards.[11]

Overall rates of firearm violence in the United States have been declining in recent years, but given the conflicting trends at the state level—some, such as California, are strengthening controls; others, such as Florida, are relaxing them—it is difficult to associate these trends with changes in policy.

Evaluations have been undertaken of specific initiatives in specific contexts.

The Brady Bill. In the United States, there have been a number of studies that have attempted to assess the impact of the Brady Bill, which required criminal record checks and a waiting period before the sale of a handgun, but as noted above, many states were exempt from its provisions, making evaluation difficult. One study of homicide and suicide rates (1985–1997) found a statistically significant reduction in the rate of firearm suicides among seniors fifty-five years of age and older; however, there was no significant effect on other age-groups. Furthermore, the reduction was more correlated to the effect of the waiting period for gun purchases than to any other aspect of the law. Finally, the study did not find a clear pattern of differences between the thirty-two states that had implemented additional restrictions associated with the law and the eighteen states that already had them in place.[12] Other studies provided evidence that the law indeed prevents sales of firearms to potentially dangerous individuals and reduces gun trafficking. Between 1994 and 2000, 689,000 firearm applications were rejected, in most cases due to the applicant's criminal history.[13]

Assault Weapons Ban. Although the CDC task force found that there was insufficient evidence to determine the effectiveness of bans on specific firearms,[14] the frequency of the use of assault weapons in crimes has dropped significantly in the United States since 1994. Between 1990 and 1994, the assault weapons named in the ban accounted for 4.82 percent of the guns traced to crimes by the Bureau of Alcohol, Tobacco and Firearms (BATF). Since the implementation of the ban, this number has been steadily falling each year, an indication that the ban's effectiveness increases annually. In 2001, the last year for which data are available, it had dropped to 1.1 percent. Using these figures, the Brady Center to Prevent Gun Violence estimates that if the ban had not been enacted, approximately 60,000 additional assault weapons would have been traced to crimes in the last ten years.[15]

Handgun Ban. Washington, D.C., passed a law in 1976 that virtually banned any new purchases or ownerships of handguns. One study found that in the first ten years after the implementation of the law, there was a 25 percent decline in both firearm homicides and suicides, while non-

Table 8.1 Firearm Deaths in the United States

Year	Firearm Suicides	Firearm Suicides Rate per 100,000	Percent Total Suicides	Firearm Homicides	Firearm Homicides Rate per 100,000	Percent of Total Homicides
1981	16,139	7.03	58	13,960	6.1	62
1982	16,560	7.15	59	12,610	5.4	60
1983	16,600	7.1	59	11,200	4.8	58
1984	17,113	7.26	58	11,190	4.7	59
1985	17,363	7.3	59	11,140	4.7	59
1986	18,153	7.56	59	12,180	5.1	59
1987	18,136	7.49	59	11,880	4.9	59
1988	18,169	7.43	60	12,550	5.1	61
1989	18,178	7.36	60	13,220	5.4	62
1990	18,885	7.57	61	15,000	6	64
1991	18,526	7.32	60	16,380	6.5	66
1992	18,169	7.08	60	16,230	6.4	68
1993	18,940	7.29	61	17,070	6.6	70
1994	18,765	7.13	60	16,330	6.3	70
1995	18,503	6.95	59	14,760	5.6	68
1996	18,166	6.74	59	13,320	5	68
1997	17,566	6.44	58	12,290	4.6	68
1998	17,424	6.32	57	11,010	4.1	65
1999	16,599	5.95	57	10,130	3.7	65
2000	16,586	5.89	56	10,180	3.7	66
2001	16,869	5.92	55	10,130	3.6	63
2002	17,108	5.94	54	10,820	3.7	67

Source: Centers for Disease Control and Prevention (CDC), *Suicide Firearm Deaths and Rates per 100,000*, WISQARS: Web-based Injury Statistics Query and Reporting Systems, http://www.cdc.gov/ncipc/wisqars/default.htm; also Kwing Hung. Firearm Statistics: Updated Tables. Department of Justice Canada, Ottawa, January 2005.

firearm homicide and suicide rates remained stable.[16] However, as in the case of other bans, guns flow easily across the border from states with less rigorous controls, such as West Virginia.

One-Gun-a-Month. An analysis of period after the implementation of the 1993 Virginia law that limited handgun purchases to one per person per

Figure 8.1 Firearm Deaths in the United States

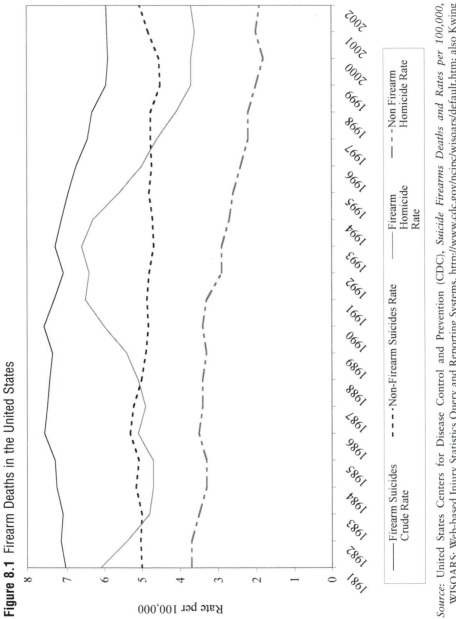

Source: United States Centers for Disease Control and Prevention (CDC), *Suicide Firearms Deaths and Rates per 100,000*, WISQARS: Web-based Injury Statistics Query and Reporting Systems, http://www.cdc.gov/ncipc/wisqars/default.htm; also Kwing Hung, Firearm Statistics: Updated Tables. Department of Justice Canada, Ottawa, January 2005.

month found that the guns recovered from crimes in other states were significantly less likely to have originated in Virginia.[17]

Saturday Night Specials. The state of Maryland banned the sale of Saturday night specials in 1988. One analysis found that the rate of firearm homicides was 9 percent lower between 1990 and 1998 than it had been during the period before the law was implemented.[18]

Zero-Tolerance Policies. Many schools have adopted a position of zero tolerance toward firearms, but the effects of this policy on school violence have not been measured. Further, no research has been done on the impact of the 1994 Gun Free Schools Act. One study found that the rate of students carrying firearms to or from schools with metal detectors was half that of other schools. However, there was no appreciable difference in the overall occurrence of violence between the two types of schools.[19]

Licensing and Registration. Studies have shown that both licensing and registration are needed to effectively prevent the diversion of firearms to illegal markets. There is no significant effect on the illicit trade in states that have only licensing or only registration. However, states with both licensing and registration are relatively infrequently the source for guns recovered at crime scenes.[20]

Criminal History Purchase Restrictions. Laws that prohibit offenders convicted of misdemeanour or felony crimes from buying handguns have been shown to have an effect on the levels of subsequent convictions. A study conducted in California found that convicted offenders of misdemeanour crimes who had been denied handgun purchases after the passage of a state law had a recidivism rate that was 29 percent lower than that of offenders who had been permitted to buy handguns prior to the passage of the law.[21]

Domestic Violence Purchase Restrictions. Screening firearm buyers for restraining orders has been shown to reduce rates of intimate partner homicide although results are not entirely conclusive.[22]

Concealed Carry Weapons (CCW) Laws. One of the most fiercely debated policies in the United States, CCW laws have been subject to a barrage of studies heavily influenced by the ideologies of their authors. Policies that facilitate the concealed carrying of firearms have had no reductive effect on homicide rates and may even have had an augmentative effect.[23]

Child Access Protection (CAP) Laws. CAP laws make firearm owners liable to felony prosecution if children are able to access their weapons due to improper storage. Adoption of such laws has been correlated to a decrease in unintentional firearm death rates among young people.

Overall, the evidence regarding the impact of firearm regulation in the United States is difficult to assess. Many studies of the same intervention reach contradictory conclusions, presenting dilemmas for policy makers. As Jens Ludwig notes, one of the key issues is to consider the source.[24] However, several conclusions are very clear when the United States is considered in the international context.

1. The United States has much higher rates of gun ownership than virtually any other country.
2. The United States has less national firearm regulation than virtually any other country.
3. The rates of firearm death and injury in the United States are much higher than in any other industrialized country.
4. U.S. guns supply illegal markets worldwide, fueling violence and crime in Canada, Mexico, the Caribbean, Northern Ireland and even as far away as Japan.

CANADA

Historically, Canada has had relatively strict controls on handguns. Changes in the 1977 Criminal Law Amendment Act distinguished among "unrestricted weapons" (rifles and shotguns), restricted weapons (primarily handguns, short-barrelled semiautomatics and grandfathered prohibited weapons) and prohibited weapons (fully automatic firearms and sawed-off shotguns). Restricted weapon permits could be issued to individuals if they were required for "lawful occupation," if they were used for target shooting under the auspices of an approved shooting club or if the weapons formed part of a collection. Permits required for self-protection were issued in very few cases: applicants had to demonstrate that their lives were in danger and that the police could not protect them. Restricted weapons were also registered. Owners were required to report loss or theft, and possession of a restricted weapon without a valid registration certificate or at a place other than the place specified on the certificate was a criminal offence. Special permits were required to transport or carry restricted weapons, defining clearly where and when the owner was allowed to have the firearm.

In contrast, the controls on rifles and shotguns—unrestricted weapons— were more limited. A firearms acquisition certificate (FAC) was required to acquire an unrestricted firearm, but screening was, in practice, limited. However, the law did confer broad powers on firearms officers, who could refuse to issue an FAC if they had information indicating that "it would not be desirable in the interests of the safety of the applicant or any other person." Although there was a safety test requirement in the law, it had never been proclaimed.[25]

New requirements introduced in 1991 with Bill C-17 strengthened the screening requirements by adding a mandatory training course, a detailed questionnaire, references, a photograph and a twenty-eight-day waiting period. It raised the age for an FAC from sixteen to eighteen years of age with provisions for minors' permits. The law also reinforced the powers of the firearms officer to refuse an FAC if it was not in the interests of the safety of the applicant or any other person by shifting the burden of proof on appeal of the decision. That is, it required that the applicant prove that the firearms officer erred in his or her refusal. This law also defined safe-storage requirements and prohibited semiautomatic versions of fully automatic weapons as well as large-capacity magazines (although there were provisions for provincial exemptions to the magazine prohibition).

However, the 1991 law did not address many of the concerns raised by public safety organizations in the wake of the killing of fourteen female engineering students at l'École Polytechnique in Montreal on December 6, 1989. In particular, concerns focused on gaps in the controls over firearm owners: the FAC was required only to obtain guns, not to possess guns, and only a third of gun owners had valid FACs. It also recognized the need to strengthen accountability for the firearms owned through registration. For example, rifles and shotguns have tended to be more frequently recovered in crime and are more often a cause of death than handguns. Consequently, an unusual alliance of more than 350 organizations—including the Canadian Association of Chiefs of Police, the Canadian Public Health Association, the Canadian Bar Association, the Canadian Criminal Justice Association, the YWCA of Canada, Victims of Violence International and others—encouraged the government to improve the controls over rifles and shotguns.[26] In addition, a series of inquests recommended the licensing of all firearm owners and the registration of all firearms.

The new government introduced the Firearms Act, Bill C-68, in 1995. After a highly publicized struggle, it received royal assent on December 5, 1995.[27] It includes

- The ability to prohibit, through order in council, firearms not "reasonably" used in hunting in an effort to broaden the ability to prohibit semiautomatic military assault weapons;
- A ban on short-barrelled and small-caliber (.25 and .32) handguns with a grandfather clause;
- Licensing of all firearm owners by 2001 (including possession only and possession/acquisition licenses);
- Registration of all firearms by 2003, and
- Production of the firearm license in order to purchase ammunition.

The law also contained a series of provisions, including the nonderogation clause, intended to accommodate aboriginal peoples' hunting rights.

The province of Alberta, along with several other provinces and gun organizations, challenged the constitutionality of the law in the Alberta Court of Appeal, arguing that while it was legitimate for the federal government to license handgun owners and register handguns, it was a violation of provincial jurisdiction to extend these provisions to long guns (rifles and shotguns). In October 1998, the Alberta Court of Appeal ruled 3–2 in favor of the federal government's position that the regulation of firearms was, in substance, a matter of public safety, falling within the federal government's right to legislate in matters of criminal law.[28] It rejected the province's assertion that the regulation of long guns was, in pith and substance, an attempt by the federal government to intrude upon the exclusive jurisdiction of the provinces to legislate in the area of property and civil rights.[29] The province of Alberta appealed to the Supreme Court of Canada but the court, in a 9–0 ruling, dismissed the appeal, maintaining that

> the gun control law comes within Parliament's jurisdiction over criminal law. The law in "pith and substance" is directed to enhancing public safety by controlling access to firearms through prohibitions and penalties. This brings it under the federal criminal law power. While the law has regulatory aspects, they are secondary to its primary criminal law purpose. The intrusion of the law into the provincial jurisdiction over property and civil rights is not so excessive as to upset the balance of federalism.[30]

In the decision, the court also confirmed that licensing cannot be separated from registration:

> The licensing provisions cannot be severed from the rest of the Act. The licensing provisions require everyone who possesses a gun to be licensed; the registration provisions require all guns to be registered. These portions of the Firearms Act are both tightly linked to Parliament's goal of promoting safety by reducing the misuse of any and all firearms. Both portions are integral and necessary to the operation of the scheme.[31]

The costs of the program have generated controversy—an average of $100 million per year has been spent for ten years, most of it on licensing firearm owners. Efforts to streamline and reduce costs have had a limited impact, as the costs of screening and continuous eligibility monitoring are expensive.[32]

Evaluation

A number of studies have examined the effects of earlier legislation on gun death and injury rates in Canada[33] and concluded that there were significant reductions. As with the Australian and British reforms, it is too early to judge the effects of the Canadian legislation. But the number and rate of firearm death and injury in Canada are now the lowest they have been in thirty years.[34] The deadline for licensing was 2001 and the deadline for registration was 2003, it is estimated that 90 percent of firearm owners in Canada have now been licensed and 90 percent of Canada's 7 million firearms have been registered. While it is too early to evaluate the impact of the most recent law, preliminary data indicate its effectiveness. Rigorous background checks led to the refusal or revocation of about 9,000 licences in the first five years of the current legislation. That number represents seventy times more revocations than were made during the last five years of the old law.

Further, law enforcement agencies have found the registry extremely useful for their investigations and prosecutions. Police access the Candian Firearms Registry On-Line around 2,000 times each day,[35] and data from the system was used to support more than 3000 affidavits in 2004.

Throughout the 1980s, an average of 1,400 people died from firearm wounds each year, at a rate of 5.5 per 100,000. The 1990s saw the average annual deaths fall to 1,200 per year, at a rate of 4.6 per 100,000. Since the law passed, firearm deaths have continued to decline, reaching 816 (2.5 per 100,000) in 2003, the last year for which there are data. The rate of homicides involving firearms has declined by more than 35 percent since 1991, but what is most significant is that the rate of murders with rifles and shotguns, the focus of the legislation in both 1991 and 1995, has plummeted from 131 (0.47 per 100,000) in 1989 to 32 (0.12 per 100,000) in 2003. Homicides with other guns, primarily handguns, have increased from 0.13 per 100,000 to 0.34 per 100,000, fuelled largely by illegal imports. The rate of firearms being used in spousal homicide has declined by nearly 80 percent since 1974,[36] and since the new legislation was passed, the number of women killed with firearms has dropped from 74 (0.53 per 100,000) to 28 (0.13 per 100,000). Further, the rate of robberies committed with firearms has declined by more than 50 percent since 1991, including a 12 percent decline in 2001 alone.[37] (See Table 8.2.)

BRAZIL

With 34,755 firearm homicides out of 49,919 total homicides in 2000, Brazil has an especially severe problem with firearm-related violence. While the number of legally registered firearms (including those held by law enforcement officers) is estimated at 7 million, the total number of firearms in circulation is probably closer to 18.5 million. Brazil's arms industry, which is the second largest in the Western Hemisphere, is largely unregulated. Lax enforcement of the rules has meant that the majority of arms confiscated by the police are Brazilian-made.[38] The newly passed Disarmament Statute identifies arms trafficking as a crime, and violators may be punished by four to ten years in prison. Brazil is the first country in South America to criminalize the illegal arms trade.[39]

Brazil's Disarmament Statute, passed in October 2003, raised the minimum age for firearm possession from twenty-one to twenty-five years of age. Further restrictions on possession include the following criteria: The applicant must declare that he or she has a legitimate need to own a gun, though he or she does not have to demonstrate this need. However, the person must present proof that he or she:

- Is of sound mental and physical health;
- Has a fixed residence;

Table 8.2 Firearm Statistics in Canada

Year	1989	1995	2003	Percent Chan;
Total firearm deaths				
Number	1,367	1,125	816	−41
Rate per 100,000	5	3.8	2.5	−48
Homicides with firearms				
Number	218	176	161	−26
Rate per 100,000	0.8	0.6	0.5	−37
Homicides with rifles and shotguns				
Number	131	61	32	−76
Rate	0.5	0.2	0.1	−80
Homicides with other guns				
Number	87	115	129	48
Rate	0.3	0.4	0.4	33
Homicides without guns				
Number	439	412	387	−12
Rate	1.6	1.4	1.2	−25
Overall firearm deaths (male)				
Number	1,207	1,028	767*	−36.5
Rate	8.9	7	4.9	−45
Overall firearm deaths (female)				
Number	157	117	49	−69
Rate	1.1	0.6	0.3	−73
Homicides of women with firearms				
Number	74	43	28	−62
Rate	0.53	0.29	0.13	−75
Homicides of women without firearms				
Number	172	152	128	−24
Rate	1.23	1.03	0.83	−32
Robberies with firearms				
Number	6,442	6,692	3,877	−40
Rate per 100,000	24	23	12	−50

*2002 data.

Source: Data from Kwing Hung, Firearm Statistics: Updated Tables, Department of Justice Canada, Ottawa, January 2005; Kathryn Wilkins, Deaths Involving Firearms. Health Reports 16, 4 Statistics Canada, Ottawa, 2005.

Figure 8.2 Firearm Deaths in Canada by Type

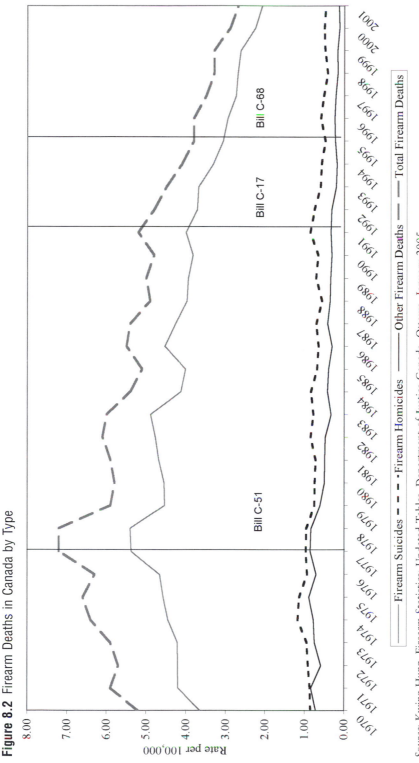

Source: Kwing Hung, Firearm Statistics: Updated Tables. Department of Justice Canada, Ottawa, January 2005.

Figure 8.3 Rate of Firearm Homicides in Canada by Weapon Type

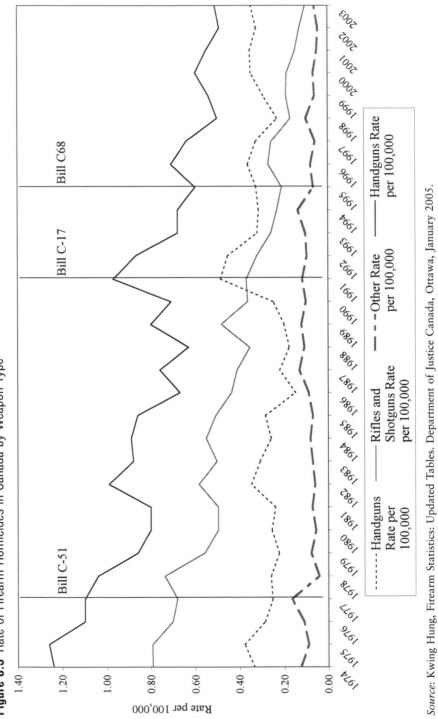

Source: Kwing Hung, Firearm Statistics: Updated Tables. Department of Justice Canada, Ottawa, January 2005.

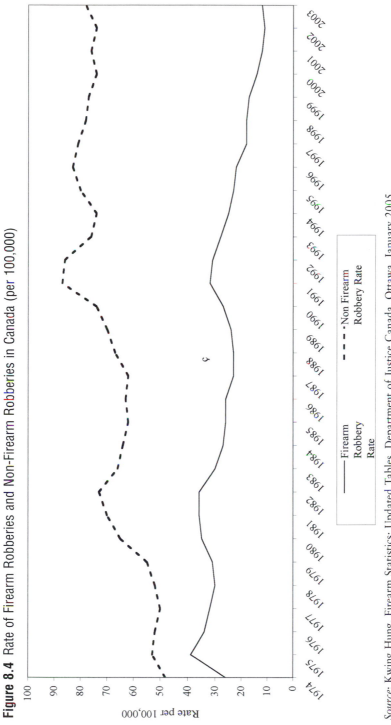

Figure 8.4 Rate of Firearm Robberies and Non-Firearm Robberies in Canada (per 100,000)

Source: Kwing Hung, Firearm Statistics: Updated Tables. Department of Justice Canada, Ottawa, January 2005.

Figure 8.5 Rate of Male/Female Firearm Homicides in Canada

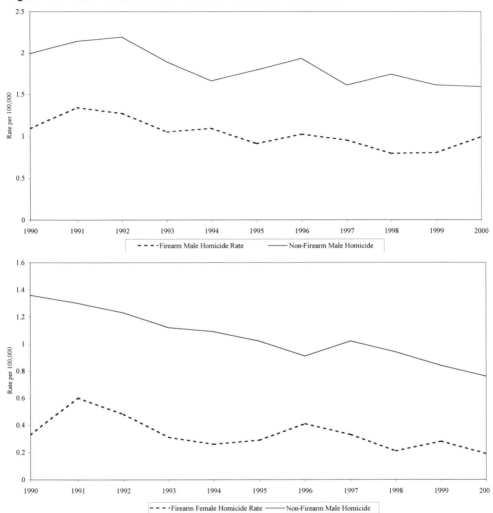

Source: Kwing Hung, Firearm Statistics: Updated Tables. Department of Justice Canada, Ottawa, January 2005.

- Has licit employment;
- Has no criminal record; and
- Can effectively handle a weapon.[40]

The law also aims at reducing firearm crime by making it illegal for any private individual to carry a firearm in public. Civilians who need to carry a weapon to perform their jobs (e.g. security officers, hunters) are exempt in limited cases determined by federal rather than state authorities. Those convicted of illegally carrying a firearm may be punished by a jail sentence without the possibility of bail. Finally, the Disarmament Statute called for a national referendum to decide whether gun sales should be banned for all Brazilian civilians to be held in October 2005.[41]

Evaluation

Rates of firearm violence in Brazil have risen dramatically over the past decade, particularly among young men. (See Figure 8.6.) The weapons-collection initiatives in Brazil have collected more than 300,000 firearms, but the impact of removing these guns from circulation is unclear. It is premature to evaluate the impact of the Brazilian firearm legislation; although studies have been undertaken on some of the community-based projects, the results are inconclusive.

Figure 8.6 Trends in Firearm Homicides in Brazil

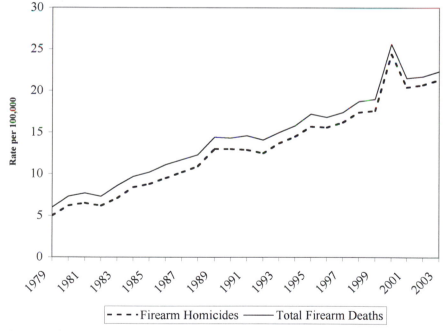

Source: Rubem César Fernandes, Benjamin Lessing, Caroline Iootty, Julio Cézar Purcena, Luciana Phebo, Marcelo de Souza Nascimento, Pablo Dreyfus, and Patricia Rivero, "Brazil: The Arms and the Victims," *Viva Rio*, Rio de Janeiro, 2005.

COLOMBIA

Colombia has one of the highest rates of gun homicide in the world, and the combination of political violence and drug-related violence with the availability of guns has created lethal results. Gun carrying is commonplace, and while licensing and registration are required, the gun laws are generally permissive. Efforts to more strongly regulate firearms have included a ban on carrying handguns in the cities of Bogotá and Cali at particular times, including on weekends, after paydays, on holidays and on election days, coupled with an aggressive enforcement strategy. Violence with firearms against women is also rampant. Groups such as Amnesty International maintain that violence against civilians is being fueled by the "Plan Colombia" of the United States which has funnelled to Colombia $600 million in 2003 and 2004 in military and police assistance. In addition to political violence, criminal violence and violence by security forces has kept mortality high and fuelled a pervasive culture of violence and instability.

Evaluation

A recent study examined the effects of a handgun ban and concluded that the homicide rate was lowered by 13 percent in Bogotá and 14 percent in Cali during the intervention periods (1993–1994 in Bogotá; 1995–1997 in Cali). Other factors may have contributed to this reduction, however.[42] The longer term outlook for the country is less encouraging. The homicide rate, already the highest reported in the world, has increased over recent years.

UNITED KINGDOM

The United Kingdom's controls on firearms are among the most restrictive in the Commonwealth and in the European Union. Citizens must obtain a permit to buy ammunition, and all firearms must be registered.[43] The Firearms Act was passed in 1937 and further amendments were passed in 1965 and 1968. Under the act, anyone who possesses or wishes to acquire a firearm or ammunition must have a firearm certificate, obtained from the local police. Possession and acquisition of a shotgun requires a shotgun certificate. Firearm certificates must be issued for each firearm, and the police must be satisfied that the applicant for a rifle or pistol certificate has a good and valid reason for owning a gun—sporting or target shooting, for example. Self-protection is not considered a valid reason, and renewal of the certificates is required every three years. Following the murder of sixteen people at Hungerford, Berkshire, in August 1987, the Firearms Act of 1988 was introduced, which expanded the class of prohibited weapons to include most semiautomatic rifles and smooth-bore shotguns as well as self-loading or pump-action shotguns.

A public inquiry on firearms regulation was undertaken following the Dunblane massacre on March 13, 1996, when sixteen primary-school children and their teacher were murdered by a member of a local gun club. In its submission to the commission, the British Home Office maintained that stricter controls on firearms in Britain had had a significant effect on public safety, contrasting the patterns of crime in Britain with those in the United States, including the homicide rates as well as the use of guns in crime.[44] A new law, passed in 1997, banned 95 percent of handguns and required that the remainder (.22-caliber) be stored at gun clubs. When the Labour Party took power, it introduced a total ban on handguns, accompanied by a buyback.[45] Citizens surrendered 162,353 firearms and 700 tonnes of ammunition,[46] which were subsequently destroyed. Despite this high success rate, the number of illicit firearms is still believed to be high and a number of arms were probably transferred to other European countries.[47] Most recently, in January 2004, the United Kingdom banned self-contained air-cartridge guns. These weapons may be easily converted to fire live ammunition. The owners of the estimated 70,000 of these air guns must have obtained a certificate from the police by April 30, 2004, to possess them, or they were permitted to turn the weapons in without compensation. After May 1, 2004, unlicensed owners could face up to ten years in prison.[48]

Evaluation

The percentage of firearm-related deaths and injuries in Great Britain is one of lowest internationally.[49] In 2000 there were approximately 200 firearm-related deaths (0.4 per 100,000).[50] In England, only 3 percent of households have firearms.[51] Of the 1,007 homicides committed in 2002–2003, 80 were committed with a firearm, and 40 were committed with a handgun.[52] Only 68 homicides were committed with a firearm in 2003–2004. Despite its strict firearm laws, the United Kingdom does not have integrated systems for licensing or registration or systematic tracing of firearms seized, so information about patterns of crime is lacking. However, it appears that there has been an increase in the use of firearms—primarily replicas as well as smuggled firearms—in violent crime. Overall homicide rates have increased more quickly than homicides with firearms. Homicides of women with firearms appear to have declined, except for a spike in 2002–2003 (see Figure 8.7), but fell again in 2003–2004.

SWITZERLAND, AUSTRIA AND GERMANY

Historically, responsibility for firearm legislation in Switzerland has rested with its twenty-six canton (state) governments, although more recently

Figure 8.7 Trends in Homicides with Firearms in England and Wales (Male and Female)

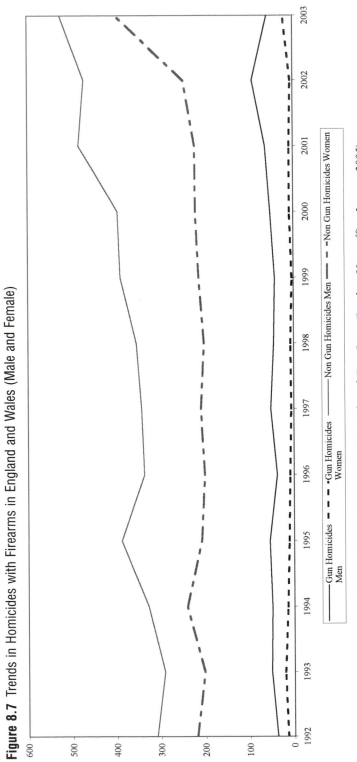

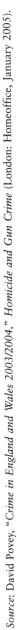

Source: David Povey, "*Crime in England and Wales 2003/2004*," *Homicide and Gun Crime* (London: Homeoffice, January 2005).

there have been considerable efforts to harmonize approaches and establish national standards.[53] In Switzerland, able-bodied men are required to undergo military training at the age of twenty and remain in the standing army until the age of forty-two. They are issued a military weapon along with a box of sealed ammunition to be kept in their home. About 70 percent of those who enter it complete basic training, but the attrition rate is fairly high—about 40 percent of Swiss are still in the army when they reach the end of eligibility.[54] Consequently, Switzerland has one of the highest rates of gun ownership in Europe. There is strict screening of army officers, and ammunition is stored in sealed boxes and inspected regularly. Other firearms are strictly regulated—a permit is required for each hunting rifle and to purchase ammunition, and most cantons require additional permits to carry firearms outside the home. Firearm sellers must verify that buyers meet certain criteria: the buyer must be at least eighteen years of age, must not present any apparent risk to him- or herself or third persons, and must not be entered in the Register of Convictions for Violent Crimes and Misdemeanors. Individuals wishing to resell or transfer their weapons to another person must document the transaction through a written contract, which they have to keep for at least ten years.[55]

A special certificate must be obtained before firearm owners may carry their arms in public. To qualify for this permit, applicants must demonstrate a legitimate need to protect themselves, other persons, or goods against specific risks. Applicants must further pass two tests, one on the correct handling of firearms and one on the legislation concerning the use of firearms. Permits are valid for five years.[56] No firearms are prohibited, but certain types of automatic and semiautomatic firearms are heavily restricted.[57] Furthermore, certain cantons require registration for particular weapons, while others do not.[58]

Switzerland has high rates of firearm death compared to other industrialized countries and has the highest firearm death rate among Western European countries.[59] Following the Zug massacre in 2001, Switzerland considered strengthening its gun laws, but with a change in government these efforts seem to have stalled.

Austria's gun laws are similar to those of most European countries in many respects. There is a strict screening process (at least on paper), including a psychological exam, in order to obtain a handgun license, and all handguns are registered. Firearms (not including handguns) are registered by dealers and not by the government. Further, only those who register for a government permit are allowed to own war weapons (e.g., automatic rifles and pistols).[60] There are restrictions on certain categories of firearms such as fully automatics, pump shotguns and the like, and there are requirements for safe storage. Firearm ownership rates are highest in rural areas, where hunting is common. At the same time, Austria, along with the United States and South Africa, is one of the few countries surveyed that has relatively permissive laws when it comes to carrying handguns for self-protection.[61]

While Austrian laws are stricter than laws in Switzerland, they are considerably more permissive than the laws in Germany. Germany passed very restrictive firearm laws in 1972 in response to growing concerns about terrorism. The fundamental principle of the 1972 legislation (Waffengsetz) is, "The number of gun owners and the number and types of guns in private property must be limited to the lowest possible level in the light of interests of public safety."[62]

Licensing requires certification of need, certification of trustworthiness, certification of technical knowledge and certification of physical fitness. The right to carry weapons in public is severely restricted and reserved to public figures who can claim that their lives are in acute danger and or who are in specific occupations.[63]

Germany requires that gun owners be citizens or be residents of the country for at least three years. Firearm owners are required to store their weapons and ammunition securely, and may only carry their firearms away from their property if the weapon is unloaded. The local licensing authority keeps records of every licensed firearm, including the serial number. Furthermore, gun collections are subject to an annual review. All licenses can be revoked or limited in order to avoid dangers concerning the public security.[64]

In April 2003, the town of Erfurt, following a highly publicized school shooting, passed legislation raising the minimum age of possession to age twenty-five (eighteen for hunters) and instituted a mandatory psychological test for all those under twenty-five.[65]

Evaluation

According to the United Nations' International Study on Firearm Regulation, the average (over five years) of nonfirearm homicide rates in Austria, Germany and Switzerland were roughly the same (1.61, 1.60 and 1.56 per 100,000, respectively). The overall homicide rates (2.14, 1.81 and 2.47) vary in accordance with the rates of firearm homicide (0.53, 0.21 and 0.91, respectively). This parallels the differences in firearm ownership rates in the three countries. While overall rates of homicide with firearms are low by American standards, they are high for Europe. Rates of children killed with guns are high in Switzerland as are suicides with firearms and domestic homicide.

FRANCE

France has a relatively high rate of gun ownership among European countries; an estimated 18.2 percent of households contain a firearm.[66] France's firearm legislation, first written in 1939, and amended in 1993, 1995, 1998 and 2001, has been criticized as inadequate and difficult to implement. There are no restrictions on the sales of hunting rifles. The buyer does not need to show the dealer any identification or hunting license. Carbines, handguns, pump-action firearms, .22-caliber long rifles and hunting carbines may also be easily obtained upon presentation of identification. A person who wishes to acquire a handgun or a semiautomatic military weapon must first obtain authorization from police headquarters. Sporting rifles require six months' membership at a sport-shooting range.[67]

Amendments have progressively strengthened the law. The 1993 and 1995 amendments banned the sale of certain arms, including shotguns, for self-protection. Following the implementation of this legislation, firearm dealers' sales dropped by 20 percent. The December 1998 amendment tightened controls over military and civilian arms held by private individuals. The 2001 decree requires arms dealers to keep a register of their transactions and to obtain authorization for their activities.[68] Firearms classified for military and defensive uses are more strictly controlled than hunting rifles and shotguns. Permits are required, and safe storage is defined. For hunting rifles, the minimal requirement is a valid hunting permit and a valid hunting license or a license issued by the sport federation. There are no specific storage requirements defined. Certain firearms must be registered with the department clerk in the firearm owner's area. There are no specific safe-storage regulations for firearms in categories 5 to 7, but specific rules apply for firearms in categories 1 to 4.[69] Detailed data on firearm death and injury are not available for France.

THE RUSSIAN FEDERATION

Firearms are strictly regulated in the Russian Federation. There are an estimated 4 million legally registered firearms in civilian hands in the Russian Federation, a country with a population of 150 million. The number of illegally held firearms is estimated to be between 300,000 and 1.5 million.[70] In the first half of 1999 alone, 20,000 units of weapons, 857 kilograms of explosives and 3,907 explosive devices were seized during the course of criminal cases.[71] In 2001, there were 13,000 reported crimes involving firearms. In the first half of 2002, there were 7,200 crimes involving firearms, and approximately half of these involved legally possessed weapons.[72]

Service and civilian firearms are regulated by the Federal Weapons Act of 1996, which establishes control of firearms at the federal level and denies regional or local regulations. In order to own a firearm, a license must be obtained; to acquire a firearm, a permit is required. For a citizen to obtain a firearm acquisition license, he or she must submit an application form, a document proving citizenship and a medical certificate stating that the applicant has no mental illness, alcohol or drug addiction or vision disorders.[73]

However, a license cannot be granted to citizens that are under eighteen years old (sixteen years old in the case of smoothbore hunting arms),[74] have not presented a medical certificate, have a previous conviction for a deliberate offence infringing on public order or established order of government, lack a fixed address or have not submitted documents to prove passing of the required safety examination.[75]

After acquiring a firearm, the citizen must register it at his or her local interior agency within two weeks from the date of acquisition. The applicant must present documentation that the firearm was acquired legally to the interior agency, which grants the firearm owner a permit either to store or to store and carry the firearm. This permit is valid for five years but may be extended.[76]

The Russian Ministry of Internal Affairs is in the process of organizing the centralized registration of missing (stolen or lost) and uncovered (confiscated, found or voluntarily surrendered) firearms. This is an international endeavour involving the Commonwealth of Independent States. A database for lost and uncovered firearms and light weapons has been set up and is updated daily.[77]

Citizens purchasing smoothbore long arms must pass an examination in the rules of the safe handling of firearms. However, individuals who have permits for storage or storage and carrying of firearms are exempt. Those purchasing smoothbore sport-shooting firearms and hunting weapons, or a document certifying the right to shoot, must also pass an examination in which they demonstrate safe handling of firearms.[78] In addition, civilians must obtain a permit to store arms. Storage must be done under conditions that ensure the firearms' safety, preventing any unauthorized persons from accessing them. The military has stricter guidelines, including alarm systems and armed guards.[79]

Evaluation

Detailed data on trends in firearm death and injury are not available for Russia, but in spite of the high-profile random shootings and political violence, overall rates of firearm death are relatively low.[80]

SOUTH AFRICA

Violence has been called "the greatest threat to human rights" in the emerging democracy of South Africa. In 1996, 3,503,573 arms were in circulation, compared to 1,933,222 licenses for possession.[81] South Africa's Arms and Ammunition Act of 1969 required that firearm owners be licensed and firearms registered, but it did not restrict the number of firearms an individual may own. In addition, South Africa is one of the few countries that has allowed widespread carrying of handguns for self-protection by civilians. Despite the emphasis on problems associated with postconflict military weapons, the vast majority of firearms recovered in crime in South

Africa are pistols, revolvers, rifles and shotguns, and not military weapons.[82] In 2000, 62 percent of firearm homicide victims were killed by handguns, while 24 percent were killed by long guns.[83] Criminal violence dwarfs political conflict as a cause of death. In 2000, 10,854 people were murdered with a firearm, accounting for 49.3 percent of all murders in that year.[84]

In 2000, South Africa passed the Firearms Control Bill, which significantly strengthened existing regulations. The minimum age to possess a firearm was raised from sixteen to twenty-one years of age. The criteria for obtaining a license were expanded to include training in the proper handling of firearms, no mental instability, no previous violent crime convictions and no dependence on narcotic substances. A license may be revoked if a firearm owner is posing a threat to him- or herself or his or her community. Finally, the act grants the minister of safety and security the discretionary power to declare certain public areas (such as schools, places of worship, bars and so forth) gun-free zones.[85]

When South Africa's domestic firearm legislation is compared to that of nine other southern African nations (Botswana, Lesotho, Malawi, Mozambique, Namibia, Swaziland, Tanzania, Zambia and Zimbabwe), some interesting contrasts emerge. Botswana, for example, presently has a total prohibition on issuing handgun licenses to individuals. Namibia's domestic firearm policy (Arms and Ammunition Act, no. 7 of 1996) allows licenses to be issued for up to four firearms, all of which are registered. Owners must be fingerprinted and a photograph issued with the license. Lesotho's Internal Security Arms and Ammunition Act of 1966 was amended in 1970, in 1971 and again in 1999. It requires firearm owners to be licensed and to obtain registration certificates, issued by local police. Rifles were banned in 1999. Malawi's Firearms Act of 1967 was amended in 1968, 1971 and 1974 and allows annual firearm licenses to be issued.

Mozambique's domestic firearm legislation was created with the Regulamento de Armas e Municoes of 1973 and requires that all firearm owners be licensed. Each license must be individually confirmed by the minister of the interior and accompanied by letters explaining the need for the firearm. Applicants are fingerprinted, and ownership is restricted to three hunting rifles and one handgun per person. It is estimated that there are only about 3,000 legal firearm owners in the country. Swaziland's Arms and Ammunition Act no. 24 of 1964 requires individuals to obtain annually renewed licenses to possess firearms and purchase ammunition. Tanzania's Arms and Ammunition Act of 1991 sets out strict processes for acquiring firearm licenses. Zambia's Firearms Act of 1969 requires both licensing and registration and restricts ownership to individuals twenty-one years of age and older. Zimbabwe's Firearms Act of 1957 requires a firearm certificate; applicants must be over the age of sixteen.[86]

Evaluation

No evaluation has been undertaken as the South African law has been implemented too recently to assess its effects. Coordinated efforts to address trafficking through the SADC protocol will also need to be assessed.

INDIA

India's domestic policy on firearms and light weapons is regulated under the Arms Act (1959) and Arms Rules (1962). Due to the severe twin problems of illicit small arms and light weapons proliferation and significant terrorist activity, India has, since 1987, limited the powers of state and district authorities to issue licences. They are no longer allowed to license the use of prohibited-bore weapons, and licenses are limited geographically. Licenses for possession of prohibited-bore weapons may only be issued, under special conditions, by the Ministry of Home Affairs.[87]

All firearm owners must be licensed. Applicants must provide, in addition to photographic identification and the prescribed fee, information regarding their date of birth, the availability of a safe place to store the firearm and ammunition, the purpose for which they require a firearm and any previous criminal record or prohibition to possess a firearm. No training certificate for private citizens is required, but certain states demand certification from professional bodies.[88]

In addition, all civilian gun owners are required to get their weapons inspected once a year by a competent authority—inspections are also recorded in the license.[89] The licensing authority may refuse to grant the license if the applicant is of unsound mind, is below the age of sixteen, is deemed by the licensing authority to be a threat to the security of the public peace, has been sentenced on conviction of any offence involving violence or has been ordered to execute a bond for keeping the peace or for good behavior.[90] The licensing authorities maintain a list of firearm owners and the firearms held by them. No centralised database is maintained about firearm ownership and the identification of firearms. Every police station maintains a register of the license holders in its jurisdiction. Licenses are renewed after a prescribed period or three years, whichever is earlier. Any police officer or other officer specially empowered by the central government can demand the production of a license from the person carrying firearms or ammunition. The licensee is required to inform the licensing authorities of any change of place of residence.[91] While the licensing legislation is stringent, its application is significantly less so. Licensing authorities usually delegate their duties to junior functionaries who do not exercise much discretion when granting licences.[92]

All firearms manufactured in India are uniquely marked by stamping to indicate the registration number, the manufacturer or factory of origin and the year of manufacture. This applies to arms that are produced for pri-

Figure 8.8 Rate of Murders with and without Firearms in South Africa

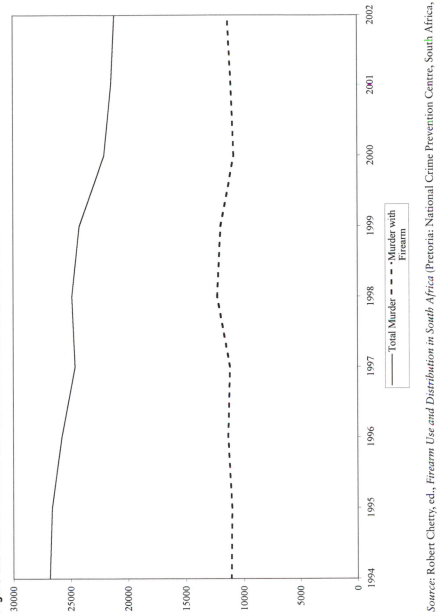

Source: Robert Chetty, ed., *Firearm Use and Distribution in South Africa* (Pretoria: National Crime Prevention Centre, South Africa, 2000), and South African Police Service, cited Rubem César Fernandes, Benjamin Lessing, Caroline Iootty, Julio Cézar Purcena, Luciana Phebo, Marcelo de Souza Nascimento, Pablo Dreyfus, and Patricia Rivero, "Brazil: The Arms and the Victims," *Viva Rio*, Rio de Janeiro, 2005, http://www.vivario.org.br/publique/cgi/cgilua.exe/sys/start.htm?sid=28&infoid=962.

vate or personal use and those that are used by armed forces, police or paramilitary forces. A record is maintained of these registration numbers by a central authority. A record of each and every weapon manufactured by the factory is kept, along with information on the concerned dealer.[93]

Evaluation

There are no formal evaluations of firearm regulation in India, but overall both levels of firearm ownership and firearm violence are relatively low. There are an estimated 40 million firearms in India, a country with more than 1 billion people. India accounts for the majority of firearm ownership in all of south Asia.[94] Firearms are often featured in ethnic conflict. In early 2002, in one of the worst massacres in recent history, nearly 2,000 Muslims were killed by ethnic Hindus.[95] For 1999, there were 12,000 reported firearm deaths (1.2 per 100,000) including 9,300 homicides, 600 suicides, and 2,400 accidents.[96]

JAPAN AND THE FAR EAST

Japan's firearm control regime is one of the strictest among industrialized countries. Following World War II, Allied forces enacted numerous orders to seize firearms and swords as part of the disarmament policy, and in 1945 the Prohibition Act for Possession of Firearms was passed, banning the possession of firearms unless otherwise permitted for official duty or hunting. In 1958, a new Firearms and Swords Control law was passed. It required permits for rifles, shotguns and air rifles (handguns are essentially prohibited; there are only fifty-eight handgun licenses for target shooting in the whole country). To qualify for a permit to acquire a rifle, an applicant must have owned a shotgun for at least ten years. Firearm owners must present their guns for inspection at the local police station when summoned, typically once a year. The law also defines safe-storage requirements, and homes may be inspected. Although Japan has one of the lowest rates of firearm ownership and violence in the world (fewer than fifty people are killed with guns in an average year), the Japanese remain concerned about what they perceive as an escalation in violence, the increasing proportion of firearm incidents involving individuals not associated with organized crime, and the flow of illegally imported firearms.[97] The country has taken a leadership role in international efforts to reduce the illicit trafficking of firearms in the context of both crime and conflict.[98]

Likewise, China severely restricts civilian possession of firearms, but does issue permits for security guards at financial institutions, hunters and target shooters. In an effort to reduce illicit firearm trafficking, China recently introduced the death penalty for those engaged in illegal trading of firearms. China prohibits the ownership of civilian handguns, while allowing hunting rifles to herdsmen and hunters who make their livelihoods from the act. This status must be proved to the county licensing body. The licensee must then obtain a "purchasing assignment certificate" from the local author-ites. Applicants must present a piece of photographic identification, pro-vide a curriculum vitae, pay the appropriate fee, undergo a background check, provide a genuine reason or a proposed aim for the use of the firearm and provide information regarding their plans for storage of the firearm. Civilian firearms must be kept in good condition, with measures taken in order to ensure their safety. Ammunition and firearms must be stored sep-arately. Airguns are permitted for "entertainment purposes."[99]

Singapore prohibits civilian possession of firearms. Singapore also main-tains the death penalty for certain firearm offences.[100]

Evaluation

Again, there does not seem to be any formal evaluation of firearm laws in the region but the extremely low rates of reported firearm violence sug-gest that laws may be one factor. (See Table 2.7.)

AUSTRALIA AND NEW ZEALAND

Firearm legislation in Australia is state controlled but is similar to, although somewhat more restrictive than, Canada's legislation. Prior to 1996, all states licensed owners, but only five of eight Australian states registered firearms. The National Committee on Violence recommended a series of measures related to firearm regulation in its 1990 report, including regis-tration of all firearms.[101] However, following the murder of thirty-five people in Port Arthur, Tasmania, on April 28, 1996, the Australian Police Ministers' Council and representatives of all Australian governments agreed to the Nationwide Agreement on Firearms, a ten-point plan for the regu-lation of firearms. Some of the elements of this plan were:

- Registration of all firearms.
- Stronger licensing provisions, including proof of genuine reason to own any firearm; uniform screening, which includes a five-year pro-hibition on owning firearms against anyone committing a domestic vi-olence act or subject to a restraining order; a safety course requirement; a minimum age of eighteen to purchase firearms; a twenty-eight-day waiting period and strict storage requirements.
- A ban on semiautomatic rifles and shotguns, except for those farmers who can prove a genuine need; the ban was accomplished through a special tax levy to raise $500 million to buy back the weapons from their owners.

- Improved controls on the trading of firearms, including a separate permit for each firearm and a ban on private and mail-order sales of firearms.[102]

By August 1997, more than 500,000 weapons had been surrendered.[103] A recent report by the Australian Centre of Criminology suggests that the new provisions have played a role in reducing lethal violence.[104]

More recently, Australia has extended the prohibitions in its law on certain types of weapons:

- Category C (prohibited except for occupational purposes): self-loading rimfire rifles with a magazine capacity of no more than ten rounds, self-loading shotguns with a magazine capacity of no more than five rounds, and pump-action shotguns with a magazine capacity no greater than five rounds; and

- Category D (prohibited except for official purposes): self-loading centrefire rifles, self-loading rimfire rifles with a magazine capacity of more than ten rounds, self-loading shotguns with a magazine capacity of more than five rounds, pump-action shotguns with a magazine capacity of more than five rounds.[105]

Since 2002, Australia has banned semiautomatic handguns with a barrel length of less than 120 millimeters and revolvers and single-shot handguns with a barrel length of less than 100 millimeters. Shot capacity is also limited to a maximum of ten. In addition, sporting pistols with a caliber over .38 are banned.[106]

New Zealand's firearm legislation also includes elements common to the legislation in Canada, Australia and the United Kingdom. It dates back to the Arms Importation Ordinance of 1845 and the Arms Act of 1920, which required that every firearm be registered with police. In 1983, the Arms Act shifted the focus from firearm registration to licensing firearm owners. Requirements depended on the class of user. For example, firearms could be acquired by those over sixteen who had satisfied police that they were a "fit and proper person." The act severely restricted access to handguns and revolvers, which, as in Canada, were classed as "restricted weapons." The law also established standards for dealers. In 1992, the Arms Amendment Act was introduced, which placed added emphasis on domestic violence and classified military-style semiautomatic weapons as restricted weapons. In addition, it created renewal requirements for firearm licenses.[107] The fact that New Zealand discontinued its manual, paper-based firearm registration system for long guns in 1983 is a point that has been used by opponents of strict gun control to "prove" that firearms registration does not work.[108] However, in response to police and public concerns, a comprehensive review of New Zealand's firearm regulations was initiated and the results were released in the summer of 1997.[109] They recommended, among other things, registration of all firearms. However, these plans were abandoned.

Evaluation

It is too early to evaluate the impact of these measures, but a recent study on firearm death (firearm suicide, homicide, accidents, legal intervention and undetermined) in Australia reported a 47 percent drop in firearm deaths between 1991 and 2001, most of it occurring after the legislative reforms.[110] (See Figure 8.9.) All firearm deaths dropped from 3.6 per 100,000 to 1.7 per 100,000, with rates for both men and women victims decreasing significantly.[111] Both firearm homicide and firearm suicide were similarly affected. One striking difference, however, was in the trends of firearm homicide. Rates for men fell from .53 per 100,000 to .34 per 100,000, but rates for women victims plummeted, from .44 per 100,000 to .14 per 100,000.[112] (See Figure 8.11.) Use of hunting rifles in homicides decreased significantly (see Figure 8.10).

CONCLUSIONS

There is no question that in some countries the regulation of civilian possession of firearms stimulates heated and often emotional debate. However, what is most striking in this review of international laws and emerging norms is how out of step the United States is with most industrialized countries and, indeed, many developing and postconflict countries. Notions of civilian rights to bear arms are not shared elsewhere in the world and, while there are other countries, particularly developing countries, that allow the carrying of firearms by civilians for self-protection in the face of high crime and inadequate policing, even countries with relatively permissive laws require licensing and registration of firearms. Although it is still early, preliminary results from Canada and Australia suggest significant declines in particular forms of gun violence targeted by their legislation. In Canada, the impacts of domestic gun laws are undermined by the flow of illegal handguns from the United States. In Great Britain, the results are uneven although it seems that gun homicides have not increased as quickly as homicides without guns, suggesting that the gun law may have had an impact. Great Britain, like Canada, is affected by the flow of illegal guns from Europe. In Europe and in the Far East gun laws are relatively strict. Nevertheless there are differences among countries. Contrary to much that has been written, Switzerland, which has a relatively high rate of gun ownership also has rates of suicide, domestic homicide and children killed with firearms that are well above European norms.

In developing countries that lack the political, policing and justice infrastructure to implement laws and where demand factors are often strong,

Figure 8.9 Firearm Deaths in Australia, 1991–2001

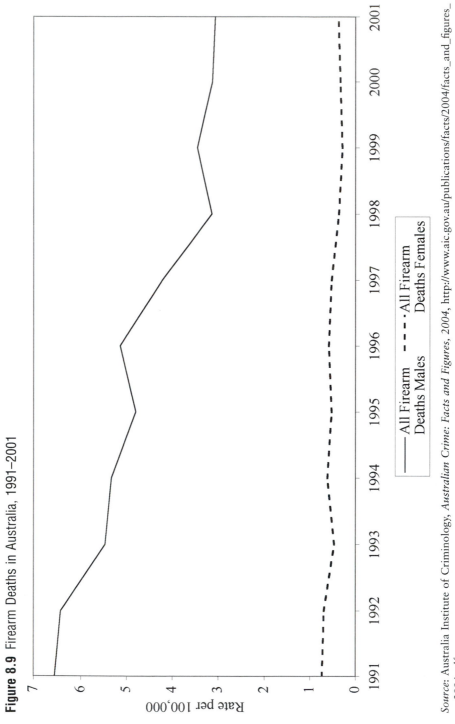

Source: Australia Institute of Criminology, *Australian Crime: Facts and Figures, 2004*, http://www.aic.gov.au/publications/facts/2004/facts_and_figures_2004.pdf.

Figure 8.10 Firearm Homicides in Australia by Type of Firearm

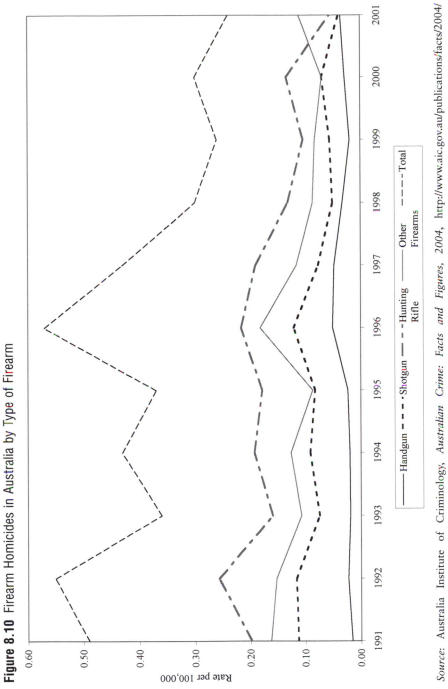

Source: Australia Institute of Criminology, *Australian Crime: Facts and Figures, 2004,* http://www.aic.gov.au/publications/facts/2004/facts_and_figures_2004.pdf.

Figure 8.11 Firearm Homicide Statistics for Australia Identified by Gender

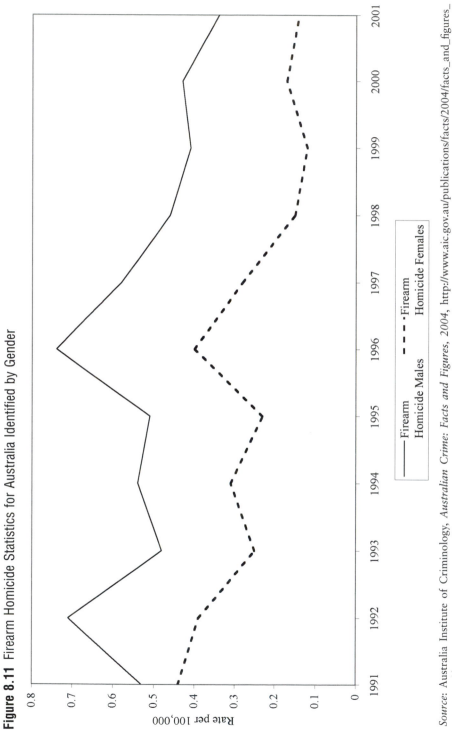

Source: Australia Institute of Criminology, *Australian Crime: Facts and Figures, 2004*, http://www.aic.gov.au/publications/facts/2004/facts_and_figures_2004.pdf.

it is often hard to assess impacts. In South Africa and Brazil it is simply too early to tell. But in Colombia, results from a small scale ban of handgun carrying were promising. What is interesting to note is that many developing countries and transitional economies with many of the factors expected to drive violence, but relatively limited supplies of firearms, have relatively low rates of gun violence. India and many countries from the former Soviet Union are a case in point in marked contrast to the Americas. The impact of legislative changes, however, seems to be clearest in countries with high incomes, stable political environments, and effective policing and judicial systems.[113] Countries with relatively strict laws, such as Brazil,[114] Jamaica[115] and South Africa,[116] have high rates of illegal firearms in circulation and high rates of lethal violence. More study is needed, but this appears to be the result of strong social, economic and political conditions fueling demand, a lack of effective enforcement capacity and accessible sources of illegal weapons. However, the international perspective shows clearly that most countries strictly regulate firearms and, at least among developing nations, there is evidence that this translates into lower rates of firearm violence and injury than is experienced in the United States.

9

Global Action: The Rise of an International Movement

As we have seen, countries' abilities to address the firearms problem are weakened by illegal trade. Firearms from countries with weak regulation often fuel the global trade in illegal guns. Over the last decade, attention has focused on global approaches to address the misuse of firearms in the context of crime and conflict. Informal cooperation among national groups working on the issue (both pro and con) has been evident for many years, but formal collaborations among governments have evolved relatively recently. Regional agreements through the Organization of American States, the European Union and the Economic Community of West African States emerged in the late 1990s, around the same time efforts to address illegal firearm trafficking began in earnest at the United Nations. Work at the United Nations has tended to proceed on parallel tracks—through the Commission on Crime Prevention and Criminal Justice, based in Vienna, and through the Disarmament Commission, based in New York.

To date, analyses of the international movement to control small arms have tended to focus on developments and activity among disarmament scholars and nongovernmental organizations (NGOs), while neglecting the work of scholars and advocates focused on civilian firearms, public health, policing and gender. This chapter examines the development of national gun control movements and their contributions to the development of a global movement.

The most obvious contribution of national gun control groups is their work on the development of firearms protocol and on marking and tracing firearms as part of the Convention on Transnational Organized Crime developed by the UN Commission on Crime Prevention and Criminal Justice. Throughout 1997 and 1998, there were NGO and Commission on Crime Prevention and Criminal Justice meetings at a series of regional consultations. Representatives from gun control organizations (Gun Control

Network, United Kingdom; Coalition for Gun Control, Canada; Trauma Foundation, United States; Gun Free, South Africa; Coalition for Gun Control, Australia) along with representatives from disarmament groups such as International Alert and British American Security Information and Co-operation (BASIC) participated. Along with the meetings in Vienna, regional meetings were held in the Ljubljana, Slovenia; Arusha, Tanzania; São Paulo, Brazil and New Delhi, India.

While firearm manufacturers and gun lobby groups have cooperated informally for many years, there is also evidence of increased coordination in and focus on international action over the past decade. The gun lobby was also well represented at the United Nations with spokespeople from the National Rifle Association (NRA) as well as national groups from other countries.

Not only have governments turned their attention to the need for collaboration, but there is an emerging global movement to control the proliferation and misuse of firearms. A number of resolutions passed by various United Nations councils and commissions have also stressed the importance of regulating civilian firearm possession as a strategy to reduce conflict, crime and human rights violations. Many states and most NGOs, including the International Action Network on Small Arms, which was founded in 1998,[1] have maintained that much more needs to be done to prevent the diversion and misuse of firearms. Since the 2001 UN conference entitled Illicit Trafficking in Small Arms and Light Weapons in All Its Aspects, there has been growing attention to the need to address the problem of regulating civilian possession. While explicit references to the regulation of civilian possession and use of small arms were deleted from the 2001 Conference Programme of Action as a result of pressure from the United States,[2] a number of the recommendations that were agreed to clearly have implications for the regulation of civilian firearm possession. One example includes the agreement to criminalize illegal possession. Most recently, the United Nations special rapporteur on human rights has stressed state obligations to adequately regulate civilian possession of firearms. In addition, many regional agreements have emerged that include harmonization of legislation regarding civilian possession.

With the growing concern about small-arms trafficking in the context of both conflict and crime in recent years, attention has focused on the need for adequate regulation of civilian possession of small arms. International forums have attempted to establish international norms and instruments. A wide range of agreements have emphasized the importance of legislation governing civilian possession, and in some cases these agreements have moved toward harmonizing laws among countries. Moreover, experience with community-based policing and community-based violence prevention has proven important for designing appropriate local solutions. Global instruments and agreements are only words on paper unless attention is paid to developing implementation strategies that work right down to the community level.

In addition, while a focus on violence against women has been critical in national gun control movements as well as the 1997 Resolution of the Commission on Crime Prevention and Criminal Justice, the discussion of gender and small arms is relatively new to disarmament groups.

GUN CONTROL: NATIONAL PERSPECTIVES

United States

The history of the gun control movement in the United States has been the subject of many books and is extremely complex. While the dominant group opposing gun control is clearly the NRA, the gun control movement is relatively fragmented, owing in large part to the multiple levels of jurisdiction—municipal, state and federal—involved in regulating firearms. In the United States, it is fair to say that the preoccupation has been domestic; relatively little attention has been paid to international developments on gun control, with a few exceptions. The assassinations of President John F. Kennedy, Robert Kennedy and Martin Luther King, Jr., all played a role in promoting stronger controls over firearms in the United States and in the passage of the Federal Gun Control Act in 1968.[3] Grassroots gun control advocacy groups emerged in the decades following.

For example, the National Coalition to Ban Handguns was formed by the Methodist Church Board of Church and Society in 1975. The organization established an impressive alliance of organizations, including the American Psychiatric Association, the American Public Health Association, the Black Women's Community Development Foundation, the American Jewish American Psychiatric Association, the National Association of Social Workers, the United States Conference of Mayors, the United States National Student Association as well as a host of faith-based, labour and community organizations.[4] The coalition supported a ban on the future private sale and possession of handguns, Saturday night specials, and assault weapons. The organization's first big accomplishment was a law adopted by the District of Columbia in 1976 that prohibited the purchasing of handguns and possession of assembled and loaded guns for self-defense.[5]

In 1979, it filed a suit against the Department of Defense, arguing that its marksman program, which required membership in the National Rifle Association, "compelled hundreds of thousands of American citizens to join an increasingly political, hard-line pro-gun organization in order to receive governmental benefits that should be available to all Americans."[6] In 1988, it played a major role in pressuring Maryland to ban the small, concealable handguns called Saturday night specials. The organization also played an important role in the California ban on military assault weapons in 1989.[7]

The National Coalition to Ban Handguns became the Coalition to Stop Gun Violence in 1990. It still has, as its ultimate goal, a ban on handguns,[8] but it now has a broader policy agenda, including licensing gun owners and registering guns, and has been a prime mover behind the gun industry lawsuits. The Coalition to Stop Gun Violence currently includes forty-five civic, professional and religious organizations and 100,000 individual members working to reduce gun violence.[9] Founder Michael Beard was a legislative aide to Robert Kennedy, and after Kennedy's assassination dedicated himself to the issue.[10]

Furthermore, the Coalition to Stop Gun Violence has actively engaged with other national gun control organizations in an effort to build the case for stronger gun control in the United States, particularly through licensing and registration. The Coalition to Stop Gun Violence has also been active in the evolving international movement to control guns, and has participated since 1998 in a range of international initiatives.

Another group that formed to raise the issue of gun control is the National Council to Control Handguns, which eventually became Handgun Control Inc. and is now the Brady Campaign. It was founded in 1974 by Mark Borinsky and businessman Pete Shields, who lost his son to gun violence. The new organization was initially a member of the National Coalition to Ban Handguns but broke with it over strategic direction. Founded by the victims of gun violence, it focused on the victims of gun violence. It gained profile and political influence when Sarah Brady joined it in 1985. Her husband, Jim Brady, President Ronald Reagan's press secretary, was disabled in an assassination attempt on the president's life in 1981, and she brought with her strong Republican ties. The organization played a major role in the passage of the 1988 Brady Bill, which made a seven-day waiting period mandatory for all handgun purchases. The law passed the House of Representatives in 1991, but part of it was ruled unconstitutional in 1994.

Handgun Control Inc. was one of the first advocacy groups in the United States to draw attention to the contrast between the United States and other countries. In 1989, it published a poster that contrasted the handgun murder rates in selected industrialized countries: The poster, with an American flag transposed onto a handgun, read, "In 1983, handguns killed 35 people in Japan, 8 in Great Britain, 27 in Switzerland, 6 in Canada, 7 in Sweden, 10 in Australia and 9,014 in the United States."[11] Viewed as a "moderate" group, Handgun Control (now the Brady Campaign) is the largest gun control organization in the United States, with a well-developed direct marketing operation, an annual budget of more than $7 million and a donor list of 1 million.[12] Partly because of its moderate stance, it was successful in forging alliances with a range of other organizations, including law enforcement. During 1989, while lobbying for a ban on assault weapons, Handgun Control was able to enlist the support of the International Association of Chiefs of Police in producing the video *The Deadly Distinction*. In 1995, Handgun Control had links with 108 national organizations, including the American Medical Association and many other proponents of strong laws.

While the NRA has been able to involve some police directly and indirectly, most mainstream police organizations support stronger gun control. They include the International Association of Chiefs of Police, the Police Executive Research Forum, the National Fraternal Order of Police and the National Association of Police Organizations.[13] The Brady Campaign also works with the Center to Prevent Handgun Violence to build links with educators and researchers. The National Education Association and the American Federation of Teachers support its work. Most major health care groups in the United States have also lined up in favor of moderate improvements to gun control. The American Academy of Pediatrics, the American Medical Association and most state medical associations are also on the side of gun control. In spite of its successes, however, the Brady Campaign's annual budget is still estimated to be only 5 percent of that of the NRA. For example, during the 1995–1996 election cycle, the Brady Campaign spent $315,000 while the NRA spent $6.6 million.[14]

The Violence Policy Center is another organization that focuses on banning handguns altogether, without compromise. The Violence Policy Center was founded by Josh Sugarman, formerly with the Coalition to Ban Handguns.[15] The Violence Policy Center criticized other groups for not going far enough in their efforts to ban handguns.[16] For example, Sugarman suggested that the Brady Campaign has actually helped the National Rifle Association by accepting the notion that citizens have the right to own handguns for legitimate purposes and by focusing on the issue of crime guns and the notion of "guns in the wrong hands." He suggested that this focus ignores the extent of the problem, including the issue of suicide.[17]

The now-defunct Ceasefire was formed with the support of *Rolling Stone* publisher Jann Wenner after the murder of former Beatle John Lennon. In addition to a plethora of state and local organizations, more recent entrants into the debate include the Bell Campaign, a victims' campaign, and the Million Mom March in 1999. Americans for Gun Safety, which has adopted a moderate stance, was sponsored by the Tides Foundation in 2000. Initially designed to be an umbrella organization, linking many of the state-based groups, it attempted to develop a position that would be accepted by the gun lobby. It now operates as a separate NGO and is probably the only procontrol group in the United States that believes that the Second Amendment guarantees the individual the right to own guns.[18] Other groups with injury prevention, peace and human rights agendas have been particularly active. The Handgun Epidemic Lowering Plan (HELP) is a health-based coalition led by pediatrician Katherine Christoffel. Join Together is a coalition that focuses not just on gun violence but also on drug abuse prevention. Physicians for Social Responsibility, a national affiliate of the International Physicians for the Prevention of Nuclear War, has been particularly active on the gun control issue along with its work against weapons of mass destruction.

In the United States, progress on strengthening gun laws has been uneven. The Brady Bill of 1998 was overturned. Similarly, the assault weapons ban of 1994 was allowed to lapse in 2004. However, significant progress has been made at the state level: a number of states have laws comparable to those of other industrialized countries.

In spite of public opinion, which generally supports stronger gun laws, there is a significant gap between public opinion and public policy in the United States, which many have interpreted as a failure of democracy.[19] Many features of government have tended to favor the NRA; these include the absence of campaign spending limits, the structure of government and the shift to conservatism. In addition, the salience of the gun control issues with supporters—the intensity of their support—pales in comparison with that of the gun lobby. While the majority of Americans support gun control, it is less likely to be an issue that determines their voting choices than it is for opponents of gun control.

Fragmentations within the gun control movement, conflicting agendas and competition for funding and the political agenda have certainly not helped. Donna Dees-Thomases, leader of the Million Mom March, has suggested that the competition for funds within the gun control movement has had a profoundly negative influence on the movement.[20] The Funders Collaborative for Gun Violence, sponsored by major donors to the gun control movement such as Soros Open Society, and the Joyce Foundation attempted to encourage more coherence and cooperation among gun control groups with limited success. Individuals and groups with particular approaches undermined the efforts of others. For example, the allies and funders of the Violence Policy Center were particularly vociferous in attacking other organizations that stopped short of banning handguns.[21] Analysts of the movement have noted that one of the challenges of the gun control movement in comparison to others has been its inability to establish "an internally consistent and culturally resonant frame sufficiently powerful to galvanize activism on a large scale or to noticeably influence public opinion."[22]

Canada

On December 6, 1989, a misogynist shot twenty-eight people at L'École Polytechnique, a Montreal engineering school, with a Ruger Mini-14, killing fourteen young women. Subsequent investigations reveal that he had a history of antisocial behavior, yet was able to legally acquire a semiautomatic military weapon with a large-capacity magazine, capable of firing thirty rounds of ammunition without reloading. After committing suicide, he was identified only after police conducted a store-by-store search in the Montreal area to see who had recently sold the rifle, because firearms were not registered except at the point of sale.[23] Like the Brady Campaign, the Coalition for Gun Control in Canada focused on building alliances with established organizations in policing, health and education. The Coalition for Gun Control developed into a collaborative effort involving 350 organizations from across the political spectrum and the country, including well-established institutional advocacy groups such as the Canadian Bar Association, the Canadian Public Health Association, the Canadian Association of Chiefs of Police and the Church Council on Justice and Corrections, as well as small issue-oriented advocacy groups such as the December 6th Foundation and a host of community organizations.

In spite of a tiny budget and small full-time staff, the coalition has been described as one of Canada's most influential advocacy groups in the justice sector.[24] In 1996, its president was the person most often cited on justice issues in Canada.[25] The coalition has also played a role in shaping and mobilizing public opinion, through the development and passage of two pieces of Canadian legislation.[26] Bill C-68, passed in 1991, strengthened screening processes, defined safe-storage requirements and banned many military assault weapons and large-capacity magazines. The 1995 legislation required all firearm owners to be licensed by 2001 and all firearms to be registered by 2003. It also banned short-barreled handguns and most semiautomatic military assault weapons (with grandfather clauses). Along with police, victims and health groups, the coalition successfully intervened to defend the law against a constitutional challenge in the Alberta Court of Appeal and the Supreme Court of Canada.[27]

The coalition has been analysed from a number of perspectives. In particular, the alignment between the organization and the complexity of environment has been an important factor. Coalition member organizations were very diverse coming from across the country and the political spectrum with representatives in many sectors (see Table 9.1). As a result, local groups and representatives could respond to local needs in terms of lobby politicians, mobilizing the community or addressing the media. This high level of decentralization was key given the diversity of the political, public and media landscapes. At the same time, the coalition is the only organization in the country devoted to gun control, and given the absence of funds, there is no competition on the issue. The principal challenge is the relative priority assigned to gun control relative to other justice and social issues.

The coalition continues to work on effective implementation of the law, and works to defend the law against efforts to erode it. In spite of a huge controversy surrounding the management and financing of the systems used to support Canada's gun control law, gun death, injury and crime in Canada have fallen dramatically with the progressive strengthening of legislation. For example, murders with rifles and shotguns have fallen by more than 60 percent, overall firearm deaths (predominantly suicides) have also fallen by 60 percent and murders of women with firearms and robberies with guns have also plummeted.[28] At the same time, murders and crimes involving handguns have remained relatively stable, fueled by the illegal trade in firearms, principally from the United States.

Consequently, international action on illicit trafficking is a key focus of the organization. The coalition is a founding member of the International

Table 9.1 Segmentation of the Coalition for Gun Control (Canada)

| Sector | Selected National Groups | Regional/Local Number of Groups (by sector) | | | | | |
		Quebec	Ontario	Maritimes	Prairies	BC
Law/justice	Canadian Bar Association Canadian Criminal Justice Association John Howard Society	3	3	2	2	1
Police	Canadian Association of Chiefs of Police Canadian Police Association (withdrew)	10	21	1	4	4
Women	YWCA Canadian Federation of University Women Catholic Women's League Jewish Women International Evangelical Lutherans	19	16	7	9	5
Health	Canadian Public Health Association Canadian Association of Emergency Physicians Trauma Association of Canada National Emergency Nurses Affiliation	24	19	1	6	1
Victims	Victims of Violence International CAVEAT December 6th Foundation	1	1			
Faith	United Church Catholic Bishops Canadian Jewish Congress Mennonite Central Committee	4	3	1	1	1

Table 9.1 (continued)

Sector	Selected National Groups	Regional/Local Number of Groups (by sector)				
		Quebec	Ontario	Maritimes	Prairies	BC
Peace	Church Council on Justice and Corrections Quaker Committee on Justice and Jails	2	2		2	
Labor	Canadian Labour Congress Canadian Auto Workers National Union of Public and General Employees	3	1			
Community	Japanese Canadians	4	2			
Education	Canadian Teachers Federation Canadian Association of University Teachers Association of Universities and Colleges of Canada	25	26	7	2	1
Municipal	Federation of Canadian Municipalities Big City Mayors	69	18	5	1	3
Safety	Canada Safety Council	163	111	38	26	16

Source: International Action Network on Small Arms, Strategic Plan, London: International Action Network on Small Arms, 2004.

Action Network on Small Arms and has acted as a consultant on gun control issues to advocacy organizations and governments around the world. Although the Canadian gun lobby is by no means as powerful as the American gun lobby, there is no doubt that there are spillover effects. The NRA has devoted considerable resources to attacking Canada's law (as well as those of Great Britain and Australia) and the president of the NRA has come to Canada in an effort to undermine support for the law.[29] Public support for gun control remains high, but as in the United States, the opponents are more highly motivated and vocal.

Australia

Efforts to strengthen gun laws in Australia were promoted by Gun Control Australia for many years, with limited success. That changed on May 10, 1996, when thirty-five people were killed and seventeen injured in Port Arthur, Tasmania, by a gun collector with military-style semiautomatic rifles. Within months, the Australian government announced a series of improvements to gun control legislation, including a buyback of semiautomatic weapons and a national licensing and registration scheme. Previously, only five of eight Australian states registered guns. Tasmania was not one of them.

Lawyers and public health organizations joined together, and a comprehensive law was adopted requiring the registration of all firearms, strengthening conditions for license acquisition, banning semiautomatic hunting rifles and shotguns and requiring a separate license for each firearm. The National Coalition for Gun Control included a number of public health experts, lawyers and women's organizations.[30] Women's groups were particularly important in applying pressure on the government.[31]

When it introduced the legislation that established national standards for licensing and registration as well as the $500 million buyback of semiautomatic weapons, the government regarded its move as a rejection of American-style gun culture. In 1998, Prime Minister John Howard said, "The gun culture is something that is abhorrent to Australians and I will do all in my power to stop it coming into this country, and I don't care who criticizes it."[32] The chair of the National Coalition for Gun Control, Rebecca Peters, went on to lead the Funders' Collaborative in the United States and was the first director of the International Action Network on Small Arms.

New Zealand

In New Zealand in the late 1990s, the New Zealand Police Association was among the groups pushing for stronger gun control.[33] Several women's groups became involved in the debate, including the National Collective of Independent Women's Refuges, the National Council of Women, the

YWCA and a wide range of sexual assault and domestic violence centres. An independent inquiry commissioned by the minister of police and led by Sir Thomas Thorp resulted in *Review of Firearms Control in New Zealand*, which recommended far-reaching revisions to the law.[34] The commission called on experts from around the world and like many other studies drew on international comparisons. However, progress in New Zealand has been stymied by a change in government and lack of coherent advocacy efforts or leadership.[35]

United Kingdom

At Hungerford on August 19, 1987, a mass shooting left sixteen people dead and fourteen injured. It also precipitated changes to the gun laws in Great Britain in 1988. In order to possess any firearms, applicants needed to prove their fitness as well as need for firearms. For the first time, all guns including shotguns were registered with the local police, and a certificate was required to purchase ammunition, giving Great Britain one of the most stringent gun laws in the world.

But on March 13, 1996, one of the most horrifying shootings in recent memory raised the bar again. In the tiny village of Dunblane, Scotland, sixteen primary-school children and their teacher were murdered and another ten were injured by a member of a local gun club who then killed himself. Following the Dunblane massacre, gun control in the United Kingdom gained momentum.[36] The Snowdrop Campaign, for example, led by Ann Pearston, Jacqueline Walsh and Rosemary Hunter, began a petition to ban handguns. Eventually, they collected 700,000 signatures, and the parents of the Dunblane children were involved in submitting the petition to parliament. Ann Pearston delivered a critical speech to the Labour Party Conference in October 1996, which resulted in the party subsequently adopting a policy banning all handguns, which they proceeded to implement when they came into power the following year. Subsequently, a broader mandate was developed by the Gun Control Network, based in London.[37] The organization played a major role in promoting the UK ban on handguns and subsequently has worked on other issues, including a ban on replica firearms. The UK gun control campaign explicitly defined itself as a rejection of American culture. Former cabinet minister David Mellor said, "What I want to see taken out are the Clint Eastwood–type guns which are an American accretion on our way of life. If we want to import the American way of life, we've got to come to terms with the American way of death."[38]

Japan

Japan has a level of community safety unmatched by most of the world and reinforced by strong cultural norms. For example, Japan had fewer gun deaths in 1995 than occur in an average day in the United States. It is interesting to note that in 1995, Japan had a total of 168 firearms shootings, in which 34 people were killed and 33 were injured. This caused the Japanese to grow concerned about what they perceived as an escalation in violence. "Gun related crimes have threatened to undermine the fabric of Japan's peaceful society. A peaceful and safe society is a common desire of the people. In order to stop the spread of firearms and prevent the tragedy of gun-related crimes, it is imperative that each person understand the danger and the anti-social nature of firearms and resolves to eliminate gun-related crimes," proclaimed the National Police Agency.[39] Awareness of the issue of firearm regulation in Japan was influenced by the murder of Japanese citizens travelling in the United States. In one instance, exchange student Yoshira Hattori was shot and killed on October 31, 1992, in Baton Rouge, Louisiana, when he made the fatal error of knocking on the wrong door. Another Japanese citizen, Kei Sunade, was killed in 1994 in New York City. Yoshi's father, Masaichi Hattori, presented a petition requesting a ban on guns signed by 1.72 million people, the largest in history, to President Clinton. Mr. Hattori and Kei's father, Koichi Sunade, formed the Association to End Gun Violence. Mr. Hattori has supported community firearms regulation initiatives. The assassination attempt on Takaji Kunimatsu, the commissioner general of the Japanese Police Agency, in March 1995, galvanized the police, citizens and government on the issue.[40] Again, advocacy against guns in Japan was seen as a rejection of American-style culture.[41] The National Police Agency sponsored a meeting of international gun control advocates from the United States, Australia and Canada in 1996 in an effort to strengthen international collaboration.

South Africa

As was the case with the Coalition to Ban Handguns in the United States, the gun control movement in South Africa grew out of a faith-based antiviolence campaign. Peter Storey, bishop of the Methodist Church of South Africa, initiated the Gun Free South Africa campaign, calling on people to turn in their guns in December 1994. While the number of guns actually turned in was relatively small—about 241 in total—the campaign played an important educative role. As the organization became formalized in 1995, it drew on other peace movements and leaders, including leaders from the Black Sash movement, an anticonscription women's movement. The organization focused its efforts on a wide range of campaigns aimed at reducing both the demand for and the supply of firearms. Some of its supporters made explicit the links between firearm possession and masculinity.[42] The campaign to create gun-free zones had buildings such as schools and hospitals, and even communities, declare themselves "gun free." While this program initially relied on voluntary compliance, the new firearm legislation passed in 2000 added the force of law to maintain these zones.

In 1999, Gun Free Zones became one of the founding members of the Gun Control Alliance, a cross-sectoral coalition modeled on successful gun control coalitions in other countries. Although there were some tensions over the long-term goal of banning all firearms and the short-term goal of supporting legislation to regulate firearms, these tensions were successfully negotiated, in contrast to the experience in other countries such as the United States. Currently, over 200 diverse national, regional and local organizations support the Charter for Gun Control, including business, health, religious, women and youth organizations. These include: Black Sash, Business against Crime, Child Accident Prevention Foundation of South Africa, Disabled People of South Africa, the Human Rights Committee, Human Rights Institute of South Africa, Quaker Peace Centre, South African Association of Youth Clubs, South African NGO Coalition, South African Society of Physiotherapy and Red Cross Children's Hospital.[43] Later in 1999, the government introduced its new Firearms Law. Over the next few years, Gun Free Zones and the Gun Control Alliance worked to refine the terms of the Firearms Law, and its attendant regulations, systems and implementation.

Women's groups also played an important role in both Gun Free South Africa and the newly founded Gun Control Alliance. The gun lobby in South Africa has vehemently opposed the legislation.[44] The prominence of women also contributed to particularly aggressive and misogynistic opposition to the new law.[45]

In addition, Gun Free South Africa has been involved in international efforts since the late 1990s. It was a member of HELP, based in Chicago, and an early participant in the International Action Network on Small Arms. In recent years a substantial portion of its funding has come from international sources.

Brazil

Viva Rio is a grassroots organization focused on bringing an end to violence. Following the shooting of street children in central Rio de Janiero and the random killing of favela residents by military police, a major campaign was organized to protest the violence. One of the organizers of the campaign, Rubem César Fernandes, went on to found Viva Rio. In its early stages, the focus of the organization was primarily grassroots mobilization and protests against violence as well as media campaigns. In 1995, for example, following a politically motivated kidnapping, Viva Rio organized a march of 400,000 people demanding an end to violence. In 1996, it began community-based programs in the favelas focused on addressing the root causes of violence and creating more opportunities for disenfranchised youth.

Firearm issues were a small part of the organization's overall activities. In 1994 Viva Rio organized its first community disarmament project, Rio Desarme, aimed at collecting firearms. In 1998, the organization initiated another gun-collection campaign. On June 24, 2001, the organization led the public destruction of 100,000 guns that had been seized by police over previous decades.

The organization was instrumental in the collection of critical information about the sources of guns recovered by police in Brazil. Working with the police, it created a database of 750,000 firearms owned or seized in the state of Rio to support better analysis and enforcement. Results from the analysis showed that many guns recovered in Brazil had previously been exported and were being illegally imported back into the country. In 1996, Brazil suspended small-arms export licenses to private dealers in Paraguay because of evidence that guns were being exported and illegally reimported.[46]

In 1999, the organization began to focus its efforts on legislative change. During that year, it collected more than 1 million signatures in support of a law to ban the sale of guns in Brazil. While the law passed, it was ruled unconstitutional. Subsequently, the organization pressed for the Disarmament Statute, which passed in 2003. The new law increases restrictions on firearm ownership and calls for a national referendum to ban all firearms.

The Viva Rio initiative looks to reduce the availability and use of firearms, notably in the poor areas of Rio de Janeiro, which have some of the highest rates of firearm death in the world. The use of firearms in violence against women in Brazil has been a significant focus of campaigning in that country. There have also been efforts to appeal to traditional notions of gender in efforts to counter gun violence. One of Viva Rio's approaches has urged, "Choose gun-free: It's your weapon or me!" The slogan seeks to mobilize the female population to refuse weapons and deconstruct the myth that firearms equate to protection.[47] Dealing with the culture of violence, and in particular attitudes toward guns, is an essential part of a strategy to counter violence whether in the context of conflict, gang warfare or family violence.[48]

Viva Rio began working with international NGOs in 1998 after a regional consultation of the UN Commission on Crime Prevention and Criminal Justice. NGOs attending the meeting, including BASIC and the Coalition for Gun Control, participated with Viva Rio in workshops and attended the high-profile gun destruction event. Subsequently, Viva Rio participated in several international events and became a founding member of IANSA. Today it works with a range of international NGOs, including International Alert, the World Health Organization, the Small Arms Survey and the Centre for Humanitarian Dialogue, based in Geneva. Over the past five years, its revenue from international sources has grown—in 2003 it received almost half its funds from international sources.[49] Data on the firearm death rates in Brazil, relative to other countries, became a key element in the organization's advocacy efforts. In the Brazilian context, the role of NGOs and the relationship with the government and the police is evolving. Advocacy efforts in this environment are dramatically different than in other contexts given the relatively recent introduction of democracy and evolving commitment to human rights and non-military policing.

GROWING INTERNATIONAL COOPERATION

The international movement to control guns evolved as a result of the coming together of a range of organizations addressing the international gun problem from very different perspectives. A number of papers have been written in recent years documenting aspects of the emerging small-arms movement,[50] but the authors tend to focus on the aspects that they know best and, as a result, provide only a partial picture. Previous analysis of the global effort to regulate small arms, comprehensively document the role of disarmament scholars and NGOs,[51] but does not address the role of sectoral groups (health, women, etc.) or scholars and organizations focusing on the firearms control.

A number of studies appeared during the early 1990s comparing firearm death and crime rates in different countries. The world victimization survey, for example, looked at gun ownership rates and crime rates. Martin Killias, a Swiss criminologist, published several papers on the subject,[52] as did both the Canadian and U.S. governments.[53] While the gun lobby used international comparisons to argue that gun ownership was inextricably tied to history and culture,[54] international comparisons were helpful to groups working on national legislation. For example, Canada's Coalition for Gun Control used international data and brought in international experts from Switzerland, Australia and England to support its efforts to develop and defend Canada's national gun control laws in 1995. Similarly, NGOs in Australia, New Zealand, Great Britain, Australia, South Africa and Japan used the experiences of countries such as Canada and the United States in formulating their gun laws.

A conference on international gun laws was organized by the New York Law School, featuring speakers from the United States, Canada and Germany, in 1994. Groups such as the Coalition against Gun Violence and HELP in the United States organized sessions as part of their annual conferences, in part to bring international perspective to bear on the U.S. problem. For example, in April 1997, HELP organized a workshop on international perspectives on gun control, drawing on experts from South Africa, New Zealand, Australia and Canada.

In February 1997, NGOs from around the world met in London to discuss the development of an international gun control network.[55] Included were the Coalition for Gun Control (Canada), Coalition for Gun Control (Australia), Gun Control Network (United Kingdom), Waffen Weg (Austria) and British American Security Information Council (BASIC). Bilateral and multilateral cooperation was common, as was information sharing through various international forums and networks. International experts were often brought in to provide support for national advocacy initiatives. In addition to being active at the national level, these groups were active in the development of the Firearms Protocol of the United Nations Convention on Transnational Organized Crime through a series of regional meetings and commission meetings in Vienna. The focus of these meetings was examining the current status of and standards for national legislation, import/export controls on commercial shipments of firearms, as well as marking and tracing standards. Regional meetings provided an opportunity to expand international cooperation among gun control organizations. For example, at the United National America's Regional Workshop on Firearms Regulation for the Purposes of Crime Prevention and Public Safety in São Paolo, Brazil, in December 1997, representatives from Canada's Coalition for Gun Control, the World Health Organization coordinating centre, BASIC and other NGOs met with Viva Rio to discuss areas of collaboration.

During the same period, groups focused on disarmament issues were attempting to address the problem of the proliferation of small arms in conflict zones, with an emphasis on controlling the arms trade among states. Researchers such as Michael Klare,[56] Aaron Karp[57] and Chris Smith[58] focused attention on the growing problem.

Several academics and policy "think tanks" published extensively on the issue. Organizations such as the Arias Foundation (Costa Rica) and Saferworld (Great Britain) were active in the advocacy related to the development of the European Union Code of Conduct, which prohibited the exports of small arms to countries likely to abuse human rights. Their primary focus was on small arms transferred between states that were fuelling conflicts. Still other organizations such as Project Ploughshares (Canada) and various disarmament groups were involved in initiatives related to weapons collection and disarmament in conflict zones as well as addressing the root causes or demand factors associated with violence.

Public health researchers and advocates had been particularly active for many years in the United States on the issue of gun control. In Canada, they also played a critical role in the development of legislation in 1991 and 1995. Similarly, in Australia, the public health perspective was often invoked. One seminal study, A Tale of Two Cities by Arthur Kellermann and colleagues, contrasted the levels of gun violence in Seattle, Washington and Vancouver, Canada, in 1998,[59] but for the most part, international research has been limited until fairly recently.[60] The International Committee of the Red Cross (ICRC) and the World Health Organization (WHO) began to explore the issue around the same time. For example, ICRC researchers published several papers in medical journals on aspects of small arms,[61] and the ICRC entered the debate.[62] A very few health-oriented advocacy organizations took a dual perspective, looking at both the national and international levels. For example, national affiliates such as Physicians for Social Responsibility in the United States and Physicians for Global Survival in Canada were also active on the international stage as part of International Physicians for the Prevention of Nuclear War. In Canada, the Canadian Public Health Association as well as the World Health Organization coordinating centre in Quebec City also saw the importance of the issue, sponsoring a session bringing health professionals together from around the world in February 1998.[63] In March 1998, a meeting in Toronto brought together gun control, public health and disarmament experts in an effort to "find common ground."[64] Subsequent workshops focused on research needs[65] resulted in the formation of the Small Arms/Firearms Education and Research Network and an effort to track total global firearm death and injury.

During the late 1990s and early years of the twenty-first century, gun control organizations continued to build international links in an effort to shape in the UN Commission on Crime Prevention and Criminal Justice deliberations on the development of a firearms protocol to address the illicit trafficking of firearms. Linkages grew among NGOs in Japan, Brazil (Viva Rio) and South Africa (Gun Free South Africa), and Philip Alpers began to distribute regular updates through the Gun Policy Network. Consultations conducted by the UN Commission on Crime Prevention and Criminal Justice in São Paolo, Vienna and other cities around the world provided opportunities for these groups to build linkages and also involved representations by growing numbers of disarmament groups, such as BASIC, who began to recognize the importance of the crime perspective.[66] A number of international and regional meetings were held to discuss the possibilities for more formal collaboration among the gun control, disarmament and public health communities.[67]

During 1997, attention to small arms also grew in prominence on the international agenda on disarmament, and NGOs began to organize around that issue. A civil society campaign to address it had started to emerge.[68] In December 1997, a meeting of NGOs in Washington, D.C., brought together representatives of twenty-three organizations that spanned fields as diverse as conflict/disarmament, human rights/humanitarian efforts, gun control and development/refugee relief.[69] In the follow-up to this meeting, Ed Laurance of the Monterey Institute of International Studies founded the Web site PrepCom to serve as a clearinghouse of information on small arms activities by both governments and NGOs. Other NGO meetings were held in London in February 1998 and in Johannesburg in May 1998.

Groups from both the firearms control and emerging small arms control movement met several times to explore the opportunities for a unifying conceptual framework. Although data were still limited, it became clear that as many deaths with firearms occurred in countries considered to be "at peace" as in conflict zones and the "costs" of small arms extended far beyond mortality and morbidity. Efforts to differentiate "crime" and "conflict" were not useful from a human security perspective. While military weapons were the problem in some regions, handguns were the weapons of choice in many others. The importance of linking firearms control and small arms control initiatives was raised by handful of academics.[70] Researchers who made the links between domestic regulation of firearms and the international small arms issue early in the process included Michael Renner,[71] Natalie Goldring,[72] Chris Smith,[73] Lora Lumpe,[74] Abdel-Fatau Musah and Niobe Thompson,[75] Wendy Cukier[76] and later, Virginia Gamba.[77] Indeed, many appeared to assiduously ignore the role of civilian firearms, for example, stressing the proliferation of postconflict AK-47s in South Africa, in spite of the fact that the evidence was clear that most of the guns fuelling violence were handguns.

Some recognized that from a public health or human security perspective, the current constructions were not particularly helpful. While data were incomplete, it was apparent that as many people were killed with firearms in regions considered "at peace" as in those "in conflict."[78] While multisectoral alliances, including community-based policing, have been an essential part of domestic gun control movements in most countries, an understanding of the importance of these alliances and "security sector" reform has come relatively recently to the small arms community. Amnesty International was one of the first international NGOs to seriously examine this dimension of the issue, even though groups such as the Institute for Security Studies in South Africa made the link between policing and security many years previously. As with domestic gun control movements, international women's organizations also proved to be important in the development of both the UN Firearms Protocol and the 2001 Programme of Action. A gender perspective on the issue erodes many of the distinctions between legal and illegal, national and international, military and civilian.[79]

THE NRA GOES GLOBAL

It almost goes without saying that the globalisation of the gun control movement was paralleled by the globalisation of the gun lobby. While the NRA was primarily focused on the United States, it had intervened in other national debates on occasion. As soon as the issue of firearms was put on the table at the United Nations, the NRA was there. For a number of years, in fact, the only NGO dedicated to the issue of firearms with Economic and Social Council consultative status at the United Nations was the NRA. Pro–gun control organizations were, for the most part, sponsored by other organizations with consultative status, such as the World Society of Victimology, International Fellowship of Reconciliation, Verification Research, Training and Information Centre (VERTIC), International Council of Women and World Society of Friends (Quakers). The NRA and its international affiliates were the NGOs most frequently participating in the

United Nations and even on the U.S. delegation.[80] As discussed in Chapter 6, the NRA has been active internationally for many years.

The NRA was active through the late 1990s during the debates over the UN Firearms Protocol. Not only did it actively participate in the proceedings, but it also used the "threat" of international controls as a key component in its domestic fund-raising. NRA executive vice president Wayne LaPierre claimed that the United Nations is engaged in nothing less than "a worldwide effort to crush any culture that does not submit to voluntary civil disarmament." The organization sent out a fund-raising letter warning that it could be only a matter of time before the United Nations "demands gun confiscation on American soil."[81]

In 1997, the NRA joined with progun groups and firearm manufacturers from eleven other countries—including France, the Netherlands, Germany, Italy and Great Britain—to establish an international lobbying group, World Forum on the Future of Sports Shooting Activities, now headquartered in Belgium. According to its Web site, "The WFSA is a proactive advocacy organization working in concert with international bodies, national governments and regulatory authorities for the worldwide promotion and preservation of sport shooting activities."[82] Currently, it represents forty member organizations in some twenty nations around the world. In the United States, members include the NRA, (Safari Club International SCI), the Single Action Shooting Society and several industry groups. The WFSA was active at both the 1993 and 1995 review conferences.[83]

The NRA is reported to have contributed money to progun political candidates in countries such as Australia and New Zealand, and waged public campaigns against gun regulation in Canada, Japan, the United Kingdom and South Africa. The Australian attorney general accused the NRA of offensive, inaccurate and outrageous tactics when it broadcast an infomercial last year, claiming that violent crime had skyrocketed after the government tightened gun laws following the Port Arthur shooting massacre that left thirty-five people dead in 1996. Recently, the gun lobby gave a Canadian politician an award for his fight against gun control.[84] The NRA and its allies have presented the United Nations processes as part of an international campaign to ban all firearms.[85] They are now actively engaging in the process, most recently prodding a Louisiana senator to sponsor a bill withdrawing financial support for the United Nations if it treads on gun owner rights.[86]

This is not new. When the Economic Community of Western African States imposed a small arms moratorium in 1998 and requested funds to help enforce it, Sen. Jesse Helms (R-NC) blocked U.S. aid. He opposed using the taxpayers' money to "promote policies in foreign countries that may very well be a violation of the Second Amendment to the U.S. Constitution." Similarly, the NRA has opposed efforts to disarm Iraqis as part of the effort to establish peace.[87]

THE EMERGENCE OF THE INTERNATIONAL ACTION NETWORK ON SMALL ARMS

The International Action Network on Small Arms (IANSA) was created in July 1998, at a meeting that involved forty-five groups representing thirty-three NGOs from nineteen countries. At that meeting, the terms of reference for the network—a network of networks—as well as the key points of IANSA's policy were hammered out: "prevent the proliferation and unlawful use of light weapons."[88] IANSA's structure was intended to support campaigns by its members, provided they relate to the organization's core objectives. Given the complexity of the small arms issues, it was concluded that a single campaign could not address the network's objectives. Rather, the network was designed to support work at the global, regional and national level. It stated,

> IANSA will provide a transnational framework under which groups and organizations, working as coalitions or otherwise, and operating at the local, national, regional and international levels, can organize around particular concerns and issues. This network facility will not only provide a range of services to the development and effective functioning of particular campaigns and initiatives, it will also provide a mechanism for overall strategic development and cohesiveness of small arms action within a framework of respect for the autonomy of local and national efforts, and with special recognition and support for regional efforts.[89]

While academics and policy organizations are part of the network, the majority of groups are small advocacy-oriented organizations, often operating at a national level. While many of the major figures involved in the early stages of the network were well known as researchers and writers in the disarmament community, there was a gap between those writing about small arms and those with grassroots advocacy experience. Denise Garcia, for example, suggests that the network was formed as a result of a deal struck between the Canadian minister of foreign affairs and eminent scholar Ed Laurence of the Monterey Institute.[90] Scholars such as Garcia,[91] Krause[92] and Laurence[93] have suggested the global small arms movement emerged from a small group of disarmament researchers, overlooking the extensive groundwork laid by firearms injury scholars and gun control groups nationally and through the UN crime commission. Many of those attempting to lead the movement had little or no grassroots advocacy experience. In fact the founding of IANSA was significant for harnessing both the small arms/disarmament scholarship and advocacy with the extensive work on preventing firearms injury and gun control movements in the Northern and Southern hemispheres the governance structure established for IANSA in 1998 and refined in 2000 was intended to provide representation at the regional level and in some ways reflected the structure of successful national gun control coalitions. Given the critical differences between the issue of small arms, which were to be regulated, and land mines which were to be banned, the founders explicitly rejected the International Committee to Ban Landmines model. Rather than focusing on a single campaign, IANSA was designed to be a "campaign of campaigns" or "network of networks."

Subsequently, key thematic interests such as public health and women were identified as requiring representation. Although developing an international network has not been without its challenges, particularly with respect to governance issues and communication, the latest round of strategic planning indicated a high level of engagement with the issues and values in the network.[94] IANSA terms of reference were refined in Brussels in October 1998 with an extended audience of 180 participants from more than 100 NGOs.[95] IANSA was formally launched at the Hague Appeal for Peace, in May 1999. By then, it included 120 members. Today the network includes 600 members from 100 different countries.[96] The 2001 Conference on the Illicit Trade in Small Arms and All Its Aspects provided a rallying point for IANSA mobilization and action. IANSA played an important role in the preparatory meetings and helped coordinate the activities of the NGOs.

Laurence's PrepCom Web site provided a useful source of information in the lead-up to the UN conference on the Illicit Trade in Small Arms, but IANSA's mandate was much broader than the 2001 UN conference and required more than information exchange. Some NGOs have focused on particular initiatives, for example, a convention on brokering or a convention on marking or the work on the Firearms Protocol. In a recent survey, many IANSA members indicated an equal or greater interest in regional, national or even community-based action. While many of the large, global, policy-oriented organizations focus primarily on activities in the United Nations, for many of the grassroots groups that are part of IANSA, the UN processes do not seem particularly relevant to their work on the ground. Indeed, while the 2001 Programme of Action is considered to be an important step forward because it represents global consensus, many of the agreements that have been struck at the regional level are more aggressive and relevant to the work of some NGOs. The network is designed to support a range of initiatives at the global, regional and national level and to provide a means of information exchange.

IANSA's action plan includes:

- Preventing and combating illicit transfers through developing legally binding instruments on marking and brokering;
- Controlling legal transfers between states to reduce the risk that weapons will be used in human rights violations;

- Controls on the availability, use and storage of small arms within states, including strong domestic firearm regulation and a ban on civilian possession of military weapons;
- Collection and destruction of surplus weapons from both civil society and regions of conflict;
- Increasing transparency and accountability;
- Resources to support effective implementation;
- Support for research and information-sharing measures to counter demand; and
- Improved coordination between government and civil society at all levels.[97]

A considerable amount of effort went into developing the position. Initially, a number of IANSA members excluded reference to regulation of the civilian possession of firearms, partly to avoid the wrath of the gun lobby, and partly because the intransigence of the U.S. government was well known. For example, the first paper in the influential Biting the Bullet series[98] made no reference to the regulation of civilian possession, in spite of the priority ascribed to this in many regions. This was remedied in two subsequent papers, which highlighted the importance of the regulation of civilian possession.[99]

Others, particularly those from the United States, were apprehensive about allying themselves with an issue as controversial as gun control and tried to maintain a narrow definition of small arms (military specification only) and to exclude any reference to regulation of domestic firearms. But others, including NGO representatives and academics, were equally resistant. In October 2001, a second, larger meeting was held in Brussels that involved 180 individuals representing more than 100 NGOs from across the globe. The purpose of this meeting was to better define the role of IANSA, and through a series of workshops and detailed discussions, the parties addressed and developed IANSA's founding document, which contained a statement of purpose, policy framework, programme of action and organizational structure.[100] As Natalie Goldring noted, the small arms agenda was almost hijacked by the NRA at this conference when the drafters of a key document amended it to state, "These measures are not aimed at banning appropriate possession and use of sporting weapons or self-defense firearms by individual citizens in strict accordance with national laws and regulations without consulting the broader group."[101] Given that few countries besides the United States allow civilian possession of small arms for self defense, the footnote would have been resisted by most countries present had they been consulted. Efforts to erode the position of IANSA continue.

Groups such as the Eminent Persons Group, led by Count Albi (Albrecht Gero Muth), worked with gun manufacturers[102] and tried to pressure

IANSA NGOs to exclude references to civilian possession of firearms. There were difficult discussions within the NGO community regarding the strategy for the 2001 conference. A survey of IANSA members, made it clear that the majority thought that regulating civilian possession was critical. In the end, the IANSA position paper for the 2001 conference included civilian possession as part of the position.[103]

As more data were collected, however, it showed (1) that there were more firearms in civilian hands than under state control, (2) that deaths from firearms in countries "at peace" were comparable to those in countries at war, and (3) that in many contexts, such as South Africa, handguns were a much greater problem than military assault weapons, the boundaries were eroded. Coupled with pressure from national groups, particularly those in arms-infested areas such as Brazil and South Africa, a number of the global organizations began to recognize the need to include civilian possession in the Programme of Action,[104] and influential scholars such as Ed Laurence noted that its omission was a serious failing in the Programme of Action.[105] Similarly, national groups focused on disarmament eventually embraced the issue. Of note, for example, is the recent intervention of Amnesty International in support of the U.S. assault weapons ban.[106]

Groups associated with IANSA cut across sectors and regions[107] including such diverse organizations as the Bonn International Center for Conversion (BICC), Human Rights Watch (HRW), International Alert (IA), Institute for Security Studies (ISS), Amnesty International (AI), Norwegian Initiative on Small Arms Transfers (NISAT), Stockholm International Peace Research Institute (SIPRI), Groupe de Recherche et D'information sur la Paix et la Sécurité (GRIP), International Peace Research Institute (PRIO), The Centre for Humanitarian Dialogue, Viva Rio, Gun Free South Africa, The Coalition for Gun Control, The Handgun Epidemic Lowering Plan, Womens International League for Peace and Freedom (WILPF), the Commission of Nobel Peace Laureates, Saferworld, International Physicians for the Prevention of Nuclear War (IPPNW), and many many others (see Table 9.2).

IANSA is significant, in part because it represents the coming together of a range of groups from many countries concerned about the problems of small arms and firearms from a variety of perspectives. Historically, the arms control, firearms control and health and development organizations had proceeded on separate tracks, but in its founding document, IANSA maintained that:

> IANSA's vision is to be instrumental in reducing the availability and misuse of small arms within a framework of human security. The measure of our collective success is the reduction in the death, injury, and suffering generated by the misuse of small arms. In order to break the cycle of underdevelopment, violence and conflict which is fuelled by the proliferation of small arms, two types of policies must be pursued simultaneously and with equal emphasis: those which address controlling or limiting the trade in and diffu-

sion of small arms; and those which are directed towards reducing the demand for these weapons.[108]

The UN Conference on the Illicit Trade in Small Arms in All Its Aspects, July 2001

On July 9, 2001, the United Nations Conference on the Illicit Trade in Small Arms and Light Weapons in All Its Aspects opened at the UN headquarters in New York. After roughly two years of preparation, the conference set out to discuss, and eventually approve, the Programme of Action to Prevent, Combat and Eradicate the Illicit Trade in Small Arms and Light Weapons in All Its Aspects (Programme of Action), which became the global reference for the efforts conducted at all levels, local, national and international, against the scourge of the illicit proliferation of small arms and light weapons. Before turning its attention to the draft programme, the conference dedicated five days to opening statements by states, regional organizations and other actors involved in the UN process. One of these opening days was entirely devoted to statements by NGOs, which included both representatives of the progun lobby, under the guidance of the U.S.-based NRA and its international counterpart, the World Forum on the Future of Sports Shooting Activities (WFSA), and representatives of IANSA.

NGO participation during the conference had been a matter hotly debated during the preparatory process. In the end, it was decided that NGOs would be able to participate with a low profile: they would be allowed in the conference room but only in the gallery; they would be excluded from the sessions of negotiation on the programme and they would be given one day to present their views.

The conference provided a crucial opportunity to address the urgent problem of the spread and misuse of small arms and light weapons. It focused on the illicit aspect of the small arms trade, as many illegal weapons in circulation were at some point legally transferred by governments or with government approval. In addition, governments have failed to rein in private traffickers. Legal sales to governments also warranted international attention as they may also lead to human rights abuses or prolong conflicts.

Furthermore, the conference aimed to negotiate and approve binding norms and implement measures to stop weapons from winding up in the hands of abusive forces, be they governments or nonstate actors. Four priority areas were looked at:

- Adoption of codes of conduct on arms transfers;
- Establishment of transparency mechanisms;
- Implementation and enforcement of arms embargoes; and
- Internationalization of norms regulating the activities of arms brokers.

At the conference, 134 statements were made by 171 countries. Some of the sixteen various measures agreed on to curb the international proliferation of guns follow:

- Ninety-five states advocated marking weapons to determine origins and transfer routes to prevent illicit diversion. Specifics differed, however, as some states wanted marking to be a national responsibility, while others wanted "agreed minimum standards"; a third group advocated negotiation of legally binding international agreements.
- Eighty states called for stricter controls on import and export licensing. Mandatory licensing was seen as central to preventing the diversion of weapons to the illicit market.
- Seventy-nine states called for the regulation of arms brokers. Again, specifics differed, as some countries wanted standards imposed, others preferred "strict regulation" and still others wanted international agreements.
- Seventy-seven states called for international information exchange to detect illicit flow of weapons and as a means of building confidence among states.
- Seventy-six agreed that specific criteria must underpin export controls so as to control decisions to transfer weapons to specific destinations. Criteria involved prohibition of transfers to zones of conflict, repressive regimes, states known to violate human rights and nonstate actors.
- Twenty-three states proposed that illicit production, transfer, possession and use be considered crimes under national legislation with according penalties.
- Fourteen states mentioned the importance of maintaining and enforcing UN arms embargoes.[109]

In July 2001, six years of work within the UN system culminated in the adoption, by consensus, of the *Programme of Action to Prevent, Combat and Eradicate the Illicit Trade in Small Arms and Light Weapons in All Its Aspects*. This is a politically binding document that, for the first time ever, establishes a comprehensive global framework for small arms action. Among the more significant commitments articulated in the Programme of Action are:

At the National Level

- strengthening laws, regulations and procedures related to small arms manufacture, export, import, stockpiling, trade and possession;
- establishing/designating national coordination agencies;

- identifying and taking action against those engaged in the illicit small arms manufacture, export, import, stockpiling, trade or possession;
- establishing or maintaining effective systems of marking and record keeping;
- establishing or maintaining effective systems of export and import licensing;
- ensuring that all confiscated or collected small arms are destroyed;
- establishing or maintaining adequate stockpile management and security practices;
- destroying surplus stocks;
- implementing effective disarmament, demobilization and reintegration (DDR) programmes, where appropriate; and
- publicizing all relevant national laws, regulations and procedures.

At the Regional Level

- establishing/designating small arms points of contact within regional and subregional organizations;
- encouraging the negotiation of legally binding regional small arms instruments;
- strengthening regional moratoria and similar initiatives;
- regional cooperation, coordination and harmonization of small arms measures and enforcement mechanisms;
- establishing, where appropriate, regional stockpile management and security mechanisms;
- supporting national DDR programmes; and
- developing voluntary transparency measures.

At the Global Level

- requesting the UN Department of Disarmament Affairs to collate and circulate small arms information provided by states;
- encouraging postconflict DDR;
- strengthening the ability of states to trace Small Arms and Light Weapons;
- encouraging cooperation among states and relevant multilateral organizations with respect to Small Arms and Light Weapons;
- developing a common understanding of the problems related to illicit brokering; and
- promoting dialogue and a culture of peace through public awareness programmes.

In the arena of implementation, international cooperation and assistance, states agreed to provide a wide range of technical support and capacity building in order to ensure that the Programme of Action produces its intended results.[110]

While the Programme of Action was heralded as an important step forward in the international campaign against the proliferation and misuse of small arms, it left many disappointed that it did not go far enough. A particular weakness was the omission of any reference to the regulation of civilian possession of firearms, in spite of the fact that more than two-thirds of the world's guns are in the hands of civilians. It was particularly disappointing, as earlier drafts of the Programme were much stronger on this point. For example, the L4 version of the Programme draft made explicit reference to the need for nations to regulate civilian possession and use as discussed in Chapter 8.

Some have stated that while the Programme of Action makes no explicit reference to controls over the sale, possession and use of civilian weapons, it is difficult to fulfill the obligations outlined in the program without these controls. This is particularly true with respect to obligations for record keeping and tracing. For example, all participating nations undertake "to adopt and implement" the legislative or other measures required to "establish as criminal offences under their domestic law the illegal manufacture, *possession*, stockpiling and trade of small arms within their areas of jurisdiction, in order to ensure that those engaged in such activities can be prosecuted under appropriate national penal codes" (emphasis added).[111] While the paragraph does not prescribe how domestic law is to regulate possession, it goes beyond "seriously considering" and actually requires that possession be subject to domestic law and that violation of such law be made a criminal offence.

Similarly, in order for states "to identify . . . groups and individuals engaged in the illegal manufacture, trade, stockpiling, transfer, *possession* . . . of illicit small arms" (emphasis added), and then pledge to "take action under *appropriate national law*, against such groups and individuals" (emphasis added), Regehr suggests, there must be domestic laws to regulate possession otherwise it is not possible to distinguish between legal and illegal possession.[112]

Regehr also notes the requirement for record keeping to support tracing and suggests that states must. Programme of Action put in place a system of comprehensive and accurate records of all small arms within its jurisdiction to enable prompt retrieval and collation. Again this has implications for national laws.[113]

The Progamme of Action includes a considerable emphasis on disarmament, demobilization and reintegration (DDR), and states that, in practice, regulation of civilian possession of firearms is a key element of DDR activities. In the postconflict context, as set out, for example, in the UN Department of Peacekeeping Operations (DPKO) guidelines on DDR, disarmament is defined not only in relation to ex-combatants but also as encompassing a broad programme for the management of arms, including, in the short term, weapons-collection programmes aimed at the general public. Regulation of civilian possession has been actively promoted as part of DDR or as part of general weapons collection and regulation efforts at the national, subregional or regional level. However, to date, implementation has been problematic due to lack of funding, among other reasons.[114]

Furthermore, despite the absence of explicit reference to regulating civilian possession of firearms, a number of countries, including Canada and Mexico have continued to press for action on this issue. Several sessions addressed it at the 2005 Biennial Meeting of States, which reviewed progress on the Programme of Action. In addition, the Programme of Action has provided a framework for important work on issues such as international standards on marking and tracing. A politically binding agreement was signed in July 2005. The United States broke the consensus that would have made it legally binding.

Still, opposition from the United States to international efforts to combat the illegal trade in small arms continues. The United States forced major changes to the Programme of Action before it would support it in July 2001, yet it appears to be backtracking even from that modest agreement, perhaps because of increased pressure from the National Rifle Association and its political allies. As recently as August 2005, the U.S. UN delegation insisted that all references to small arms be deleted from the agreement that was scheduled to be signed by more than 170 world leaders at a UN World Summit, September 12–14, 2005. The provisions to which the United States objected, the only provisions in the agreement dealing with small arms, were to: (1) "Adopt and implement an international instrument to regulate the marking and tracing, illicit brokering, trade and transfer of small arms and light weapons"; and (2) Implement the 2001 UN Programme of Action, an early step by the international community toward controlling the trade in small arms. More than 140 States had expressed support during the negotiations for the inclusion of one or both of these commitments on small arms in the measures to be agreed by the summit.

While the focus on many IANSA NGOs remains the Programme of Action and its implementation, it is by no means the only focus of efforts. The Control Arms Campaign, initiated by IANSA, Amnesty International and Oxfam, is focused on promoting the development of a Framework Convention on the Arms Trade. The measures go beyond the Programme of Action, and the campaign aims to have the international community adopt a global arms trade treaty in time for the next UN arms conference in 2006. The treaty would create legally binding arms controls and ensure that all governments control arms to the same basic international standards, for example, preventing transfers to those likely to use the arms in human rights violations.

A subset of IANSA NGOs has been active in the development of the arms trade treaty and the International Control Arms Campaign with Oxfam and Amnesty International.

Work is also under way to explore other initiatives left out of the Programme of Action, for example, international standards on civilian possession and possibly a prohibition on the unregulated possession by civilians of military assault weapons. In fact, in the lead-up to the 2005 review conference, the issue of controlling civilian possession moved to the forefront of both NGO and government agendas. Groups such as the Centre for Humanitarian Dialogue[115] in Geneva and the Small Arms Working Group in Canada have now embraced the issue, sponsoring conferences and publishing reports. In part, this has been driven by the fact that in spite of the omission of references to civilian possession in the Programme of Action, many governments referenced civilian possession in their reports.

While the UN 2001 conference was the primary focus of some NGOs participating in IANSA, for many others who were focused on regional or national initiatives, it was secondary. The recent survey on strategic planning priorities of IANSA members, for example, indicated relatively even distribution among priorities at the global and national level.

While the United Nations Programme of Action on the Illicit Trade in Small Arms and follow-up review conferences has been an important focal point for advocacy, it is only one of IANSA's priorities.

CONCLUSION: THE GLASS IS HALF FULL

Considerable effort has been directed at capacity building and at community-based initiatives addressing the demand for small arms. The evolution of the international small arms movement is consistent with developments in advocacy networks, which have become increasingly internationalized in response to the globalization of various political interests. The limited research to date on IANSA has tended to examine it from an international relations or policy perspective, noting that it is a reflection of the "new multilateralism." Laurence, for example, maintains that while national governments remain central to the solution of problems, policy making now includes a full range of actors—NGOs, business, media and other experts—that contribute to the making of "epistemic communities" on critical social issues. In this context, collaboration and partnering are critical. Problems are multidimensional and multidisciplinary, and there is increased pressure for transparency. Norms evolve through a complex interplay between governments and nongovernmental organizations.[116]

Understanding the evolution and impact of IANSA in the context of transnational social movement and advocacy organizations provides a different perspective. The movement has emerged from the convergence of disparate interests including players from the disarmament, development, human rights domain, as well as domestic gun control, policing, public health and women's organizations. While policy-oriented academics and NGOs see IANSA as a vehicle for policy development and implementation, particularly of global instruments, others see it as a network of networks or campaign of campaigns aimed at promoting information sharing and capacity building. Indeed, as we have seen, many IANSA NGOs are primarily interested in using the network to support their efforts at the local or national level. In this regard, the literature on other transnational organizations and networks is instructive. In an environment characterized by great uncertainty and constant change, coalitions create capacity to respond dynamically to challenges by generating flexible, emergent organizing strategies in response to environmental uncertainty and complexity. Technology has certainly played a major role in promoting the emergence of new organizational forms. The Internet and e-mail have provided international advocacy networks like IANSA with low-cost means of organizing internationally, but also present significant challenges in contexts where language, literature and infrastructure are highly variable and where complex negotiations and trust building are required.[117]

Apart from the academic debate about the process, progress is clearly being made on a global basis in reducing the global gun epidemic. Some of this progress is reflected in the development of new international instruments and agreements such as the UN's Firearms Protocol and 2001 Programme of Action. Even more progress has been made at the regional level, particularly in Africa, where countries have come together in an effort to establish standards and harmonize legislation. And there is no question that regardless of the progress that the Programme of Action has made, most countries in the world are moving forward in strengthening their controls over firearms. While the United States remains a major problem—in terms of its role as a supplier of legal and illegal firearms as well as an exporter of gun ideology and opposition to gun control—it is increasingly being left behind as more and more countries around the world explicitly reject "gun culture" on a number of levels.

In addition to the progress being made through global, regional and national measures aimed at reducing the misuse of guns, there has been significant progress in our understanding and awareness of the problem, the factors that contribute to the misuse of guns and the capacity of organizations at all levels to develop appropriate potential solutions bringing to bear experience in other jurisdictions and best practices. There is both a stronger understanding emerging of the need for integrated and comprehensive approaches and a recognition of the common ground among disarmament, public health and gun control approaches to the issue. There is also a more nuanced understanding of the issue and the importance of context. The

Table 9.2 Segmentation of the International Action Networks on Small Arms

Sector	Organization	International	Africa and Middle East	North America and Caribbean	Region Central and South America	Asia	Eastern Europe	Western Europe	Pacific Region
Gun control	Coalition for Gun Control			X					
	Campaign Against Arms Trade							X	
	Viva Rio				X				
	Gun Free South Africa		X						
	Coalition for Gun Control (Australia)								X
	Gun Control Network (UK)							X	
Faith	Quakers	X	2	1				2	
	Pax Christi	X				X	X	3	
Children/youth	Ecumenical Service for Peace		X						
	Cameroon Youths & Students Forum for Peace		X						
	Child Watch		X						
	Watchlist on Children & Armed Conflict			X					
	Children and Youth in Organised Armed Violence				X				
	Coalición Latinoamericana para Acabar con la Utilización de Niños Soldados				X				
	Bangladesh Coalition for Childs Rights					X			

	Organization								
Health	Save the Children—Europe Group							X	X
	International Physicians for Prevention of Nuclear War	X	1	4	4			X	1
	Trauma Centre of Cameroon			X			X		
	Croatian Red Cross						X		
Research and education	Security Research & Information Centre	X		X					
	Small Arms Firearms Education Research Network			X					
	Centro de Estudios Estratégicos				X				
	Center for Research and Global Communication		X						
	Groupe de Recherche et d'Information sur la Paix et la Sécurité							X	
	Archivio Disarmo							X	
Women	Women's Institute for Alternative Development			X					
	Caribbean Association for Feminist Res. and Action			X					
	Leitana Nehan Women's Development Agency								X
Human rights/ democracy	Amnesty International	X	6	2			X	5	
	Center for Human Rights & Rehabilitation		X						

Table 9.2 (continued)

Sector	Organization	International	Africa and Middle East	North America and Caribbean	Central and South America	Asia	Eastern Europe	Western Europe	Pacific Region
	Martin Luther King Center for Democracy & HR					X			
	Human Rights Center						X		
	Center for Democracy & Development		X						
Landmines	Kenya Coalition Against Landmines		X						
	Adopt-A-Minefield			X					
	Abkhazian Committee to Ban Landmines					X	X		
Conflict resolution/peace	OXFAM	X	X	2				3	
	PeaceNet Kenya		X						
	Center for Conflict Resolution		X						
	Foundation for Peace in Central Asia					X			
	National Peace Campaign					X			
	Swisspeace							X	
	Peace Movement Aotearoa								X
	World Environmental Movement for Africa		X						
	One Sky			X					

	Poverty reduction/ development		
World Vision	X	1	1
African Environmental and Human Development Agency	X		
Centre for Environment & Community Development	X		
Institute for Development Cooperation		X	
WIKH Foundation		X	

Source: International Action Network on Small Arms, www.iansa.org

level of knowledge development and information exchange has been important in institutionalizing concern about the issue, a shared understanding of the need for action as well as the engagement of more and more governments, NGOs and private citizens. The emergence of a relatively influential international movement linking academics, policy organizations, advocacy organizations and grassroots organizations working on various aspects of the issue is also a positive outcome of the work over recent years.

Conclusion

Small arms and light weapons cause the vast majority of violence-related death and injury throughout the world. This is true not only in war situations and in what have been called "terrorist" situations, but in times of peace as well. Firearms are used frequently without cause, in the escalation of disputes, in suicides, in the commission of crimes and in the actions of law enforcement officers. While other weapons may be used in violence, the widespread availability, portability, and simplicity of use of firearms make them a "weapon of choice" in a wide variety of situations that might have otherwise resulted in little or no violence and in no death or injury.

Many of the deaths and injuries caused by small arms around the world have their origin in the United States. Annually, the United States manufactures more guns than does any other country in the world. The guns manufactured in the United States largely end up, through legal or illegal sales or other routes, in the hands of residents of the United States. Within the United States, there are more guns, and more guns per capita, than in any other country in the world. The United States also has the highest annual rate of gun deaths per capita in the industrialized world. But the United States is also the largest supplier of guns to people in the rest of the world, through both legal and illegal transfers. These exported guns are a major cause of worldwide death, injury and disability.

Culture in the United States, particularly male culture, reinforces the link between masculinity and guns. Many young men in the United States, and some young women, grow up using model guns as toys, using real guns for hunting and reading dramatic tales about the ownership and use of guns. The U.S. media and the U.S. gun lobby export this gun culture worldwide, adding to worldwide acceptability and use of guns.

Laws on gun ownership and gun transfer in the United States are among the most lax in the world. And the United States has persistently undermined international efforts and efforts within other countries to address problems of gun ownership and gun transfer. Pressure by the gun lobby is a major factor in the laxity of laws in the United States and in the elements of U.S. foreign policy that seek to limit control of guns. The combination of pressure by the gun lobby and the reluctance of the current administration to enter into multilateral agreements leads to great difficulties in the adoption of effective controls on gun ownership and use. The result is a larger number of gun-related deaths and gun-related injuries than would be the case if laws on gun ownership in every country and international restrictions on gun transfer were more stringent.

In this book, gun transfer, gun ownership and gun use in the United States and other countries and regions of the world are discussed in depth. It is our conclusion that deaths and injuries from guns are far higher than they would be if stringent restrictions were adopted in every nation and internationally. The United States bears a significant share of the blame for the situation worldwide, but failure to act responsibly by international bodies and by many countries and regions exacerbates the problem.

This book also discusses the actions that are available for individuals, for government and regulatory bodies at every level, and for civil society (nongovernmental organizations) in the United States and elsewhere to address this problem. We must continue to raise awareness of the impact of firearm violence and the risks associated with firearms. We need to continue to push for minimum international standards, regional agreements and national laws. We need to implement integrated, community-based strategies. The time has come to curb the carnage.

Notes

Preface

1. Austin Bradford-Hill, "The Environment and Disease: Association or Causation," *Proceedings of the Royal Society of Medicine* 58, May 1965: 297.

Chapter 1

1. Charles Montaldo, "Six Killed in Wisconsin Hunting Incident: Chai Vang Arrested in Shooting," November 24, 2004, http://crime.about.com/od/news/a/vang041122.htm.

2. "Police Arrest 2 Suspects In Arby's Double Homicide," The Milwaukee Channel.com, October 26, 2004, http://www.themilwaukeechannel.com/news/3856144/detail.html.

3. "Man Shoots Wife, Friend, Then Self," The WBALChannel.com, October 22, 2004, http://www.thewbalchannel.com/beachandbayforecast/3842864/detail.html.

4. David Bruser and Tracey Huffman, "There Was No Choice: Silence, a Rifle Cracks, a Woman Is Saved," *Toronto Star*, August 26, 2004: A1, A10.

5. "B.C. Shooting Leaves 3 Dead, 3 Injured," *CBC News*, November 2, 2004, http://www.cbc.ca/story/canada/national/2004/11/01/penticton_homicide041101.html.

6. Royal Canadian Mounted Police, "Shooting Leaves Four RCMP Officers Dead," March 3, 2005, http://www.rcmp-grc.gc.ca/news/n_0508_e.htm.

7. "Notebook: Renato Is Shot, Killed," *Seattle Times,* October 6, 2004, http://seattletimes.nwsource.com/html/sports/2002055285_soccer06.html.

8. *Associated Press*, "Pro-Aristide Rally Turns Violent in Haiti," Friday, October 1, 2004, http://www.foxnews.com/story/0,2933,134184,00.html.

9. "4 Die In Argentina School Shooting," CBS News, September 28, 2004, http://www.cbsnews.com/stories/2004/09/28/world/main646126.shtml.

10. Laura Scott, "Baby Girl Injured in a Car Gun Attack," *Evening Standard News* October 12, 2004, http://news.scotsman.com/uk.cfm?id=1189862004.

11. "Forbes Editor Murdered," International Freedom of Expression Exchange, July 9, 2004, http://www.ifex.org/en/layout/set/print/content/view/full60036/.

12. "High Death Toll in Russia Siege," *BBC News*, September 4, 2004, http://news.bbc.co.uk/1/hi/world/europe/3624024.stm.

13. Shameem Mahmud, "Two Youths First Threw Grenades from Ground," *Daily Star*, vol. 5. no. 91, http://www.thedailystar.net/2004/08/25/d4082501055.htm

14. "Phillipines: Reporter Murdered," Archivo De Crónicas, October 20, 2004, http://www.ifex.org/es/content/view/archivefeatures/159.

15. World Health Organization (WHO), "Resolution WHA 49.25 (The Prevention of Violence: A Priority for Public Health) Geneva: WHO, 1996," http://www.who.int/violence_injury_prevention/pdf/WHA49en.pdf, internal document quoted as: WHA 49/1996/Rec/1.

16. Robin Coupland, "The Effect of Weapons on Health," *Lancet* 347 (February 17, 1996): 450–451.

17. International Committee of the Red Cross (ICRC), *Arms Availability and the Situation of Civilians in Armed Conflict* (Geneva: ICRC, 1999).

18. D. Meddings, "Weapons Injuries during and after Periods of Conflict," *British Medical Journal* 315 (November 1997): 1417–1420; J.H. Sloan, A.L. Kellermann, D.T. Reay, J.A. Ferris, T. Koepsell, F.P. Rivara, C. Rice, et al., "Handgun Regulations, Crime, Assault, and Homicide: A Tale of Two Cities," *New England Journal of Medicine* 319, no. 19 (1988): 1256–1262.

19. United Nations, *International Study on Firearms Regulation* (Vienna: United Nations, 1997).

20. Wendy Cukier and Antoine Chapdelaine, *Global Trade in Small Arms: Public Health Effects and Interventions*, A Joint Publication of International Physicians for the Prevention of Nuclear War (IPPNW) and SAFER-Net, March 2001, http://www.research.ryerson.ca/SAFER-Net/issues/GlobAbs3.html.

21. International Committee of the Red Cross (ICRC), *Arms Transfers and International Humanitarian Law* (September 1997).

22. M. Shaw and Antoinette Louw, "South Africa's Urban Poor: Major Victims of Crime," *Habitat Debate* 4, no. 1 (1998), http://www.unhabitat.org/HD/hdmar98/forum1.htm#poor.

23. Y. Dandurand, "Peacebuilding and Criminal Justice: Assisting Transitions from Power to Authority," in Restorative Justice Issues (Centre for Foreign Policy, 1997).

24. British American Security Information Council (BASIC), *Africa: The Challenge of Light Weapons Destruction during Peacekeeping Operations*, no. 23 (December 1997), http://www.basicint.org/pubs/Papers/BP23.htm.

25. South African Truth and Reconciliation Commission, *Final Report*, 5 vols. (Cape Town: Juta and Co., 1999).

26. Alexander Chloros, Joel Johnston, Katherine Joseph, and Rachel Stohl, British American Security Information Council, *Breaking the Cycle of Violence: Light Weapons Destruction in Central America*, no. 24 (December 1997), http://www.basicint.org/pubs/Papers/BP24.htm.

27. Wendy Cukier, "Small Arms and Light Weapons: A Public Health Approach," *Brown Journal of World Affairs* 9, no. 1 (Spring 2002): 261–280; Coali-

tion for Gun Control, Small Arms/Firearms Effects, http://www.guncontrol.ca/Content/international.html.

28. T. Miller and M. Cohen, "Costs of Gunshot and Cut Stab Wounds in the United States with some Canadian Comparisons," *Accident Analysis and Prevention* 29, no. 3 (1997): 329–341.

29. T. R. Miller, M. A. Cohen and B. Wiersema, *Victim Costs and Consequences: A New Look* (Washington, DC: U.S. Department of Justice, National Institute of Justice, 1996), NCJ 155282.

30. Victor W. Sidel, *Towards a Better World: The International Arms Trade and Its Impact on Health,* British Medical Journal 311, no. 7021 (December 23–30, 1995): 1677–1680; R. Coupland, "The Effect of Weapons on Health," *Lancet*, vol. 347 (1996): 450–451.

31. M. Renner, "Small Arms Big Impact: the Next Challenge of Disarmament," *Worldwatch,* October 1997.

32. A. L. Kellerman, F. P. Rivara, G. Somes, D. T. Reay, J. Francisco, J. G. Banton, J. Prodzinski, et al., "Suicide in the Home in Relation to Gun Ownership," *New England Journal of Medicine* 327 (1992): 467–472.

33. Gilliat Falbo, Roberto Buzzetti, and Adriano Cattaneo, "Homicide in Children and Adolescents: A Case Control Study in Recife, Brazil," *Bulletin of the World Health Organization* 79, no. 1 (2001): 2–7.

34. Martin Killias, John van Kesteren, and Martin Rindlisbacher, "Guns, Violent Crime, and Suicide in 21 Countries," *Canadian Journal of Criminology* 43/4: (2001): 429–448.

35. Jan J. M. van Dijk, "Criminal Victimisation and Victim Empowerment in an International Perspective," Ninth International Symposium on Victimology, Amsterdam, the Netherlands, August 25–29, 1997.

36. Graduate Institute of International Studies, *Small Arms Survey 2001: Profiling the Problem*, Oxford University Press, 2001.

37. K. McKenzie, *Domestic Gun Control in Ten SADC Countries* (Pretoria: Gun Free South Africa, 1999).

38. Cukier, "Small Arms and Light Weapons," Coalition for Gun Control, Small Arms/Firearms Effects.

39. Jacklyn Cock, "Fixing Our Sights: A Sociological Perspective on Gun Violence in Contemporary South Africa," *Society in Transition* (1997): 1–4.

40. Rosemary Gartner, *Affidavit of Rosemary Gartner*, Alberta Court of Appeal, in Reference Re: Firearms Act, vol. 39 (1998): ABCA 305.

41. Cited in *Firearm Violence in America: An Annotated Bibliography* (Eastern Association for the Surgery of Trauma, Violence Prevention Task Force, 1994).

42. P. Culross, "Legislative Strategies to Address Firearm Violence and Injury," *Journal of Family Practice* 42, no. 1 (1996): 15–17.

43. P.D.C. Cummings, F. P. Rivara Grossman, and T. D. Koepsell, "State Gun Safe Storage Laws and Child Mortality Due to Firearms," *Journal of the American Medical Association* 278 (1997): 1041–1126.

44. Public programs to discourage keeping guns in the home have been extensive in the United States. For example, Project Lifeline is a public service campaign

of the HELP Network, Physicians for Social Responsibility and the Center to Prevent Handgun Violence. Their advertisements show a handgun pointed out from a picture with the caption "The person most likely to kill you with a handgun already has the keys to your house," American Public Health Association, 1996. The Nation's Health.

45. The impact of these programs has been questioned. For example, see C. M. Callahan, F. P. Rivara, and T. D. Koepsell, "Money for Guns: Evaluation of the Seattle Buy-Back Program," *Public Health Reports* 109 (1994): 472. See also M. T. Plotkin, ed., *Under Fire: Gun Buy-Backs, Exchanges and Amnesty Programs* (Washington: Police Executive Research Forum, 1996). Such programs may, however, have educational effects, which have not been measured.

46. R. J. Flinn and L. G. Allen, "Trigger Locks and Firearm Safety: One Trauma Centre's Prevention Campaign," *Journal of Emergency Nursing* 21, no. 46 (1995): 296–298.

47. Center for Preventing Handgun Violence, *Legal Action Project, Outline of Gun Manufacture and Seller Liability Issues*, Center for Preventing Handgun Violence (Washington, DC, 1995).

48. (IANSA London, 2000), *Focusing Attention on Small Arms: Opportunities for the UN 2001 Conference on the Illicit Trade in Small Arms and Light Weapons.*

49. W. Cukier, D. Miller, H. Vazquez, and C. Watson, *Regulation of Civilian Possession of Small Arms and Light Weapons and the Centrality of Human Security*, Biting the Bullet Series (London, July 2003).

50. Natalie Goldring, "A Glass Half Full," UN Small Arms Conference, Council on Foreign Relations, Roundtable on the Geo-Economics of Military Preparedness, New York, September 26, 2001.

Chapter 2

1. Howard Jones, *Death of a Generation: How the Assassinations of Diem and JFK Prolonged the Vietnam War* (Oxford: Oxford University Press, 2003).

2. "The RFK Assassination: The Crime," http://homepages.tcp.co.uk/~dlewis/crime.htm.

3. Robert F. Kennedy, Speech on Martin Luther King, Jr.'s Death, Indianapolis, Indiana, April 4, 1968, http://members.iquest.net/~reboomer/kensp.htm.

4. Lynda Hurst, "10 Years Later, How a Massacre Changed us All," *Toronto Star*, November 27, 1999.

5. Honourable Lord Douglas Cullen, *The Public Inquiry into the Shootings at Dunblane Primary School on 13 March 1996*, Great Britain Scottish Office, October 16, 1996, http://www.archive.official-documents.co.uk/document/scottish/dunblane/dunblane.htm.

6. Margaret Scott, *Port Arthur: A Story of Strength and Courage* (Milson's Point: Random House Australia), 1997.

7. Jennifer Rosenberg, "The Columbine Massacre," About.com, http://history1900s.about.com/library/weekly/aa041303a.htm.

8. Conrad Johnson, "Profiles: Lives Shattered by Sniper," CNN, October 23, 2002, http://www.cnn.com/2002/US/South/10/15/shooting.victims/index.html.

9. BBC News, "Swiss Mourn Gun Rampage Victims," September 27, 2001, http://news.bbc.co.uk/1/hi/world/europe/1567632.stm.

10. BBC News, "Shock at Brazil Journalist's Killing," June 10, 2002, http://news.bbc.co.uk/1/hi/world/americas/2035822.stm; Reporters without Borders, "Tim Lopes, TV Globo," http://www.rsf.fr/artkilled_2002.php3?id_article=2514.

11. Graduate Institute of International Studies (GIIS), *Small Arms Survey 2001: Profiling the Problem* (Oxford: Oxford University Press, 2001).

12. Wendy Cukier, "International Small Arms/Firearms Control," *Canadian Foreign Policy* 6, no. 1 (Fall 1998): 73–89.

13. Étienne G. Krug, Linda L. Dahlberg, James A. Mercy, Anthony B. Zwi, and Rafael Lozano, eds., *World Report on Violence and Health* (Geneva: WHO, 2002), http://www.who.int/violence_injury_prevention/violence/world_report/wrvheng/en/; United Nations Development Programme (UNDP). *UNDP Human Development Report 2000* (New York: Oxford University Press, 2000), 36, http://hdr.undp.org/reports/view_reports.cfm?year=2000; A. Reza, J. A. Mercy, and E. G. Krug, "Epidemiology of Violent Deaths in the World," *Injury Prevention* 7 (2001): 104–111; World Health Organization, "Small Arms and Global Health" (World Health Organization contribution to the UN Conference on Illicit Trade in Small Arms and Light Weapons, New York, July 9–20, 2001), http://www5.who.int/violence_injury_prevention/download.cfm?id=0000000158.

14. United Nations, *International Study on Firearm Regulation* (New York: United Nations, 1998).

15. World Health Organization, Collaborating Centre for Safety Promotion and Injury Prevention, International Workshop on Small Arms and Firearms Injury: Finding a Common Ground for Public Health, Québec City, Canada, February 7, 1998.

16. Robin Coupland, "The Effect of Weapons on Health," *Lancet* 347 (February 17, 1996): 450–451.

17. Project Ploughshares, *Armed Conflicts Report 1996* (Waterloo, Ontario: Institute of Peace and Conflict Studies, 1996), http://www.ploughshares.ca/images articles/ACR02/ACRmonitorSpring02.map.pdf.

18. International Committee of the Red Cross, *Arms Availability and the Situation of Civilians in Armed Conflict* (Geneva: International Committee of the Red Cross, 1999).

19. See Firearm Death, Injury and Crime, http://www.ryerson.ca/SAFER-Net, for updated statistics.

20. David B. Kopel, Paul Gallant, and Joanne D. Eisen, "Global Deaths from Firearms: Searching for Plausible Estimates," *Texas Review of Law and Politics* 8, no. 1 (Fall 2003): 114–141.

21. Graduate Institute of International Studies (GIIS), *Small Arms Survey 2004: Rights at Risk* (Oxford: Oxford University Press, 2004).

22. Ibid.

23. See for example, Small Arms Firearms Education Research Network (SAFER-Net), Master Deaths Table, 2003, http://www.ryerson.ca/SAFER-Net/issues/globalfirearmdeaths.html.

24. Centers for Disease Control and Prevention (CDC), *National Vital Statistics Report* 50, no. 15 (September 16, 2002).

25. Centers for Disease Control and Prevention, "Rates of Homicide, Suicide and Firearm Related Death among Children: 26 Industrialized Countries," 46, no. 5 (February 7, 1997): 101–105.

26. United Nations, *United Nations International Study on Firearm Regulation* (New York: UN, 1998).

27. E. G. Krug, K. E. Powell, and L. L. Dahlberg, "Firearm-Related Deaths in the United States and 35 Other High- and Upper-Middle-Income Countries," *International Journal of Epidemiology* 27 (1998): 214–221.

28. E. G. Krug, L. L. Dahlberg, and K. E. Powell, "Childhood Homicide, Suicide, and Firearm Deaths: An International Comparison," *World Health Stat Q* 49, no. 4 (1996), in Centers for Disease Control and Prevention, "Rates of Homicide, Suicide and Firearm Related Death among Children—26 Industrialized Countries," *CDC Weekly Report* 46, no. 5 (1997).

29. Étienne G. Krug, Linda L. Dahlberg, James A. Mercy, Anthony B. Zwi, and Rafael Lozano, eds., *World Report on Violence and Health* (Geneva: WHO, 2002).

30. Ibid.

31. J. C. Campbell, D. W. Webster, J. Koziol-McLain, C. R. Block, D. W. Campbell, and M. A. Curry, "Risk Factors for Femicide within Physically Abusive Intimate Relationships: Results from a Multi-site Case Control Study," *American Journal of Public Health* 93 (2003): 1089–1097.

32. Scott Simmie, "Too Often, Domestic Violence Is No Surprise: Even Professionals Miss Warning Signs," Office of the Chief Coroner of Ontario, 2002, cited *Toronto Star,* April 1, 2004, A1, 8.

33. L. E. Saltzman, J. A. Mercy, P. W. O'Carroll, M. L. Rosenberg, and P. H. Rhodes, "Weapon Involvement and Injury Outcomes in Family and Intimate Assaults," *The Journal of the American Medical Association (JAMA)* 267 (1992): 3043–3047.

34. Rosemary Gartner, "Cross Cultural Aspects of Interpersonal Violence: A Review of the International Empirical Evidence" (paper given at the International Conference on Crime and Violence: Causes and Policy Responses, Bogotá, World Bank, May 2000).

35. Carlos Carcach and Marianne James, "Homicide between Intimate Partners in Australia," *Trends and Issues in Crime and Criminal Justice* 90 (July 1998): 1–6.

36. E. Ryan, *Gun Violence against Women: South African Women Speak* (Johannesburg: Gun Free South Africa, June 1998).

37. U.S. Department of Justice, "Intimate Homicide," *Homicide Trends in the U.S.,* Bureau of Justice Statistics, http://www.ojp.usdoj.gov/bjs/homicide/intimates.htm.

38. Violence Policy Center, *When Men Murder Women: An Analysis of 2000 Homicide Data*, Washington, DC, 2002, in Johns Hopkins Center for Gun Policy and Research (JHCGPR), "Fact Sheet: Firearms and Intimate Partner Violence," October 2003, http://www.jhsph.edu/gunpolicy/IPV_firearms2.pdf.

39. United Nations, *International Study on Firearm Regulation,* 1998.

40. D. Hemenway, T. Shinoda-Tagawa, and M. Miller, "Firearm Availability and Female Homicide Victimization Rates across 25 Populous High-Income Countries," *Journal of the American Medical Women's Association* 57 (2002): 100–104.

41. S. Essex, Testimony to the Standing Committee on Justice and Legal Affairs, Guelph, YWCA of Canada, May 16, 1995.

42. H. Ozcebe, "Firearm Deaths in Turkey" (paper given at the Role of Public Health in the Prevention of War-Related Injuries Conference, Montreal, Canada, May 9–11, 2002).

43. Simon Chapman, *Over Our Dead Bodies: Port Arthur and Australia's Fight for Gun Control* (Annandale, New South Wales, Australia: Pluto, 1998).

44. Women's Services Network (WESNET), "Domestic Violence in Regional Australia: A Literature Review" (report for the Commonwealth Department of Transport and Regional Services under the Partnerships against Domestic Violence Programme, June 2000), http://www.padv.dpmc.gov.au/oswpdf/dv_regional.pdf.

45. Ryan, *Gun Violence against Women.*

46. Dansys Consultants Inc., *Domestic Homicides Involving the Use of Firearms* (Ottawa: Department of Justice, 1992).

47. Krug, Dahlberg, Mercy, Zwi, and Lozano, *World Report on Violence and Health*, 90–91.

48. Cock, "Fixing Our Sights: A Sociological Perspective on Gun Violence in Contemporary South Africa," *Society in Transition* 28, no. 1–4 (1997): 70–81.

49. Human Rights Watch (HRW), "Women in Conflict and Refugees," *World Report 2001*, http://www.hrw.org/wr2k1/women/women3.html.

50. Chen Reis, K. H. Lyons, B. Vann, L. Arnowitz, V. Iacopina, B. Mansaray, A. M. Akinslure-Smith, and L. Taylor, "The Prevalence of War-Related Sexual Violence and Other Human Rights Abuses among Internally Displaced Persons in Sierra Leone" (Role of Public Health in the Prevention of War-Related Injuries Conference, Montreal, Canada, May 9–11, 2002).

51. "Gun Control: Public Support for Regulating Firearm Ownership in Canada," *Reid Report* 8, no. 9 (1993).

52. Vanessa Farr and Kiflemariam Gebre-Wold, eds., *Gender Perspectives on Small Arms and Light Weapons: Regional and International Concerns* (Bonn: Bonn International Center for Conversion, 2002).

53. David Hemenway, "The Epidemiology of U.S. Firearm Injuries," *Journal of Public Health Policy* 24, nos. 3–4 (2003): 380–386.

54. Kwing Hung, *Firearm Statistics* (Ottawa: Department of Justice, 1997).

55. Johanna Birchmayer and David Hemenway, "Suicide and Firearm Prevalence: Are Youth Disproportionately Affected?" *Suicide and Life Threatening Behaviour* 31, no. 3 (2001): 303–311.

56. Donna L. Hoyert, Elizabeth Arias, Betty L. Smith, Sherry L. Murphy, and Kenneth D. Kochanek, "Deaths: Final Data for 1999," *CDC National Vital Statistics Reports* 49, no. 8 (2001): 68.

57. Thomas Gabor, *The Impact of the Availability of Firearms on Violent Crime, Suicide and Accidental Death* (Ottawa: Department of Justice, 1994).

58. A. L. Kellerman, F. P. Rivara, G. Somes, D. T. Reay, J. Francisco, J. G. Banton, J. Prodzinski, C. Flinger, and B. B. Hackman, "Suicide in the Home in Relation to Gun Ownership," *The New England Journal of Medicine* 327, no. 7 (August 13, 1992): 467–472.

59. Peter Carrington and Sharon Moyer, "Gun Availability and Suicide in Canada: Testing the Displacement Hypothesis," *Studies on Crime and Crime Prevention* 3 (1994): 168–178.

60. Ted R. Miller and Mark Cohen, "Costs of Gunshot and Cut/Stab Wounds in the United States with Some Canadian Comparisons," *Accident Analysis and Prevention* 29, no. 3 (1997): 329–341.

61. R. Simon, M. Chouinard, and C. Gravel, "Suicide and Firearms: Restricting Access in Canada" (paper given at the 29th Annual Conference, American Association of Suicidology. St. Louis, Missouri, 1996).

62. David Hemenway and Matthew Miller, "Association of Rates of Household Handgun Ownership, Lifetime Major Depression and Serious Suicidal Thoughts with Rates of Suicide across US Census Regions," *Injury Prevention* 8 (2002): 313–316.

63. Martin Killias, "A Response to Professor Mauser," *Canadian Journal of Criminology* 38, no. 2 (1996): 215–216.

64. Antoon Leenaars and David Lester, "Psychological Reports 1993," *Association Quebecoise de Suicidologie Projet de loi C-68, Memoire* 72 (1995): 787–790; Carrington and Moyer, "Gun Availability and Suicide in Canada."

65. S. Canetto and I. Sakinofsky, "The Gender Paradox in Suicide," *Suicide and Life-Threatening Behaviour* 28, no. 1 (1998): 1–23.

66. Geoffrey A. Jackman, Mirna M. Farah, Arthur Kellermann, and Harold K. Simon, "Seeing Is Believing: What Do Boys Do When They Find a Real Gun," *Pediatrics* 107, no. 6 (June 2001): 1247–1250.

67. U.S. Department of Justice, Bureau of Justice Statistics, "Crimes Committed with Firearms, 1973–2002," December 13, 2003, http://www.ojp.usdoj.gov/bjs/glance/tables/guncrimetab.htm.

68. Canadian Centre for Justice Statistics, Statistics Canada, *Canadian Crime Statistics 2001* (Ottawa: Statistics Canada, 2001), http://dsp-psd.communication.gc.ca/Collection-R/Statcan/85-205-XIE/0000185-205-XIE.pdf.

69. R. Chetty, ed., *Firearm Use and Distribution in South Africa* (Pretoria: National Crime Prevention Centre, 2000).

70. Graduate Institute of International Studies (GIIS), *Small Arms Survey 2003: Development Denied* (Oxford: Oxford University Press, 2003).

71. T. R. Miller, M. A. Cohen, and B. Wiersema, *Victim Costs and Consequences: A New Look* (Washington, DC: U.S. Department of Justice, National Institute of Justice, 1996), NCJ 155282.

72. Ibid.

73. "Residents of Dangerous Areas Are Less Likely to Exercise," *Washington Post,* February 26, 1999: A7.

74. Graduate Institute of International Studies, *Small Arms Survey 2003.*

75. Krug, Dahlberg, Mercy, Zwi, and Lozano, *World Report on Violence and Health,* 215.

76. Graduate Institute of International Studies, *Small Arms Survey 2001.*

77. GIIS, *Small Arms Survey 2005: Weapons at War* (Geneva, 2005).

78. International Committee of the Red Cross, *Arms Availability and the Situation of Civilians in Armed Conflict.*

79. Ibid.

80. M. Kuzman, B. Tomic, R. Stevanovic, M. Ljubicic, D. Katalinic, and U. Rodin, "Fatalities in the War in Croatia, 1991 and 1992: Underlying and External Causes of Death," *JAMA* 270 (1993): 626–628.

81. International Committee of the Red Cross, *Arms Availability and the Situation of Civilians in Armed Conflict.*

82. Ibid.

83. Ibid.

84. Ibid.

85. Saving Women's Lives, "Focusing on Women and Armed Conflict," June 2002, http://www.savingwomenslives.org/factsheet_women_and_armed_conflict.htm.

86. Robin Coupland and David Meddings, "Mortality Associated with Use of Weapons in Armed Conflicts, Wartime Atrocities, and Civilian Mass Shootings: Literature Review," *The British Medical Journal (BMJ)* 319 (1999): 407–410.

87. Wendy Cukier and A. Chapdelaine, "Small Arms, Explosives and Incendiaries," in *Terrorism and Public Health: A Balanced Approach to Strengthening Systems and Protecting People*, ed. Barry Levy and Victor Sidel (Oxford: Oxford University Press in cooperation with the American Public Health Association, 2002).

88. Ibid.

89. Ibid.

90. World Bank, *Curbing the Epidemic: Governments and the Economics of Tobacco Control* (Washington, DC: World Bank, 1999), http://www1.worldbank.org/ tobacco/reports.asp. See also World Bank, "Tobacco Control at a Glance," June 2003, http://www1.worldbank.org/tobacco/pdf/AAG%20Tobacco%206-03.pdf.

91. Krug, Powell, and Dahlberg, "Firearm Related Death in the United States and 35 Other High- and Upper-Middle-Income Countries."

92. Miller and Cohen, "Costs of Gunshot and Cut/Stab Wounds in the United States."

93. Ibid.

94. Ted Miller, "Costs Associated with Gunshot Wounds in Canada in 1991," *Canadian Medical Association Journal* 153 (1995): 1261–1268.

95. Miller and Cohen, "Costs of Gunshot and Cut/Stab Wounds in the United States."

96. Ibid.

97. Philip J. Cook and Jens Ludwig, *Gun Violence: The Real Costs* (Oxford: Oxford University Press, 2000).

98. Andrew J. Buck, Simon Hakim, and J. Uriel Speigel, "Endogenous Crime Victimization, Taxes and Property Values," *Social Science Quarterly* 73, no. 2 (1993): 334–348.

99. Bonnie Fisher, "A Neighborhood Business Area Is Hurting: Crime, Fear of Crime and Disorder Take Their Toll," *Crime and Delinquency* 37, no. 3 (1991): 363–373.

100. Cook and Ludwig, *Gun Violence.*

101. World Bank, "The Causes and Consequences of Conflict in Developing Countries," http://www.worldbank.org.research.conflict/motivation/htm.

102. Robert L. Ayres, *Crime and Violence as Development Issues in Latin America*, Latin America and Caribbean Studies (Washington, DC: World Bank, 1998); D. K. Gupta, *The Economics of Political Violence: The Effect of Political Instability on Economic Growth* (New York: Praeger, 1990).

103. Leslie W. Kennedy and Vincent F. Sacco, *Crime Victims in Context* (Los Angeles: Roxbury, 1998).

104. Fisher, "A Neigborhood Business Area Is Hurting."

105. Mark Shaw and Antoinette Louw, "South Africa's Urban Poor: Major Victims of Crime," *Habitat Debate* 4, no. 1, United Nations Centre for Human Settlement (March 1998).

106. Beth Moore Milroy, Philippa Campsie, Robyn Whittaker, and Zoe Girling, "Who Says Toronto Is a 'Good' City?" in *World Class Cities: Can Canada Play?* ed. C. Andrews, P. Armstrong, and A. Lapierre (Ottawa: International Council for Canadian Studies and the University of Ottawa Press, 1999), 159–194.

107. David Savageau and Richard Boyer, *Places Rated Almanac: Your Guide to Finding the Best Places to Live in North America* (New York: Prentice Hall Travel, 1993); Marion Joppe, "Toronto's Image as a Destination: A Comparative Importance Satisfaction Analysis," and S. Shoemaker, "Segmenting the US Travel Market," *Journal of Travel Research* 32, no. 3 (1994).

108. Fisher, "Neighbourhood Business Area Is Hurting."

109. Richard Freeman, "Crime and the Job Market," Working Paper 4910 (Cambridge, MA: National Bureau of Economic Research, 1994).

110. Chris McCormick, ed., *Constructing Danger: The Mis/representation of Crime in the News* (Halifax: Fernwood Publishing, 1995); Stephen Rattien, "The Role of the Media in Hazard Mitigation and Disaster Management," in *International Disaster Communications: Harnessing the Power of Communications to Avert Disasters and Save Lives*, ed. F. H. Cate (Washington, DC: Annenberg Washington Program in Communications Policy Studies of Northwestern University, 1994), http://www.annenberg.nwu.edu/pubs/disas/disas7.htm.

111. Margie Peden, "The Cost of Treating Firearm Victims," National Trauma Research Programme of the South Africa Medical Research Council Report, 1997. See also M. Peden and J. W. van der Spuy, "The Cost of Treating Firearm Victims," *Trauma Review* 6, no. 2 (1998): 4–5.

112. Ibid.

113. Victor W. Sidel, "The International Arms Trade and Its Impact on Health," *The British Medical Journal* 311 (1995): 1677–1680, http://bmj.bmjjournals.com/cgi/content/full/311/7021/1677; Coupland, "The Effect of Weapons on Health."

114. Ibid.

115. "Possibilities to Reduce the Number of Weapons and the Practice of Using Weapons to Solve Problems in Cambodia," *STAR Kampuchea*, July 23, 1998.

116. Cindy Collins, interviews at UN Headquarters (prepared for the Office for the Coordination of Humanitarian Affairs [OCHA], Humanitarian Implications of Small Arms and Light Weapons, New York, July 1998).

117. Cock, "Fixing Our Sights."

118. Andrew D. Herz, "Gun Crazy: Constitutional False Consciousness and the

Dereliction of Dialogic Responsibility," *Boston University Law Review* 75, no. 1 (1995): 57.

119. Diane Archer and Rosemary Gartner, *Violence and Crime in Cross-National Perspective* (New Haven: Yale University Press, 1987).

120. Y. Dandurand, "Peacebuilding and Criminal Justice: Assisting Transitions from Power to Authority," *Restorative Justice Issues*, Centre for Foreign Policy, March 31, 1997.

121. British American Security Information Council (BASIC), "Africa: The Challenge of Light Weapons Destruction During Peacekeeping Operations," no. 23 (December 1997), http://www.basicint.org/pubs/Papers/BP23.htm.

122. Alexander Chloros, Joel Johnston, Katherine Joseph, and Rachel Stohl, BASIC, "Breaking the Cycle of Violence: Light Weapons Destruction in Central America," no. 24 (December 1997), http://www.basicint.org/pubs/Papers/BP24.htm.

123. Ryan, *Gun Violence Against Women*.

124. Krug, Dahlberg, Mercy, Zwi, and Lozano, *World Report on Violence and Health*, 322.

125. William Godnick, Robert Muggah, and Camilla Waszink, *Stray Bullets: The Impact of Small Arms Misuse in Central America*, Small Arms Survey Occasional Paper No. 5 (Geneva: Small Arms Survey, 2002), 11.

126. Centers for Disease Control and Prevention, *National Vital Statistics* 49, no. 12 (October 9, 2001), http://www.cdc.gov/nchs/data/nvsr/nvsr49/nvsr49_12.pdf.

127. See preliminary 2000 figures in Centers for Disease Control and Prevention, *National Vital Statistics* 49, no. 12 (2001), http://www.cdc.gov/nchs/data/nvsr/nvsr49/nvsr49_12.pdf.

128. Ibid.

129. U.S. Bureau of Justice Statistics, "Crimes Committed with Firearms, 1973–2002," December 13, 2003, http://www.ojp.usdoj.gov/bjs/glance/tables/guncrimetab.htm.

130. Hemenway, "The Epidemiology of U.S. Firearm Injuries."

131. K. Hung, "Firearm Statistics: Updated Tables," Department of Justice, Canada, March 2004.

132. A. Chapdelaine, E. Samson, M.D. Kimberley, and L. Viau, "Firearm-Related Injuries in Canada: Issues for Prevention," *Canadian Medical Association Journal* 145, no. 10 (1991): 1217–1223.

133. Graduate Institute of International Studies, *Small Arms Survey 2004*.

134. Ibid., table 6.7.

135. Chapdelaine, Samson, Kimberley, and Viau, "Firearm-Related Injuries in Canada: Issues for Prevention"; Graduate Institute of International Studies, A. Mercy, Anthony B. Zwi, and Rafael Lozano, eds., *World Report on Violence and Health* (Geneva: World Health Organization, 2002), http://www.who.int/violence_injury_prevention/violence/world_report/wrvheng/en/.

136. Centers for Disease Control and Prevention, "Homicide Trends and Characteristics—Brazil, 1980–2002," Morbidity and Mortality Weekly Report (*MMWR*) 53, no. 8 (March 5, 2004): 169–171, http://www.cdc.gov/mmwr/preview/mmwrhtml/mm5308a1.htm.

137. Ibid.

138. Ibid.

139. Ibid.

140. Ibid.

141. United Nations, *International Study on Firearm Regulation,* Centers for Disease Control and Prevention, "Homicide Trends and Characteristics—Brazil, 1980–2002."

142. Ibid.

143. Ibid.

144. Ibid.

145. Ibid.

146. Ibid.

147. R. B. Barradas and M. C. Ribeiro, "Correlation between Homicides Rates and Economic Indicators in Sao Paulo, Brazil, 1996," *Revista Panamericana De Salud Publica* 7 (2000): 118–123; C. C. Beato Filho, R. M. Assunção, B. F. Silvia, F. C. Marinho, I. A. Reis, and M. C. Almeida, "Homicide Clusters and Drug Traffic in Belo Horizonte, Minas Gerais State, Brazil from 1995 to 1999," *Cadernos de Saúde Pública* 17 (2001): 1163–1171.

148. J. A. Mercy, E. G. Krug, L. L. Dahlberg, and A. B. Zwi, "Violence and Health: The United States in a Global Perspective," *American Journal of Public Health* 93 (2003): 256–261.

149. Wendy Cukier and Antoine Chapdelaine, "Global Trade in Small Arms: Public Health Effects and Interventions," International Physicians for the Prevention of Nuclear War (IPPNW) and SAFER-Net, Ryerson University, Toronto (March 2001); Ibid.

150. Graduate Institute of International Studies, *Small Arms Survey 2003.* Development Denied.

151. J. M. Cruz and M. A. Beltrán, "Las armas en El Salvador: diagnóstico sobre su situación y su impacto" (trans. "Arms in El Salvador: Diagnosis of the Situation and Impact"), University Institute of Public Opinion (IUDOP Publication), Central American University for the Arias Foundation for Peace and Human Progress, http://www.arias.org.cr/fundarias/cpr/armasliv

152. United Nations, "Police: Crimes Recorded in Criminal (Police) Statistics, by Type of Crime Including Attempts to Commit Crimes," Seventh United Nations Survey on Crime Trends and the Operations of Criminal Justice Systems (1998–2000), March 31, 2004, http://www.unodc.org/pdf/crime/seventh_survey/7sv.pdf.

153. Graduate Institute of International Studies, *Small Arms Survey 2002: Counting the Human Cost* (Oxford: Oxford University Press, 2002), appendix 4.1, 195.

154. Ibid.

155. Krug, Dahlberg, Mercy, Zwi, and Lozano, *World Report on Violence and Health,* http://www.who.int/violence_injury_prevention/violence/world_report/wrvheng/en/.

156. All rates taken from Ibid., Table A.10, pp. 322–323, with the exception of Switzerland, which was taken from United Nations, "Police: Crimes Recorded in Criminal (Police) Statistics."

157. Killias, "A Response to Professor Mauser."

158. Krug, Dahlberg, Mercy, Zwi, and Lozano, *World Report on Violence and Health*.

159. "Illegal Arms Trade Remains Threat to Russian Security," *RIA* (Moscow), June 16, 1999, http://www.nisat.org.

160. "Russian Council Gives Figures for Crime with Guns, Bombs," *Itar-Tass* (Moscow), April 24, 2000, http://www.nisat.org.

161. Maxim Pyadushkin with Maria Haug and Anna Matveeva, *Beyond the Kalashnikov: Small Arms Production, Exports and Stockpiles in the Russian Federation*, Geneva, Small Arms Survey Occasional Paper No. 10, August 2003.

162. United Nations, *International Study on Firearm Regulation*.

163. Krug, Powell, and Dahlberg, "Firearm-related Deaths in the United States and 35 Other High- and Upper-Middle-Income Countries."

164. United Nations, "Police: Crimes Recorded in Criminal (Police) Statistics."

165. Ibid.

166. Ibid.

167. *National Report of Latvia on the Implementation of the United Nations' Small Arms and Light Weapons Programme of Action, 2002* (submitted to the UN Department of Disarmament Affairs), http://disarmament.un.org/cab/salw-nationalreports.html.

168. United Nations, "Police: Crimes Recorded in Criminal (Police) Statistics."

169. Ibid.

170. United Nations, *International Study on Firearm Regulation*.

171. Graduate Institute of International Studies, *Small Arms Survey 2002*.

172. Ibid.

173. Gun Free South Africa, "Statistics Sheet: Latest Statistics May 2002," May 2002, http://www.gca.org.za/facts/statistics.htm.

174. Stephanie Burrows, Brett Bowman, Richard Matzopoulos, and Ashley van Niekerk, *A Profile of Fatal Injuries in South Africa, 2000. Second Annual Report of the National Injury Mortality Surveillance System*, October 2001. For an online summary of the contents, see Gun Free South Africa, "Statistics Sheet: Latest Statistics May 2002."

175. United Nations, "Police: Crimes Recorded in Criminal (Police Statistics)."

176. "Small Arms Firearms Education Research Network (SAFER-Net) Country Profile: Japan," September 13, 2001, http://www.research.ryerson.ca/SAFER-Net/.

177. Graduate Institute of International Studies, *Small Arms Survey 2004*.

178. "Scholar: Targeting the Cease-fire," *Chennai the Hindu* (India) (March 16, 2001): 12, http://www.nisat.org.

179. Bangladesh Development Partnership Centre, *Study on Illegal Small Arms and Violence in Bangladesh*, Dhaka, Bangladesh, 2000.

180. Niobe Thompson and Devashish Krishnan, "Small Arms in India and the Human Costs of Lingering Conflicts," in *Over a Barrel: Light Weapons and Human Rights in the Commonwealth*, ed. A. F. Musah and N. Thompson (London: Commonwealth Human Rights Initiative, November 1999), 38, 60, 94–96.

181. Ibid.

182. H. A. Chotani, J. A. Razzak, and S. P. Luby, "Patterns of Violence in Karachi, Pakistan," *Injury Prevention* 8 (2002): 57–59.

183. Jenny Mouzos and Catherine Rushford, "Firearm-Related Deaths in Australia, 1991–2001," *Trends and Issues in Crime and Criminal Justice* 269 (2003): 1–6.

184. Graduate Institute of International Studies, *Small Arms Survey 2004.*

185. Philip Alpers and Conway Twyford, *Small Arms in the Pacific*, Geneva, Small Arms Survey Occasional Paper No. 8 (2003): 33.

186. Philip Cook and Jens Ludwig, *Gun Violence: The Real Costs* (New York: Oxford University Press, 2000).

Chapter 3

1. V. P. Bunge, "National Trends in Intimate Partner Homicides, 1974–2000," *Juristat* 22 (2002): 5.

2. E. G. Krug, L. L. Dahlberg, J. A. Mercy, A. Zwi, and R. Lozano, eds., World Health Organization (WHO): *World Report on Violence and Health* (Geneva: WHO, 2002).

3. Ibid.

4. Jeffrey Boutwell and Michael T. Klare, "A Scourge of Small Arms. Special Report: Waging a New Kind of War," *Scientific American* 282, no. 6 (2000): 30–35.

5. International Physicians for the Prevention of Nuclear War (IPPNW), (Aiming for Prevention: International Medical Conference on Small Arms, Gun Violence and Injury, Helsinki, Finland, September 28–30, 2001).

6. A. Lilenfeld and D. Lilenfeld, *Foundations of Epidemiology* (2nd ed.) (New York: Oxford University Press, 1980); A. L. Kellermann, R. K. Lee, J. A. Mercy, and J. Banton, "The Epidemiologic Basis for the Prevention of Firearm Injuries," *Annual Review of Public Health* 12 (1991): 17–40.

7. Ibid.

8. L. S. Robertson, *Injuries: Causes, Control Strategies, and Public Policy* (Lexington, MA: Lexington Books, 1983); D. Hemenway, S. J. Solnick, and D. R. Azrael, "Firearm Training and Storage," *Journal of the American Medical Association* 273, no. 1 (1995): 46–50.

9. David Hemenway, *Public Health, Private Guns* (Ann Arbor: University of Michigan Press, 2004), 24.

10. N. Prabha Unnithan, L. Huff-Corzine, and Hugh Whitt, "Cross-National Patterns of Lethal Violence," in *The Currents of Lethal Violence*, ed. N. Prabha Unnithan, L. Huff-Corzine, Jay Corzine, and Hugh Whitt (Albany: University of New York Press, 1994).

11. A. McAlister, "Homicide Rates and Attitudes towards Killing in Fifteen Nations" (Aiming for Prevention, Helsinki, Finland, October 28–30, 2001).

12. R. V. Clarke, ed., *Situational Crime Prevention: Successful Case Studies* (Albany, NY: Harrow and Heston, 1992).

13. Martin Killias, "Gun Ownership, Suicide, and Homicide: An International Perspective," *Understanding Crime: Experiences of Crime and Crime Control*, ed. Anna del Frate, Uglijesa Zvekic, and Jan J. M. van Dijk (Rome: United Nations Interregional Crime and Justice Research Institute, 1993), 289–303.

14. GPC Research, *Fall 2000 Estimate of Firearms Ownership* (Ottawa: Justice Canada, 2001).

15. David Hemenway and Matthew Miller, "Firearm Availability and Homicide Rates across 26 High Income Countries," *Journal of Trauma-Injury Infection & Critical Care* 49, no. 6 (December 2000): 985–988.

16. Peter Herby, "Arms Availability and the Situation of Civilians in Armed Conflict," *International Review of the Red Cross*, no. 835 (September 30, 1999): 669–672.

17. Michael Renner, "Small Arms, Big Impact, The Next Challenge of Disarmament," Worldwatch Paper 117 (Washington, DC: Worldwatch Institute, 1997), 11–14.

18. *International Committee of the Red Cross* position, "Arms Transfers, Humanitarian Assistance and International Humanitarian Law" (February 19, 1998): 669–672.

19. Katherine McKenzie, *Domestic Gun Control Policy in 10 SADC Countries* (Gun Free South Africa, 1999).

20. Renner, "Small Arms, Big Impact."

21. Antoine Chapdelaine, "Firearms Injury Prevention and Gun Control in Canada," *Canadian Medical Association Journal* 155, no. 9 (1996).

22. A. L. Kellermann, R. K. Lee, J. A. Mercy, and J. Banton, "The Epidemiologic Basis for the Prevention of Firearm Injuries," *Annual Review of Public Health* 12 (1991): 17–40.

23. T. R. Miller and M. A. Cohen, "Costs of Gunshot and Cut/Stab Wounds in the United States, with Some Canadian Comparisons," *Accident Analysis and Prevention* 29, no. 3 (1997): 329–341.

24. Franklin E. Zimring and Gordon Hawkins, *Crime Is Not the Problem: Lethal Violence in America* (New York: Oxford University Press, 1997).

25. E. D. Shenassa, S. N. Catlin, and S. L. Buka, "Lethality of Firearms Relative to Other Suicide Methods: A Population Based Study," *Journal of Epidemiology and Community Health* 57 (2003): 120–124.

26. A. L. Kellerman, F. P. Rivara, N. B. Rushforth, J. G. Banton, D. T. Reay, J. T. Francisco, A. B. Locci, B. B. Hackman, and G. Somes, "Gun Ownership as a Risk Factor for Homicide in the Home," *New England Journal of Medicine* 329 (1993): 1084–1091.

27. A. L. Kellerman, F. P. Rivara, G. Somes, D. T. Reay, J. Francisco, J. G. Banton, J. Prodzinski, C. Flinger, and B. B. Hackman, "Suicide in the Home in Relation to Gun Ownership," *The New England Journal of Medicine* 327, no. 7 (August 13, 1992): 467–472.

28. D. A. Brent, J. A. Perper, C. J. Allman, G. M. Moritz, M. E. Wartella, and J. P. Zelenak, "The Presence and Accessibility of Firearms in the Homes of Adolescent Suicides," *Journal of the American Medical Association* 266 (1991): 2989–2995.

29. J. H. Sloan, A. L. Kellermann, D. T. Reay, J. A. Ferris, T. Koepsell, F. P. Rivara, C. Rice, L. Gray, and J. LoGerfo, "Handgun Regulations, Crime, Assaults and Homicide: A Tale of Two Cities," *New England Journal of Medicine* 319 (1985): 1256–1262.

30. Miller and Cohen, "Costs of Gunshot and Cut/Stab Wounds in the United States."

31. Ibid.

32. Martin Killias, "International Correlations between Gun Ownership and

Rates of Homicide and Suicide," *Canadian Medical Association Journal* 148 (May 1993): 1721–1725.

33. Pat Mayhew and Jan J. M. van Dijk, *Criminal Victimization in Eleven Industrialized Countries*, WODC Report (The Hague: Ministry of Justice of the Netherlands, 1997), 162.

34. J. Hintikka, H. Lehtonen, and H. Viinamaki, "Hunting Guns in Homes and Suicides in 15–24 Year Old Males in Eastern Finland, Australia and New Zealand," *Journal of Psychology* 31 (1997): 858–861.

35. G. Falbo, R. N Buzzetti, and A. Cattaneo, "Homicide in Children and Adolescents: A Case Control Study in Recife, Brazil," *Bulletin of the World Health Organization* 79, no. 1 (2001): 2–7.

36. Wendy Cukier, "Firearms Regulation: Canada in the International Context," *Chronic Diseases in Canada* 19, no.1 (1998): 25–34; Hemenway and Miller, "Firearm Availability and Homicide Rates across 26 High-Income Countries": 985–988; Martin Killias, John van Kesterten, and Martin Rubndisbacker, "Guns, Violent Crime and Suicide in 21 Countries," *Canadian Journal of Criminology* 43 (2001): 429–448.

37. Centers for Disease Control and Prevention (CDC), "First Reports Evaluating the Effectiveness of Strategies for Preventing Violence: Firearms Laws: Findings from the Task Force on Community Preventive Services," *Morbidity and Mortality Weekly Report* 3 (October 2003).

38. International Action Network on Small Arms, "The United States," http://www.iansa.org/regions/namerica/namerica.htm usa.

39. U.S. Bureau of Justice Statistics, *Sourcebook of Criminal Justice Statistics 2000* (Washington, DC: Department of Justice, 2001).

40. P. J. Cook and J. Ludwig, *Guns in America: Results of a Comprehensive National Survey on Firearms Ownership and Use* (Washington, DC: U.S. Department of Justice, National Institute of Justice, 1996).

41. Environics Research Group, "Majority Support for Gun Control; Majority Support Continuation of National Firearms Registry," February 21, 2003, http://erg.environics.net/news/default.asp?aID=513.

42. M. Wallace, "Crime Statistics in Canada, 2002." Statistics Canada, Catalogue 85002 XIE, Canadian Centre for Justice Statistics, vol. 22, no. 5 (2003).

43. United Nations, *United Nations International Study on Firearm Regulation*, Database Update, 1999.

44. Miller and Cohen, "Costs of Gunshot and Cut/Stab Wounds in the United States."

45. L. Saltzman, J. Mercy, P. O'Carroll, M. Rosenberg, and P. H. Rhodes, "Weapon Involvement and Injury Outcomes in Family and Intimate Assaults," *JAMA* 267: 3043–3047.

46. Hemenway and Miller, "Firearm Availability and Homicide Rates across 26 High-Income Countries."

47. T. Christoffel and S. S. Gallagher, *Injury Prevention and Public Health: Practical Knowledge, Skills and Strategies* (Galtersburg, MD: Aspen Publishers, 1999).

48. S. Lab, *Crime Prevention: Approaches, Practices, Evaluations* (Cincinnati, OH: Anderson, 1997).

49. Philip J. Cook and Jens Ludwig, *Gun Violence: The Real Costs* (New York: Oxford University Press, 2000).

50. Ibid.

51. B. Stuart, "Gun-Free Zones Backed," *Citizen*, August 24, 2000.

52. A. Villaveces, P. Cummings, V. Espitia, T. D. Koepsell, B. McKnight, and A. Kellermann, "Effect of a Ban on Carrying Firearms on Homicide Rates in Two Colombian Cities," *Journal of the American Medical Association* 283 (2000): 1205–1209.

53. Primer foro Centroamericano sobre la proliferaction de armas livianas (trans. First Central American Forum on the Proliferation of Small Arms), Antigua, Guatemala, June 26–29, 2000, http://www.arias.or.cr/fundarias/cpr/armsliv.

54. D. W. Webster, J. S. Vernick, and L. M. Hepburn, "Relationship between Licensing, Registration and Other Gun Sales Laws and the Source State of Crime Guns," *Injury Prevention* 7 (2001): 184–189.

55. Ibid.

56. J. Mouzosz, "Firearm-Related Violence: The Impact of the Nation-wide Agreement on Firearms," *Trends & Issues in Crime & Criminal Justice*, no. 116, Australian Institute of Criminology, Canberra (May 1999): 6.

57. K. Hung, *Firearm Statistics. Supplementary Tables* (Ottawa: Research and Statistics Division, Department of Justice, 2000).

58. Mouzoz, "Firearm-Related Violence."

59. International Committee of the Red Cross, *Arms Availability and the Situation of Civilians in Armed Conflict.*

60. Ibid.

61. Gary Mauser, "Are Firearms a Threat to Public Health? The Misuse of Science in Medical Research" (paper presented to the Canadian Law Society Association, St. Catherine's, Ontario, Brock University, June 1–4, 1996).

62. David Hemenway, "Survey Research and Self-Defense Gun Use: An Explanation of Extreme Overestimates," *Journal of Criminal Law and Criminology (Northwestern)* 87 (1997): 1430.

63. John Lott and D. B. Mustard, *More Guns, Less Crime: Understanding Crime and Gun-Control Laws* (Chicago: University of Chicago Press, 1998).

64. J. Donohue, "The Impact of Concealed-Carry Laws," in *Evaluating Gun Policy: Effects on Crime and Violence* (Washington, DC: Brookings Institution Press, 2003), 287–341.

65. A. Altbeker, "Guns and Public Safety: Gun-Crime and Self-Defence in Alexandra and Bramley January–April 1997," *Gun Free South Africa*, http://www.gca.org.za/facts/briefs/46.htm#3.

66. Mauser, "Are Firearms a Threat to Public Health?"

67. Gary Mauser, *The Failed Experiment: Gun Control and Public Safety in Canada, Australia, England and Wales* (Vancouver: Fraser Institute, 2003), http://www.sfu.ca/~mauser/index1.html.

68. D. Kopel, *The Samurai, the Mountie and the Cowboy: Should America Adopt the Gun Controls of other Democracies?* (Buffalo, NY: Prometheus, 1992).

69. M. Killias, "Gun Ownership and Violent Crime: The Swiss Experience in International Perspective," *Security Journal* 1, no. 3 (1990): 169–174.

70. Cukier, "Firearms Regulation."

71. Hemenway and Miller, "Firearm Availability and Homicide Rates across 26 High Income Countries."

72. Franklin E. Zimring and Gordon Hawkins, *Crime Is Not the Problem: Lethal Violence in America* (New York: Oxford University Press, 1997).

73. A. McAlister, "Homicide Rates and Attitudes Towards Killing in Fifteen Nations" (Aiming for Prevention, Helsinki, Finland, October 28–30, 2001).

74. Miller and Cohen, "Costs of Gunshot and Cut/Stab Wounds in the United States."

75. Maria Fernanda Tourinho Peres, *Firearm-Related Violence in Brazil: Summary Report* (Sao Paulo, Brazil: Centre for the Study of Violence, University of Sao Paulo, 2004).

76. Tom Christoffel and Susan Scavo Gallagher, *Injury Prevention and Public Health: Practical Knowledge, Skills and Strategies* (Gaithersburg, MD: Aspen, 1999).

77. Zimring and Hawkins, *Crime Is Not the Problem.*

78. David Foot and Daniel Stoffman, *Boom, Bust and Echo 2000: Profiting from the Demographic Shift in the New Millenium* (Toronto: Stoddart, 2000).

79. D. Hemenway, "The Public Health Approach to Motor Vehicles, Tobacco and Alcohol with Applications to Firearms Policy," *Journal of Public Health Policy* 22, no. 4 (2001): 381–402.

80. Ibid.

81. A. L. Kellermann, "Comment: Gunsmoke—Changing Public Attitudes Towards Smoking and Firearms," *American Journal of Public Health* 87 (1997): 910–913.

82. Hemenway and Miller, "Firearm Availability and Homicide Rates across 26 High-Income Countries."

83. Villaveces, Cummings, Espitia, Koepsell, McKnight, and Kellermann, "Effect of a Ban on Carrying Firearms on Homicide Rates in Two Colombian Cities."

84. Falbo, Buzzetti, and Cattaneo, "Homicide in Children and Adolescents."

85. Ibid.

86. Neil Boyd, "A Statistical Analysis of the Impacts of the 1977 Firearms Control Legislation: Critique and Discussion" (Ottawa: Justice Canada, 1996).

Chapter 4

1. Jeffrey Boutwell and Michael Klare, "A Scourge of Small Arms," http://www.pugwash.org/reports/pim/pim21.htm.

2. U.S. Department of Labor, *Congressional Record* 139 (November 3, 1993): S16, 936, cited in J. Dixon, "On Lemon Squeezers and Locking Devices: Consumer Product Safety and Firearms, a Modest Proposal," *Case Western Reserve Law Review* 47 (1997): 990–991.

3. UN Expert Panel on Small Arms, cited in Joseph Di Chiaro, *Reasonable Measures: Addressing the Excessive Accumulation and Unlawful Use of Small Arms* (Bonn: Bonn International Centre for Conversion [BICC], August 1998).

4. Tom Diaz, *Making a Killing: The Business of Guns in America* (New York: The New Press, 1999).

5. Graduate Institute of International Studies, *Small Arms Survey 2004: Rights at Risk* (Oxford: Oxford University Press, 2004).

6. "Guns in America; Home on the Range," *Economist* (March 26, 1994): 23.

7. Graduate Institute of International Studies, *Small Arms Survey 2004.*

8. Ibid.

9. Graduate Institute of International Studies, *Small Arms Survey 2003: Development Denied* (Oxford: Oxford University Press, 2003).

10. International Committee of the Red Cross, *Arms Availability and the Situation of Civilians in Armed Conflict* (Geneva: International Committee of the Red Cross, 1999).

11. Peter Lock, "Armed Conflicts and Small Arms Proliferation," *Policy Sciences* 30, no. 3: 117–132.

12. Graduate Institute of International Studies, *Small Arms Survey 2003: Development Denied* (Oxford: Oxford University Press, 2003).

13. "Guns in America"; See also Philip Cook and Ludwig, "Guns in America: National Survey on Private Ownership and Use of Firearms."

14. Boutwell and Klare, "A Scourge of Small Arms."

15. Graduate Institute of International Studies, *Small Arms Survey 2003.*

16. United States, Department of Justice. 2005. *Annual Firearms Manufacturing and Export Report* (2003). Prepared by the Office of FEA, Bureau of Alcohol, Tobacco, and Firearms (Washington: Department of Justice, 2005), http://www.atf.treas.gov/firearms/stats/afmer/afmer2003.pdf.

17. Alok K. Chakrabarti, *An Analysis of the US Firearms Industry* (Newark, NJ: New Jersey Institute of Technology, 2000).

18. Ibid.

19. Robert Haas, cited in William C. Symonds, Lorraine Woellert, and Susan Garland, "Gunmakers under Fire," *Business Week*, August 16, 1999.

20. Ibid.

21. John Lott, Jr. and Grover Nordquist, "Gun Suit Reform Could Still Be Shot Down," *Fox News Online*, February 25, 2004, http://www.foxnews.com/story/0,2933,112545,00.html.

22. Shailagh Murray, "Senate Passes Bill Barring Gun Suits 65–31 Vote After Heated Debate," *Washington Post* (Saturday, July 30, 2005): A08.

23. Diaz, *Making a Killing.*

24. Lynn Hamilton, "Light Triggers, Hefty Profits," *MotherJones.com*, January 26, 2000, http://www.motherjones.com/news/feature/2000/01/glock.html.

25. *Small Arms Survey 2003.*

26. Maxim Pyadushkin, Maria Haug, and Anna Matveeva, "Beyond the Kalashnikov: Small Arms Production, Exports, and Stockpiles in the Russian Federation," *Small Arms Survey: Occasional Paper No. 10* (August 2003).

27. Ibid.

28. *Small Arms Survey 2002.*

29. Rubem Cesar Fernandes, Bejamin Lessing, Carolina Iootty, Juloi Cesar

Purcena, Luciana Phebo, Marcelo de Souza Nascimento, Pablo Dreyfus, Patricia Rivero, "Brasi; *The Arms and the Victims*," *Viva Rio*, 2005.

30. *Small Arms Survey 2002.*

31. Diaz, *Making a Killing.*

32. Ibid.

33. International Committee of the Red Cross, *Arms Availability and the Situation of Civilians in Armed Conflict* (Geneva: International Committee of the Red Cross, 1999).

34. Ibid.

35. Brian Wood and Johan Peleman, *The Arms Fixers: Controlling the Brokers and Shipping Agents*, British American Security Information Council, no. 99.3 (November 1999), http://www.nisat.org/publications/armsfixers/default.htm.

36. Ibid.

37. Bureau of Alcohol, Tobacco, and Firearms, *Firearms Commerce in the United States: 2001/2002.*

38. J. Dixon, "On Lemon Squeezers and Locking Devices."

39. "Guns in America; Home on the Range," *Economist*, March 26, 1994: 23, 25.

40. Ibid.

41. Bureau of Alcohol, Tobacco, and Firearms (BATF), *Commerce in Firearms in the United States* (Washington, DC: U.S. Department of the Treasury, Bureau of Alcohol, Tobacco, and Firearms, 2000).

42. Diaz, *Making a Killing.*

43. Ibid.

44. R. J. Spitzer, *The Politics of Gun Control* (Chatham, NJ: Chatham House Publishers, 1995), 73.

Chapter 5

1. Smuggling Work Group, *Report of the Smuggling Work Group* (Ottawa: Justice Canada, 1995).

2. Rubem Cesar Fernandes, Bejamin Lessing, Carolina Iootty, Juloi Cesar Purcena, Luciana Phebo, Marcelo de Souza Nascimento, Pablo Dreyfus, Patricia Rivero, "Brasil *The Arms and the Victims*" (*Viva Rio*, 2005); G. Khatchik, P. Leandro, and L. Carneiro, *Connecting Weapons with Violence: The South American Experience*, monograph no. 25 (Halfway House, South Africa: Institute for Security Studies, 1998) claimed that Paraguay was a major source, but subsequent empirical studies showed that this was only the partly the case. A survey conducted by the Brazilian Institute for Higher Studies on Religion (ISER), released on August 2, 1999, showed that 83.12 percent of 44,437 firearms seized in the state of Rio de Janeiro from 1994 to March 1999 were manufactured in Brazil. Indeed, of the seized weapons, 72 percent (32,143 guns) were manufactured by two Brazilian firearms manufacturers, Taurus and Rossi. The ISER study, based on registries of the Arms and Explosives Control Department of the Rio de Janeiro Civilian Police, dispelled a long-held public security view that weapons used by Brazilian criminals were mostly foreign made.

3. R. Chetty, ed., *Firearm Use and Distribution in South Africa* (National Crime Prevention Centre, Secretariat of Safety and Security, Pretoria, South Africa: 2000).

4. For a thorough discussion of the limitations of data sources, see the *United Nations International Firearms Study* (Vienna: United Nations, 1998).

5. Ibid.

6. Glenn L. Pierce, LeBaron Briggs, and David Carlson, *The Identification of Patterns in Firearms Trafficking Implications for Focused Enforcement Strategies: A Report to the United States Department of Treasury, Bureau of Alcohol, Tobacco and Firearms* (Chicago: Northwestern University, 1995).

7. Joseph Vince, *Disarming the Criminal* (Washington, DC: Bureau of Alcohol, Tobacco, and Firearms, 1996).

8. S. Handleman, *Comrade Criminal: Russia's New Mafia* (New Haven, CT: Yale University Press, 1995).

9. W. M. Leary, *Perilous Missions: Civil Air Transport and CIA Covert Operations in Asia* (University of Alabama Press, 1984); F. Lert, *Les Ailes de la CIA* (The Wings of the CIA) (Paris: Histoire & Collections, 1998).

10. Office of Inspector General, *Allegations of Connections between CIA and the Contras in Cocaine Trafficking to the United States*, Report of Investigations, *Volume II: The Contra Story* (Washington, DC: Central Intelligence Agency, 1998), www.odci.gov/cia/publications/cocaine2/index.html.

11. Brian Wood and Johan Peleman, "The Arms Fixers: Controlling the Brokers and Shipping Agents," British American Security Information Council, no. 99.3 (November 1999), http://www.nisat.org/publications/armsfixers/default.htm.

12. Andreas Von Bulow, *Im Namen des Staates: CIA*. BND und die kriminellen Machenschaften des Geheimdienste (Munich: Piper, 1998): 624.

13. Violence Policy Center, *Credit Card Armies—Firearms and Training for Terror in the United States* (Washington, DC: Violence Policy Center, 2002), http://www.vpc.org/graphics/creditcardarmies.pdf.

14. Wood and Peleman, "The Arms Fixers."

15. Ibid.

16. C. Smith, P. Batchelor, and J. Potgieter, *Small Arms Management and Peacekeeping in Southern Africa* (Geneva: United Nations Institute for Disarmament Research, Disarmament and Conflict Resolution Project, 1996).

17. Alexander Chloros, Joel Johnston, Katherine Joseph, and Rachel Stohl, BASIC *Breaking the Cycle of Violence: Light Weapons Destruction in Central America*, no. 24 (December 1997), http://www.basicint.org/pubs/Papers/BP24.htm.

18. Christopher Smith, "The Impact of Light Weapons On Security: A Case Study of South Asia," *Stockholm Peace Research Institute Yearbook 1995* (London: Oxford University Press, 1995).

19. W. Cukier, A. Chapdelaine, P. De Villiers, B. Ford, and V. Westwick, "Combatting the Illicit Trafficking and Misuse of Firearms: A Submission to the United Nations Commission on Crime Prevention and Criminal Justice and the Ad Hoc Committee on Transnational Organized Crime (IOC) Convention (Vienna, April 27–May 4, 1999).

20. Tom Diaz, *Making a Killing: The Business of Guns in America* (New York: The New Press, 1999).

21. C. Collins, *Liberalization of the Global Small Arms Trade* (manuscript, 2000).

22. T. Crawford-Browne, *The R30 Billion Defence Procurement Proposal and Industrial Participation Programme* (Cape Town: Coalition for Defence Alternatives, 1998).

23. P. Cook and J. Leitzel, "Perversity, Futility and Jeopardy: An Economic Analysis of the Attack on Gun Control," *Law and Contemporary Problems* 59, no. 1 (1996): 91–118.

24. Philip J. Cook, Stephanie Molliconi, and Thomas B. Cole, "Regulating Gun Markets," *Journal of Criminal Law & Criminology* 86 (Fall 1995): 59–92.

25. D. W Webster, J. S. Vernick, and L. M. Hepburn, "Relationship between Licensing, Registration, and Other Gun Sales Laws and the Source State of Crime Guns," *Injury Prevention* 7 (2001): 184–189.

26. D. R. Meddings, "Weapons Injuries During and After Periods of Conflict: Retrospective Analysis," *British Medical Journal* 315 (1997): 1417–1420; International Committee of the Red Cross, *Arms Availability and the Situation of Civilians in Armed Conflict* (Geneva, 1999).

27. W. Cukier, "International Fire/Small Arms Control," *Canadian Foreign Policy* 6, no. 1 (1998): 73–89.

28. Michael Klare and David Andersen, *Scourge of Guns: The Diffusion of Small Arms and Light Weapons in Latin America* (Washington, DC: Federation of American Scientists, 1996).

29. D. Garcia-Peña Jaramillo, "Linkages between Drugs and Illicit Arms Trafficking: Issues of Current Concern to Colombia" (paper prepared for the workshop Weapons Collection and Integration of Former Combatants into Civil Society: The Experiences of Guatemala, El Salvador, Honduras, Nicaragua, and Columbia, UN Department for Humanitarian Affairs, November 18, 1998). The drugs-guns link has also been identified as a major problem in South Africa. See T. Ryan, *Drugs, Violence and Governability in the Future South Africa* (Pretoria: Institute for Security Studies, 1997).

30. Canadian Association of Chiefs of Police, "Gun Control Resolution," Annual Conference, Hamilton, 1999.

31. P. Williams, "Transnational Organized Crime and International Security: A Global Assessment," in *Society Under Siege, Crime Violence and Illegal Weapons* (Halfway House Institute for Security Services, 1998).

32. Cukier, "International Fire/Small Arms Control."

33. M. Killias, "International Correlations between Gun Ownership and Rates of Homicide and Suicide," *Canadian Medical Association Journal* 148, no. 10 (1992): 1721–1725.

34. Cook, Molliconi, and Cole, "Regulating Gun Markets."

35. Cook and Leitzel, "Perversity, Futility and Jeopardy."

36. R. Jamieson, N. South, and I. Taylor, *Economic Liberalisation and Cross-Border Crime: The North American Free Trade Area and Canada's Border with the*

US (London: Institute for Social Research of the University of Salford, 1997); Christina Eigel, "Internal Security in an Open Market: The European Union Addresses the Need for Community Gun Control (Ninth Annual European Law Issue)," *Boston College International and Comparative Law Review* 18, no. 2 (Summer 1995): 429–441.

37. P. Williams, "Drugs and Guns," *Bulletin of the Atomic Scientists* 55, no. 1 (January/February 1999): 46–48.

38. R. T. Naylor, "Loose Cannons: Covert Commerce and Underground finance in the Modern Arms Black Market," *Crime Law and Social Change* 22 (1995): 1–57.

39. W. Cukier, "Marking Tracing and Tracking: The Role of Information in Controlling the Misuse of Firearms" (Toronto: *American Society of Criminology*, 1999).

40. Chetty, *Firearm Use and Distribution in South Africa.*

41. Adam Graycar, *Small Arms Project: An Australian Perspective* (CSCAP Working Group on Transnational Crime, 1998).

42. Canada Newswire, "Illegal Handgun Seizure Largest in Years," November 26, 2001.

43. United Nations, International Study on Firearms Regulation, August 30, 1999 [last update], http://www.uncjin.org/Statistics/firearms.

44. "Gangland Armourer Facing Long Jail Term," *Times*, January 21, 1999 (London: Black Market Archive), www.nisat.org.

45. Cook, Molliconi, and Cole, "Regulating Gun Markets."

46. G.L. Pierce, L. Briggs, and D. Carlson, *The Identification of Patterns in Firearms Trafficking: Implications for Focused Enforcement Strategies* (Boston, MA: Northeastern University).

47. M. Hallowes, *Operation ABONAR* (London: Metropolitan Police, Directorate of Intelligence, 1999).

48. N. Goldring, *Domestic Laws and International Controls*; Jeffrey Boutwell and Michael Klare, eds., *Light Weapons and Civil Conflict: Controlling the Tools of Violence* (Lanham, MD: Rowman and Littlefield, 1999).

49. United Nations, International Study on Firearms Regulation.

50. G. Francis, "Illicit Firearms in Canada: Sources, Smuggling and Trends," *RCMP Gazette* 57, no. 2 (1995): 22–24.

51. L. Lumpe, "The US Arms Both Sides of Mexico's Drug War," *Covert Action Quarterly* 61 (1998): 39–46.

52. Garcia-Peña Jaramillo, "Linkages between Drugs and Illicit Arms Trafficking."

53. United Nations, *International Study on Firearms Regulation.*

54. Ibid.

55. Cook and Leitzel, "Perversity, Futility and Jeopardy."

56. Chetty, *Firearm Use and Distribution in South Africa.*

57. Rocco Parascandola, "Stolen Uzi Cache Turning Up in All the Worst Places," *New York Post*, July 5, 1998, Black Market Archive, www.nisat.org.

58. Adam Graycar, *Small Arms Project: An Australian Perspective* (Kuala Lumpur: Council for Security Cooperation in the Asia Pacific, Working Group on Transnational Crime, 1998).

59. C. Whitlock, "Gun Thefts Put UPS in the Cross Hairs," *Washington Post*, December 24, 1999.

60. H. Woolcott, "UPS Is Taking Aim at Gun Thefts," *Los Angeles Times*, November 8, 1999.

61. C. Sorensen, "Mail-Order Guns Worry Canadian Officials," *Hamilton Spectator*, January 4, 2004: A09.

62. Graycar, *Small Arms Project*.

63. Chetty, *Firearm Use and Distribution in South Africa*.

64. B. Vobejda, D. Ottaway, and S. Cohen, "Recycled DC Police Guns Tied to Crimes," *Washington Post*, November 12, 1999.

65. Investigators were able to purchase such parts at thirteen of the fifteen gun shows they targeted. U.S. General Accounting Office, *Small Arms Parts: Poor Controls Invite Widespread Theft*, report GAO/NSIAD-94-21, 1994.

66. Dana Priest and Roberto Suro, "More Arrests, Charges are seen by FBI and Defense Department," *The Washington Post*, October 18, 1997: A10, Black Market Archive, www.nisat.org.

67. "Russia: Army Servicemen Detained for Illegal Trafficking of Firearms," *Moscow RIA in Russian* 13 (December 2000, FBIS Translated Text), Black Market Archive, www.NISAT.org.

68. "Mexico Drug Trafficking Groups 'Promoting' Arms Trafficking," Mexico City La Jornada, September 27, 1996, FBIS Translated Text from Black Market Archive, www.NISAT.org

69. J. Duncanson, and Jim Rankin, "3000 Guns Go 'Missing' from Police," *Toronto Star*, September 10, 1997.

70. Wood and Peleman, "The Arms Fixers."

71. U.S. Department of Justice, Export Control Enforcement Unit, *Significant Export Control Cases*, September 5, 1997.

72. U.S. Department of the Treasury, *International Traffic in Arms* (Washington, DC: Bureau of Alcohol, Tobacco, and Firearms, 1991).

73. United Nations, *International Study on Firearms Regulation*.

74. Lora Lumpe, "The US Arms Both Sides of Mexico's Drug War," *Covert Action Quartely*, no. 61 (Summer 1997): 39–46.

75. Reuters, "Four Arrests in Suspected Irish Gun-Smuggling Ring," July 27, 1999, Black Market Database, www.nisat.org.

76. Tom Godfrey, "Have Gun Will Travel," *Toronto Sun*, October 30, 2002.

77. Wood and Peleman, "The Arms Fixers."

78. J. Vince, *Disarming the Criminal* (Washington, DC: Firearms Enforcement Division, Department of the Treasury, Bureau of Alcohol, Tobacco, and Firearms, 1996).

79. S. McCaffrey, "Report Traces Gun Sales," Associated Press, December 20, 1999.

80. Vince, *Disarming the Criminal*.

81. Ibid.

82. Smuggling Work Group, *Report of the Smuggling Work Group*.

83. J. Thompson, *Misfire* (Toronto: McKenzie Institute, 1995).

84. Toronto Police Services, "Minutes of the Board Meeting," January 22, 2004, www.torontopoliceboard.on.ca/minutes/2004/040122pmm.pdf.

85. Smuggling Work Group, *Report of the Smuggling Work Group*.

86. T. Godfrey, "Have Gun Will Travel," *Toronto Sun*, October 30, 2002.

87. Tim Wiener and Ginger Thompson, "US Guns Smuggled into Mexico Aid Drug War," *New York Times*, May 19, 2001.

88. Graduate Institute of International Studies, *Small Arms Survey 2003: Development Denied* (Oxford: Oxford University Press, 2003).

89. Ibid., 118.

90. DEFAE. Investigación: Brazilian Institute of Higher Studies on Religion (ISER), Rio de Janeiro, released on August 2, 1999.

91. Ibid.

92. Graduate Institute of International Studies, *Small Arms Survey 2003*.

93. Ibid.

94. Oxfam and Amnesty International, *Shattered Lives: The Case for Tough International Arms Control* (London: Oxfam and Amnesty International, 2003).

95. Ibid.

96. Margaret Coker, "Illegal Soviet Weapons Fuel Wars around World," Special Reports: Small Arms, Mass Destruction, *Atlanta Journal-Constitution*, July 8, 2001, http://www.nisat.org.

97. Oxfam and Amnesty International, *Shattered Lives*.

98. S. Handleman, *Comrade Criminal: Russia's New Mafia* (New Haven, CT: Yale University Press, 1995).

99. Wendy Cukier, "Vuurwapens: legale en illegale kanalen" (Firearms: licit/illicit links), *Tijdschrift voor—Criminologie,* translation of 43, no. 1 (2001): 27–41, http://www.ryerson.ca/SAFER-Net.

100. Ibid.

101. Ibid.

102. Michael Hallowes, *Operation ABONAR*. London: Metropolitan Police, Directorate of Intelligence, 1999.

103. Court Reporter, Duo get six years for selling guns, New Shopper, 14 September 2004, http://www.newsshopper.co.uk/news/lewgreennews/display.var.527321.0.duo_get_six_years_for_selling_guns.php.

104. Jeevan Vasagar, "East European gunrunners boost UK gang weaponry," The Guardian (London), July 2, 2003: 8.

105. M. Chachiua, "Arms Management Programme: Operations Rachel 1996–1999," ISS Monograph 38, (Pretoria): Institute for Security Studies, (June 1999): 6; British American Security Information Council (BASIC), The *Illicit Traffic in Small Arms: Submission to UN Department of Disarmament Affairs*, July 1999.

106. BASIC, *Illicit Traffic in Small Arms: Submission to UN Department of Disarmament*, July 1999, http://www.basicint.org/WT/smallarms/unrecsfinal.pdf. "The easy availability of AK-47s in Mozambique and Angola has flooded South Africa with illicit automatic weapons and made South Africa one of the largest centres of illicit light weapons trafficking. In turn, more and more crimes in South Africa involve the threat or use of a firearm. By January 1999, there was an average of 30

gun related deaths per day in South Africa." However, the empirical evidence presented by Chetty, *Firearm Use and Distribution in South Africa,* shows the vast majority of the criminal acts and murders in South Africa involve handguns, not AK-47s.

107. Chetty, *Firearm Use and Distribution in South Africa.*

108. K. McKenzie, *Domestic Gun Control in Ten SADC Countries* (Johannesburg: Gun Free South Africa, 1999).

109. Anthony Minnaars, *Policing the Ports: Reducing Illicit Trafficking in South Africa* (Pretoria: Institute for Security Studies), no. 84, www.iss.co.za/Pubs/Monographs/No84.

110. Ibid.

111. Graduate Institute of International Studies, *Small Arms Survey 2003,* 117.

112. Niobe Thompson and Devashish Krishnan, "Small Arms in India and the Human Costs of Lingering Conflict," *Over a Barrel: Light Weapons and Human Rights in the Commonwealth,* Abdel Fatau-Musah and Niobe Thompson, eds. (New Delhi: Commonwealth Human Rights Initiative, 1999).

113. L. Lumpe, *Running Guns: The Global Black Market in Small Arms* (London: Zed Books, 2000).

114. Graduate Institute of International Studies, *Small Arms Survey 2002: Counting the Human Cost* (Oxford University Press, 2002).

115. United Nations, *International Study on Firearms Regulation.*

116. David Capie, *Small Arms Production and Transfers in Southeast Asia,* Canberra Paper on Strategy and Defence No. 146 (Canberra: Strategic Defence Studies Center, Australian National University, 2002).

117. Ibid.

118. Philip Alpers and Conor Twyford, *Small Arms in the Pacific,* Occasional Paper No. 8, *Small Arms Survey,* March 2003.

119. Ibid.

Chapter 6

1. Rosemary Gartner, "Affidavit of Rosemary Gartner."

2. United Nations, *International Study on Firearm Regulation,* (Vienna: United Nations, 1998).

3. M. Killias, "Gun Ownership, Suicide and Homicide: An International Perspective," 1992.

4. A. Smith, "Shooting Industry Market Trend Analysis," *Industry in Review* (December 1993): 144.

5. James T. Dixon, "On Lemon Squeezers and Locking Devices," *Case Western Reserve Law Review* 47 (1997): 979.

6. U.S. Bureau of the Census, Department of Commerce, *The National Data Book, Statistical Abstract of the United States* (Washington, DC: Government Printing Office, 1994, 205–316.

7. P. Cook, S. Molliconni, and T. Cole, "Regulating Gun Markets," *Journal of Criminal Law and Criminology* 86 (1995): 59, 81.

8. Kurt Kluin, "Gun Control: Is it a Legal and Effective Means of Controlling Firearms in the United States?" *Washburn Law Journal* 21, no. 92 (1982): 254–255.

9. A.L. Kellermann, F.P. Rivara, R.K. Lee, and J.G. Banton, "Injuries and Deaths Due to Firearms in the Home," *Journal of Trauma: Injury, Infection and Critical Care* 45, no. 2 (1998): 263–267.

10. Richard Block, *Firearms in Canada and Eight Other Western Countries: Selected Findings of the 1996 International Crime (Victim) Survey* (Ottawa: Department of Justice Canada, 1998).

11. L. Montgomery, "NRA Alters Aim, and Its Targets, in a Slow Revolt," *Seattle Times*, May 21, 1995: A3.

12. Environics Research Group, "Majority Support for Gun Control; Majority Support Continuation of National Firearms Registry," press release on results of a Focus Canada Survey conducted January 2–14, 2003, http://erg.environics.net/news/default.asp?aID=513.

13. This estimate was generated based on a large 1991 poll conducted by the Angus Reid Group for the Department of Justice Canada and other polls conducted in the 1990s. The estimate was published in United Nations, International Study on Firearm Regulation, August 1999, http://www.uncjin.org/Statistics/firearms.

14. Graduate Institute of International Studies, *Small Arms Survey 2004: Rights at Risk* (Oxford: Oxford University Press, 2004).

15. Graduate Institute of International Studies, *Small Arms Survey 2002: Counting the Human Cost* (Oxford: Oxford University Press, 2002).

16. Graduate Institute of International Studies, *Small Arms Survey 2003: Development Denied* (Oxford: Oxford University Press, 2003).

17. Wendy Cukier, *Emerging Global Norms in the Regulation of Civilian Possession of Small Arms* (Toronto: SAFER-Net, 2003).

18. Associated Press, "Yemen Bans Firearms from Streets," February 5, 2002, http://story.news.yahoo.com/news?tmpl=story&u=/ap/20020205/ap_on_re_mi_ea/yemen_arms_2 AHMED AL-HAJ.

19. Ilene R. Prusher, "Fear of Crime Holds Up US Effort to Disarm Iraq," *Christian Science Monitor*, June 2, 2003, http://www.csmonitor.com/2003/0602/p01s03-woiq.html.

20. J. Anderson, *Inside the NRA: Armed and Dangerous: An Exposé* (Beverly Hills, CA: Dove Books, 1996).

21. Kevin O'Neill, "I Need a Hero: Gender and the Rhetorical Dimension of the NRA's Use of Media," http://beard.dialnsa.edu/~treis/pdf/NRA%20use%20of%20Media.pdf.

22. Ibid.

23. Robert J. Spitzer, *The Politics of Gun Control* (Chatham, NJ: Chatham House, 1995).

24. M. Udulutch, "The Constitutional Implications of Gun Control and Several Realistic Gun Control Proposals," *American Journal of Criminology* 17, no. 14 (1989): 19, 21.

25. Anderson, *Inside the NRA*.

26. E. Eckholm, "The Riots Bring a Rush to Arm and New Debate," *New York Times*, May 17, 1992: S4.

27. T. Hargrove, "Focus on Stopping Violence," *Atlanta Journal-Constitution*, November 22, 1995: A4.

28. J. Lenzen, "Liberalizing the Concealed Carry of Handguns by Qualified Civilians: The Case for 'Carry Reform,'" *Rutgers Law Review* 47, no. 4 (1995): 1503–1504.

29. Anderson, *Inside the NRA*.

30. Tom Diaz, *Making a Killing: The Business of Guns in America* (New York: The New Press, 1999).

31. Violence Policy Center, *Female Persuasion: A Study of How the Firearms Industry Markets to Women and the Reality of Women and Guns* (Washington, DC: Violence Policy Center, December 1994).

32. South African Gunowner's Association, "About SAGA," http://www.saga .org.za/about_saga.htm.

33. Paul Peake, "Self Defence," 1998, http://www.ssaa.org.au/ilanov98.html.

34. Diaz, *Making a Killing,* 120.

35. Dixon, "On Lemon Squeezers and Locking Devices," 172.

36. Anderson, *Inside the NRA*.

37. National Firearm Association, "The Lioness Method of Rape Prevention: For Women Only!" 1999, http://www.nfa.ca/publications/lioness.pdf.

38. Tiia Rajala, "Guns 'R' Us: Building of an NRA Membership," 2001, http:// www.uta.fi/laitokset/historia/sivut/ylhitutsem2001/RajalaTiia.pdf.

39. A. Jones, "Is This Power Feminism?—The Push to Get Women Hooked on Guns," *Ms.*, May–June 1994.

40. Philip J. Cook and Jens Ludwig, *Guns in America: Results of a Comprehensive Survey on Private Firearms Ownership and Use* (Washington, DC: National Institute of Justice, 1997); Angus Reid Group, *Gun Control: Public Support for Regulating Firearm Ownership in Canada*, 1993.

41. W. Cukier, *Ceasefire: Guns and Violence against Women* (Canadian Advisory Council on the Status of Women, 1991). See also "Women and Firearms in the International Context," *International Peace Update* 65, no. 3 (2000).

42. Will Lester, "Women, Men Differ on Gun Control," September 7, 1999, Associated Press.

43. Angus Reid Group, *Gun Control*.

44. Environics Research Group, "Majority Support for Gun Control."

45. Lester, "Women, Men Differ on Gun Control."

46. Jones, "Is This Power Feminism?"

47. C. Jefferson, *Attitudes to Firearms: The Case of Kwa Mashu, Tsolo-Qumbo and Lekoa-Vaal* (Pretoria: Institute for Security Studies, 2001).

48. D. Kappell, Y. C. Lin, and S. O. Yem, "Risk Factors for Wanting a Gun in Phnom Penh, Cambodia" (paper presented at the Role of Public Health in the Prevention of War-Related Injuries, Montreal, Canada, May 9–11, 2002).

49. Diaz, *Making a Killing*.

50. Arthur J. Kellermann, "Comment: Gunsmoke—Changing Public Attitudes

towards Smoking and Firearms," *American Journal of Public Health* 87, no. 6 (1997).

51. National Firearms Association, "Gun-Proofing Your Child," 1999, http://www.nfa.ca/publications/gunproof.pdf.

52. Coalition for Gun Control, "Kids and Guns," http://www.guncontrol.ca/Content/Kids.html.

53. Jacklyn Cock, "Fixing Our Sights: A Sociological Perspective on Gun Violence in Contemporary South Africa," *Society in Transition* 1–4: 70–81.

54. Oxfam, Amnesty International, and International Action Network on Small Arms (IANSA), *Shattered Lives: The Case for Tough International Arms Control* (London, 2003).

55. Vanessa Farr and Kiflemariam Gebre-Wold, eds., *Gender Perspectives on Small arms and Light Weapons: Regional and International Concerns* (Bonn: Bonn International Conversion Centre, 2002).

56. Oxfam, Amnesty International, and IANSA, *Shattered Lives*.

57. Jacklyn Cock, "Fixing Our Sights: A Sociological Perspective on Gun Violence in Contemporary South Africa."

58. Joshua S. Goldstein, *War and Gender: How Gender Shapes the War System and Vice Versa* (Berkley: University of California Press, 2001).

59. B. Bruce Briggs, *The Great American Gun War*. The Public Interest, Fall 1976.

60. Cited in Dan Kahan, Donald Braman, and John Gastil, "Gun Litigation: A Culture Theory Critique," unpublished manuscript, http://research.yale.edu/cultural cognition/documents/cultural_critique_gun_litigation.pdf.

61. Barbara Frey Cited in Oxfam and Amnesty International. *The Impact of Guns on Women's Lives* (London: Oxfam and Amnesty International, 2005), http://www.oxfam.org.uk/what_we_do/issues/conflict_disasters/women_guns.htm.

62. Rosemary Gartner, "Cross Cultural Aspects of Interpersonal Violence: A Review of the International Empirical Evidence," International Conference on Crime and Violence: Causes and Policy Responses, World Bank, May 2000, http://www.worldbank.org/.

63. Andrew McAlister, "Homicide Rates and Attitudes Towards Killing in Fifteen Nations," (paper presented at Aiming for Prevention, Helsinki, Finland, International Physicians for the Prevention of Nuclear War, October 28–30, 2001), http://www.ippnw.org/Helsinki2ndAnnB.pdf.

64. Dov Cohen, "Law, Social Policy, and Violence: The Impact of Regional Cultures," *Journal of Personality and Social Psychology* 70, no. 5 (1996): 961–978.

65. Quaker United Nations Office, "Curbing the Demand for Small Arms: Focus on Southeast Asia" (summary report from the workshop held in collaboration with the Centre for Humanitarian Dialogue, the Quaker United Nations Office, the Quaker International Affairs Programme, Southeast Asia, and the Working Group on Weapons Reduction, Phnom Penh, Cambodia, May 26–31, 2002).

66. D. Kopel, *The Samurai, the Mountie and the Cowboy: Should America Adopt the Gun Controls of other Democracies?* (Buffalo, NY: Prometheus, 1992).

67. Ibid.

68. Alexander MacLeod, "A Shot in the Dark? Antigun Lobby in Britain Aims for Ban on Handguns," *Christian Science Monitor*, August 5, 1996: 1.

69. Lester, "Women, Men Differ on Gun Control."

70. Jefferson, *Attitudes to Firearms*.

71. Environics Research Group, "Majority Support for Gun Control."

72. Dov Cohen, "Culture, Social Organization, and Patterns of Violence," *Journal of Personality and Social Psychology* 75, no. 2 (1998): 408–419.

73. Cohen, "Law, Social Policy, and Violence."

74. American Academy of Pediatrics, Committee on Public Education, "Media Violence," *Pediatrics*, November 2001.

75. Ibid., 4.

76. Paul J. Lynch, Douglas A. Gentile, Abbie A. Olson, and Tara M. van Brederode, "The Effects of Violent Video Game Habits on Adolescent Aggressive Attitudes and Behaviors" (paper presented at the Biennial Conference of the Society for Research in Child Development, Minneapolis, Minnesota, April 19–22, 2001).

77. J. L. Sherry, "The Effects of Violent Video Games on Aggression: A Meta-Analysis," *Human Communication Research* 27, no. 3 (2001): 409–431.

78. Cecilia Von Feilitzen and U. Carlsson, *Children in the New Media Landscape: Games, Pornography, Perceptions* (Göteborg, Sweden: The UNESCO International Clearinghouse on Children and Violence on the Screen at Nordicom, 2000).

79. Cited in Jackson Katz, "Advertising and the Construction of Violent White Masculinity," in *Gender, Race and Class in Media: A Text Reader*, ed. G. Dines and J. Humez (Thousand Oaks, CA: Sage Publications, 1995).

80. Robert Arjet, *Gunplay: Men, Guns and Action Films in the United States* (Atlanta: Emory University, 2002).

81. B. S. Centerwall, "Television Violence: The Scale of the Problem and Where We Go from Here," *JAMA* 267 (1992): 3059–3063.

82. George Gerbner and L. Gross, "Living with Television: The Violence Profile," *Journal of Communication* 30, no. 3 (1980): 10–29.

83. Cukier, *Ceasefire*.

84. Elizabeth C. Hirschman, "Men, Dogs, Guns and Cars: The Semiotics of Rugged Individualism," *Journal of Advertising* 32, no. 1 (Spring 2003): 9–22.

85. O'Neill, "I Need a Hero."

86. Ibid.

87. Katz, "Advertising and the Construction of Violent White Masculinity."

88. Ibid.

Chapter 7

1. Will Lester, "Women, Men Differ on Gun Control," *Associated Press*, September 7, 1999.

2. Thomas Hartley and Josephine Mazzuca, "Seven out of Ten Canadians Support National Firearms Registry" Gallup Poll, 61.77 (2001).

3. Lester, "Women, Men Differ on Gun Control."

4. Angus Reid, "Gun Control: Public Support for Regulating Firearm Ownership in Canada," *The Reid Report* 8, no. 9 (October 1993).

5. Stephen Lab, *Crime Prevention: Approaches, Practices, Evaluations* (Cincinnati: Anderson, 1997).

6. Cited in Philip J. Cook and Jens Ludwig, *Gun Violence: The Real Costs* (Oxford: Oxford University Press, 2000), 35.

7. Jacqueline Cohen and Jens Ludwig, "Policing Crime Guns," in *Evaluating Gun Policy*, ed. Philip Cook and Jens Ludwig (Washington, DC: Brookings Institution Press, 2003), 217–250.

8. Wendy Cukier, *Gun Violence in Toronto: Towards a Fact Based Strategy* (Toronto: SAFER-Net, 2003).

9. Villaveces, Cummings, Espitia, Koepsell, McKnight, and Kellermann, "Effect of a Ban on Carrying Firearms on Homicide Rates in Two Colombian Cities," *Journal of the American Medical Association* 283 (2000): 1205–1209.

10. W. Cukier, A. Bandeira, R. Fernandes, J. Kamenju, A. Kirsten, and C. Walker, "Combating the Illicit Trade in Small Arms and Light Weapons: Strengthening Domestic Regulations" (Biting the Bullet Briefing 7–London: International Alert, Saferworld, 2001).

11. P. J. Cook and J. Ludwig, *Gun Violence: The Real Costs* (Oxford: Oxford University Press, 2000), 118.

12. Cukier, Bandeira, Fernandes, Kamenju, Kirsten, and Walker, "Combating the Illicit Trade in Small Arms and Light Weapons."

13. D.W. Webster, J. S. Vernick, and L. M. Hepburn, "Relationship between Licensing, Registration, and Other Gun Sales Laws and the Source State of Crime Guns," *Injury Prevention* 7 (2001): 184–189.

14. United Nations Wire, *Despite US Resistance, States Agree on Pact*, July 27, 2001, http://www.unwire.org/UNWire/20010723/16179_story.asp.

15. United Nations, *International Study on Firearm Regulation* (New York: United Nations, 1998).

16. Wendy Cukier, David Lochhead, Justyna Susla, and Alison Kooistra (revised), *Emerging Global Norms in the Regulation of Civilian Possession of Small Arms* (Toronto: SAFER-Net, Ryerson, 2005), http://www.research.ryerson.ca/SAFER-Net/.

17. OSCE, *Best Practice Guide on National Controls over Manufacture of Small Arms and Light Weapons* (Vienna: OSCE, 2003).

18. John S. Milne, S. Hargarten, A. L. Kellerman, and Garen Wintemute, "Effect of Current Federal Regulations on Handgun Safety Features," *Annals of Emergency Medicine* 41, no. 1 (2003): 1–9.

19. David Hemenway, *Public Health, Private Guns* (Ann Arbor: Michigan University Press, 2004).

20. Ibid.

21. Ilhan Berkol, "Marking and Tracing Small Arms and Light Weapons: Improving Transparency and Control," Groupe de recherché et d'information sur la paix et la sécurité (GRIP), 2002. Translated and updated from the French "Marquage et traçage des armes légères: Vers l'amélioration de la transparence et du contrôle," GRIP, 2000–2002.

22. United Nations, *International Study on Firearm Regulation.*

23. White House, Office of the Press Secretary, "President Clinton to Partici-

pate in Launching Maryland's Landmark New Gun Safety Law," April 11, 2000, http://clinton4.nara.gov/WH/New/html/20000411_15.html.

24. Philip Alpers and Conor Twyford, *Small Arms in the Pacific*, Occasional Paper No. 8 (Geneva: Small Arms Survey, March 2003).

25. "Brazil Wants Tighter Gun Laws: Disarmament Statute Passed in Congress Yesterday," Viva Rio press release, October 24, 2003.

26. United Nations, *International Study on Firearm Regulation*.

27. United Nations, *International Study on Firearm Regulation*, 1998.

28. Ibid., Tables 1.2 and 1.4.

29. Katherine Kramer, *Legal Controls on Small Arms and Light Weapons in Southeast Asia*, Occasional Paper No. 3 (Geneva: Small Arms Survey, Nonviolence International and International Alert, 2001), 7.

30. W. Cukier, "The Feasibility of Increased Restrictions on the Civilian Possession of Military Assault Weapons at the Global Level," Research Report, The Peacebuilding and Human Security: Development of Policy Capacity of the Voluntary Sector Project for the Canadian Peacebuilding Coordinating Committee (CPCC), 2005.

31. Violence Policy Center, "The Campaign to Ban Assault Weapons," March 31, 2004, http://www.vpc.org.

32. Canada, Firearms Act (1995): c. 39, http://laws.justice.gc.ca/en/F.11.6.

33. United Nations, *International Study on Firearm Regulation*, 1998.

34. United Kingdom, National Audit Office, "Home Office: Handgun Surrender and Compensation," February 26, 1999, http://www.nao.org.uk/pn/9899225.htm.

35. United Nations, *International Study on Firearm Regulation*, 1998.

36. Coalition for Gun Control, "Discussion on the Proposed Amendments Contained in Bill C-15B" (briefing to the Standing Committee on Justice and Human Rights), October 2001, http://www.guncontrol.ca/Content/Brie.c15.cgc%5B2%5D .FINAL.PDF.

37. "Factsheet: Guns in the Home," www.jhsph.edu/gunpolicy/Guns_in_Home.pdf.

38. James B. Jacobs, *Can Gun Control Work?* (Oxford: Oxford University Press, 2002).

39. Soros Foundation and Open Society Institute, *Gun Control in the United States: A Comparative Survey of State Firearm Laws* (New York: Soros Foundation, 2000).

40. International Crime Victimization Survey, 1996, cited in Richard Block, *Firearms in Canada and Eight Other Western Countries: Selected Findings of the 1996 International Crime (Victim) Survey* (Ottawa: Department of Justice, January 1998).

41. Richard Block, *Firearms in Canada and Eight Other Western Countries: Selected Findings of the 1996 International Crime (Victim) Survey* (Ottawa: Justice Canada, 1998).

42. Barise Hassan, "Arms Banned on Mogadishu Streets," BBC, January 24, 2002.

43. H.E. John McCarthy, "Illicit Trade in Small Arms and Light Weapons in All Its Aspects" (Japan: Pacific Islands Countries Regional Seminar, January 20–22, 2003).

44. William Godnick, Robert Muggah, and Camilla Waszink, "Stray Bullets: The Impact of Small Arms Misuse in Central America," *Small Arms Survey*, Occasional Paper No. 5 (October 2002), http://www.smallarmssurvey.orgOPs/OP05Central America.pdf.

45. Ibid., 7.

46. Alpers and Twyford, *Small Arms in the Pacific*.

47. Clare Jefferson and Angus Urquhart, "Firearm Indicators: The Impact of Small Arms in Tanzania: Results of a Country Study," *Institute for Security Studies (ISS) Monograph Series* 70 (2002): 45–60.

48. R. Chetty, ed., *Firearm Use and Distribution in South Africa* (Pretoria: National Crime Prevention Centre, 2000).

49. United Kingdom Home Office, *Firearms Law: Guidance to the Police 2002* (London: Her Majesty's Stationary Office, 2002), http://www.homeoffice.gov.uk/docs/policeguide.pdf.

50. Katherine McKenzie, *Domestic Gun Control Policy in Ten SADC Countries* (Johannesburg: Gun Free South Africa, 1999).

51. United Nations, *International Study on Firearm Regulations*, August 1999.

52. Ibid., 64.

53. Coalition for Gun Control, "Canada's Gun Control Laws 2004," http://www.guncontrol.ca/Content/GunControlLaws.html.

54. Kramer, *Legal Control on Small Arms and Light Weapons in Southeast Asia*, 8.

55. United Nations, *International Study on Firearms Regulations*, 1997.

56. Task Force on Community Preventative Services, "First Reports Evaluating the Effectiveness of Strategies for Preventing Violence: Firearm Laws," *Morbidity and Mortality Weekly Report*, October 3, 2003: 11–20, http://www.cdc.gov/mmwr/preview/mmwrhtml/rr5214a2.htm.

57. Evelyn Nieves, "California Strengthens Handgun Laws and Partners' Rights," *New York Times* October 16, 2001: A16.

58. Small Arms Firearms Education Research Network (SAFER-Net), "Country Profile: Argentina," 2001, http://www.ryerson.ca/SAFER-Net.

59. Handgun-Free America, "General Information: France," http://www.handgunfree.org/HFAMain/research/abroad/france.htm.

60. United Nations, *International Study on Firearm Regulation*, August 1999, http://www.uncjin.org/Statistics/firearms.

61. Ibid.

62. Ibid.

63. R. Chetty, ed., *Firearm Use and Distribution in South Africa*.

64. SAFER-Net, "Country Profile: South Africa," 2001, http://www.ryerson.ca/SAFER-Net.

65. SAFER-Net, "Country Profile: Namibia," 2001, http://www.ryerson.ca/SAFER-Net.

66. SAFER-Net, "Country Profile: Malawi," 2001, http://www.ryerson.ca/SAFER-Net.

67. Katherine McKenzie, *Domestic Gun Control Policy in Ten SADC Countries*.

68. Ibid.

69. SAFER-Net, "Country Profile: Zambia," 2001, http://www.ryerson.ca/SAFER-Net.

70. Wendy Cukier, "Firearms Legislation in Arab League Nations," SAFER-Net, 2005, http://www.research.ryerson.ca/SAFER-Net/.

71. SAFER-Net, "Country Profile: Bangladesh," 2001 http://www.ryerson.ca/SAFER-Net.

72. "102 Bodies to Sniff Out Arms Licence Flaws," *Daily Star* December 2, 2002, http://www.dailystarnews.com.

73. This information was gathered from SAFER-Net country profiles of Japan, France, Russia, New Zealand and India, 2001, http://www.ryerson.ca/SAFER-Net.

74. United Nations, *International Study on Firearm Regulations*, August 1998, Table 3.4, 57.

75. Kramer, *Legal Controls on Small Arms and Light Weapons in Southeast Asia*.

76. Alpers and Twyford, *Small Arms in the Pacific*.

77. Canadian Association of Chiefs of Police, "Canada's Firearms Licensing and Registration System Is Working to Make Communities Safer," press release, Halifax, January 21, 2004.

78. This information was taken from SAFER-Net country profiles for Brazil, Australia, Japan, India, Germany and Austria, http://www.ryerson.ca/SAFER-Net.

79. Soros Foundation and Open Society Institute, *Gun Control in the United States*.

80. Commission of Firearms, Annual Report, 2004 (Ottawa: Canadian Firearms Centre, 2005), http://www.cfc-cafc.gc.ca/media/reports/rapport2004report/default_e.asp.

81. Handgun Free America, "Country Factsheet: France," March 2004, http://www.handgunfree.org/HFAMain/research/abroad/france.htm.

82. SAFER-Net, "Country Profile: New Zealand," 2001, http://www.ryerson.ca/SAFER-Net.

83. SAFER-Net, "Country Profile: Mexico," 2001, http://www.ryerson.ca/SAFER-Net.

84. Kramer, *Legal Controls on Small Arms and Light Weapons in Southeast Asia*.

85. Ibid.

86. Jefferson and Urquhart, "Firearm Indicators."

87. "Uganda Embarks on Full-Scale Regulation of All Guns," Xinhuanet, June 29, 2002.

88. Joan Mugenzi, "Government to Computerize Firearms Registration," *New Vision Uganda*, 2002.

89. SAFER-Net, "Country Profile: Bangladesh" (January 9, 2004), http://www.ryerson.ca/SAFER-Net.

90. A. L. Kellermann, F. P. Rivara, G. Somes, D. T. Reay, J. Francisco, J. G. Banton, J. Prodzinski, C. Fligner, and B. B. Hackman, "Suicide in the Home in Relation to Gun Ownership," *The New England Journal of Medicine* 327, no. 7 (August 13, 1992): 467–472.

91. United Nations, *International Study on Firearm Regulation* (New York: United Nations, 1998).

92. Kramer, *Legal Controls on Small Arms and Light Weapons in Southeast Asia.*

93. Ibid.

94. SAFER-Net, "Country Profile: Czech Republic," 2001, http://www.ryerson.ca/SAFER-Net.

95. SAFER-Net, "Country Profile: Estonia," 2001, http://www.ryerson.ca/SAFER-Net.

96. SAFER-Net, "Country Profile: Greece," 2001, http://www.ryerson.ca/SAFER-Net.

97. SAFER-Net, "Country Profile: Japan," 2001, http://www.ryerson.ca/SAFER-Net.

98. SAFER-Net, "Country Profile: Australia," 2001, http://www.ryerson.ca/SAFER-Net.

99. Kramer, *Legal Controls on Small Arms and Light Weapons in Southeast Asia.*

100. Alpers and Twyford, *Small Arms in the Pacific,* 72.

101. Ibid., 117.

102. Kramer, *Legal Controls on Small Arms and Light Weapons in Southeast Asia.*

103. Edward Laurence and William Godnick, "Weapons Collection in Central America: El Salvador and Guatemala," in *Managing the Remnants of War: Micro Disarmament as an Element of Peace-Building,* ed. Sami Faltas and Joseph de Chiaro III (Baden-Baden: Nomos Verlag, 2001), 6.

104. Max Loria, "Costa Rica: Diagnostico Armas de Fuego" ("The Firearms Problem"), trans. Greg Puley (San Jose: Arias Foundation for Peace and Human Progress, 2000).

105. Gabriela Lopez, "Mexican State Launches Guns-for-Food Exchange," Reuters, May 5, 2001.

106. T.M. Thorp, "Review of Firearms Control in New Zealand," January 27, 2004, http://www.police.govt.nz/resources/1997/review-of-firearms-control/.

107. S. Lab, *Crime Prevention: Approaches, Practices and Evaluations* (Cincinnati: Anderson, 1997).

108. Ibid.

109. Ibid.

110. SAFER-Net, "Country Profile: Australia," 2001, http://www.ryerson.ca/SAFER-Net.

111. SAFER-Net, "Country Profile: Canada," 2001, http://www.ryerson.ca/SAFER-Net.

112. SAFER-Net, "Country Profile: Estonia," 2001, http://www.ryerson.ca/SAFER-Net.

113. SAFER-Net, "Country Profile: Greece," 2001, http://www.ryerson.ca/SAFER-Net.

114. W.K. Hastings, "International Perspectives on Gun Control," *New York Law School Journal of International and Comparative Law* 15 (1999): 2–3.

115. SAFER-Net, "Country Profile: Russia," 2004, http://www.ryerson.ca/SAFER-Net.

116. Alpers and Twyford, *Small Arms in the Pacific.*

117. Ibid.

118. Brendan Nicholson, "Bid to Halt Illegal Arms Trafficking," *Age*, December 1, 2002.

119. Drilon Pimental, "Bat for Stiffer Penalties vs Gun Ban Violators," *Manila Bulletin*, February 9, 2003.

120. Guangya Wang, "Protocol Plays Pivotal Role against Firearms Trafficking," *People's Daily*, December 10, 2002.

121. Shyamol Nazimuddin, "50,000 Arms in the Hands of Chittagong Underworld," *Independent*, January 17, 2003.

122. Farah Mihlar Ahamad, "Lankan Firearms Amnesty a Damp Squid," *Times of India*, January 20, 2002.

123. R. Mickleburgh, "Moses Brings Gun Gospel North," *Globe and Mail*, April 14, 2000: A1, A8.

124. U.S. Constitution, Second Amendment.

125. See, for example, *United States v. Cruikshank*, 92 U.S. 542 (1875); *United States v. Miller*, 307 U.S. 174 (1939); *Lewis v. United States*, 445 U.S. 55 (1980), all of which hold that the Second Amendment of the American Constitution does not guarantee any individual the right to possess firearms. For a more complete discussion, see J.D. Ingram and A.A. Ray, "The Right (?) to Keep and Bear Arms," *New Mexico Law Review* 27 (1997): 491.

126. O.H. Stephens, Jr., and J.M. Scheb II, *American Constitutional Law* (Minneapolis/St. Paul, MN: West Publishing Co., 1993), 473.

127. Lord Cullen, "Public Enquiry into the Shootings at Dunblane Primary School," October 16, 1996, http://www.official-documents/co/uk/document/scottish/dunblane/dunblane.htm.

128. *Police v. Goodwin* cited in W. Cukier, T. Sarkar, and T. Quigley, "Firearm Regulation: International Law and Jurisprudence," *Canadian Criminal Law Review*, vol. 6, no. 1 (December 2000): 99–123.

129. *R. v. Hasselwander*, 81 C.C.C. (3d) 471 (S.C.C.) (1993) at 479.

130. W. Cukier, T. Sarkar, and T. Quigley, "Firearm regulation: international law and jurisprudence" the Canadian Criminal Law Review, vol. 6, no. 1 (December 2000): 99–123.

131. Barbara Frey, The question of the trade, carrying and use of small arms and light weapons in the context of human rights and humanitarian norms. United Nations Commission on Human Rights. Fifty-fourth session. May 30, 2002.

132. United Nations General Assembly, Fifty-Fourth Session, Disarmament and International Security, Supplement Number 42 (A/54/42). December 1999, http://disarmament.un.org:8080/Library.nsf/0/63de2b694fe172e385256ce500761a4e/$FILE/dc54.42.pdf.

133. United Nations Commission on Crime Prevention and Criminal Justice, Sixth Session. Criminal Justice Reform and Strengthening of Legal Institutions Measures to Regulate Firearms. Resolution L.19 E/CN.15/1997/L.19/Rev.1. May 1997.

134. United Nations, General Assembly, Fifty-Fifth Session, Protocol Against the Illicit Manufacturing and Trafficking in Firearms. Their Parts and Components and Ammunition, Supplementing the United Nations Convention against Transnational Organized Crime. June 8, 2001, http://www.unodc.org/pdf/crime/a_res_55/255e.pdf.

135. United Nations, "Draft Programme of Action to Prevent, Combat and Eradicate the Illicit Trade in Small Arms and Light Weapons in All Its Aspects," Version L4 Rev 1, 2001.

136. United Nations, "UN Draft Programme of Action to Prevent, Combat and Eradicate the Illicit Trade in Small Arms and Light Weapons in All Its Aspects," Third session. March 19–30, 2001.

137. Ernie Regehr, "The UN and a Small Arms Program of Action: Measuring Success," *Ploughshares Monitor* (December, 2001), http://www.ploughshares.ca/CONTENT/MONITOR/Monitor01list.html.

138. First Continental Meeting of African Experts on the Illicit Proliferation, Circulation and Trafficking of Small Arms and Light Weapons, May 17–19, 2000. Addis Ababa, Ethiopia. http://129.194.252.80/catfiles/2852.pdf.

139. Bamako Declaration on an African Common Position on the Illicit Proliferation, Circulation and Trafficking of Small Arms and Light Weapons, November 30–December 1, 2000. Bamako, Mali. http://www.state.gov/t/ac/csbm/rd/6691.htm.

140. The Nairobi Declaration on the Problem of the Proliferation of Illicit Small Arms and Light Weapons in the Great Lakes Region and the Horn of Africa, March 15, 2000. http://www.smallarmsnet.org/docs/saaf04.pdf.

141. Declaration Concerning Firearms, Ammunition and Other Related Materials in the Southern African Development Community, March 9, 2001. http://www.smallarmssurvey.org/source_documents/Regional%20fora/Africa/SADCdecl090301.pdf.

142. Andean Plan to Prevent, Combat and Eradicate Illicit Trade in Small Arms and Light Weapons, June 25, 2003. http://www.comunidadandina.org/ingles/treaties/dec/D552e.htm.

143. South Pacific Chiefs of Police Conference (SPCPC) Working Group. The Nadi Framework—Legal Framework for a Common Approach to Weapons Control, March 10, 2000. Nadi, Fiji. www.globalpolicy.org/security/smallarms/regional/nadi.rtf.

144. Joint Action of the European Communities Council, December 1998. http://www.eu-asac.org/and_cambodia/First%20EU%20Joint%20Action%20December%201998.pdf.

Chapter 8

1. IANSA, "The United States," http://www.iansa.org/regions/namerica/namerica.htm#usa.

2. Brady Campaign to Prevent Gun Violence, "State Gun Laws: Frequently Asked Questions: Licensing and Registration," April 2, 2004, http://www.stategunlaws.org.

3. Open Society Institute, *Gun Control in the United States: A Comparative Survey of State Firearm Laws* (New York: Open Society Institute, 2000).

4. Brady Campaign to Prevent Gun Violence, "State Gun Laws: Frequently Asked Questions: Carrying Concealed Weapons 2002," April 2, 2004, http://www.stategunlaws.org.

5. Open Society Institute, *Gun Control in the United States*.

6. Ibid.

7. Brady Campaign to Prevent Gun Violence, "State Gun Laws: Frequently Asked Questions 2002," April 2, 2004, http://www.stategunlaws.org.

8. Violence Policy Center, "The Campaign to Ban Assault Weapons," March 31, 2004, http://www.vpc.org.

9. Brady Campaign to Prevent Gun Violence, "State Gun Laws: Frequently Asked Questions 2002."

10. I. Berkol, "Marking and Tracing Small Arms and Light Weapons: Improving Transparency and Control," *GRIP Report*, special issue, 2002.

11. The following section has been adapted from Johns Hopkins Center for Gun Policy and Research, "Factsheet: Firearm Injury and Death in the United States," January 2004, http://www.jhsph.edu/gunpolicy/US_factsheet_2004.pdf.

12. Philip Cook and Jens Ludwig, "Homicide and Suicide Rates Associated with the Implementation of the Brady Handgun Violence Prevention Act," *Journal of the American Medical Association* 284 (2000): 585–591.

13. Robert A. Hahn, Oleg O. Biluka, A. Crosby, M. Fullilove, A. Liberman, E. Mosckcki, S. Snyder, F. Tuma, and Peter Briss, "First Reports Evaluating the Effectiveness of Strategies for Preventing Violence: Firearms Legislation," *Morbidity and Mortality Weekly Report,* October 3, 2003: 11–20.

14. Ibid.

15. Brady Center to Prevent Gun Violence, "On Target: The Impact of the 1994 Federal Assault Weapons Act," http://www.bradycampaign.org/xshare/200403/on_target.pdf.

16. Johns Hopkins Center for Gun Policy and Research, "Factsheet: Firearm Injury and Death in the United States."

17. David Hemenway, *Private Guns, Public Health* (Ann Arbor: University of Michigan Press, 2004).

18. Johns Hopkins Center, "Factsheet."

19. Hahn, Biluka, Crosby, Fullilove, Liberman, Mosckcki, Snyder, Tuma, and Briss, "First Reports Evaluating the Effectiveness of Strategies for Preventing Violence."

20. D. W. Webster, J. S. Vernick, and L. M. Hepburn, "Relationship between Licensing, Registration, and Other Gun Sales Laws and the Source State of Crime Guns," *Injury Prevention* 7 (2001): 184–189.

21. Johns Hopkins Center for Gun Policy and Research, "Factsheet: Firearm Injury and Death in the United States."

22. Elizabeth Richard Vigdor and James A. Mercy, "Disarming Batterers: The Impact of Domestic Violence Firearm Laws," in *Evaluating Gun Policy*, eds. Philip Cook and Jens Ludwig (Washington, DC: Brookings Institution Press, 2003): 157–214.

23. David McDowall, Colin Loftin, and Brian Wiersema, "Easing Concealed Firearm Laws: Effects on Homicide in Three States," *Journal of Criminal Law and Criminology* 86 (1995): 193–206. See also Jens Ludwig, "Concealed-Gun Carrying Laws and Violent Crime: Evidence from State Panel Data," *International Review of Law and Economics* 18 (1998): 239–254.

24. Jens Ludwig, "Evaluating Gun Policy Evaluations," *Criminology and Public Policy* 2, no. 3 (July 2003): 411–418.

25. William Bartlett, *Gun Control Legislation in Canada, the United Kingdom and the United States* (Ottawa: Library of Parliament, 1990).

26. Coalition for Gun Control: Endorsers, 1997.

27. Firearms Act (Canada), 1998, 128 CCC (3d) 225 (Alta. CA).

28. Ibid.

29. Ibid.

30. Ibid., paragraph 3.

31. Ibid.

32. W. Cukier, "A Reality Check on the Gun Registry: Canada's Gun Control Law Is a Long-Term Investment in Our Security," *Hill Times* 680 (2003).

33. Peter Carrington, and Sharon Moyer, "Gun Availability and Suicide in Canada: Testing the Displacement Hypothesis," *Studies on Crime and Crime Prevention* (1994); Antoon Leenaars and Lester David, "Gender and Impact of Gun Control on Suicide and Homicide," *Archives of Suicide Research* 2 (1996): 223–234.

34. K. Hung, Firearm Statistics: Updated Tables.

35. Canada Firearms Centre, "Fact Sheet: Canada's Gun Control Program: Keeping Firearms Out of the Wrong Hands," February 21, 2003, http://www.cfc-ccaf.gc.ca/en/general_public/news_releases/feb21-2003/factsheet.asp.

36. Bunge, "National Trends in Intimate Partner Homicide."

37. Josée Savoie, *Crime Statistics in Canada, 2001* (Ottawa: Canadian Centre for Justice Statistics, 2001).

38. Pablo Dreyfus, Carolina Iootty de Paiva Dias, Benjamin Lessing, and William Godnick, "Small Arms Control in MERCOSUR, Security and Peacebuilding Programme, Monitoring the Implementation of Small Arms Control in Latin America." Viva Rio Press Release Series No. 3, 2003.

39. "Brazil Wants Tighter Gun Laws: Disarmament Statute Passed in Congress Yesterday," Viva Rio Press Release, October 24, 2003, http://www.vivario.br.

40. Ibid.

41. Ibid.

42. A. Villaveces, P. Cummings, V. Espitia, T.D. Koepsell, B. McKnight, and Arthur Kellermann, "Effect of a Ban on Carrying Firearms on Homicide Rates in 2 Colombian Cities," *JAMA* 283, no. 9 (2000): 1205–1209.

43. Berkol, "Marking and Tracing Small Arms and Light Weapons."

44. Lord Cullen, "Public Enquiry into the Shootings at Dunblane Primary School," October 16, 1996, http://www.official-documents/co/uk/document/scottish/dunblane/dunblane.htm.

45. United Kingdom, Secretary of State, "The Government Reply to the Second Report from the Home Affairs Committee Session," *Controls over Firearms*, 1999–2000.

46. United Kingdom, National Audit Office, "Home Office: Handgun Surrender and Compensation," February 26, 1999, http://www.nao.org.uk/pn/9899225.htm.

47. Berkol, "Marking and Tracing Small Arms and Light Weapons."

48. "Gun Ban Will Cause Illegal Ownership," *Evening Post*, January 24, 2004.

49. See Table 6.1.

50. See Table 2.4.

51. Berkol, "Marking and Tracing Small Arms and Light Weapons."

52. Povey, *Crime in England and Wales.*

53. Ordonnance sur les armes, les accessoires d'armes et les munitions (trans. "Law on Arms Accessories and Ammunition"), September 21, 1998.

54. M. Killias, "Gun Ownership and Violent Crime: The Swiss Experience in International Perspective," *Security Journal* 1, no. 3 (1990): 169–174.

55. Swiss Embassy to the U.S. Gun Ownership in Switzerland, January 2004, http://www.eda.admin.ch/washington_emb/e/home/legaff/Fact/gunown.html.

56. Ibid.

57. United Nations, *International Study on Firearm Regulation*, August 1999, updated database, http://www.uncjin.org/Statistics/firearms.

58. BBC News Online, "Switzerland and the Gun," September 27, 2001, http://news.bbc.co.uk/1/hi/world/europe/1566715.stm.

59. See Table 2.4.

60. United Nations, *International Study on Firearm Regulation*, August 1999.

61. Waffen weg—der gewarlfrei Weg (trans. "Ban Guns"), http://members .aon.at/waffen-weg/.

62. Joachim J. Savelsberg, "Gun Control and Gun Violence: Lessons from a German Comparison," *New York Law School Journal of International and Comparative Law* 15, nos. 2, 3 (1995).

63. Ibid.

64. United Nations, *International Study on Firearm Regulation*, August 1999.

65. "Erfurt Tries Tougher Youth Gun Ownership Laws," Deutsche-Welle World Service, June 7, 2003, http://www.dw-world.de/english/0,3367,1430_A_920826_ 1_A,00.html.

66. See Table 6.1.

67. SAFER-Net, "Country Profile: France," 2001, http://www.ryerson.ca/ SAFER-Net.

68. Ibid.

69. Ibid.

70. Maxim Pyadushkin, Maria Haug, and Anna Matveeva, "Beyond the Kalashnikov: Small Arms Production, Exports, and Stockpiles in the Russian Federation," *Small Arms Survey*, Occasional Paper No. 10, August 2003.

71. "Weapons 'Black Market' Expands Over Past 3 Years," Itar-Tass (Moscow), August 10, 2000, http://www.nisat.org.

72. Pyadushkin, Haug, and Matveeva, "Beyond the Kalashnikov."

73. United Nations, *International Study on Firearm Regulation,* August 1999.

74. Pyadushkin, Haug, and Matveeva, "Beyond the Kalashnikov."

75. United Nations, *International Study on Firearm Regulation*, August 1999.

76. Ibid.

77. United Nations Department of Disarmament Affairs, *National Report of the Republic of the Russian Federation on the Implementation of the United Nations'*

Small Arms and Light Weapons Programme of Action, 2002–2003, http://disarm ament2.un.org/cab/salw-nationalreports.html.

78. United Nations, *International Study on Firearm Regulation*, August 1999.

79. United Nations Department of Disarmament Affairs, *National Report of the Republic of the Russian Federation*.

80. William A. Pridemore, "Social Structure and Homicide in Post-Soviet Russia" (PhD diss., University of Albany, 2002).

81. Gun Free South Africa, "Statistics Sheet: Latest Statistics," May 2002, http://www.gca.org.za/facts/statistics.htm.

82. Jaclyn Cock, "Fixing Our Sights: A Sociological Perspective on Gun Violence in Contemporary South Africa," *Society in Transition* 1–4: 70–81.

83. R. Chetty, ed., *Firearm Use and Distribution in South Africa*.

84. Ibid.

85. Firearms Control Act No. 60 of 2000, November 22, 2001, http://www.gov.za/documents/00sublist.htm.

86. Katherine McKenzie, "Domestic Gun Control in Ten SADC Countries," report commissioned by Gun Free South Africa, 1999.

87. United Nations, National Report of India on the Implementation of the United Nations' Small Arms and Light Weapons Programme of Action, http://dis armament.un.org/cab/salw-nationalreports.html.

88. United Nations Department of Disarmament Affairs, *International Study on Firearm Regulation*, August 1999.

89. United Nations Department of Disarmament Affairs, National Report of India on the Implementation of the United Nations' Small Arms and Light Weapons Programme of Action.

90. Williams Arputharaj, Chamila James, Hemmathagama Thushani, and Nanayakkara Saradha, *A Comparative Study of Small Arms Legislation in Bangladesh, India, Nepal, Pakistan and Sri Lanka* (Colombo, Sri Lanka: South Asia Partnership International, 2003).

91. United Nations, *International Study on Firearm Regulation*, August 1999.

92. Arputharaj, Hemmathagama, and Nanayakkara, *Comparative Study of Small Arms Legislation*.

93. United Nations Department of Disarmament Affairs, National Report of India on the Implementation of the United Nations' Small Arms and Light Weapons Programme of Action.

94. International Action Network on Small Arms, "South and Central Asia," http://www.iansa.org/regions/scasia/scasia.htm.

95. Graduate Institute of International Studies, *Small Arms Survey 2003*.

96. See Table 2.7.

97. National Police Agency National Symposium to End Gun Violence, Tokyo, Japan, 1996.

98. Japan, Firearms Division, National Police Agency, "Firearms Control in Japan" and "Firearm Laws and Regulations and Enforcement Strategy in Japan," Japan National Police Agency, 1997.

99. United Nations, *International Study on Firearm Regulation*, August 1999.

100. "Amnesty International's: Report on Singapore," May 28, 2002, http://www.singapore-window.org/sw02/020528ai.htm.

101. National Committee on Violence, *Violence: Directions for Australia* (Canberra: Australian Institute for Criminology, 1990).

102. Australasian Police Ministers' Council, *Consolidated Resolutions Relating to Legislative Issues*, May 10, 1996 and July 17, 1996.

103. Australia, Attorney-General and Minister for Justice, "Thanks to Participants in Firearms Buyback," August 26, 1997, http://www.gun.law.gov.au.

104. J. Mouzos, *Firearm-Related Violence: The Impact of the Nationwide Agreement on Firearms, Trends and Issues in Crime and Criminal Justice*, no. 116 (Canberra: Australian Institute of Criminology, 1996).

105. Rowena Johns, *Australian Parliament Briefing Paper. Firearms Restrictions: New Developments*, March 2004, http://www.parliament.nsw.gov.au/prod/web/PHWebContent.nsf/PHPages/ResearchBf032004?OpenDocument.

106. United Nations Department of Disarmament Affairs, National Report of Australia on the Implementation of the United Nations' Small Arms and Light Weapons Programme of Action, 2002–2003, http://disarmament2.un.org/cab/salw-nationalreports.html.

107. William K. Hastings, "International Perspectives on Gun Control," *New York Law School Journal of International and Comparative Law* 15, nos. 2, 3 (1995).

108. G. Mauser, *Gun Control Is Not Crime Control* (Vancouver: Fraser Institute, 1995).

109. Sir Thomas Thorpe, Review of Firearms Control in New Zealand, 238–254.

110. Australian Institute of Criminology, *Australian Crime: Facts and Figures 2003* (Australia: 2003); Jenny Mouzos and Catherine Rushforth, "Firearm Related Deaths in Australia, 1991–2001," *Australian Institute of Criminology: Trends and Issues* 269 (November 2003).

111. Ibid.

112. Ibid.

113. Wendy Cukier, "Firearms Regulation: Canada in the International Context," *Chronic Diseases in Canada* 19, no. 1 (1998).

114. L. Flávio Gomes, and W. T. Oliveira, *Leis das armas de fogo no Brasil* (trans. "The Firearms of Brazil") (São Paulo: 1999).

115. World Bank Report, *Controlling the Jamaican Crime Problem: Peace Building and Community Action*, 2000.

116. United Nations, *International Study on Firearm Regulation*, August 1999.

Chapter 9

1. International Action Network on Small Arms, *Focusing Attention on Small Arms: Opportunities for the UN 2001 Conference on the Illicit Trade in Small Arms and Light Weapons* (London: IANSA, 2000); Saferworld, "Biting the Bullet Briefings: International Alert."

2. N. Goldring, "A Glass Half Full: The UN Small Arms Conference," Coun-

cil on Foreign Relations, Roundtable on the Geo-Economics of Military Preparedness, September 26, 2001.

3. Robert J. Spitzer, *The Politics of Gun Control* (Chatham, NJ: Chatham
House, 1995).

4. National Coalition to Ban Handguns, Statement on the Second Amendment,
June 26, 1981, http://www.guncite.com/journals/senrpt/senrpt27.html.

5. Don Kates, "Gun Control = Gun Prohibition," *Clinton Gun-Ban.com*, NRA-
ILA, March 1998, http://www.clintongunban.com/Articles.aspx?i=59&a=Articles.

6. Josh Sugarman, *NRA: Money, Firepower and Fear* (Washington, DC: National Press, 1992).

7. Hon. Lawrence J. Smith, The Fifteenth Anniversary of the National Coalition to Ban Handguns, Remarks in the House of Representatives, Wednesday, May
24, 1989, http://thomas.loc.gov/cgi-bin/query/z?r101:E24MY9-194:.

8. Donna Dees-Thomases, *Looking for a Few Good Moms* (New York: Rodale,
2004).

9. The Coalition to Stop Gun Violence, http://www.csgv.org.

10. Dees-Thomases, *Looking for a Few Good Moms.*

11. Sugarman, *NRA.*

12. Spitzer, *Gun Control.*

13. Gregg Lee Carter, *The Gun Control Movement* (New York: Twayne, 1997).

14. Spitzer, *Gun Control.*

15. Carter, *The Gun Control Movement.*

16. Ibid.

17. Josh Sugarman, "The NRA is Right but We Still Need to Ban Handguns,"
The Washington Monthly (June 1987).

18. Americans for Gun Safety Foundation, http://www.agsfoundation.com/
debate.html.

19. Spitzer, *Gun Control.*

20. Dees-Thomases, *Looking for a Few Good Moms.*

21. Carter, *The Gun Control Movement.*

22. Constance A. Nathonson and Laury Oaks, "Smoking and Guns: Social
Movements as Catalysts for Change," Johns Hopkins School of Public Health,
Working Paper Series, 1996, http://www.jhsph.edu/popcenter/publications/
abstracts/WP96-11.

23. Coalition for Gun Control, "The Gun Control Story," http://www.
guncontrol.ca/Content/TheGunControlStory.html.

24. Tim Falconer, *Watchdogs and Gadflies: Activism from Marginal to Mainstream* (Toronto: Viking, 2001).

25. Lydia Miljan, "Reactions to Violent Crime," Fraser Forum, June 1994.

26. Falconer, *Watchdogs and Gadflies.*

27. Coalition for Gun Control, "The Gun Control Story," http://www.
guncontrol.ca/Content/TheGunControlStory.html.

28. Wendy Cukier and Neil Thomlinson, *The Year of Missing Information: The
Construction of the Billion Dollar Registry* (Winnipeg: Canadian Communications
Association, Winnipeg 2004).

29. Canadian Press, "Freedom Lost without Right to Own Guns, Charlton Heston tells B.C. Convention," *The Ottawa Citizen*, April 14, 2000.

30. Simon Chapman, *Over Our Dead Bodies: Port Arthur and Australia's Fight for Gun Control* (Sydney: Pluto Press, 1998).

31. Margaret Hartley, "Report on the Round Table Meeting," June 12, 1996, Canberra, http://www.wisenet-australia.org/ISSUE42/roundtab.htm.

32. *Sydney Morning Herald/The Age*, 1998, cited in David Hemenway, *Private Guns, Public Health*.

33. New Zealand Police, *Review of Firearms Control in New Zealand*, June 1997, report of an Independent Inquiry Commissioned by the Minister of Police 1997, http://www.police.govt.nz/resources/1997/review-of-firearms-control/.

34. T. M. Thorp, Review of Firearms Control in New Zealand: Summary and Conclusions (June 1997): 3.

35. Philip Alpers (gun policy researcher), interview with the author, October 10, 1999.

36. Michael North, whose daughter Sophie was killed in the Dunblane massacre, interview with the author, September 27, 1999.

37. Mick North, *Dunblane: Never Forget* (Edinburgh: Mainstream, 2000).

38. Cited in Alexander MacLeod, "A Shot in the Dark? Antigun Lobby in Britain Aims for Ban on Organization," *Christian Science Monitor*, August 5, 1996.

39. National Police Agency, Firearms Division. *Firearms Control in Japan*, Tokyo, Japan, 1996.

40. Wendy Cukier, T. Sarkar, and T. Quigley, "Firearm Regulation: International Law and Jurisprudence," *The Canadian Criminal Law Review*, December 2000.

41. M. Jordan, "Guns and the Japanese: A People's Fear and Fascination," *International Herald Tribune,* March 18, 1997.

42. Jacklyn Cock, "Fixing our Sights: A Sociological Perspective on Gun Violence in Contemporary South Africa," *Society in Transition* 1–4: 70–81.

43. Adele Kirsten, "The Role of NGOs in the Control of Light Weapons Proliferation and the Reversion of Violence: A Case Study of Gun Free South Africa," in *Society Under Siege III: Managing Arms in South Africa*, ed. Virginia Gamba and Clare Hansmann, 2000, http://www.iss.co.za/Pubs/Books/SocietyIII Blurb.html.

44. Juan de Groot, "The Role of NGOs in the Control of Light Weapons: A Case Study of the South African Gunowners Association," in *Society Under Siege III: Managing Arms in South Africa*, ed. Virginia Gamba and Clare Hansmann, 2000, http://www.iss.co.za/Pubs/Books/SocietyIIIBlurb.html.

45. Adele Kirsten, cited in *In the Line of Fire: A Gender Perspective on Small Arms Proliferation, Peace Building and Conflict Resolution* (Women's International League for Peace and Freedom, Palais des Nations, Geneva, March 7–8, 2001), http//www.reachingcriticalwill.org/social/genderdisarm/WILPFSMALLARMS.html.

46. "Small Arms: On the UN Conference on the Illicit Trade in Small Arms and Light Weapons and in all its Aspects," *Disarmament Times* (special issue), Summer 2001, http://disarm.igc.org/DisarmTimes/DT-SmallArms.pdf.

47. R. Fernandes, L. Phebo, and P. Dreyfus, "Vivia Rio" (paper presented at the

Role of Public Health in the Prevention of War-Related Injuries, Montreal, May 9–11, 1999).

48. Rubem César, "Civil Society, Human Security and Public Security Policies: The Experience of Viva Rio, Brazil" (paper presented at the Fourth Ministerial Meeting, Human Security Network, Santiago de Chile, July 2–3, 2002). See also http://www.desarme.org.

49. Viva Rio, Annual Report, Rio de Janiero, 2003, http://www.vivario.org.br/AnnualReport/2003/PAGES/slide_eng27.htm.

50. Silvia Cattaneo and Keith Krause, "A Voice for Whom? Legitimacy, Representation and Advocacy in the International Action Network on Small Arms," International Studies Association Annual Convention, Montreal, March 17–20, 2004.

51. Edward Laurence, *The History of the Global Effort to Regulate Small Arms* (Monterey Institute of International Studies, 2002); Denise Garcia, *Making New International Norms, The Small Arms Case* (Unpublished, April 2004).

52. Martin Killias, "Gun Ownership, Suicide and Homicide: An International Perspective," *Canadian Medical Association Journal 148* (April 1993): 1,721–1,725.

53. William Bartlett, *Gun Control Legislation in Canada, the United Kingdom and the United States* (Ottawa: Government of Canada, Library of Parliament, 1990).

54. David Kopel, *The Samurai, the Mountie, and the Cowboy* (Buffalo, NY: Prometheus Books, 1992).

55. Gun Control Network. Achievements, http://www.gun-control-network.org/GCN08.htm.

56. Michael Klare, "Small Arms—The New Major Weapons," in *Lethal Commerce, The Global Trade in Small Arms and Light Weapons*, ed. Jeffrey Boutwell, Michael Klare, and Laura W. Reed (Cambridge: American Academy of Arts and Sciences, 1995).

57. Aaron Karp, "The Arms Revolution: The Major Impact of Small Arms," vol. 17, no. 4, The Washington Quarterly, (Autum 1994): 65–77.

58. Christopher Smith. "Light Weapons—The Forgotten Dimension of the Arms Trade," in *Brassey's Defence Yearbook*. Kings College London. Centre for Defence Studies, (1994): 271–284.

59. J. H. Sloan, A. L. Kellermann, D. T. Reay, J. A. Ferris, T. Koepsell, F. P. Rivara, C. Rice, L. Gray, and J. LoGerfo, "Handgun Regulations, Crime, Assaults, and Homicide: A tale of Two Cities," *The New England Journal of Medicine 319*, no. 19 (November 10, 1988): 1256–1262.

60. Wendy Cukier, "Firearms Regulation: Canada in the International Context," *Chronic Diseases in Canada* 19, no.1 (1998): 25–34; and E. G. Krug, K. E. Powell and L. L. Dahlberg, "Firearm Related Death in the United States and 35 Other High- and Upper-Middle Income Countries," *International Journal of Epidemiology* 27 (1998): 214–221.

61. Robin Coupland, "The Effect of Weapons on Health," *Lancet* 347 (February 17, 1996): 450–451; and D. Meddings, "Weapons Injuries During and After Periods of Conflict: Retrospective Analysis," *British Medical Journal* 315 (1997): 1417–1420.

62. Peter Herby, "Arms Availability and the Situation of Civilians in Armed Conflict," *International Review of the Red Cross,* no. 835 (September 30, 1999): 669–672.

63. "Public Health Perspectives on Firearms and Small Arms" (report on an international workshop, Quebec City, World Health Organization Coordinating Centre, February 7, 1998).

64. Cukier, "International Small Arms/Firearms Control: Finding Common Ground," *Canadian Foreign Policy* 6, no. 1 (Fall 1998): 73–89.

65. Small Arms Firearm Education Research Network (SAFER-Net), *Small Arms/Firearms Epidemiology and Research Workshop Report* (Toronto: Ryerson Polytechnic University, 1998).

66. Cukier, "Small Arms/Firearms."

67. Ibid.

68. Keith Krause, "Norm-Building in Security Spaces: The Emergence of the Light Weapons Problematic" (February 1999): 1–28. Edward Laurance and Rachel Stohl, *Making Global Public Policy: The Case of Small Arms and Light Weapons,* International Alert Occasion Paper No. 7 (December 2002).

69. Krause, Norm-Building in Security Spaces.

70. Natalie Goldring, "Domestic Laws and International Controls," in *Light Weapons and Civil Conflict,* ed. Jeffrey Boutwell and Michael T. Klare (New York: Carnegie Commission on Preventing Deadly Conflict, 1999), 101–125.

71. Michael Renner, *Small Arms, Big Impact: The Next Challenge of Disarmament* (Washington: The Worldwatch Institute, October 1997).

72. Susannah L. Dyer and Natalie J. Goldring, "Controlling Global Light Weapons Transfers: Working Toward Policy Options" (Annual Meeting of the International Studies Association, San Diego, California, April 16–20, 1996); Natalie J. Goldring, "Links between Domestic Laws and International Light Weapons Control (American Academy of Arts and Sciences Carnegie Commission on Preventing Deadly Conflict: Controlling the Global Trade in Light Weapons, Washington, DC, December 11–12, 1997).

73. Christopher Smith, Peter Batchelor, and Jackie Potgieter, *Small Arms Management and Peacekeeping in Southern Africa,* United Nations Institute for Disarmament Research (UNIDIR), Disarmament and Conflict Resolution Project, 1996.

74. Lora Lumpe, ed., *Running Guns: The Global Black Market in Small Arms* (London: Zed Books, 2000).

75. Abdel-Fatau Musah and Niobe Thompson, eds., "Small Arms in India and the Human Costs of Lingering Conflicts," *Over a Barrel: Light Weapons and Human Rights in the Commonwealth* (London and New Delhi: Commonwealth Human Rights Initiative [CHRI], November 1999), 38, 60, 94–96.

76. Cukier, "Small Arms/Firearms."

77. Virginia Gamba, ed., *Society Under Siege: Crime, Violence and Illegal Weapons vol. 1, Crime Violence and Illegal Weapons* (Halfway House, South Africa: Institute for Strategic Studies, 1997).

78. Cukier, "Small Arms/Firearms."

79. Wendy Cukier, "Global Effects of Small Arms: A Gendered Perspective," *In*

the Line of Fire: A Gender Perspective on Small Arms Proliferation, Peace Building and Conflict Resolution (Conference, Palais des Nations, Geneva, Women's International League for Peace and Freedom, March 7–8, 2001).

80. United Nations, "List of Participants" (United Nations Conference on the Illicit Trade in Small Arms and Light Weapons in All Its Aspects, New York, July 9–20, 2001).

81. Mark Strauss, "The NRA's Love-Hate Relationship: New World Order," *Foreign Policy*, July 19, 2001, http://slate.msn.com/id/112137/.

82. World Forum on the Future of Sport Shooting Activities. About the Forum, http://www.wfsa.net/Home.htm.

83. World Forum on the Future of Sport Shooting Activities. Documents, http://www.wfsa.net/UN_&_Legislative_documents.htm.

84. M. P. Garry Breitkreuz named "Sport Shooting Ambassador of the Year," Canadian Shooting Sports, CILA Institute for Legislative Action.

85. Ronald Bailey, "Global Gun Grabbers," *Weekly Standard*, February 23, 1998.

86. "National Rifle Association Is Turning to World Stage to Fight Gun Control," *New York Times*, April 2, 1997.

87. Natalie J. Goldring, "The NRA Goes Global," *Bulletin of the Automatic Scientists 55*, no. 1 (January–February 1999).

88. International Action Network on Small Arms (IANSA), "Founding Document," 1998, http://www.iansa.org/about/m1.htm.

89. Ibid.

90. Denise Garcia, "Making New International Norms: The Small Arms Case," BCSIA Discussion Paper 2003–13 (Kennedy School of Government, Harvard University, April 2004).

91. Ibid.

92. Silvia Cattaneo and Keith Krause, "A Voice for Whom? Legitimacy, Representation and Advocacy in the International Action Network on Small Arms 45, (International Studies Association Annual Convention, Montreal, March 17–20, 2004).

93. Edward Laurence, *The History of the Global Effort to Regulate Small Arms.* Monterey Institute of International Studies, 2002.

94. International Action Network on Small Arms, "Participation, Accountability and Action the Future of IANSA's Governance. A Discussion Paper," June 2003, http://www.iansa.org/about/m1.htm.

95. Groupe de Recherche et D'information sur la Paix et la Sécurité (GRIP).

96. International Action Network on Small Arms, "Contacts by Region," http://www.iansa.org/regions/index.htm.

97. International Action Network on Small Arms. "Background Information: International Actions Network on Small Arms Ltd.," http://www.iansa.org/about/selection/background_info.htm.

98. Owen Greene with Elizabeth Clegg, Sarah Meek and Geraldine O'-Callaghan, *Framework Briefing: The UN 2001 Conference—Setting the Agenda; Biting the Bullet Project Briefing* No. 1; BASIC, International Alert and Saferworld (London, February 2000).

99. Wendy Cukier, Derek Miller, Helen Vazquez, and Charlotte Watson, *Regulation of Civilian Possession of Small Arms and Light Weapons and the Centrality of Human Security, Biting the Bullet Series* (London, July 2003).

100. International Action Network on Small Arms, "Background Information," http://www.iansa.org/about/selection/background_info.htm.

101. Goldring, "The NRA Goes Global."

102. Statement of the Rt. Hon. the Count Albi, executive director, Eminent Persons Group, before the WFSA Workshop on Defining "Small Arms" as they Pertain to "Firearms" for the 2001 UN Conference on Small Arms, Imperial War Museum, London, April 27, 2001, http://www.geocities.com/eminentpersons group/Un6.html.

103. International Action Network on Small Arms, "Focusing Attention on Small Arms," December 2000, http://www.guncontrol.ca/Content/Temp/iansa.pdf.

104. Wendy Cukier, with contributions from: Antonio Bandeira, Rubem Fernandes, Lt-Col (ret) Jacob Kamenju, Adele Kirsten, Greg Puley, and Carlos Walker, "Combating the Illicit Trade in Small Arms and Light Weapons: Strengthening Domestic Regulations," *Biting the Bullet* (2001a).

105. Edward Laurance and Rachel Stohl, *Making Global Public Policy: The Case of Small Arms and Light Weapons*, International Alert Occasion Paper No. 7 (December 2002).

106. Amnesty International, USA, "Amnesty International Supports Renewal of Assault Weapons Ban," Press Release September 15, 2004, http://www.amnestyusa.org/arms_trade/news.do.

107. IANSA, http://www.iansa.org/issues/index.htm.

108. International Action Network on Small Arms, "Participation, Accountability and Action: The Future of IANSA'S Governance, A Discussion Paper," http://www.iansa.org/about/participation_accountability.htm.

109. Graduate Institute of International Studies, *Small Arms Survey 2001*.

110. United Nations, *Draft Programme of Action to Prevent, Combat and Eradicate the Illicit Trade in Small Arms and Light Weapons in All Its Aspects*.

111. Ernie Regehr, "The UN and a Small Arms Program of Action: Measuring Success," *Ploughshares Monitor,* December 2001, http://www.ploughshares.ca/CONTENT/MONITOR/Monitor01list.html.

112. Ibid.

113. Ibid.

114. Peggy Mason, personal communication, 2002.

115. Centre for Humanitarian Dialogue Missing Pieces, Geneva, HDC, 2005, http://www.hdcentre.org/.

116. Laurance and Stohl, *Making Global Public Policy*.

117. W. Cukier and A. Zohar, "Complex Environments and Emergent Order in International Advocacy," International Society Third Sector Research (ISTR) Conference, Ryerson University and York University Toronto, Canada, July 11–14, 2004.

Selected Resources

Australian Bureau of Statistics (ABS). *Underlying Cause of Death.* 2002. http://www.abs.gov.au/Ausstats/abs@.nsf/0/EC202352E78808AECA2569B1 007AB774?Open.

Australian Institute of Criminology (AIC). *Australian Crime: Facts and Figures 2004.* Australia: AIC, 2004. http://www.aic.gov.au/publications/facts/2004/facts_and_figures_2004.pdf.

Bonn International Center for Conversion. http://www.bicc.de.

The Brady Campaign to Prevent Gun Violence, Brady Center. http://www.brady campaign.org/

Brent, D. A., J. A. Perper, C. J. Allman, G. M. Moritz, M. E. Wartella, and J. P. Zelenak. "The Presence and Accessibility of Firearms in the Homes of Adolescent Suicides." *Journal of the American Medical Association* 266, no. 21 (1991): 2989–2995.

Bunge, V. P. "National Trends in Intimate Partner Homicides, 1974–2000." *Juristat* 22, no. 5 (2002).

Campbell, J. C., D. W. Webster, J. Koziol-McLain, Carolyn Block, Doris Campbell, Mary Ann Curry, Faye Gary, et al. "Risk Factors for Femicide in Abusive Relationships: Results from a Multisite Case Control Study." *American Journal of Public Health* 93, no. 7 (2003): 1089–1097.

Canetto, S., and I. Sakinofsky. "The Gender Paradox in Suicide." *Suicide and Life-Threatening Behaviour* 28, no. 1 (1998): 1–23.

Carcach, Carlos, and Marianne James. "Homicide between Intimate Partners in Australia." *Trends and Issues in Crime and Criminal Justice* 90 (July 1998): 1–6.

Carrington, Peter, and Sharon Moyer. "Gun Availability and Suicide in Canada: Testing the Displacement Hypothesis." *Studies on Crime and Crime Prevention* 3 (1994): 168–178.

Carter, Gregg Lee. *The Gun Control Movement.* New York: Twayne, 1997.

Center for Gun Policy and Research, Johns Hopkins School of Public Health. http://www.jhsph.edu/gunpolicy.

Centers for Disease Control and Prevention (CDC). "Homicide Trends and Characteristics—Brazil, 1980–2002." *Morbidity and Mortality Weekly Report (MMWR)* 53, no. 8 (March 5, 2004): 169–171. http://www.cdc.gov/mmwr/preview/mmwrhtml/mm5308a1.htm.

———. *National Vital Statistics Report* 50 (September 2002): 15–16. http://www.cdc.gov/nchs/products/pubs/pubd/nvsr/50/50-16.htm.

———. *National Vital Statistics Report* 53, no. 15 (February 28, 2005). http://www.cdc.gov/nchs/pressroom/05facts/lifeexpectancy.htm.

———. "Rates of Homicide, Suicide, and Firearm-Related Death Among Children—26 Industrialized Countries." *Morbidity and Mortality Weekly Report* 46, no. 5 (1997): 101–105 (last update May 2, 2001). http://www.cdc.gov/mmwr/preview/mmwrhtml/00046149.htm.

Chapdelaine, Antoine. "Firearms Injury Prevention and Gun Control in Canada." *Canadian Medical Association Journal* 155, no. 9 (1996): 1285–1289.

Chapdelaine, Antoine, E. Samson, M. D. Kimberley, and L. Viau. "Firearm-Related Injuries in Canada: Issues for Prevention." *Canadian Medical Association Journal* 145, no. 10 (1991): 1217–1223.

Chapman, Simon. *Over Our Dead Bodies: Port Arthur and Australia's Fight for Gun Control.* Annandale: Pluto Press, 1998.

Chetty, R., ed. *Firearm Use and Distribution in South Africa.* Pretoria: National Crime Prevention Centre, South Africa, 2000.

Christoffel, T., and S. S. Gallagher. *Injury Prevention and Public Health: Practical Knowledge, Skills and Strategies.* Galtersburg, MD: Aspen Publishers, 1999.

Clarke, R. V., ed. *Situational Crime Prevention: Successful Case Studies.* Albany, NY: Harrow and Heston, 1992.

Coalition for Gun Control. http://www.guncontrol.ca.

The Coalition to Stop Gun Violence. http://www.csgv.org/

Cock, Jacklyn. "Fixing Our Sights: A Sociological Perspective on Gun Violence in Contemporary South Africa." *Society in Transition* 28, no. 1/4 (1997): 70–81.

Cohen, D. "Culture, Social Organization, and Patterns of Violence." *Journal of Personality and Social Psychology* 75, no. 2 (1998): 408–419.

Cook, Philip J., and Jens Ludwig. *Guns in America: Results of a Comprehensive National Survey on Firearms Ownership and Use.* Washington, DC: U.S. Department of Justice, National Institute of Justice, 1996.

———. *Gun Violence: The Real Costs.* New York: Oxford University Press, 2000.

Cook, Philip J., S. Molliconi, and T. B. Cole. "Regulating Gun Markets." *Journal of Criminal Law and Criminology* 86 (Fall 1995): 59–92.

Coupland, Robin. "The Effect of Weapons on Health." *Lancet* 347 (February 17, 1996): 450–451.

Coupland, Robin, and David Meddings. "Mortality Associated with Use of Weapons in Armed Conflicts, Wartime Atrocities, and Civilian Mass Shootings: Literature Review." *British Medical Journal* 319 (August 14, 1999): 407–410.

Cukier, Wendy. "Firearms Regulation: Canada in the International Context." *Chronic Diseases in Canada* 19, no. 1 (1998): 25–34.

———. "International Small Arms/Firearms Control." *Canadian Foreign Policy* 6, no. 1 (Fall 1998): 73–89.

———. "Small Arms and Light Weapons: A Public Health Approach." *The Brown Journal of World Affairs* 9, no. 1 (Spring 2002): 261–280.

———. "Vuurwapens: legale en illegale kanalen" [Firearms: Licit/Illicit links], edited by H. J. Frankie and E. S. de Wijs. *Tijdschrift voor—Criminologie* 43, no. 1 (2001): 27–41.

Cukier, Wendy, and Antoine Chapdelaine. "Small Arms, Explosives and Incendiaries." Chap. 9 in *Terrorism and Public Health: A Balanced Approach to Strengthening Systems and Protecting People*, edited by Barry Levy and Victor Sidel. Oxford: Oxford University Press, 2002.

Cukier, Wendy, D. Miller, H. Vazquez, and C. Watson. *Regulation of Civilian Possession of Small Arms and Light Weapons and the Centrality of Human Security*. Biting the Bullet Series. London, July 2003.

Dansys Consultants, Inc. *Domestic Homicides Involving the Use of Firearms*. Ottawa: Department of Justice, 1992.

Dauvergne, Mia. "Homicide in Canada, 2003." Statistics Canada, Catalogue no. 85-002-XPE, *Juristat* 24, no. 8. http://www.statcan.ca/english/preview/85-002-XIE/P0080485-002-XIE.pdf.

Diaz, Tom. *Making a Killing: The Business of Guns in America*. New York: The New Press, 1999.

Dodd, Tricia, Sian Nicholas, David Povey, and Alison Walker. *Crime in England and Wales 2003/2004*. July 2004. http://www.homeoffice.gov.uk/rds/pdfs04/hosb1004.pdf.

Donohue, J. "The Impact of Concealed-Carry Laws." In *Evaluating Gun Policy: Effects on Crime and Violence*, edited by Jens Ludwig and Philip Cook, 287–341. Washington, DC: Brookings Institution Press, 2003.

Falbo, Gilliat, Roberto Buzzetti, and Adriano Cattaneo. "Homicide in Children and Adolescents: A Case-Control Study in Recife, Brazil." *Bulletin of the World Health Organization* 79, no. 1 (2001): 2–7.

Fernandes, Rubem César, Benjamin Lessing, Caroline Iootty, Julio Cézar Purcena, Luciana Phebo, Marcelo de Souza Nascimento, Pablo Dreyfus, and Patricia Rivero. "Brazil: The Arms and the Victims." *Viva Rio*, 2005. http://www.vivario.org.br/publique/cgi/cgilua.exe/sys/start.htm?sid=28infoid=962.

Gartner, Rosemary. "Cross Cultural Aspects of Interpersonal Violence: A Review of the International Empirical Evidence." Paper presented at the International Conference on Crime and Violence: Causes and Policy Responses, World Bank. May 2000.

Goldring, Natalie. "Domestic Laws and International Controls." In *Light Weapons and Civil Conflict: Controlling the Tools of Violence*, edited by Jeffrey

Boutwell and Michael Klare, 101–125. Lanham, MD: Rowman & Little-field, 1999.

Graduate Institute of International Studies (GIIS). *Small Arms Survey 2004: Rights at Risk*. Oxford: Oxford University Press, 2004.

———. *Small Arms Survey 2003: Development Denied*. Oxford: Oxford University Press, 2003.

———. *Small Arms Survey 2002: Counting the Human Cost*. Oxford: Oxford University Press, 2002.

———. *Small Arms Survey 2001: Profiling the Problem*. Oxford: Oxford University Press, 2001.

Gun Policy Network. http://www.gunpolicy.org.

Hahn, Robert A., Oleg O. Biluka, A. Crosby, M. Fullilove, A. Liberman, E. Moscicki, S. Snyder, F. Tuma, and Peter Briss. "First Reports Evaluating the Effectiveness of Strategies for Preventing Violence: Firearms Laws." *Morbidity and Mortality Weekly Report* 52 (October 3, 2003): 11–20.

Handgun Epidemic Lowering Plan. http://www.helpnetwork.org/

Harvard Injury Control Research Center, Harvard University. http://www.hsph.harvard.edu/hicrc.

Hemenway, David. "The Epidemiology of U.S. Firearm Injuries." *Journal of Public Health Policy* 24, no. 3/4 (2003): 380–386.

———. *Public Health, Private Guns*. Ann Arbor: University of Michigan Press, 2004.

———. "Survey Research and Self-Defense Gun Use: An Explanation of Extreme Overestimates." *Journal of Criminal Law and Criminology* 87, no. 4 (1997): 1430.

Hemenway, David, and Matthew Miller. "Association of Rates of Household Handgun Ownership, Lifetime Major Depression, and Serious Suicidal Thoughts with Rates of Suicide across US Census Regions." *Injury Prevention* 8 (December 2002): 313–316.

———. "Firearm Availability and Homicide Rates across 26 High-Income Countries." *Journal of Trauma—Injury, Infection and Critical Care* 49, no. 6 (December 2000): 985–988.

Hemenway, David, T. Shinoda-Tagawa, and Matthew Miller. "Firearm Availability and Female Homicide Victimization Rates across 25 Populous High-Income Countries." *Journal of the American Medical Women's Association* 57, no. 2 (2002): 100–104.

Herz, Andrew D. "Gun Crazy: Constitutional False Consciousness and Dereliction of Dialogic Responsibility." *Boston University Law Review* 75, no. 1 (1995).

Hintikka, J., H. Lehtonen, and H. Viinamaki. "Hunting Guns in Homes and Suicides in 15–24-Year-Old Males in Eastern Finland." *Australian and New Zealand Journal of Psychology* 31, no. 6 (1997): 858–861.

International Action Network on Small Arms (IANSA). http://www.iansa.org.

International Alert. http://www.international-alert.org.

International Committee of the Red Cross (ICRC). *Arms Availability and the Situation of Civilians in Armed Conflict*. Geneva: ICRC, June 1999.

————. *Arms Transfers and International Humanitarian Law.* Geneva: ICRC, September 1997.

International Physicians for the Prevention of Nuclear War (IPPNW). "Aiming for Prevention: International Medical Conference on Small Arms, Gun Violence, and Injury." Helsinki, Finland, September 28–30, 2001. http://www.ippnw.org/Helsinki.html.

Jackman, Geoffrey A., Mirna M. Farah, Arthur Kellermann, and Harold K. Simon. "Seeing Is Believing: What Do Boys Do When They Find a Real Gun?" *Pediatrics* 107, no. 6 (June 2001): 1247–1250.

Join Together, Boston University School of Public Health. http://www.jointogether.org/home/.

Kellermann, A. L. "Comment: Gunsmoke—Changing Public Attitudes towards Smoking and Firearms." *American Journal of Public Health* 87, no. 6 (1997): 910–913.

Kellerman, A. L., F. P. Rivara, N. B. Rushforth, J. G. Banton, D. T. Reay, J. T. Francisco, A. B. Locci, B. B. Hackman, and G. Somes. "Gun Ownership as a Risk Factor for Homicide in the Home." *New England Journal of Medicine* 329, no. 15 (1993): 1084–1091.

Kellerman, A. L., F. P. Rivara, G. Somes, D. T. Reay, J. Francisco, J. G. Banton, J. Prodzinski, C. Flinger, and B. B. Hackman. "Suicide in the Home in Relation to Gun Ownership." *New England Journal of Medicine* 327, no. 7 (1992): 467–472.

Killias, Martin. "International Correlations between Gun Ownership and Rates of Homicide and Suicide." *Canadian Medical Association Journal* 148 (May 1993): 1721–1725.

Killias, Martin, J. Van Kestern, and M. Rindlisbacher. "Guns, Violent Crime, and Suicide in 21 Countries." *Canadian Journal of Criminology* 156 (October 2001): 429–448.

Krug, Étienne G., Linda L. Dahlberg, James A. Mercy, Anthony B. Zwi, and Rafael Lozano, eds. *World Report on Violence and Health.* Geneva: WHO, 2002. See esp. 310, 312, 316, 318, 322, 323. http://www.who.int/violence_injury_prevention/violence/world_report/wrvheng.

Krug, Étienne G., Linda L. Dahlberg, and K. E. Powell. "Childhood Homicide, Suicide, and Firearm Deaths: An International Comparison." *World Health Statistics Quarterly* 49, no. 3/4 (1996): 230–235.

Krug, Étienne G., K. E. Powell, and Linda L. Dahlberg. "Firearm Related Death in the United States and 35 Other High- and Upper-Middle-Income Countries." *International Journal of Epidemiology* 27 (1998): 214–221.

Lab, S. *Crime Prevention: Approaches, Practices, Evaluations.* Cincinnati: Anderson, 1997.

Ludwig, Jens. "Concealed-Gun-Carrying Laws and Violent Crime: Evidence from State Panel Data." *International Review of Law and Economics* 18 (September 1998): 239–254.

————. "Evaluating Gun Policy Evaluations." *Criminology & Public Policy* 2, no. 3 (2003): 411–418.

Ludwig, Jens, and Philip Cook, eds. *Evaluating Gun Policy: Effects on Crime and Violence.* Washington, DC: Brookings Institution Press, 2003.

Lumpe, L. *Running Guns: The Global Black Market in Small Arms.* London: Zed Books, 2000.

McDowall, David, Colin Loftin, and Brian Wiersema. "Easing Concealed Firearm Laws: Effects on Homicide in Three States." *Journal of Criminal Law and Criminology* 86, no. 1 (1995): 193–206.

Meddings, David. "Weapons Injuries during and after Periods of Conflict: Retrospective Analysis." *British Medical Journal* 315 (November 1997): 1417–1420.

Meddings, David, and S. Connor. "Circumstances around Weapon Injury in Cambodia after Departure of a Peacekeeping Force: Prospective Cohort Study." *British Medical Journal* 319 (August 1999): 412–415.

Mercy, James A., Étienne G. Krug, Linda L. Dahlberg, and Anthony B. Zwi. "Violence and Health: The United States in a Global Perspective." *American Journal of Public Health* 93 (February 2003): 256–261.

Mercy, James A., Anthony B. Zwi, and Rafael Lozano, eds. *World Report on Violence and Health.* Geneva: WHO, 2002.

Miller, Matthew, Deborah Azarel, and David Hemenway. "Community Firearms, Community Fear." *Epidemiology* 11, no. 6 (2000): 709–714.

———. "Rates of Household Firearm Ownership and Homicide across US Regions and States, 1988–1997." *American Journal of Public Health* 92 (December 2002): 1988–1993.

Miller, Ted. "Costs Associated with Gunshot Wounds in Canada in 1991." *Canadian Medical Association Journal* 153 (November 1995): 1261–1268.

Miller, Ted, and M. Cohen. "Costs of Gunshot and Cut Stab Wounds in the United States with Some Canadian Comparisons." *Accident Analysis and Prevention* 29, no. 3 (1997): 329–341.

Mouzos, Jenny, and Catherine Rushford. "Firearm-Related Deaths in Australia, 1991–2001." *Trends and Issues in Crime and Criminal Justice* 269 (November 2003): 1–6.

Musah, A. F., and N. Thompson, eds. *Over a Barrel: Light Weapons and Human Rights in the Commonwealth.* London and New Delhi: Commonwealth Human Rights Initiative (CHRI), November 1999. See esp. 38, 60, 94–96.

Naylor, R. T. "Loose Cannons: Covert Commerce and Underground Finance in the Modern Arms Black Market." *Crime, Law and Social Change* 22 (1995): 1–57.

The Norwegian Initiative on Small Arms Transfers (NISAT). http://www.nisat.org.

Pierce, Glenn L., LeBaron Briggs, and David Carlson. *The Identification of Patterns in Firearms Trafficking: Implications for Focused Enforcement Strategies.* A report to the United States Department of Treasury, Bureau of Alcohol, Tobacco and Firearms. Northeastern University, 1995.

Povey, David. *Crime in England and Wales 2003/2004.* Supplementary Volume 1, *Homicide and Gun Crime.* (London: Home Office, 2005).

The Program on Security and Development, Monterey Institute of International Studies. http://sand.miis.edu/

Renner, M. "Small Arms, Big Impact: The Next Challenge of Disarmament." *Worldwatch Papers.* October 1997.

Reza, A., James A. Mercy, and Étienne G. Krug. "Epidemiology of Violent Deaths in the World." *Injury Prevention* 7 (2001): 104–111.

Saferworld. http://www.saferworld.co.uk.

Saltzman, L.E., James A. Mercy, P.W. O'Carroll, M.L. Rosenberg, and P.H. Rhodes. "Weapon Involvement and Injury Outcomes in Family and Intimate Assaults." *Journal of the American Medical Association* 267 (June 1992): 3043–3047.

Sapnas, K.G. "The Context of Violence in Women Hospitalized for Gunshot Wounds in Cape Town, South Africa." *Journal of Multicultural Nursing & Health* 10, no. 1 (2004): 34–41.

Sauvé, Julie. "Crime Statistics in Canada, 2004." Statistics Canada, Catalogue no. 85-002 XIE, *Juristat* 25, no. 5 (2005).

Scottish Executive. *Statistical bulletin CrJ/2003/5: Firearm Certificate Statistics, Scotland, 2002.* July 2003. http://www.scotland.gov.uk/stats/bulletins/0-0263-00.asp.

Sloan, J.H., A.L. Kellermann, D.T. Reay, J.A. Ferris, T. Koepsell, F.P. Rivara, C. Rice, L. Gray, and J. LoGerfo. "Handgun Regulations, Crime, Assaults and Homicide: A Tale of Two Cities." *New England Journal of Medicine* 319 (November 1988): 1256–1262.

Small Arms/Firearms Education and Research Network (SAFER-Net). http://www.research.ryerson.ca/SAFER-Net/index.html.

Smallarmsnet, Institute for Security Studies. http://www.smallarmsnet.org.

Small Arms Survey, Graduate Institute of International Studies. www.smallarmssurvey.org.

Spitzer, R.J. *The Politics of Gun Control.* New Jersey: Chatham House Publishers, 1995.

Statistics Canada. "Canadian Crime Statistics, 2003." *Juristat* 24, no. 6 (2004). http://www.statcan.ca/Daily/English/040728/d040728a.htm.

Thorp, T.M. *Review of Firearms Control in New Zealand: June 1997.* http://www.police.govt.nz/resources/1997/review-of-firearms-control/.

United Kingdom. Bureau of National Statistics. http://www.statistics.gov.uk/census2001/profiles/727.asp.

United Nations (UN). The Eighth International Crime Victims Survey, 2000. Prepared by the Interregional Crime and Justice Research Institute, 2003. http://www.unicri.it/wwd/analysis/icvs/data.php.

———. International Study on Firearm Regulation. New York: UN, 1997 (last update August 30, 1999). http://www.uncjin.org/Statistics/firearms.

———. International Study on Firearm Regulation. New York: UN, 1998. http://www.ojp.usdoj.gov/bjs/glance/tables/guncrimetab.htm.

———. The Seventh United Nations Survey on Crime Trends and the Operations of Criminal Justice Systems, 1998–2000. http://www.unodc.org/unodc/crime_cicp_survey_seventh.html.

U.S. Department of Justice. *Annual Firearms Manufacturing and Export Report,*

2003. Prepared by the Office of FEA, Bureau of Alcohol, Tobacco, Firearm, and Explosives. Washington, DC: Department of Justice, March 31, 2005. http://www.atf.treas.gov/firearms/stats/afmer/afmer2003.pdf.

———. Bureau of Justice Statistics. "Crimes Committed with Firearms, 1973–2002" (last update December 13, 2003). http://www.ojp.usdoj.gov/bjs/glance/guncrime.htm.

Villaveces, A., P. Cummings, V. Espitia, T. D. Koepsell, B. McKnight, and Arthur Kellermann. "Effect of a Ban on Carrying Firearms on Homicide Rates in Two Colombian Cities." *Journal of the American Medical Association* 283 (March 2000): 1205–1209.

Wallace, M. "Crime Statistics in Canada, 2003." Statistics Canada, Catalogue no. 85002 XIE, *Juristat* 24, no. 6 (2004). http://www.statcan.ca:8096/bsolc/english/bsolc?catno=85-002-X20040068405.

Webster, D. W., J. S. Vernick, and L. M. Hepburn. "Relationship between Licensing, Registration, and Other Gun Sales Laws and the Source State of Crime Guns." *Injury Prevention* 7 (September 2001): 184–189.

Wellford, C. F., J. V. Pepper, and C. V. Petrie, eds. Committee on Law and Justice, National Research Council. *Firearms and Violence: A Critical Review.* Washington, DC: The National Academies Press, 2004.

Wiebe, D. J. "Homicide and Suicide Risks Associated with Firearms in the Home: A National Case-Control Study." *Annals of Emergency Medicine* 41, no. 6 (2003): 771–782.

Wilkins, Kathryn. "Deaths Involving Firearms." Statistics Canada, *Health Reports* 16, no. 4 (2005).

Wood, Brian, and Johan Peleman. *The Arms Fixers: Controlling the Brokers and Shipping Agents.* Norwegian Initiative on Small Arms Transfers (NISAT). November 20, 1999.

World Forum on the Future of Sport Shooting Activities: Members and Links (last update 2001). http://www.wfsa.net/Links.htm.

World Health Organization (WHO). Collaborating Centre for Safety Promotion and Injury Prevention. *International Workshop on Small Arms and Firearms Injury: Finding a Common Ground for Public Health.* Québec City, Canada, February 7, 1998.

World Health Organization. *Small Arms and Global Health.* Geneva: WHO, 2001.

Zimring, Franklin E., and Gordon Hawkins. *Crime Is Not the Problem: Lethal Violence in America.* New York: Oxford University Press, 1997.

Index

The letter "f" indicates figures; "t" indicates tables.

international measures (*see* international gun control movement)
in Japan, 216–17, 217–18
national measures, 9–10, 206–7, 230–31, 235
in New Zealand, 215–16
regional measures, 168–70, 231
in United Kingdom, 216
U.S. controversy over, 131
U.S. movement for, 208–11
U.S. opposition to, 131, 136–37, 166, 167, 207, 208, 227, 233, 235, 242
See also firearm regulation; firearms: attitudes toward; postconflict conditions, firearms in: control of
gun culture
and firearms demand, 126–27
and gun lobby, 114
and masculinity, 124–26, 130, 241
and media, 121–22, 125, 128–30
overview of, 8–9, 109–10
regional variations in, 127–28
rejecting, 235
in United States, 125, 126–27, 241
See also firearms: attitudes toward
gun-free-zones, 61, 217–18
gun industry and trade, global
arms trade, 50
overview of, 7, 68–69
supply and demand, factors of (*see* firearms: demand factors; firearms: supply factors)
trends, 87
in United States, 74–76
See also civilian possession and use of firearms; firearm marketing and promotion; government firearm markets; illegal firearm markets; military firearm markets; term illegal firearm trade in *under country*
gun lobby
American, 66, 87, 114–15, 121–22, 160–61, 207, 211, 242 (*see also* National Rifle Association (NRA))

Australian, 115, 121
Canadian, 211
international, 116–21, 224, 227
South African, 115, 218
gun owners
profile of, 8–9, 109
screening and licensing of, 146–52, 147t, 148t, 162t–163t, 191, 196, 198–99, 200
gun ownership
firearm deaths linked to, 6–7, 23–24, 55, 57f, 95
limiting and requirements, 58–63, 181, 186
organizations promoting, 116t–121t
overview of, 109–10
purposes, legal, 146t
regional variations in, 110–14, 111t–112t, 130
and suicide rates, 23–24
gun running, 7–8
See also illegal firearm markets
gun shows, 108, 140
gun violence
reducing, 132
response to, U.S. versus other nations, 43, 46
risk factors for, 63, 132 (*see also* firearm availability/death link)

Haiti, gun violence in, 33
Handgun Control Inc., 209
handguns
ban on, 144, 174, 175, 198, 216
features of, 71
prevalence of, 223
recovery of, 104
regulations concerning, 144–45
in United States, 112, 144
use of, 105–6
Harris, Eric, 12
Hasina, Sheikh, 2
Hattori, Yoshira, 217
health care and gun violence. *See* public health aspects of gun violence

About the Authors

WENDY CUKIER is Professor of Justice Studies and Information Technology Management at Ryerson University in Toronto. She is a cofounder of Canada's Coalition for Gun Control, a founding member of the International Action Network on Small Arms, and coordinates the Small Arms Firearms Education and Research Network. In 2000 she was awarded the Governor General's Meritorious Service award, one of Canada's highest honors.

VICTOR W. SIDEL is Distinguished University Professor of Social Medicine at the Montefiore Medical Center and Albert Einstein College of Medicine in the Bronx, and Adjunct Professor of Public Health at Weill Medical College of Cornell University. He is a former president of the American Public Health Association, and a cofounder and past president of Physicians for Social Responsibility and International Physicians for the Prevention of Nuclear War (which won the Nobel Peace Prize in 1985).